FREE AFRICAN-AMERICANS OF MARYLAND 1832

INCLUDING ALLEGANY, ANNE ARUNDEL, CALVERT, CAROLINE, CECIL, CHARLES, DORCHESTER, FREDERICK, KENT, MONTGOMERY, QUEEN ANNE'S, AND ST. MARY'S COUNTIES

Jerry M. Hynson

HERITAGE BOOKS
2007

HERITAGE BOOKS
AN IMPRINT OF HERITAGE BOOKS, INC.

Books, CDs, and more—Worldwide

For our listing of thousands of titles see our website
at
www.HeritageBooks.com

Published 2007 by
HERITAGE BOOKS, INC.
Publishing Division
65 East Main Street
Westminster, Maryland 21157-5026

Other Heritage Books by Jerry M. Hynson:

Absconders, Runaways and Other Fugitives in the Baltimore City and County Jail

Baltimore Life Insurance Company Genealogical Abstracts

District of Columbia Runaway and Fugitive Slave Cases, 1848-1863

Maryland Freedom Papers, Volume 1: Anne Arundel County

Maryland Freedom Papers, Volume 2: Kent County

*Maryland Freedom Papers, Volume 3: Maryland Colonization Society
Manumission Book, 1832-1860*

*The African American Collection: Anne Arundel County, Maryland
Marriage Licenses, 1865-1888*

The African American Collection: Cecil County, Maryland Indentures, 1777-1814

*The African American Collection: Kent County, Maryland
Marriages , 1865-1888*

International Standard Book Number: 978-1-58549-483-5

Table of Contents

Introduction

Among the legislative actions of the Maryland General Assembly of 1831 was the passage of "*An act relating to the People of Color in this state.*" Although the primary intent of the act was to achieve the removal of free African Americans from the state of Maryland in their entirety, actions relating to the application of law yielded other results. First, the state of Maryland found itself playing a strong role in the founding of the colony of Liberia. Secondly, the enumeration of the African American population of the state, as required by the act, resulted in a thorough recording of the African American population of 1832.

It is not known whether or not such a recording was made in every political subdivision of the state. Lists for several counties were held at the Maryland Historical Society. However between 1937 and 1970, the lists were lost.

The only censuses known to exist for many years were those for Harford, Somerset, and Talbot Counties. These were compiled and published by the late Mary K. Meyer in her work entitled *Free Blacks in Harford, Somerset, and Talbot Counties, Maryland*, published in 1991.[1] Shortly before her untimely demise in 1997, Mrs. Myer made me aware of the existence of the microfilm copies of the censuses of Allegany, Anne Arundel, Calvert, Caroline, Cecil, Charles, Dorchester, Frederick, Kent, Montgomery, Queen Ann's, and St. Mary's Counties among the papers of the Maryland State Colonization Society. With her encouragement, this compilation was undertaken.

In using the lists that follow, be aware that they are the result of reading many frames of microfilm of varying condition, bearing many forms of handwriting and spelling. The user is encouraged to make use of the microfilm at The Maryland Historical Society for personal determination.[2]

My thanks go to Francis O'Neill of the Maryland Historical Society Library, Pat Melville of the Maryland State Archives, and F. Edward Wright of the Maryland Genealogical Society for their assistance and encouragement in

---

[1]Meyer, Mary K., *Free Blacks in Harford, Somerset, and Talbot Counties, Maryland, 1832*. Pipe Creek Publications, Mt. Airy, Maryland, 1991. Available from Family Line Publications, 65 E. Main St. Westminster, MD.

[2]See Maryland Historical Society Collection entitled *Maryland State Colonization Society Papers*, Roll 32

preparing this work.

Special thanks go to my wife, Yvonne T. Hynson for her encouragement and assistance in proofing and preparing the text.

Jerry M. Hynson
August, 1998

An Act Relating to the People of Color
In this State

Section 1. Be it enacted by the General Assembly of Maryland, That the governor and council shall as soon as conveniently may be after the passage of this act, appoint a board of managers, consisting of three persons, who shall, at the time of their appointment, be members of the Maryland State Colonization Society, whose duty it shall be to remove from the state of Maryland , the people of color now free, and such as shall hereafter become so , to the colony of Liberia, in Africa, or such other place or places out of the limits of this state, as they may approve of, and the person or persons so to be removed , shall consent to go to according to the provisions of this act , and to provide for their establishment and support as far as necessary, and to discharge the other duties required of them by this act ; and before the said managers shall proceed to act they shall severally give bond to the state of Maryland, in the penalty of ten thousand dollars, conditioned for their faithful accounting for all monies that may come to their hands; which bond shall be approved by one of the judges of Baltimore county court, and sent to the treasurer of the western shore of this state.

Section 2. And be it enacted, That it shall be the duty of the treasurer of the western shore, to pay to the board of managers, as appointed hereinafter directed, such sums as they shall, from time to time, require, not exceeding in all, the sum of twenty thousand dollars during the present year, to be applied by them as they, in their discretion, shall think best , in removing or causing to be removed , such slaves as my hereafter become free, and such people of color as are now free, and may be willing to remove out of the state to the colony of Liberia, on the coast of Africa, or to such other place or places, out of the limits of the state, as they may think best, and as the said persons to be removed, so may consent to go to, in the manner hereinafter provided \; and the said board may, from time to time, make such preparations at the said colony of Liberia, as they may think best, which shall seem to them expedient for the reception and accommodation and support of the said persons so to be removed until they can be enabled to support themselves, and shall also take such measures as may seem to them necessary and expedient to place before the people of color of the state of Maryland, full and correct information of the condition and circumstances of the colony of Liberia, or such other place or places, to which they may recommend their removal, and shall return a faithful account of their expenditures of the said sums, and make a full report of all their proceedings to the next general assembly of this state.

Section 3. And be it enacted, that it shall hereafter be the duty of every clerk of a county in this state, whenever a deed of manumission shall be left in his office for record, and every register of wills, in every county of this state, whenever a will, manumitting a slave or slaves , shall be admitted to probate, to send within five days thereafter, (under a penalty of ten dollars for each and every omission so to do, to be recovered before any justice of the peace, one half whereof shall go to the informer and the other half to the state; an extract from such deed or will, stating the names, number, and ages of slaves so manumitted, a list

list whereof , in the case of a will do proved , shall be filed therewith, by the executor or administrator) to the board of managers for Maryland, for removing the people of color of said state; and it shall be the duty of the said board, on receiving the same, to notify the American Colonization Society, or the Maryland State Colonization Society thereof, and to propose to such society that they shall engage, at the expense of such society, to remove said slave or slaves so manumitted to Liberia; and if the said society shall so engage, then it shall be the duty of the said board of managers to have the said slave or slaves delivered to the agent of such society, at such place as the said society shall appoint, for receiving such slave or slaves, for the purpose of such removal, at such time as the said society shall appoint; and in case the said society shall refuse so to receive and remove the person or persons so manumitted and offered or in case the said person or persons shall refuse so to be removed, then it shall be the duty of the said board of managers to remove the said person or persons to such other place or places, beyond the limits of this state, as the said board shall approve of, and the said person or persons shall be willing to go to, and to provide for their reception and support, such place or places as the said board may think necessary until they are able to provide for themselves, out of any money that may be earned by their hire, or may be otherwise provided for that purpose; and in case the said person or persons shall refuse to be removed to any place, beyond the limits of this state, and shall persist in remaining therein, then it shall be the duty of the said board to inform the sheriff of the county wherein such person or persons may be, of such refusal, and it shall be the duty of the said sheriff forthwith to arrest or cause to be arrested the said person or persons so refusing to emigrate from this state, and transport the said person or persons beyond the limits of this state; and all slaves shall be capable of receiving manumission, for the purpose of removal as aforesaid, with their consent, of whatever age, any law to the contrary notwithstanding.

Section 4.   And be it enacted, , that in case any slave or slaves so manumitted cannot be removed without separating families, and the said slave or slaves so unwilling on that account to be removed shall desire to renounce the freedom so intended by the said deed or will to be given, than it shall and may be competent to such slave or slaves, to renounce, in open court, the benefit of said deed or will, and to continue to be a slave.

Section 5.   And be it enacted, That it shall and may be competent for the orphan's court of this state and for Baltimore City Couty, to grant annually a permit to any slave or slaves so permitted as aforesaid, to remain as free in said county, in cases where the said courts may be satisfied by respectable testimony, that such slave or slaves so manumitted deserve such permission on account of their extraordinary good conduct and character; *Provided*, such permit shall not exempt any manumittor or his representatives, or his estate, from any liability to maintain any hereafter emancipated slaves, who, at the time his or her right to freedom accrues, who may be able top gain a livelihood, or be over forty-five years of age at said time, and afterwards become unable to maintain himself and herself.

Section 6.   *And be it enacted,* That the said board of managers, shall in all cases where the removal of a slave or slaves manumitted as aforesaid shall devolve upon them, have full power and authority, whenever the same shall be necessary, and can be done with advantage, to hire out such slave or slaves so manumitted and so to be removed, until their wages shall produce a sufficient sum to defray all expenses attending their removal, and necessary support at the place or places of such removal.

Section 7.   *And be it enacted,* That the treasurer of the western shore is hereby authorized and required, for the purpose of paying for the transportation of the colored population of this state, to borrow, on the credit of the state, in certificates of stock, not less than one thousand dollars each, the sum of twenty thousand dollars, redeemable at the expiration of fifteen years, at a rate of interest not exceeding five per cent per annum; and the faith of the state is hereby pledged for the payment of said principal when due, and the interest accruing semi-annually until paid; and the money so borrowed, is hereby appropriated to pay for the removal of the free colored population of the several counties of this state; and the said treasurer is also required to borrow, on similar terms, and payable at the lapse of fifteen years from the date of the loan, such further sum or sums as muy be require to pay the expenses incurred under this law, in removing the free people of color to Liberia or elsewhere, beyond the limits of this state; *Provided always,* that the amount of loans made, shall not exceed two hundred thousand dollars.

Section 8.   *And be it enacted,* That for the purpose of raising a fund to pay the principal and interest of the loans authorized and required by this act, the levy courts or commissioners of the several counties of this state, as the case may be, and the mayor and city council of Baltimore are hereby authorized annually during the continuance pf this act, to levy on the assessable property within their respective counties, clear of the expense of the collection severally, as follows: -- on Somerset county, the sum of three hundred and sixty nine dollars and thirty three cents; on Worcester county, the sum of three hundred and twenty – seven dollars and thirty three cents; on Dorchester county, the sum of three hundred sixty seven dollars and thirty three cents; on Talbot county the sum of two hundred and seventy six dollars; on Queen Anne' s county, the sum of three hundred and seventy five dollars and thirty three cents; on Caroline county, the sum of one hundred and fifty dollars; on Kent county, the sum of two hundred and eighty – one dollars; and on Cecil county , the sum of three hundred and ninty - six dollars and sixty – six cents; on Harford county. The sum of three hundred and fifty – six dollars and sixty – six cents; on Baltimore county the sum of three thousand two hundred and forty four dollars and sixty six cents; on Anne Arundel county, the sum of six hundred and fifty four dollars; on Prince George's county, the sum of five hundred and twelve dollars and sixty six cents; on Calvert county, the sum of one hundred and sixty dollars and sixty six cents; on St. Mary's county, the sum of two hundred and sixty three dollars and thirty three cents; on Charles county, the sum of four hundred and forty six dollars and sixty six cents; non Montgomery county the sum of three hundred and forty dollars and sixty six cents; on Frederick county, the sum of nine hundred and forty four dollars and sixty six cents; on Washington county, the sum of four hundred and ninty one dollars and thirty one cents; and on Allegany county, the sum of one hundred and fifty eight dollars which said amount or sum shall be collected in the same manner , and by the same collector or collectors as county charges are collected, the levy courts or commissioners as the case may be, and the mayor and city council of Baltimore respectively, taking bond with sufficient security from each collector for the faithful collection and payment of money in the treasury of the eastern or western shore as the case may be , at the time of paying other public moneys to, and for the use of the state.

Section 9   *And be it enacted ,* That the sheriffs of the several counties of this state , shall be, and they are hereby required to cause the number of the free people of color inhabiting their respective counties to be taken , and cause to be made a list of the names of the said free people of color residing in their respective counties; the said enumeration shall distinguish the sexes of said free people of color, and the said list shall state the ages of such free people of color, for effecting which the said sheriffs aforesaid, shall have power and are hereby required to appoint one or more assistants in their respective counties, the said lis5t of names and the said enumeration shall be made by an actual enquiry by such sheriff or his assistants at every dwelling house, or by personal enquiry of the head of every family; the said listing and enumeration shall commence on the first day of June next, and the said sheriffs shall make out two copies of the said list and enumeration stating the names, sexes, and ages of the free people of color, in their respective counties, and shall deliver one copy to the clerk of their respective counties, whose duty it shall be to record the same in a book by him to be kept for that purpose, and the other copy shall be by said sheriffs transmitted to the board of managers appointed under this act, and every sheriff failing to comply with the duties prescribed in this section , shall forfeit two hundred dollars, to be recoverable in the county court of their respective counties by action of debt or indictment.

Section 10.   *And be it enacted,* That the compensation of every sheriff and assistant shall be at the rate of two dollars and twenty five cents for every fifty persons by him returned, except where such person resides in the city of Baltimore, when such sheriff or assistant shall receive at the rate of one dollar and twenty five cents for every three hundred persons over three thousand residing in the city of Baltimore, which said compensation shall be levied on the assessable property within the respective counties, and shall be collected in the same manner and by the said collector or collectors, as the county charges are collected, and be by them paid over to the person entitled to receive the same; *Provided,* that the levy courts or commissioners of the respective counties and the mayor and the city council of Baltimore as the case may be , may, if they deem the compensation hereby allowed inadequate, allow such further compensation as they may deem proper.

Section 11   *And be it enacted,* That the several sheriffs of the counties of this state , from time to time, make report to the said board of managers of such , of said free people of color in their said counties as they shall find willing to remove from the state, stating therein the names ages and circumstances of such persons, and the place or places beyond the limits of this state to which they are willing to remove, and whether they are or are not able to defray the expenses of such removal; whether any such means are provided; and it shall be the duty of the board of managers whenever they shall ascertain by the said reports of the said sheriffs or otherwise, that such persons of color are willing to remove from the state, and to make a register of their names and ages, and take such measures as they may think necessary for their removal as soon as practicable, either to the colony of Liberia, or to such other place or places beyond the limits of this state which the said board may approve of, and to which they may be willing to go, and it shall be offered to them more then they can send in one year, from the different counties as aforesaid, to apportion the same among the said counties, according to the number respectively of their free people of color, as appears by the last census.

Section 12.   *And be it enacted,* Than nothing in this act shall be taken or construed to extend to any slave or slaves who may be entitled to his, her, or their freedom hereafter, by virtue of any deed of manumission executed or recorded according to then law, prior to the passage of this act, or last will and testament duly admitted to probate before the passage of said act, unless he, she, or they shall consent thereto.

Passed by the General Assembly of Maryland 12 March 1832.

Free African Americans of Maryland - 1832

A List of the Free People of Allegany County with their Ages and Names

Samuel Moton, 55
Henry Waugh, 14
John H. Moton, 12
William Moton, 10
Joseph Sifton, 13
William Sifton, 10
Samuel Hill, 44
Baker Parker, 80
James Harris Jr.25
James Harris Sr, 45
Sam'l Harris,35
William Harris, 10
Edward Harris, 1
James Walters, 40
William Bias, 58
John Smith, 47
Henry Smith, 17
Thompson Smith, 16
Francis Gordon Sr,
    45
Jas Gordon, 13
William Gordon, 9
Francis Gordon Jr, 4
Jerry Wilson, 26
*James Johnson, 16
John T. Alexander, 3
William Holley, 39
Thomas Holley, 17
James M. Holley, 15
Wm. Porter, 30
Benjamin Bates, 24
Nehemiah Bates, 61
William Bates, 15
Nehemiah Bates, 61
Nehemiah Bates, 14
Josias Bates, 10
John Bates, 10
William Campbell, 30
Robert Campbell, 4
Wm. Campbell2
London Satterfield,
    65
Benjamin Campbell,
    22
John Campbell, 23
Louis Buchanan, 46
Joseph Jones, 27
Basil Perry, 54
Joseph West, 40
John Butler, 4

John Smith, 46
Aora Smith, 17
Thomas Smith, 15
James Henry, 11
Wm. Henry, 4
William Hamilton, 23
John Davis, 30
Solomon Butler, 16
John Male, 17
Wilmore Male, 41
James, 15
Luke Male, 13
Wilmore Male Jr, 11
George Male, 9
Isaac Male7
Adam Male
Barney Craky, 14
Samuel Davis, 25
John T. Davis 8
Henry Hogan, 30
Moses Hogan 70
Robert Johnson, 14
Isaac Coates, 55
Joseph Waugh, 4
Lloyd Waugh, 4
Jeremiah Johnson,
    28
Otho Johnson 25
Thomas Johnson, 19
Pere Mitchell, 40
Isaac Sweet, 35
John H. Sweet, 5
Females
Susan Parker, 70
Mary Moten, 54
Priscilla Moten, 7
Margaret Moten, 6
Susan Moten, 3
Louisa Sifton, 65
Sophia Sifton, 16
Harriett Hill, 37
Casy Jenny, 12
Louisa Jenny, 9
Rebecca Parker, 53
Rosana Parker, 21
Temperance
Harris, 34
Anna Harris, 38
Henrietta Harris, 9
Mary Harris, 30

Sarah Harris, 8
Ester Jones, 18
Hannah Bias, 27
Harriett Smith, 12
Louisa Smith, 7
Elizabeth Smith, 10
Henny Butler, 42
Maria Campbell, 28
Lavinia Campbell, 5
Susan Bates, 48
Mary A. Bates, 7
Ann Holley, 13
Susan Moten, 3
Louisa Sifton, 65
Sophia Sifton, 16
Harriett Hill, 37
Casy Jenny, 12
Louisa Jenny, 9
Rebecca Parker, 53
Rosana Parker, 21
Temperance
Harris, 34
Anna Harris, 38
Henrietta Harris, 9
Mary Harris, 30
Sarah Harris, 8
Ester Jones, 18
Hannah Bias, 27
Harriett Smith, 12
Louisa Smith, 7
Elizabeth Smith, 10
Henny Butler, 42
Maria Campbell, 28
Lavinia Campbell, 5
Susan Bates, 48
Mary A. Bates, 7
Ann Holley, 13
Milly Blue, 50
Eliza Hogan, 27
Charlotte Davis, 65
Charlotte
Campbell, 26
Mary Barnes, 14
Priscilla Russell, 14
Rebecca Johnson, 23
Cornelia Coates, 10
Mary Hogan, 72
Isaac Sweet, 35
Fanny Waugh, 17
Lydia Gorden, 28

Allegany County

Fanny Massy, 37
Rebecca Butler, 14
Lavinia Butler, 10
Mary Male, 5
Elizabeth Chase, 13
Lucy Smith, 8
Chloe Henry, 45
Elizabeth Gordon, 7
Jane Butler, 44

Elsy Brooks, 37
Catherine Hamilton,
  45
Catherine Sweet, 11
Joana Butler, 17
Elizabeth Male, 18
Priscilla Male, 3
Margaret Brooks, 6
Ann Mitchell, 30
Mary A. Sweet, 9

Lucretia Sweet, 16

Elizabeth Campbell,
  55
Harriet Smith, 10
Elizabeth Smith, 6
Letty Wakly, 13

Taken by Moses
Rawlings,
Sheriff, Allegany
County

****

ANNE ARUNDEL COUNTY
CENSUS OF FREE AFRICAN AMERICANS 1832

Bushrod W. Merriott.
Sheriff of Anne Arundel County.

A list of free Negroes residing in Anne Arundel County and the City of
Annapolis in the year 1832 whose names, ages have been registered by
the Sheriff of said County agreeably to an act of the Legislature passed at
December session, 1831

Thomas Garrett, 45
Rosetta, 28
Dinah, 24
Juliet, 26
Rose, 47
Minty, 34
Abigail, 50
Nancy, 37
Minty, 30
Avarilla, 30
Rosetta, 10
Juliet, 8
Toney Bias, 50
Arrang, 26
Jacob, 22
Richard, 21
Powall, 25
William Court, 44
Thomas Court, 21
Charles Court, 18
Joseph Court, 15
John Court, 13
Issac Thomas, 45

Fielder Bracy, 23
Henry Clarke, 19
Jack Owens, 60
Benjamin James, 35
Edward Smothers,
  48
Nathan James, 45
George Sharpe, 33
James Sharpe, 28
James Ennis, 25
David Randall, 45
Riley Hawkins, 19
James Owens, 46
Thomas Owens, 23
Orange Gambrill, 46
Sammy Hill, 40
William, 60
Moses Shorter, 46
Gassaway Chew, 25
William Diggs, 20
Thomas Diggs, 16
Thomas, 25
Alexander Pratt, 54

Frederick, 56
George Jenkins, 57
David Lynn, 64
Jack, 35
Ned, 37
Benjamin Brown, 22
John Brown, 18
John, 15
Charles, 24
Thomas, 20
Suddy, 18
Margaret,
Dinah, 40
*Elizabeth, 23
Washington, 22
David, 18
Nathan, 24
Rosetta, 20
Airy, 88
Thomas, 12
Henry, 23.
Frances, 22
Elizabeth, 50

2

Anne Arundel County - 1832

*Ellen, 60
Tilghman, 11
Peter Brown, 35
Ann, 31
Thomas, 22
Cale, 40
Ann Walls, 30
Rebecca, 30
Jane, 15
Caroline, 14
Thomas, 10
David, 30
Anthony, 28
Juliet, 28
Dinnah, 30
John, 40
Ellen, 46
Thomas, 23
William, 18
Sudy, 16
Elizabeth, 4
Sophia, 10
Henry, 19
Hannah, 23
John, 30
Catherine, 14
Sarah Ann, 13
Dolly, 10
John, 6
George, 8
Sophia, 6
Charles, 28
*Mary, 28
James, 15
Cator, 14
Warssen Brown, 45
Jerry Pratt, 35
Edward Wooton, 30
Washington, 25
Clem Hill, 51
Charles Bradley, 37
Flora Hawkins, 75
Thomas, 43
Sarah Sprigg, 35
Thomas, 4
Ann, 13
John, 23
Catherine, 16
John, 40
Ellen, 34
Enoch, 16
Elijah, 13
John, 11
Elizabeth, 15
Sophia, 12
William, 5

Richard, 4
Artridge, 4
Charles, 40
Philis, 30
Pheby, 14
Nicholas, 12
Henry, 10
Ellen, 8
Eliza, 6
*George, 4
William, 2
Robert, 2
James, 30
Sarah,
Leonard, 16
Charlotte, 16
Jeremiah Smith, 40
Sarah, 46
Elizabeth, 41
Harriot, 10
Rachel, 8
Jacob, 5
James, 55
John, 2
Jasper, 22
David, 56
Darky, 56
Charles, 30
Joseph, 25
Patience, 17
Henry, 42
James, 60
Elizabeth, 60
Margaret, 24
Sarah, 8
William, 6
Violetta, 46
Phillip, 22
Rachel, 32
James, 20
Phillip, 6
Charles, 4
Benjamin, 12
Susan, 15
Darky, 14
Sarah, 13
Mary, 4
*Juliet, 3
James Stewart, 66
Ruth, 18
Caly Kelly, 6
Sarah Brown, 75
Lucy Smith, 41
William Creeke, 40
Susan, 22
Milly, 5

Wesenoy, 2
Philes, 24
Eliza, 8
William, 5
Grace, 1
Washington
Samuel, 35
Ann, 27
Elizabeth, 14
Elizabeth Ann, 13
Robert, 9
Mary, 7
Cressey, 45
Ruth, 52
Charles, 33
William, 29
Frederick, 28
Diannah, 26
James, 3
Patemac, , 17
Sophia Walls, 19
Minty Hall, 45
Thomas Brown, 27
Henry Brown, 28
James Brown, 12
John Brown, 8
Hezekiah Brown, 7
Eliza Brown, 3
Samuel Brown, 1
*John Brown, 8
Francis Howard, 60
Stephen Ennis, 40
Priscilla Ennis, 34
George Ennis, 14
James Ennis, 10
Grace, 40
Thomas, 5
William, 9
Thomas Turner, 30
Rebecca, 20
George, 3
Susan, 12
Lucy, 50
George, 52
Mary, 16
Sarah, 12
Frances Barnett, 47
Nancy Barnett, 48
Mary Barnett, 18
William Barnett, 16
Henrietta Barnett, 14
Susan Barnett, 12
Eliza, 10
Ellen Barnett, 8
Matthew Barnett, 2
Anthony, 30

Free African Americans of Maryland - 1832

Sophia, 27
Jacob, 4
John Chew, 48
Charles Chew, 23
Jane, 19
Henry Chew, 17
Elizabeth Chew, 15
Mary Chew, 14
John Chew, 12
Sarah Chew, 11
*Eliza Chew, 10
William Chew, 8
Susan Chew, 6
Ann, 3
Richard, 37
Dinah, 28
Daniel, 12
Henry, 10
Hannah, 8
Rebecca, 5
Eliza, 3
Lewis, 4
Minty, 45
Ellen Hill, 25
William Hill, 4
Aatho, 20
Harriot, 19
Thomas,
Thomas,
William Servince, 27
James Barnet, 23
Samuel Barnet, 23
Andrew, 40
Rhoda, 34
Charles, 6
Carrial, 3
Caroline, 77
Hagar, 45
Sarah, 31
Sarah Jane, 10
Thomas, 13
Margaret, 3
Rachel, 3
Philip, 17
Susan, 4
John, 60
Dolly, 24
Elizabeth, 17
*Sarah, 3
John, 2
Eliza, 12
Jane, 9
Mary Smothers, 24
Jane Ellen, 2
Julian, 1
Thomas, Turner, 45

Alley, Turner
Henry Turner, 14
Pheley Turner, 12
Ellen Turner, 10
Elizabeth Turner, 7
Ellen, 45
Margaret, 55
Thompson, 54
Thompson, 28
Ann Thompson, 18
Elizabeth, 26
Mary, 14
Kinsey, 14
Margaret, 3
John, 4
Emerson, 22
Sarah, 21
George, 5
Thomas, 3
Nancy, 2
David Lynn, 65
Elizabeth, 45
Sandy, 14
Richard, 16
Maria Diggs, 22
William, 45
Dinah, 42
Henrietta, 18
Sophia, 56
Rachel, 4
*Elizabeth, 9
William, 3
Dennis, 4
Sarah,
Jane, 21
Margaret, 6 months
Charles Calvert, 45
Margaret Calvert, 42
Mary, 24
George Calvert, 17
Rachel, 5
John, 3
David Chew, 50
Nancy Chew, 42
Crissy, 17
Warssen Brown, 47
Samuel Hawkins, 67
Flora Hawkins, 60
Ann, 26
Matilda, 24
Henrietta, 22
Washington, 20
Cidney, 16
William, 23
Mary, 13
William, 14

Airey, 33
Rachel, 33
Sarah, 14
Milly Ann, 7
Benjamin, 30
Robert, 81
Mary, 3
Margaret, 5
John, 1 month
Hillery, 6 months
Benjamin, 11
Dinah, 55
Thomas, 11
Maria, 60
Sarah, 40
Ann, 24
Washington, 3
Philip, 45
Catherine, 60
Rachel, 20
Catherine. 10
John, 6 months
Minty, 60
Dinnah, 24
Charles, 2
Elizabeth, 19
Mary, 21
Anthony, 23
David, 50
Ann, 17
Crissey, 28
Fanny Parker, 40
Elizabeth Parker, 23
Ann Parker, 14
Mary Parker, 12
Althea Parker, 10
James Parker, 2
John, 50
Ann, 60
Ellen, 37
Margaret, 24
Henry, 20
Mary, 18
Thomas, 15
John, 13
Margaret, 42
Priscilla, 23
Daniel, 19
Matthew, 7
Dinah, 4
Henry, 6
*Matthew, 1 month
Rachel, 35
Alexander, 4
Moses, 2
Thomas, 9

4

Anne Arundel County - 1832

Anthony, 8
Cidwell Brown, 60
Alley Brown, 62
William, 20
Alfred, 35
Thomas, 1
George, 16
Ann, 17
Charles, 40
Rebecca, 34
Sophia, 7
Charlotte, 6
John, 4
Thomas, 2
Ellen, 24
Mary, 19
Margaret Ann, 2 months
Washington, 7
Ann, 11
Alley, 12 months
William Darnell, 35
Phillip Darnell, 31
Benjamin James, 49
Ned, 46
Joseph Harris, 22
Minty, 70
Deborah, 22
Dinah, 43
George, 17
Sarah Ann, 13
Charles, 6
Harriot, 3
Catherine, 7 Days
Elizabeth, 34
Perry, 7
Matilda, 25
Elizabeth Boothe, 45
Elisha Boothe, 14
Charles, 40
Ellen, 40
James, 4
William, 2
Camel, 4
Wilson, 3
Avarilla, 2
Daniel, 6
Harriot, 5
James, 2
Toney, 24
Charles, 40
Clarissa, 45
Thomas, 7
Richard, 5
Rachel, 2
Richard, 10

Sophia, 29
James, 12
Sarah, 11
Mary, 19
Clarissa, 2
Singleton, 40
William, 26
Flora, 35
Mary, 2
Ned, 35
Sarah, 37
Henry, 13
Rachel, 21
Hannah, 10
William, 7
Ned, 6
Margaret, 3
George, 6
Sandy, 13
Kitty, 23
John, 2
Washington, 31
Rebecca, 50
Jane, 2
Fanny, 7
Elsa, 27
William, 11
Francis, 12
Clarissa, 8
Samuel, 6
John, 2
Joseph, 9
Joseph, 8
Lafayette, 6
Benjamin, 3
James, 1
Betty, 80
Fanny, 40
Richard, 45
Henry, 41
Sophia, 6
John, 5
Mary, 1
Louisa, 14
William, 7
Benjamin, 5
Henry, 3
Richard, 4 months
Ann, 60
*Charity, 70
James, 50
Henry, 60
William, 5
Sophy, 37
John, 22
Pleasant, 21

Jane, 18
Ellen, 15
Henry, 13
Richard, 10
Sophy, 8
Benjamin, 4
Cornelia, 30
William, 2
Henry, 45
Jane, 49
Thomas, 43
Elizabeth, 16
Ann, 145
Darkey, 10
Charles, 6
Thomas, 9
Sophy, 3
Rachel, 2
Richard, 5
William, 4
Court, 41
Dinah, 40
Susan, 14
Judy, 12
Benjamin, 12
Jane, 11
Mary, 10
Elizabeth, 8
Ann, 4
Fanny, 3
Pleasant, 2
Henry, 47
Jane, 50
Jane, 10
Clarissa, 14
Charlotte, 40
Henrietta, 14
Daniel, 14
Hager, 13
Harriet, 3
Thomas, 2
Caton, 52
Ann, 40
Margaret, 42
Susan, 2
Nelson, 43
Kinzy, 40
William, 13
Susan, 10
Mary, 1
Sophy, 4
Minty, 2
Mary, 30
Susan, 4
Catherine, 32
Napoleon, 4

5

Free African Americans of Maryland - 1832

Rachel, 2
Brasilla, 17
Richard, 55
Rachel, 28
Ellen, 21
Richard, 3
Ellen, 5
Hasley, 45
Maria, 42
Betsy, 15
John, 12
Ann, 6
Elizabeth, 4
Grace, 41
Adeline, 31
Mary, 7
James, 5
Sophia, 4
Thomas, 1 month.
Walter F. Cowen, 36
David, 19
Caesar, 66
Catherine, 60
Jane, 62
James, 35
Ellen, 53
Walter, 18
Rhoda, 17
Lewis, 15
Rachel, 6
Abigail, 55
Minty, 56
Alexander, 60
Daphas, 65
William, 23
Susannah, 14
John, 42
Dolly, 33
James, 6
Sarah, 5
Mary, 60
Orange, 60
Henry, 50
Rachel, 30
William, 80
John Gante, 30
Ann, 35
Washington, 9
Dennis, 7
Joseph, 4
Mary, 4
Peter, 70
Phillip, 35
Teny, 75
Joseph, 78
Mary, 27

John, 24
Philip, 16
Henrietta, 5
Thomas, 19
Fanny, 17
John, 15
Catherine. 13
Benjamin, 41
Eustes, 10
Rachel, 8
John, 3
Mary, 4
Isaac, 22
Henry, 35
illegible, 30
John, 10
Lucinda, 8
Susan, 6
Henry, 3
George,2
Mary, 1
Matilda, 17
Sarah, 10
Edward, 6
Richard, 4
Allen, 2
Letty, 40
Dinah, 26
Peter, 27
Mary, 24
Susan, 15
Clarissa, 19
Sarah, 40
Dinah, 24
Festus, 25
Richard, 21
Daniel, 18
George, 16
Frank, 14
Fancy, 9
Caesar, 5
Richard, 32
Sarah, 28
Richard, 6
Jacob, 4
Allien, 3
Sarah, 1
John, 37
Isaac, 45
Susannah, 44
Eliza, 19
Henry, 16
Jane, 14
Jacob, 12
William, 10
Eliza, 6

Stevens, 6
Minty, 4
Kinsey, 3
Enoch, 2
Thomas, 1
Roderick, 36
Rachel, 31
Julia Ann, 2
Samuel, 44
Caesar, 32
Lloyd, 30
James, 10
Jane, 8
Benjamin, 6
Elizabeth, 1
Mary, 15
Lucy, 17
Ana, 32
Hetty, 34
David, 14
Thomas, 13
Henry, 11
Mary, 9
Titus, 57
Lucy, 7
William Garrett, 69
Sarah Garrett, 60
William Garrett Jr, 42
Samuel Garrett31
Sarah Garrett, 18
John Garrett, 67
Ruth Garrett, 65
John Garrett Jr. 33
Mary Garrett, 20
Jerry Allen, 22
Nat Allen, 20
William, Allen, 18
Richard Pearman, 46
David Cann, 62
William Brooks, 62
Francis Brooks, 60
Francis Brooks, 19
Hester Aleen, 44
Richard Garrett, 23
Delily Allen, 18
Richard Allen, 10
Richard Garrett,10
Edward Brooks, 28
John Beard, 53
Hager Jackson, 31
Samuel Datson, 38
Sarah Matthews, 62
*Amos Garrett, 20
Henry Datson, 40
Henry Datson, 32

Anne Arundel County - 1832

Mary Galloway, 21
Lydia Galloway, 5
Margaret, Galloway, 4
Hester Galloway, 2
Mary E. Galloway, 1 month.
Rebecca Allen, 12
Jane Allen, 8
Eliza Allen, 6
William Allen, 3
Eliza Brown, 36
Rose Brown, 13
Jane Brown, 11
Adam Brown, 8
Charles Brown, 6
Brice Brown, 4
Washington Brown, 11 months, 5 days.
Ann Taylor, 28
Alice Taylor, 11
Juliet Taylor, 9
Moses Taylor, 3
Priscilla Boston, 90
Washington Taylor, 8
Richard Taylor, 5
Priscilla Hanson, 23
Grace Hanson, 6
Nace Hanson, 4
Isaac Henson, 2
Cassy Brewer, 46
Henry Brewer, 8
Henney Fowler, 18
James Fowler, 9
James Parker, 45
Dinah Parker, 25
Harriet Parker, 15
*Nancy Parker, 13
Matilda Parker, 11
Peter Parker, 7
Martha Parker, 9
Henry Turner, 6
John H. Parker, 2 months
Sarah Johnson, 56
John Johnson, 62
Sarah Osborn, 31
George Osborn, 4
Thomas Jennings, 37
Loving Jennings, 35
Stephen Jennings, 12
Clarissa Jennings, 11
William Jennings, 9

Thomas Jennings, 8
Elizabeth Jennings, 7
Mary Jennings, 5
Sophia Jennings, 2
--------, Jennings, 2 months.
Leah Simmons, 70
Samuel Dorsey, 51
Ruth _____, 65
Nicholas Duggins, 55
Henry Hunt, 25
-------- Hunt, 21
Ellen Boston, 9
Maria Burgan, 43
Nat Burgan, 2
Aquila Casker, 22
Daniel Watkins, 45
Sophia Watkins, 45
Jane Watkins, 18
Henrietta Watkins, 16
Margaret Watkins, 8
Daniel Watkins, 4
Catherine Johnson, 10
Charles Simmons, 30
*Joseph Whittington, 15
Samuel Watkins, 3_
David Boston, 27
Susan Emerson, 49
Dennis Emerson, 10
Thomas Emerson, 8
Daniel Emerson, 6
Emanuel Emerson, 4
William Johnson, 29
Rose Johnson, 33
Elizabeth Johnson, 7
Sophia Johnson, 4
Susan Johnson, 2
Lucy Johnson, 24
Mary E. Johnson, 4
Dealy A. Johnson,,2
Mary Johnson, 65
Milly Jummer, 63
Antoinette Moore, 30
Margaret Perry, 40
James Caslinger, 60
Thomas Anderson, 29
Rebecca Anderson, 27
Betsy Anderson, 8

Henry Anderson, 9 months
Nicholas Harwood, 44
Hannah Harwood, 29
Eliza Harwood, 11
Hannah Harwood 4
Mary Harwood, 2
Harcel Harwood, 8 months
William Harwood, 7
Andrew Bancroft, 6
Betsy Beall, 90
Washington Bowser, 17
John Branfoot, 22
Isaac Parker, 17
*Priscilla Queen, 43
Elizabeth Queen, 16
Susan Queen, 14
Edward Queen, 8
Thomas Queen, 4
William Queen, 6
Martha Queen, 2
Edward Bowan, 45
Susan Bowan, 55
Elizabeth Bowan, 14
Daniel Parker, 33
Henry Parker, 25
Peter Parker, 8
Harriot Parker, 6
Susan Parker, 3
Joseph Parker, 1
Edward Thomas, 35
Thomas Thomas, 35
Jerry A. Plummer, 30
Joshua Henson, 20
Abraham Short, 35
Philis Queen, 60
Mary Miers, 30
James Taylor, 21
Sarah Hammond, 55
Charles Hammond, 27
Mary Hammond, 22
Richard Hammond, 90
Nace Hammond, 18
Wilson Garrett, 19
A____ Garrett, 17
Edward Garrett, 12
Hester Berry, 42
Sarah Berry, 13
Margaret Berry, 10
Matilda Berry, 3
Charles Brooks, 18

Free African Americans of Maryland - 1832

Henry Brooks, 15
*Leonard Brooks, 13
Nancy Brooks, 23
Sarah Brooks, 2
Francis Brooks, 9
    months
Isaac Parker, 13
M____, Parker, 10
Elisha Dotson, 13
Henry Dotson, 11
John Dotson, 9
Solomon Dotson, 7
David Dotson, 5
Thomas Dotson, 3
John Thomas, 40
Harriet Parker, 23
Sarah Parker, 1
Basil Queen,
Ann Queen, 35
William Queen, 14
Martha Queen, 11
Eleanor Queen, 9
Susan Queen, 7
Daniel Queen, 5
Eliza Queen, 3
Edward Queen, 2
Charity Queen, 45
Susan Queen, 12
Milly Queen, 34
Edward Queen, 7
Ellick Toogood, 34
Harriet Toogood, 27
Washington Taylor,
    10
Joshua Toogood, 45
Joseph Queen, 47
Mary Queen, 36
Margaret Queen, 14
Thomas Queen, 12
Nancy Queen, 9
*Moses Queen, 30
Nicholas Queen, 6
William Queen, 1
Betsy Taylor, 31
John Tyler, 9
William Queen, 30
Mary Queen, 70
Hannah Queen ,18
Nelly S____, 24
Betsy S____, 4
Robert S___, 2
Samuel Dorsey, 45
Jacob Williams, 60
B____ Savoy, 65
Jacob West, 45
Sarah West, 40

William West, 16
Lydia West, 14
Thomas West, 9
George West, 7
Henry Prout, 18
Priscilla Toogood, 36
Nace Toogood, 11
Rachel Toogood, 7
James Toogood, 5
Eleanor Toogood, 3
Mary Johnson, 62
George Eager, 36
Lucretia Eager, 28
Nathan Eager, 13
John H. Eager, 10
Mary A. Eager, 8
Maranda Eager, 2
Sarah Eager, 7
Caroline Eager, 16
*Jerry Wilson, 33
Samuel Sprigg, 35
Lucy Sprigg, 30
John Lane, 44
Sarah Burgess, 70
Dinah Burgess, 43
John Burgess, 28
Judia Burgess, 37
Lucretia Burgess, 17
William Burgess, 9
Eleanor Burgess. 5
Alec Burgess, 3
Emily Burgess, 7
James Nash, 39
Jacob Cook, 35
David Waters, 45
Jerry Walls, 30
Judia Parker, 70
George Philips, 67
Sarah Dulany, 14
Francis Diggs, 6
Emily Diggs, 6
Hannah Diggs, 6
Eliza Diggs, 4
William Diggs, 2
Edward Parker, 40
Richard Bladen, 47
Henry Bladen, 42
Susan Bladen, 8
Martha Bladen,4
Solomon Matthews,
    27
Betsy Jones, 40
Philip Dulany, 33
Mary Dulany, 33
Robert Dulany, 14
Margaret Dulany, 10

Hester Dulany, 8
Eleanor Dulany, 6
Henrietta Dulany, 4
Martha E. Dulany, 2
Hester Clarke, 30
Sarah Clarke, 10
Henry Chase, 17
Offer Chew, 15
Peggy Boston, 75
Nelly Williams, 70
Nancy Turner, 33
Matilda Turner, 6
    months.
Jacob Brown, 22
Ann Garrett, 30
John Offer, 35
Nancy Offer, 32
Wesley Offer, 7
John Henry Offer, 5
William Offer, 7
Betsy Offer, 1
Maria S____, 35
Hannah S____, 13
Henry S____, 6
James S___, 2
Dinah Scott, 50
John Scott, 15
Sophia Johnson, 67
Richard Johnson, 22
Susan Scott, 28
Henry Scott, 3
Benjamin Anderson,
    60
William Johnson, 28
Samuel Johnson, 20
Stephen Watkins, 19
Stephen Johnson, 14
Peter Boston, 48
Sarah Boston, 40
Violetta Boston, 23
Mary Boston, 18
Susan Boston, 16
Isaac Boston, 14
Daniel Boston, 10
Anthony Boston, 18
Eliza Boston, 6
Elias Boston, 13
Charles Brown, 10
Charles Parker, 18
William Jennings, 27
Grace Jennings, 26
Harriet Clarke, 6
Willy Clarke
Christmas Beans, 11
Tilghman Beans, 10
Joseph Beans, 7

Anne Arundel County - 1832

Mary Beans, 3
Charles Beans, 2
Otho Gray, 35
John Johnson, 21
Frank Johnson, 14
Priscilla Simms, 17
Thomas Johnson, 31
Ambrose Queen, 57
June Queen, 55
Mary Queen, 24
Nicholas Queen, 4
Henry Queen, 2
Kitty A. Queen,
Harriet Queen, 22
Elias Queen, 2
Sarah Queen, 14
James Queen, 16
William Branfot, 27
Dealy Branfot, 26
George Branfot, 4
James Branfot, 2
Charles Parker, 21
Benjamin Anderson,
    62
*Jacob Price, 22
Jeremiah Elwood, 48
Dennis Johnson, 23
Kenneth Diggs, 7
Isaac Oliver, 52
Sophia Oliver, 7
Ezekial Oliver, 5
William Oliver, 3
Nancy Powell, 35
Lucy Anderson, 90
Joseph Powell, 5
Mary Queen, 70
Ann Queen, 20
Nicholas Boston, 20
Sib Boston, 48
Anderson Parker, 48
Elizabeth Parker, 50
Gabriel Queen, 35
Nancy Parker, 42
Lucy Parker, 60
Eliza Parker, 27
Sarah Parker, 39
Margaret Parker, 37
Betsy Parker, 35
Dalia Parker, 8
Margaret Parker, 5
Eleanor Parker, 3
Elizabeth Parker, 7
    months
Edward Parker, 10
Peter Parker, 3
Isaac Parker, 11

Lewis Bryan, 11
Juliet Jones, 7
Thomas Queen, 10
Joseph Thomas, 37
Linda Ann Parker,
    12
Albert Parker, 10
John H. Parker, 8
*Joseph Parker, 5
Mary A. Parker, 3
Sophia Parker, 3
    months
Charlotte Parker, 16
Elias Parker, 14
Hannah Parker, 14
Mary A. Parker, 8
Lucy Parker, 6
John Parker, 4
Thomas Parker, 2
Isaac Green, 44
Nelly Branfot, 44
Mary Toogood, 3
Joseph Branfot, 48
Kitty A. Parker, 17
Eli Queen, 16
Lydia Parker, 16
Joseph Parker, 12
Patience Parker, 7
Henry Parker, 4
Philip Prout, 42
Lloyd Scott, 25
William Queen, 20
William, 16
Henry Wallace
    (Mathew), 15
William Snowden, 13
Minty Wells, 44
Louisa Wells, 14
Jane W____, 20
Nancy Queen, 11
Robert Queen, 13
Archibald Hawkins,
    39
Mary Hawkins, 30
Richard Hawkins, 14
Archibald Hawkins
    Jr, 8
Gassaway Hawkins,
    6
Mary Jane Hawkins,
    4
Flavilla Hawkins, 2
*Eliza Hawkins, 4
Samuel Prout, 29
Eliza Brown, 27
Nancy Brown, 8

Mary Jane Brown, 6
Betsy Scott, 23
Nancy Ann Scott, 7
James Scott, 4
William F. Scott, 9
Charles Watkins, 40
William Watkins, 45
Priscilla Eager, 20
Margaret A. Eager, 5
Thomas Eager, 4
Hester Eager, 3
James Eager, 2
Catherine Eager, 9
Sarah Eager, 18
Mary A. Eager, 6
Kitty Calvert, 38
Maria Calvert, 11
Priscilla Calvert, 7
Martha A. Calvert, 7
Eli Queen, 30
Margaret Queen, 28
Sarah Queen, 10
Gabriel Queen, 8
Chapman Queen, 7
Mary A. Queen, 5
Isaac Snowden, 40
Rebecca Watkins, 42
Henry Watkins, 13
Sibby Watkins, 8
Mary Rebecca
    Watkins, 2
Dinah Watkins, 50
Henry Price, 65
James Toogood, 40
*Jane Snowden, 60
Susan Snowden, 30
Juliet Snowden, 4
Peter Snowden, 10
Amy Snowden, 28
Ann Snowden, 5
Mary Snowden, 3
Charles Snowden, 2
John Davis, 29
Susan Davis, 27
Cecilia Davis, 46
Samuel Davis, 1
Thomas Gault, 36
Flower Gault, 30
Martha Ann Mitchell,
    6
Eliza Mitchell, 12
Kato Bias, 22
Harriet Turner, 30
James Turner, 44
Philis Turner, 48
Mary Turner, 17

9

Free African Americans of Maryland - 1832

James Turner, 13
Susan Beard, 25
Mary Green, 20
Eliza Wilson, 15
Juliet Wilson, 14
Jane Young, 45
Mary Young, 18
Fanny Young, 14
Nancy Young, 7
Henry Denkins, 55
Mary Denkins, 44
Hannah Denkins, 14
Mary Denkins, 13
Maria Denkins, 13
Sophia Denkins, 8
Edward Denkins, 9
Jacob York, 14
*Janetta, 16
Sarah, 10
Robert Johnson, 50
Nancy Johnson, 40
Edward Johnson, 17
Elizabeth Johnson, 17
John Johnson, 14
Mathias Johnson, 10
Samuel Johnson, 6
Jerry Hammond, 43
Mary Hammond, 30
Ben Boston, 7
Delilah Scott, 60
Benjamin Toogood, 44
Eleanor Toogood, 45
Ann Toogood, 16
Kitty Toogood, 14
Eleanor Toogood, 8
Jane Toogood, 9
Sarah Toogood, 3
Isaac Hood, 49
Sarah Hood, 42
Nancy Allen, 22
Eleanor Allen, 3
Richard Boston, 35
Henry Boston, 30
Lucy Boston, 10
Charles Boston, 9
Richard Boston, 7
Stephen Boston, 3
George Johnson, 10
Edward Smothers, 16
Thomas B Burley, 45
Ann Burley, 35
John Thomas Burley, 16

Nelson Warfield, 20
Isaac Toogood, 13
Thomas Boston, 7
*Kitty Butler, 70
Henry Hall, 18
Lucy Taylor, 45
Gassaway Taylor, 14
Eleanor Burley, 13
Richard Shorter, 64
Thomas Shorter, 62
Frederick Parker, 30
Henry Parker, 33
Eleanor Burley, 30
Eleanor Burley, 5
Mary E. Burley, 10
Joshua Burgess, 26
Mary Burgess, 30
Isaac Blackson, 44
Ann Anderson, 39
Wesley Anderson, 4
Maria Boston, 55
Jane Hamilton, 60
Mary Boston, 20
John Boston, 2
George Boston, 2 months
Edward Cook, 30
Richard Smothers, 18
F____ Patterson, 65
Charles Rolls, 44
Nancy Rolls, 46
Samuel Rowles, 6
Eliza Rowles, 4
Henny Rowles, 3 months
William Smothers, 19
Charles Smothers, 14
Nancy Paterson, 36
Richard Patterson, 8
Hester Patterson, 7
John Patterson, 5
James Patterson, 4
*Fanny Griffith, 33
Abraham Griffith, 9
Peter Griffith, 6
Mary Jane Griffith, 4
James Griffith, 2
Arianna Griffith, 2 months
Aria Brown, 46
John Lane, 27
Sarah Ann Brown, 7
Mary A. Newman, 27

James Henry Newman, 2
L__ Harper, 13
Darkey Bladen, 76
Lucy Hall, 32
Mary Johnson, 15
Kitty Matthews, 10
Susan Hall, 6
Thomas Hall, 4
Rachel Hall, 2
Frank Hall, 20 days
Margaret Harrison, 24
Charity Parker, 47
Elisha Parker, 16
Ariana Parker, 12
Jane E. Parker, 6
Juliet Parker, 12
Elias Parker, 5
William H. Parker, 3
Rebecca Heckman, 27
Caesar Davis, 62
Caroline Parker, 18
Milly Parker, 10
Mary Parker, 30
Aaron Rawlings, 60
Philes Rawlings, 60
Thomas Wilson, 95
Sarah Wilson
William Jennings, 30
*Grace Jennings, 30
Rebecca Jennings, 7
Linda Jennings, 4
Charles Jennings, 2
Rachel Jennings, 2
Louisa Jennings, 1 month
Thomas Davis, 12
Rachel Yorke, 24
Charity Snowden, 25
Charles Hooper, 63
George Phillips, 60
Susan Phillips, 75
Harriet Turner, 10
William Turner, 10
Anna Turner, 8
John Turner, 6
Rebecca Turner, 4
Henry Turner, 2
Betsy Allen, 24
Ann Allen, 7 months
Teney Boston, 44
Rebecca Boston, 46
William Brashears, 56

10

Anne Arundel County - 1832

Nancy Brashears, 56
William Brashears,
36
Betsy Brashears, 14
Jane Brashears, 12
Eveline Brashears, 4
John Brashears, 28
William Boston, 28
Robert Foot, 38

3rd. & 4th. District
Samuel Anderson,
35
John Anderson, 2
John Queen, 41
Daniel Queen, 45
Augustin Queen, 13
*Sylvester Queen, 11
Daniel Queen Jr, 3
Thomas Queen, 4
months.
Isaac Oliver, 15
Jeremiah Hawkins,
12
George Hawkins, 10
Augustin Hawkins,
21
Owen Brown, 26
Aaron Brown, 15
George Brown, 5
M___ Cooper, 60
Thomas Harden, 4
George Harden, 2
John Haines, 14
Thomas Haines, 75
Isaac Hawkins, 24
John Green, 12
David Queen, 35
Kitty Anderson, 23
Christy Anderson, 4
Eliza Anderson, 2
months
Nelly Queen, 53
Susan Queen, 17
Henny Queen, 5
Hannah Queen, 35
Sarah Ann Queen,
18
Eleanor Queen, 11
Margaret Queen, 9
Mary E. Queen, 7
Lucy Alias, 12
Sarah Gaither, 20
Mary Gaither, 19
Alice Brown, 57
Emeline Brown, 41

Cassey Cooper, 28
*Cassey Gaines, 16
Priscilla Queen, 22
Mary Ann Bowie, 3
Dolly Sheppard, 12
Mary Ann Sheppard,
12
Elizabeth Sheppard,
4
William Bowie, 7
Hazel Haines, 27
Sarah Bordley, 50
Samuel Green, 24
Henry Smith, 57
Philis Barnes, 50
Thomas Barnes, 12
Jack Barnes, 10
Samuel Barnes, 6
James Barnes, 8
Joseph Barnes, 1
Anna Garret, 75
Mary Scott, 33
Charles Matthews,
40
Aaron Carroll, 50
Jenny Carroll, 45
Sarah Ann Carroll,
10
Jesse Carroll, 10
James Carroll, 8
Henry Carroll, 4
Henry M____, 23
Vashel Williams, 45
Matthew ____, 28
Isaac Harwood, 45
Lucy Topping, 73
D____ Edwards, 30
Samuel Braydon, 32
Henry Hanson, 60
Hannah Hanson, 50
Eliza Hanson, 15
Lucy Hanson, 22
Charlotte Hanson,
15
Hannah Hanson, 18
Maria Richards, 23
Mary Richards, 6
Hannah Richards, 8
James Brown, 7
Henry Jackson, 4
Joshua Hanson, 4
Samuel Jackson, 3
Gabriel Burley, 23
Nicholas Matthews,
29
Joseph Walker, 22

Shadderick Isaac, 32
Joseph Rideout, 40
John Edwards, 26
Louisa Edwards, 21
Noah Edwards, 4
Sarah Edwards, 3
Dennis Edwards, 1
Harriet Rutting, 27
Philis Rutting, 12
Benjamin Rutting, 5
Alec Rutting, 3
Rachel Sanders, 50
William Sanders, 18
Richard Sanders, 10
Samuel Herbert, 23
Benjamin Bacon, 52
Mary Bacon, 35
Benjamin Bacon Jr,
1 month.
Susan Clarke, 19
Henry Clarke, 16
Samuel Jones, 40
Priscilla Jones, 40
Flavilla Jones 15
Eliza Ann Jones, 12
John H. Jones, 8
Mary Jane Jones, 4
John Brooks, 74
*Kitty Brooks, 35
Samuel Brooks, 16
Sarah Brooks, 14
Henry Brooks, 12
Caroline Brooks, 10
Anna Brooks, 4
Ann Brooks, 3
Frank Lowns, 65
Ellen Gaither, 21
James Gaither, 32
Rachel A. Gaither, 1
Richard Sanders, 35
Charles Kess, 55
Sarah Kess, 49
Henry Kess, 8
Ely Kess, 7
Charles Kess Jr. 5
Mary Kess, 11
Margaret Kess, 1
Rachel Green, 19
Joshua Toogood, 36
Perr Meir, 45
Nace ___, 65
Levin Gross, 32
Priscilla Gross, 45
David ___, 50
Nelly ___, 70
Henry Reese, 80

Free African Americans of Maryland - 1832

Samuel Hall, 55
Charles Cromwell, 70
Jerry Walker, 45
Washington James, 25
Perry Wright, 51
Susan Wright, 46
Joseph Wright, 10
Perry Wright Jr. 8
*Emory Wright, 6
Caesar Hindsman, 36
Rodu Hindsman, 21
Richard Hindsman, 13
Jacob Hindsman, 12
Elizabeth Hindsman, 9
Nancy Hindsman, , 7
Hessey Hindsman, 6
William Hindsman, 3
Dela Hindsman, 1
Louisa Maynard, 1
George Powell, 45
Charlotte Powell, 31
Mary Ann Powell, 12
Charles Powell, 1
Paul Queen, 40
Patsy Queen, 25
John Queen, 6
Isaac Queen, 4
Jack Queen, 70
Betty Green, 60
James Green, 35
Stephen Thomas, 36
Nicholas Scott, 40
Wilson Johnson, 23
Andrew Hutton, 21
Edward Reed, 23
John Queen, 21
Ann Stomp, 25
James Butler, 33
Joseph Pea, 26
Samuel Wade, 19
Amos Tyler, 30
Julia Pea, 30
Ned , 45
John Brown, 50
Charles Brown, 18
Phebe Matthews, 15
*John Brown, 50
Charles Brown, 18
Philis Matthews, 35
Hester Matthews, 15
Phoebe Brown, 3

Jacob Madden, 45
Sophia Madden, 37
John Madden, 20
Ann Madden, 18
Caroline Madden, 17
Jonas Madden, 14
Hannah Madden, 11
Eliza Madden, 7
Israel Madden, 5
Gerard Madden, 4
Adeline Madden, 1
Phillip Wright, 50
Peggy Wright, 38
John Bell, 15
Susan Bell, 9
Samuel Redman, 50
Hester Redman, 29
Charles Sheppard, 7
Emanuel Queen, 22
Julia Queen, 1 month
Donsies Fisher, 14
Nicholas John, 40
Robert Fisher, 40
Jerry Anderson, 21
Jacob Queen, 28
Gerrard Gray, 13
William Thompson, 12
Matilda Queen, 18
Patty Queen, 2 months.
Richard Fisher, 17
Lydia Hopkins, 45
Henry Primrose, 12
Robert Hopkins, 2
Samuel Butler, 52
William Butler, 19
Daniel Butler, 15
Joseph Butler, 18
Samuel Butler, 15
Daniel Butler, 12
Peter Butler, 11
Thomas Butler, 8
Henry Butler, 7
Catherine Butler, 14
Susan Isaac, 18
Mike Thompson, 56
Samuel Butler, 22
William Butler, 19
Joseph Butler, 18
Samuel Butler Jr, 15
Daniel Butler, 12
Peter Butler, 11
Thomas Butler, 8
Henry Butler, 7

Catherine Butler, 14
Susan Isaac, 18
Ann Hammond, 45
Rachel Hammond, 35
Joseph Hammond, 3
John Hammond, 4
Jane Hammond, 1
Polly Taylor, 60
Ann Taylor, 20
Treasy Taylor, 17
Mary Taylor, 15
Richard Jacob, 25
Dela Toogood, 40
Ann Toogood, 5
Blind Abbey, 60
Saraha Howard, 50
Addison Hall, 24
Henry Hall, 14
*Molly Baldwin, 13
Kitty Green, 35
Sarah Green, 6
Jane Green, 4
Anna Green, 24
Samuel Green, 2
James Green, 2
Charles Williams, 35
Ann Williams, 22
Rachel Williams, 3
Malinda Williams, 1
Fielder Gray, 40
Judy Gray, 11
Emeline Gray, 10
Charlotte Gray, 7
Albert Gray, 6
Nancy Gray, 5
Philip Gray, 4
John Gray, 3
James Pea, 60
Priscilla Pea, 52
Harriet Butler, 17
Synthia Butler, 22
Julia Butler, 3
William Harrison,, 4
Cato Matthews, 60
Rachel Matthews, 25
Mary Matthews, 20
Charity Powell, 70
Bob Chesly, 70
Rachel Waters, 50
Richard Waters, 10
William Waters, 7
Maria Waters, 12
Philes Waters, 23
John Waters, 14
Rachel Waters, 4

Anne Arundel County - 1832

Mary Williams, 25
*Beck Williams, 2
Daniel Willliams, 4 months
Nelly Simms, 18
Nancy Brooks, 45
Lucy Brooks, 16
Mary Brooks, 13
Ann Brooks, 9
Eliza Brooks, 9
Henry M___, 24
Samuel Bell, 36
Sally Harkens, 23
Peter Harkens, 6
Julia Matthews, 25
John Matthews, 5
Solomon Matthews, 4
Sarah Matthews, 37
Alice Matthews, 10
Marion Matthews, 4
Darkey Gardner, 40
Barbury Gardner, 1 month
Matilda Johnson, 18
Henry Matthews, 4
John Johnson, 3 months
Peter Madden, 65
Mary Butler, 20
Sally Bell, 6
Polly Bell, 25
Mary Bell, 7
Richard Bell, 3
Martha Bell, 56
Henry Matthews, 54
Rachel Matthews, 1
Lydia Matthews, 60
Abraham Matthews, 17
Richard Matthews, 29
Jacob Matthews, 22
Bill Matthews, 8
Peggy Matthews, 11
*George Matthews, 8
Nachel Peterson, 14
Kitty Gardner, 11
Lydia Gardner, 14
Nelly Gardner, 19
Ann Hanson, 65
Sally Smith, 50
Juda Matthews, 23
John Matthews, 4
Solomon Matthews, 1

Henry Bull, 65
Rachel Matthews, 25
Thomas Waters, 30
Polly Matthews, 50
Margaret Jones, 5
Joseph Waters, 1
Jerry Madden, 55
Vachel Rutland, 45
Mary Brown, 65
Thomas Jackson, 23
William Jackson, 17
John Jackson, 16
Polly Jackson, 50
Polly Mans, 60
India Mans, 26
Harriet Hill, 20
Henry Mans, 6
Elizabeth Mans, 3
William Mans, 2
Nace Mans Jr, 1
Thomas Brown, 40
Julia Brown, 40
Haze Kiah Duff, 35
Jane Duff, 30
Helen Reely, 29
Samuel Time, 45
Rachel Time, 40
Henry Crowner, 40
*Ann Crowner, 40
Rachel Hammond, 22
Nat Hill Jr, 34
Joshua Richards, 42
Hannah Richards, 45
Hannah Hill, 28
John Boon, 35
Harriet Boon, 20
Juda Wallace, 75
Nat Hill Senior, 74
B___ Hill, 65
Thomas Hill, 24
Dela Hill, 25
Sarah Hill, 21
Stephen Hill, 7
Nathan Hill, 29
Hager, Mans, 29
Charlotte Mans, 12
Lucy Mans, 4
Nathaniel Johnson, 8
Charles Lee, 50
Julia Lee, 60
Mary Lee, 7
Charles L___, 65
William Gross 7

Thomas Queen, 70
Milly Queen, 56
Noah Hawkins, 35
P___ Hawkins, 24
Lewis Hawkins, 6
Charlotte Hawkins, 2
Philes Hawkins, 55
Mary Hawkins, 19
Charlotte Hawkins,10
Rachel Mills, 23
Flora Thomas, 23
Mary Queen, 16
*Susan Thomas, 9
Nelly Thomas, 5
Mary Thomas, 3
Joshua Toogood, 43
Priscilla Toogood, 33
Jacob Thomas, 11
Joshua Thomas, 6
Emeline Thomas, 5
Charles Thomas, 2
John Burley, 21
Mary Thomas, 55
Daniel Thomas, 21
Mary Thomas, 18
Noah Waters, 37
Maria Waters, 27
Margaret Waters, 10
Eliza Waters, 8
Rachel Waters, 5
Hester Waters, 2
Ellen Waters, 1 month
Abraham Brogden, 72
Solomon Brogden, 30
Lucy Brogdon, 30
Henry Brogden, 16
Abraham Brogden Jr, 11
Eveline Brogden, 13
Kitty Brogden, 9
Henry Brogden, 7
Henrietta Brogden, 5
Rachel Brogden, 3
Hannah Brogden, 2
Dennis Queen, 40
Mary Queen, 26
Betsy Queen, 8
Louisa Queen, 6
Susan Queen, 2
Nelly Queen, 38
Nicholas Burley, 38
*Rachel Burley, 24

Free African Americans of Maryland - 1832

Gabriel Burley, 3
Eliza Burley, 5
John Burley, 1
Addison, Hall, 25
Ann Burley, 23
Nicholas Burley, 22
Nace Baldwin, 65
Pricilla Baldwin, 36
John Baldwin, 18
Eliza Baldwin, 18
Fanny Baldwin, 4
Thomas Boston, 50
Polly Boston, 50
Charles Boston,
Thomas Boston Jr,
  17
Louisa Fisher, 12
George Fisher, 6
William Fisher, 8
Hannah Hawkins, 45
Eliza Hawkins, 17
Lewis Hawkins, 25
Larkin Hawkins, 6
Henry Hawkins, 4
Jane Nicholson, 50
Priscilla Nicholson, 5
Ellen Brooks, 40
Mary Brooks, 16
Lawson Clarke, 30
Sarah Clarke, 20
Washington Clarke,
  4
Rachel Clarke, 10
Susan Harris, 50
Henry Harris, 8
Jane Harris, 6
Maria Cotton, 28
Robert Cotton, 6
Alvide Cotton, 1
  month
Mary Montgomery,
  58
Peter Montgomery,
  25
Betsy Cooke, 22
Israel Cooke, 3
Thomas Waters, 40
Jane Waters, 40
George Waters, 4
Richard Waters, 1
Julia Howard, 16
William Stewart, 11
Nancy Bias, 71
Peter Bias, 39
Clarissa Bias, 40
Elizabeth Bias, 21

John Bias, 2
Peter Williams, 20
Henry Williams, 12
Joseph Williams, 6
Clem Williams, 3
Polly Ramsey, 50
John Ramsey, 18
William Ramsey, 18
Margaret Ramsey, 12
Walter Reed, 50
Nancy Scott, 40
Fanny Scott, 12
Pansy Scott, 4
Ellen Scott, 4
Philes Scott, 3
  months
John Jones, 30
Jane Jones, 31
Henry Jones, 14
Zachariah Jones, 7
Thomas Jones, 5
Mary Jones, 6
  months
Susan Jones, 22
Susan Pennington,
  22
William Matthews,
  20
Matilda Matthews,
  25
Margaret Matthews,
  5
Frank Matthews, 3
Thomas Curtis, 11
Mary Stewart, 11
Lorenzo Wallace, 7
Eliza Wallace, 5
Anderson Wallace,
  10 months
Ned Wallace, 50
Maria Wallace, 10
Kitty Wallace, 8
Lydia Wallace, 12
Joseph Smith, 40
Fanny Queen, 30
William Queen, 11
Ellen Queen, 10
Ann Queen, 9
Susan Queen, 6
Joseph Queen, 1
Mary Queen, 14
Dela Queen, 25
Ruth Queen, 60
Arthur Brown , 2
Eliza Brown, 4
Columbus Cooke, 5

Phillip Cooke, 30
Henny Hooper, 70
Maria Hooper, 73
Ezekiel Hooper, 35
Washington
  Johnson, 3
Daniel Matthews, 45
Rebecca Matthews,
  18
Bill Matthews, 16
Nace Wallace, 30
Betsy Wallace, 35
Lydia Benjamin, 30
Isaac Benjamin, 39
Eliza Matthews, 16
Milly Jackson, 25
William Jackson, 33
Thomas Jackson, 25
Abraham Jackson,
  19
Benjamin Williams,
  25
Andrew Welch, 28
Robert Andrews, 41
Rachel Adams, 40
George Adams, 17
Susan Adams, 15
James Adams, 14
Nace Adams, 12
John Adams, 9
Elbridge Adams, 5
Benjamin Adams, 3
  months
Jason Wallace, 50
Mary Wallace, 50
Sally Hill, 40
Ann Hill, 3
Thomas Hawk, 35
Joseph Hawk, 20
Augustus Hawk, 16
William Hawk, 9
James Hawk, 4
Sophia Runnels, 23
James Runnels, 30
Vachel Harrison, 45
Robert Downes, 20
Edward Scott, 19
John R___, 28
Emory R___, 29
Thomas Rainer, 24
John Hawk, 26
Louisa Hawk, 18
John Hawk Jr. 4
Saul Rainer , 48
Saul Rainer Jr, 22
William Rainer, 20

14

Anne Arundel County - 1832

Henry Rainer, 12
Priscilla Rainer, 10
Nancy Rainer, 16
Emily Rainer, 8
Kitty Rainer, 4
Eliza Rainer, 2
Bill Rainer, 3
Monaka Queen, 50
Noah Queen, 28
Thomas Queen 25
Bill Queen 20
Isaac Queen, 10
William 25
Sally Queen, 16
Bett Queen 8
Edward Queen, 2
Edward 1
Milly Queen, 40
Lloyd Hill, 50
Ann Hill, 30
Dinah Brown, 49
Lewis Brown, 51
Eliza Lily, 22
Peter Lily, 23
Bill Williams, 50
Sally Williams25
Lucy Johnson, 40
Samuel C. Johnson
6
Washington
Johnson, 4
Samuel Prout, 28
Rachel Barnes, 26
Charles, 5
Ann Hall, 23
John Hall, 2
Dinah Barnes, 20
*Edward Jackson, 18
Charlotte Williams,
50
Stephen Ready, 9
Bill Williams, 40
Charlotte Williams,
35
Thomas Johnson, 15
John Johnson, 13
Margaret Johnson,
11
George Williams, 8
Henry Williams, 6
Thomas Ready, 36
Mary Ready, 60
William, 10
Eliza Lucas, 7
Pere Ready, 20
Philip Stevenson, 45

Ann Brown, 26
Peter Johnson, 37
Joseph Queen, 35
Samuel Gaither, 24
Tobias Toogood, 50
Ann Wilkinson, 60
Joseph Benson, 13
Julia Gray, 12
William Isaac, 40
Peter Gambrill, 47
Lucy Gambrill, 44
George, 21
William Gambrill, 17
John Gambrill, 11
Frederick Gambrill, 9
Lorenzo Gambrill, 4
Orlando Gambrill3
Mahala Gambrill, 3
Asa Gambrill, 2
Mary Gambrill, 1
George Toogood, 45
Dela Toogood, 25
*John Toogood, 5
Sarah Toogood, 3
Ellen Toogood
Jacob Toogood, 75
Jacob Johnson, 45
Charity Johnson, 22
Margaret Johnson, 3
Julia Johnson, 2
Levi Johnson, 1
Charles Kess, 50
Susan Kess, 40
Henry Kess, 8
Eli Kess, 7
Charles Kess, Jr, 6
Mary Kess, 4
Margaret Kess, 2
Rachel Whent, 10
Mary Whent, 5
Fannie Hains, 60
Wesley Simms, 16
Charles Simms, 55
Betsy Simms, 40
Mary Simms, 17
Betsy Simms, 16
John Simms, 6
Elizabeth Simms, 3
Joseph Simms, 2
Charles Simms, Jr, 1
Dinah Williams, 40
Aaron Williams, 12
Wesley Williams, 4
Maranda Williams, 3
ThomasWilliams, 6
Nachel Williams Jr, 8

Margaret Williams, 6
Ann Williams, 2 1
Richard Shouss, 18
William H. Williams,
1
*Sarah Williams, 22
Malow Williams, 22
Cassey Williams, 50
Leatha Williams, 13
Maria Isaac, 55
Eliza Isaac, 25
William Isaac, 10
Benjamin Isaac, 8
Basil Isaac, 7
Emeline Isaac, 5
Maria Isaac, 10
months
Billy Williams, 35
Harriet Williams, 20
Elizabeth Williams, 2
Ellen Brooks, 30
George Brooks, 35
Mary Brooks, 13
Margaret Brooks, 8
Elizabeth Brooks, 6
Sarah Brooks, 1
Vachel Williams, 40
Caroline Gray, 27
Leatha Gray, 14
Rachel Gray, 8
Lucy Gray, 3 months
Samuel Gray, 3
George Gray, 7
William Tilghman, 50
Kitty Tilghman, 30
Elizabeth Tilghman,
7
Gabriel Tilghman, 4
Eliza Tilghman, 2
John Tilghman, 10
Henry Bowie, 55
George Long, 50
Lucy Long, 25
Robert Johnson, 25
Betsy Johnson, 16
*John Johnson, 15
Bill Johnson, 10
Nicholas Johnson,
60
Fanny Johnson, 30
Anthony Robinson,
60
Ann Robinson, 55
Anthony Robinson
Jr, 12
Susan Robinson, 16

Free African Americans of Maryland - 1832

Betsy Robinson, 25
Ann Robinson, 28
James Pack, 60
Lydia Pack, 45
Nelly Pack, 23
Eliza Pack, 22
Walter Pack, 30
Pompey Pack, 22
Jane Pack, 3
Abraham Franklin,
  21
Henry Franklin, 40
Betsy Jackson, 16
Hester Jackson, 2
  months
James Franklin, 15
Levy Franklin, 14
Robert Franklin, 5
Edward Franklin, 2
Peter Franklin, 60
Nicholas Snowden,
  30
Delilah Snowden, 30
Richard Job, 70
Pomphrey Williams,
  32
John Tilghman, 32
Ben Wright, 24
Henry Snowden, 40
Henrietta Snowden,
  7
Lloyd Snowden, 3
Ann Snowden, 3
Basil Jacob, 35
Nacky Jacob, 30
*Rachel Jacob, 10
James Jacob, 8
Daniel Jacob, 6
John Jacob, 1
Priscilla Gray, 1
James Titus, 60
Sarah Titus, 45
Peter Bryan, 65
Lydia Bryan, 45
Fanny Bryan, 14
Mary Bryan, 6
Henry Barnes, 30
July Barnes, 25
Samuel Goodwin, 55
Bill Lee, 40
Nancy Gross, 35
John Gross, 9
Basil Gross, 6
David Gross, 2
Priscilla Gross, 25
Rachel Gross, 5

Ned Gross 3
Saul Watts, 45
Ephriam Gray, 60
Patience Gray, 36
Richard Gray, 23
Samuel Gray, 18
Green Gray, 13
Mary Gray, 10
Hammond Gray9
Stephen Gray, 70
Patty Lee, 70
Ann Lee, 20
Jacob Guest, 30
*Bill Howard, 40
Milly Howard, 40
Mary Howard, 8
Jane Howard, 7
Bill Howard Jr, 6
Richard Howard, 5
Sarah Howard, 4
Lucy Ross, 40
Adeline Ross,16
Charlotte Ross, 10
Emily Ross, 2
Harriet Richardson,8
Susan Richardson, 7
James Richardson, 1
Hannah Guest, 70
Thomas Miller, 24
William Wright, 26
Kitty Wright, 21
Henny, 1
Stephen Cromwell,30
Paul Jones, 10
Ann Jones, 5
Thomas Johnson, 40
Hannah Ijams, 60
Kitty Lee, 20
Sophia Stephens, 45
Maria Stephens, 16
Victor Stephens, 1
Lewis Lee, 21
Dinah Brown, 55
Henry Johnson, 36
Sally Johnson, 36
Mary Johnson, 13
John Johnson, 14
Jane Johnson, 10
Rachel Richardson,
  36
John Richardson, 18
*Elizabeth
  Richardson, 15
Crazy Rachel, 75
Charity Johnson, 40
Jacob Gibbs, 85

Phillip Johnson, 60
George Gill, 70
Fanny Gill, 65
Isaac Williams, 24
Abraham Hammond,
  50
Jane Hazelwood, 40
Sarah Barton, 40
Jane Johnson, 40
Jesse Grinnage, 50
David Johnson, 35
William Maynard, 20
Michael Hall, 45
Samuel Green, 50
Lydia Green, 40
Kitty Green, 20
Caroline Green, 23
Thomas Green, 3
Richard Green, 1
Jane Hall, 33
Bill Howard, 40
Samuel Howard, 2
George Howard, 9

ANNAPOLIS
Henry Price, 39
Lucy Hawkins, 15
William Shorter, 17
Basil Miller, 37
Susan Sands, 30
Peter Brown, 35
Sarah Brown, 65
Dinah Jackson, 60
Adeline Jackson, 62
Matilda Jackson, 20
John Jackson, 10
Dolla Belt, 35
George Larkins, 40
Charlotte Watson, 16
Mary Watkins, 12
Fanny Watson, 6
Anthony Watson, 10
Susan Jackson, 23
Clarke Franklin, 35
Jane Chew, 22
Sally Chew, 11
John James, 6
William Price, 4
Mary Johnson, 25
Moses Johnson, 2
Henrietta Davis, 34
Ann Davis, 12
Thomas Price, 5
George Price, 1
Ann Stephens, 65
Isaac Stephens, 25

Anne Arundel County - 1832

Charles shorter, 42
Charity Shorter, 35
William Shorter, 15
Daniel Shorter, 13
John Shorter, 9
Ann Shorter, 7
Lewis Shorter, 4
Elizabeth Shorter, 2
Polly Brown, 30
Jane Brown, 12
Charles Brown, 8
Ann Brown, 6
Rebecca Brown, 4
William Brown, 3
Nelly Diggs, 40
Dennis Diggs, 35
*Mary Hall, 55
Jane Bias, 27
Kitty Davis, 3
Mathias Bias, 23
Rebecca Offer, 55
Hannah Stewart, 47
Sally Johnson, 37
Hester Johnson, 5
Lucy Johnson, 3
Peter Johnson, 1
John Offer, 60
Sarah Lee, 60
Kitty Lee, 33
Rebecca Smith, 26
Elizabeth Harrison, 24
William Smith, 20
William Smith, Jr, 9
Nancy Smith, 6
Eliza Smith, 3
Henry Harrison, 5
John Harrison, 3
William Garrett, 7
Henry Garrett, 4
John A____, 7
Phillip Jacobs, 50
Nancy Johnson, 17
Cassy Kent, 40
Matilda Jackson, 16
Peter Davidge, 40
Julia Wade, 38
Priscilla Richardson, 80
Eliza Fosset, 18
Susan Butler, 30
Mary Mills, 13
Osborn Harwood, 35
Debby Cane, 25
Thomas Cane, 1
Patty Brisgdon, 30

*William Harrison, 25
Valentine Williams, 65
Thomas Johnson, 75
Priscilla Cook, 12
Frisby Miller, 43
Henry Price, 15
John Price, 13
Sally Price, 10
Alexander Price, 6
Sidney Chew, 20
Ann Price, 35
James Miller, 58
Christopher Kess, 57
Benjamin Offer, 35
Mary Offer, 25
Harriet Calder, 55
Ann Miller, 20
Louisa Miller, 15
Rachel Ford, 70
William Bowser, 7
Mary Harrison, 29
Nelly Parker, 40
Sophia Johnson, 17
Ann Bragdon, 12
Eliza Watkins, 16
Betty Carter, 44
Robert Carter, 2
Phillip Boston, 30
Ann Joles, 29
Elizabeth Matthews, 35
Henry Matthews, 40
Caroline Dorsey, 16
Harriet Chew, 12
William Ennis, 12
Charity Bishop, 38
William Bishop, 30
*John Bishop, 9
William Bishop, Jr, 8
James Bishop, 7
Horace Bishop, 6
Nicholas Bishop, 4
Rebecca Bishop, 2
Charity Folks, 76
Mary Blake, 46
Lucy Williams, 28
Rachel Ireland, 30
Charlotte Ford, 23
Ann Kent, 20
Debby Ford, 23
William Ford, 9
Sarah Ford, 4
Henry Tasker, 10
Mary Tasker, 7

William Tasker, 5
Jim Tasker, 4
Henrietta Tasker, 1
Edward Ford, 26
Harriet Johnson, 24
Aaron Johnson, 26
Margaret Boston, 30
Mary Blackson, 8
William Phelps, 4
Rebecca Boston, 2
John Boston, 6 months
Betta Cooks, 20
Ruthy Cooks, 45
Betsy Hanson, 16
Horace Hawkins, 5
Margaret Hawkins, 4
Jane Hawkins, 3
James Hawkins, 2
Darky Cooke, 25
Henry Cooke, 9
Sarah Boston, 22
*Debora Boston, 2
Anne Evans, 44
Mary Evans, 11
Hannah Fisher, 50
Mary Frazier, 60
William James, 45
Sarah Frazier, 60
Susan Brown, 40
Mary Brown, 16
Thomas Brown, 14
Harriet Brown, 11
Louisa Brown, 10
Rachel Brown, 9
Henrietta Brown, 5
Charles Brown, 4
Thomas Brown, 45
Sarah Jackson, 50
William Jackson, 65
Dinah Jackson, 18
Sarah Jackson, 5
Charity Gordon, 55
George Robinson, 60
Mary Prout, 22
Rachel Prout, 4
Joannah Prout
Anthony Belt, 50
Mary Harris, 18
Charlotte Watson, 16
Nora Watson, 29
Fanny Watson, 9
Anthony Watson, 14
Sally Lane, 50
Jane Troy, 70
Henrietta Brown, 45

17

Free African Americans of Maryland - 1832

Simpsey Lucy, 50
Mary I. Miller, 8
John Ennis, 35
John Harris, 27
Horace Bishop, 27
*John Brogden, 24
Eliza Hanson, 7
Daniel Hanson, 38
Henrietta Harrison, 27
James Hanson,6
Margaret Hanson, 1
Mary Johnson, 8
Hager Jacobs, 35
Harriet Jacobs, 12
Lilly Forty, 6 months
Margaret Forty, 9
Matilda Forty, 20
Dotty Pully, 9
Henry Pully, 12
Rachel Pully, 14
Ann Pully, 12
Andrew Harris, 45
Kitty Harris, 40
Lucretia Ward, 30
Elizabeth Ward, 14
Sophia Ward, 10
Martha Ward. 4
Jefferson Stewart, 22
Richard Joice, 17
Mary Brooks, 14
Charles Lovenden, 19
Sarah Lovenden, 15
George March, 16
Thomas Johnson, 70
Sarah Johnson, 70
Richardson Fanny, 60
Harriet Short, 30
Mary Stewart, 30
Alexander Stewart, 10
Mary I. Stewart, 2
Mary F. Stewart, 7
Rebecca Hall, 40
Harriet Hall, 12
*Martha Williamson, 4
Nancy Timmons, 43
Anne Robinson, 60
Charlotte Harrison, 48
John Carroll, 58
Mary Hanson, 15
Henny Hanson, 22

William Hanson, 12
John Hanson, 21
Henry Hanson, Jr, 18
William Chew, 13
Kitty Joice, 30
Dover Green, 45
Mary A. Green, 11
William H. Green, 5
Rebecca Duke, 6
Prissy Toogood, 70
Moses Butler, 66
Lucy Butler, 60
Susan Brown, 40
Anne Stewart, 70
James Stewart, 75
Dinah Chew, 30
Cloey Chew, 20
James Chew, 8
Richard Chew, 3
Thomas Chew, 4
Margaret Chew, 5
Mary Larkins, 30
William Larkins, 10
Rachel Larkins, 3
Julia Larkins, 1
Henrietta Chew,
  Rebecca Chew, 4
Harriet Harris, 35
*Isabella Harris, 14
Ann I. Harris, 10
Emily Harris, 9 months
Rebecca Harris, 13
Gracy Hemming, 60
Mary Stewart, 45
Rebecca Bishop, 24
Thomas Blackson, 15
Thomas Harris, 34
Mary Harris, 25
Daniel Harris, 5
John Harris, 4 months
Jim Harris, 45
Moses Lako, 35
Anne Johnson, 35
Benjamin Offer, 30
Betsy Peterson, 55
Eliza Diggs, 15
John Smith, 40
Elizabeth Smith, 13
William Smith, 10
Richard Smith, 8
Isabella Smith, 4
Josephine Smith, 4

Maria Smith, 4 months
Julia Peterson, 20
Adeline Jackson,20
Stephen Jones, 29
Maria Diggs, 12
Julia West, 16
Fanny Lowrey, 35
Mary Tillson, 40
Susan Butler, 40
Isaac Watkins, 20
Barney Taylor, 13
*Francis Neale, 30
John Cooke, 25
George Ford, 36
John Butler, 35
Ally Fidd, 50
Charles Butler, 27
Noble Butler, 70
Susan Butler, 30
Stephen Butler, 6
Josephine Butler, 6
Matilda Butler, 8
Eliza Butler, 3
John Maynard, 20
Mary Chase, 17
Adrian Bowie, 28
William Bowie, 10
Anne Green, 20
Sarah Garrison, 26
Fanny Garrison, 11
Priscilla Wallace, 55
Fanny Edwards, 30
Nelly Edwards, 2
Sarah Matthews, 60
Charlotte, 35
Milly, 30
Mary Phelps, 40
Henry Forty, 65
John Forty, 60
Henrietta Howard, 13
Maria Moss, 26
Maria Watkins, 30
Noble Watkins, 7
Harriet Watkins, 13
Joseph Watkins, 6
Thomas Johnson, 50
Kitty Johnson, 13
Betsy Lee, 14
Mary A. Thomas, 17
Eleanor S____, 7 months
William Davis, 70
Sarah Hawkins, 45
Charlotte Frost, 30

Anne Arundel County - 1832

Henrietta Frost, 14
Susan Wilkes, 40
Sarah Wilkes, 80
John Wilkes, 38
Margaret Watkins,
    15
Prissy Matthews, 38
Alexander Matthews,
    35
Priscilla Matthews3
Anne Anderson, 35
Richard Anderson, 4
Nancy Hawkins, 60
Frank Davidge, 70
Henry Young, 12
James Cane, 33
Matilda Howard, 25
Dinah Jackson, 50
Nancy Osborn, 60
Sophia Ward, 13
Jeremiah Kess, 14
Mary Sinott, 21
Sally Johnson, 22
Stephen Johnson, 8
Lucy Runnells, 70
Stephen Runnells,
    51
William Calder, 45
Charity Williams, 50
Minty Sewell, 45
Polly Gibson, 38
Anne Gibson, 14
Sally Gibson, 7
Thomas Gibson, 4
Jane Richardson, 65
Mary Fisher, 35
Thomas Fisher, 39
*George Fisher, 14
James Fisher, 12
William Fisher, 8
Anne Fisher, 5
Henry Fisher, 4
Emily Fisher, 2
Lydia Larkins, 35
Solomon Larkins, 35
Mary Larkins, 10
James Larkins, 13
Sally Larkins, 4
Rosey Thomas, 70
Alexander Thomas,
    19
Mary Thomas, 16
Eleanor, S___, 9
James Jackson, 50
Linda Jackson, 37
Henry Jackson, 17

Eliza A. Jackson, 13
James R. Jackson,
    12
Nicholas Jackson, 10
Daniel Jackson, 7
Benjamin Jackson, 4
Richard Jackson, 2
Lucy Wilson, 40
Milly Cann, 56
Charles Cann, 6
Elizabeth Cann, 20
Joseph Brown, 75
Lucy Smith, 87
John Smith, 80
Henrietta Hanson,
    35
Charles Hanson, 5
William Brown, 15
William Jackson, 16
Nelly Wilson, 30
Henry Wilson, 6
Cynthia Wright, 6
Henrietta Hall, 30
Samuel Wilson, 25
Mary Wilson, 20
Nancy Wilson, 20
Samuel Wilson, 25
William Cooke, 45
Kitty Cooke, 38
Rachel Cooke, 11
William Cooke, Jr,
    10
Priscilla Cooke, 8
James Cooke, 5
John Cooke, 3
Rosetta Hindman, 16
Mary Ennis, 13
William Ennis, 12
Fanny Ennis, 7
Leah Ennis, 6
Emily Ennis, 4
Sarah I. Ennis, 2
John Ennis, 2
    months
Sarah Ennis, 2
    months
James Bishop, 70
Leonard Bishop, 18
Sarah A. Lucas, 29
Jane Pully, 60
Ned Pully, 4
Maria Thomas, 50
Thomas Thomas, 60
Cassy Merrikin, 25
Hannah Johnson, 4
    months

Tamar Williams, 36
Joseph Williams, 46
Milly French, 40
Ridy Covenden, 38
Phillis Green, 35
Eliza Lossit, 18
Susan Lofton, 38
*John Lofton, 4
Anne Spencer, 22
Emanuel Hall, 70
Grace Hall, 50
Hannah Bordley, 60
Henny Bordley, 15
Isabella French, 6
Mary Mitchell, 27
Elizabeth Williams,
    15
Sarah Jones, 45
Aaron Jones, 55
Susan Richardson,
    21
Richard Richardson,
    4
Sarah Richardson, 2
John Boston, 20
Charles Johnson, 48
William Collins, 18
Milly Jenkins, 19
Pompey Tasks, 65
Henrietta Henry, 30
Stansbury James, 38
Goldsbourgh Gibson,
    35
Thomas Thomas, 38
Samuel Green, 40
Nick Hunt, 43
James Johnson, 18
Henry Stansbury, 9
John Stansbury, 7
Eliza Stansbury, 3
James Stansbury, 5
Charles Johnson, 50
Samuel Gambrill, 36
John Rhodes, 47
Cleo Rhodes, 46
Nancy Wood, 68
Agnes Harding, 38
*Elijah Harding, 8
Betsy Harding, 16
Thomas Harding, 6
Edward Harding, 3
Eliza Harding, 12
Jane Johnson, 45
Nancy Johnson, 57
Harriett Costs, 24
Bill Costs, 4

Free African Americans of Maryland - 1832

Isaac Dorsey, 58
Judy Dorsey, 51
Susannah Dorsey, 17
David Dorsey, 23
Harriett Dorsey, 16
Fanny Brown, 46
Ned Thornton, 50
John Brown, 60
Anne Brown, 50
Mary Ann Brown, 15
John Brown, 23
David, 21
Benjamin Stewart, 50
Henry Griffin, 24
Owen Walker, 22
Gabriel, 64
Ephriem, 50
Rezin Snowden, 40
William Pellton, 23
Jerry Brian, 60
Henry Brian, 64
Grange Green, 54
Samuel Anderson, 57
Anthony Parks, 34
Mary Parks, 33
Priscilla Parks, 3
Henry Parks, 18
Samuel Allen, 35
David Hawkins, 40
*Charles Gaither, 46
Polly Gaither, 45
Rachel Green, 55
Nancy Anderson, 40
Nelly Sipity, 80
Henry Ryston, 52
Esther Ryston, 41
Maria Ryston, 14
James Williams, 9
John Hanson, 4
Reuben Wesley, 3
Rebecca Ryston, 2
Kitty Pelton, 46
Regin Pelton, 18
James Pelton, 13
Owen Pelton, 8
Anne Pelton, 20
Maria Anderson, 45
Mary Anderson, 12
Sophia Anderson, 10
Ellen Anderson, 7
Charles Anderson, 5
Joseph Anderson, 17
Moses, 18

James Sylvester, 38
Mary Sylvester, 38
Tilghman Sylvester, 8
Lagnetty Sylvester, 5
Louis Sylvester, 3
Mary Cooke, 21
Samuel Stower, 60
James Smith, 68
Henry Smith, 60
Jane Smith, 50
Susan Smith, 30
Henry Smith, 9
Harriett, 4
John Henry Smith, 4
*Julia Ann Cooke, 30
Abraham Thomas, 28
Christopher Perry, 22
Maria Dorsey, 23
Abraham Jones, 40
Minty Jones, 39
Lydia Powell, 50
Maria Powell, 20
Ann Eliza Powell, 19
Louisa Powell, 15
John Powell, 13
Betsy Powell, 13
James Wesley, 9
Lydia Ann, 6
Washington Powell, 5
William Powell, 4
John Wesley, 5
Ann Elizabeth Powell, 1
Jimia Powell, 4 months
Eliza Woodward, 50
Hanson Munty, 8
Rebecca Munty, 6
John Munty, 2
Eliza Munty, 36
Henry Munty, 12
William France, 35
John Green, 53
Maria Green, 45
Hetty Green, 9
Washington, 11
Rosanna, 12
William Brown, 36
Cassy Williams, 60
Fancy Williams, 55
Sally Williams, 13
Washington Williams, 17

Samuel Watkins, 53
*Kitty Watkins, 40
Manuel Hawkins, 60
Violetta Hawkins, 53
Rezin Green, 45
Jane Green, 50
Joseph Green, 16
Robert Green, 13
Eli Green, 11
Allen Oliver, 25
Milly Oliver, 22
Jane Oliver, 9 months
Elijah Oliver, 1
Eliza Oliver, 1 month
John Dorsey, 32
Timothy Johnson, 38
Lloyd Johnson, 22
Elias Johnson, 9
Bill Johnson, 26
Cornelious Johnson, 19
Louisa Johnson, 21
Harriet Dorsey, 12
Abraham Dorsey, 9
John Dorsey, 7
Charles Dorsey, 4
Nicholas Dorsey, 2
Hannah Matthews, 23
Charles Matthews, 8
Mary Matthews, 5
Jane Matthews, 1
Maria Adams, 35
John Adams, 8
Isiah Adams, 6
Levi Adams, 3
Deanna Pelton, 21
Priscilla Cooke, 20
Mary Cooke, 16
*Letty Cooke, 69
Harriet Chesline, 22
Esther Dorsey, 62
Anne Thomas, 32
Rachel Thomas, 15
Charlotte Thomas, 9
Mary Thomas, 5
Harriet Boon, 40
Rachel Boon, 12
John Boon, 11
Dennis Boon, 11
Anne Boon, 10
Boston Savoy, 65
Elizabeth Dulaney, 16
Stephen Gross, 30

Anne Arundel County - 1832

Cornelius Savoy, 11
Rachel Savoy, 28
Edward Addison, 24
Joseph Addison, 25
Henry Addison, 23
Dennis Addison, 15
Mary Addison, 19
Emily Addison, 19
Nancy Addison, 14
Levy Addison, 8
Darkey Joice, 28
John Addison, 16
Thomas Clifford, 53
Edward Baker, 25
Jane Baker, 25
Dennis Green, 20
Pheby Hall, 95
Lemuel Tooney, 33
John Matthews, 26
Rachel Matthews, 20
John Horsey
    Matthews, 1
William Hawkins, 4
Kitty Matthews, 50
Leonard Hawkins, 2
Thomas Hawkins, 1
Nelly Hawkins, 22
William Rhodes, 21
Nancy Green, 42
Samuel Dorsey, 48
Ned Sugars, 58
Charles Sugars, 20
Samuel Sugars, 18
Fanny Sugars, 15
Matilda Sugars, 14
Mary Sugras, 9
Henry Sugars, 11
Andrew Sugars, 6
William Sugars, 2
Charles Smith, 33
Claney Smith, 32
Gabriel Smith, 19
Jane Brooks, 34
Samuel Brooks, 6
Milly Johnson, 60
Sarah, 80
Dinah Todd, 50
Sarah Tyler, 51
Dick Tyler, 60
Bill Cave, 56
Emily Tyler, 12
John Tyler, 9
Bill Tyler, 7
David S___, 25
Betsy Matthews, 32

Abraham Todd, 33
Basil Todd, 32
Achsah Green, 34
Rezin Green, 3
Peter Green, 34
Dinah Green, 27
Martha Anne Green, 8
Henson Green, 6
Basil Henry Green, 1
Charles Cooke, 20
Anne Bell, 16
James Brickard, 35
Mary Ann Brickard, 25
William Brickard, 6
Eleanor Brickard, 4
James Brickard, 2
Joseph, 14
Robert Ryan, 35
Bill Williams, 55
Rachel Williams, 32
James Williams, 9
Harry, 32
Sally Watkins, 36
William Watkins, 36
Maria Watkins, 13
Anne Watkins, 9
Susan Watkins, 8
Hetty Watkins, 7
Thomas Watkins, 9
    months
Charles Joice, 28
Charles Hall, 14
Robert Mahoney, 70
Capa Walker, 40
Adeline Walker, 14
Anne Walker, 6
Thomas Walker, 4
Anne Thomas, 25
Charles Thomas, 4
Sally Sands, 52
Maria Pinkney, 40
Rachel Watkins, 30
Mary Parks, 4
Priscilla Parks, 4
Dinah Boone, 15
Robert Price, 50
Hager Price, 40
Thomas Fisher,
    Louisa Fisher, 17
Andrew Hall, 22
Margaret Hall, 25
John Hall, 2
Joseph Hall, 1
George White, 23

Nancy Callander, 27
Gabriel Callander, 33
Susan Pumphrey, 40
Maria Pumphrey, 16
Harriet Pumphrey, 13
George Pumphrey, 4
W____ Hall, 38
Harriet Hall, 13
Basil Hall, 6
Caroline Hall, 4
Elias Hall, 17
George Johnson, 33
Elizabeth Johnson, 33
Agnes Johnson, 9
George Johnson, 8
John Johnson, 7
Sarah Johnson, 5
Elizabeth Johnson3
Sophia Johnson, 1
John Williams, 19
James Green, 13
Isaac Johnson, 31
Nathaniel Hall, 36
Susannah Hall, 25
Arenah Hall, 3
Eleanor Hall, 1
Sarah Wright, 19
Adam Tallana, 70
Nicholas Dorsey, 61
*Ezekial Porter, 45
Matilda Owings, 25
Maria Pinkney, 28
Percy Downes, 45
Mary Downes, 30
Maria Downes, 11
Rachel Downes, 9
Charles Downes, 5
Lucy Downes, 1
Caroline Owings, 8
    months
Hazel Burgess, 40
Joseph Burgess, 20
Celia Burgess, 36
Mary Brown, 12
Bill Brewer, 14
Abraham Brewer, 10
Vachel Howard, 30
James Powers, 50
Juliet Powers, 50
Antoinette Powers, 15
Judy Ann Powers, 10
Peter B____, 49
James Lewis, 50

Free African Americans of Maryland - 1832

Joseph Savoy, 20
John Johnson, 20
Dianna, 33
Lucretia Thornton, 25
William Hall, 6
William Lily, 19
Susan M. Brown, 25
Maria Cooper, 50
Charity Williams, 22
Rachel Giles, 30
Louisa Giles, 22
Charles Gibbons, 11
Ephriam Genson, 50
George A____, 19
*Rilate Johnson, 45
Rachel Johnson, 40
Hamilton Johnson, 16
Stephen Brown, 35
Benjamin Johnson, 14
Stephen Brown, 35
Leonard Tooney, 30
Henry Smith, 35
Peter Hopkins, 20
Gusta Dorsey, 30
Ellen Dorsey, 25
Elizabeth Dorsey, 5
Jane Dorsey, 3
Gusta Dorsey, 11
Jacob Johnson40
Sally Johnson, 35
Reuben Johnson, 13
John Johnson, 10
Artimus Johnson, 8
Elizabeth, 6
Alfred Johnson, 11
James Williams, 3
Harry, 25
James Johnson, 62
Mary Johnson, 60
Prissy Prises, 40
James Prises, 30
Arah Neal, 25
Perry Hall, 40
Harry, 20
James Williams, 45
Abraham Haines, 70
William, 36
Ann Snowden, 35
Eliza Snowden, 18
Kitty Snowden, 16
William Snowden16
Wesley Snowden, 10

Benjamin Snowden, 8
*James Snowden, 6
Maria Snowden, 4
Andrew Snowden, 53
Marina Snowden, 57
Jane Snowden, 18
Sally Snowden, 17
Nancy, 8
John Gassoway, 15
John Griffith, 9 months
Henry Griffith, 22
Sally Hammond, 7
Elizabeth Hammond, 3
Cyrus Johnson, 53
Nancy Johnson, 60
Ben Stewart, 35
Basil Matthews, 57
Harriet Matthews, 45
William Matthews16
Edward Matthews, 13
Ellen Matthews, 6
Thomas Matthews, 4
Andrew Matthews, 3
Harriet Green, 14
Richard Green, 11
Frank Harris, 60
Debby Lasko, 40
Anna, 11
Leah Nugra, 12
Lucy Nugra, 8
Caroline Nugra, 5
Elizabeth Nugra, 8
Lydia Nugra, 7 months
Cassa Nugra, 26
I___ Nugra, 6
Sally Nugra, 6
William Nugra, 2
Titus Mumphrey, 70
Rachel Mumphrey, 60
Larkin Mumphrey, 45
Rosa Mumphrey, 28
Mary Mumphrey, 11
Ben Mumphrey, 9
Nicholas Mumphrey, 8 months
Richard Cooke, 48
Jethro Hanady, 30
Bill Flood, 45
Gustav Dorsey, 36

Clem Watkins, 40
Thomas King, 60
Milly King, 10
Charles, 9
Becky, 3
Harriet, 6
John James Brown,40
Arter C__ Dorsey, 11
Alfonsa Ellen Dorsey, 11
James William Dorsey, 3
N_Ben Plummer, 74
James _ Washington, 32
Ma Will Roddy, 65
Pere Edward Johnson, 60
Lucy Johnson, 40
Aaron, 60
Rachel, 35
Sarah, 35
Paul Thomas, 60
William, 1
Rachel Talbot, 30
Betsy Johnson, 35
Joseph Johnson, 7
Susan Johnson, 5
Archibald Johnson, 3
Frederick Johnson, 9 months
Lily Dorsey, 55
James, 11
Samuel Kelly, 34
Anthony Franklin, 40
Isaac Valentine, 40
Samuel Hardy, 30
Bill Crab, 50
Peggy Brown, 65
Caroline, 3
Rachel Hardy, 18
Kitty Hardy, 9
Isaac Hardy, 2
Mary Hardy, 4
Hezekiah Johnson, 65
Elizabeth Johnson, 17
Milly Jackson, 22
Samuel Jackson, 25
Bill Jackson, 2 months

Anne Arundel County - 1832

Susan Green, 13
Cate Elford, 70
William Elford, 50
Thomas Bell, 35
Susan Bell, 13
Anne Bell, 70
Lydia Whassing, 5
Billy Bell, 5
Judy Ann Bell, 30
George Howard, 30
Phill Howard, 60
Mary Scott, 26
Frank Scott, 30
Dover Call, 56
Ben Manly, 44
Rachel Manly, 40
Sampson Frasser, 53
Titus Sheaff, 50
Maria, 60
Hannah, 50
Mary, 30
William, 30
Kitty Cole, 40
Priscilla Cole, 9
Harriet Cole, 7
Thomas Cole, 2
Eliza Cole, 2
Hannah Gradner, 39
Polly Disson, 25
    Wellam Wes.
    Gardner, 4
George W. Gardner,
    2
Elias Gardner, 7
Richard Aims, 2
Matthew Thomas, 35
Washington Waters,
    28
Vachel Waters, 21
Hetty Gardner, 26
Hannah Matthews,
    26
Sally Matthews, 91
Sarah Waters, 4
Mary Waters, 1
Samuel I Matthews,
    1
George W. Waters, 1
Barbara Boston, 35
Marry Matthews, 17
Ede A. Matthews, 11
William Matthews, 7
Priscilla Matthews, 8
Nicholas Matthews, 4
Thomas Henry, 9
    months

Cassy Boules, 19
Elizabeth Browne, 5
Rebecca Lucinda, 4
Louisa, 2
Lewis Henry, 5
Sarah Williams, 16
Kitty Matthews, 16
Thomas Chambers,
    40
Fanny Chambers, 12
Perry Chambers, 8
Nicholas Calvert, 8
John Boston, 42
Darkey Boston, 32
Samuel Boston, 18
Margaret Boston, 16
Mary Ann Boston, 5
John Boston, 3
Elizabeth Boston, 1
James Boston, 46
Samuel Baker, 16
Robert Sims, 50
Sarah Sims, 56
Ann Williams, 25
Sophia Williams, 5
Perry Williams, 3
Amos Sanders, 30
Aohsah Sanders, 27
Alexander Sanders, 2
Amos Sanders, 1
Priscilla Sanders, 17
Charlotte Burgess,
    40
Emanuel Burgess,
    50
Mary Jane Burgess,
    10
Elizabeth Ellen
    Burgess, 7
Emily Sophia
    Burgess, 6
Betsy Matthews, 90
Ann Snell, 28
Jonathon Matthews,
    56
Elizabeth Ellen, 7
Benjamin, 4
Matilda Boston, 30
Elizabeth Peach, 86
Jerry Wilson, 27
*Eliza Carry, 8
David Nelson, 42
Annie Matthews, 45
John Matthews, 4
Elizabeth Matthews,
    1

Dick Donaldson, 50
Caroline Jones, 15
Louisa Jones, 13
Rachel, 39
Rainer Holly, 50
Charles Stone, 20
Peter Warfield, 56
Katy Warfield, 45
Daniel Warfield, 20
James Warfield, 19
Hester Fisher, 11
Isaac France, 53
Rebecca France, 53
Frisby France, 14
Thomas France, 13
Edward Johnson, 60
Louisa Johnson, 40
Dinah Boon, 40
William Boon, 6
Hercules Smith, 60
Paul Talbot, 70
William Lasko, 32
Harry Smith, 30
Dennis Powells, 32
Guest Holton, 96
Caleb Snowden, 19
Richard, 48
Jerry Fisher, 50
Sarah Fisher, 45
Ned Fisher, 15
Betsy Fisher, 14
Margaret Fisher, 10
Dennis Fisher, 7
*Mary Fisher, 5
Charles Fisher, 3
Sarah Fisher, 3
Polly Cose/Case, 30
Sally Cose/Case, 17
Isaac Rhodes, 60
Jane Rhodes, 60
Marcinda Green, 14
Charles Turner, 24
Milly Turner, 25
Bill Mars, 65
Alexander Mars, 16
Benjamin Frasier, 37
John Crowner, 25
John Frank, 45
Rachel Hawkins, 40
Joseph Hawkins, 8
Henry Hawkins, 6
Eliza Hawkins, 4
Jacob Hawkins, 2
Jerry, 22
Mary, 14
George Martin, 60

Free African Americans of Maryland - 1832

Ben Brown, 45
Kediah Brown, 35
Anne, 16
Louisa, 14
Samuel Jones, 50
Samuel Clark, 40
Maria Clark, 38
Emily Clark, 22
Cassa Clarke, 12
Edward Clarke, 6
Rachel Clarke, 2
Henry Mercer, 45
Lily Mercer,, 35
James Mercer, 11
*Margaret, 6
Masshae Stevenson, 66
Hester Stevenson, 60
Mary Stevenson, 30
Nathan Stevenson, 28
Rebecca Stevenson, 3
Susannah Stevenson, 9
Mary Jones, 60
Mary Jones, 30
Amos Jones, 9
Jonas Jones, 8
Mary Jones, 5
Deborah Jones, 6 months
Samuel Jones, 31
Eliza Jones, 25
Aish Jones, 8
Harry Jones, 6
Agnes Jones, 4
Fanny Jones, 3
Anetta Jones, 9 months
Edward Matthews, 35
Cornelius Warfield, 30
Ellen Warfield, 27
July Ann Warfield, 5
Fanny Warfield, 1
Maria Pinkney, 25
Caleb Davis, 42
Providence Davis, 38
Judy Ann Davis, 5
Joseph Davis, 1
Charity Riley, 40
Louisa Ann, 25
Matilda, 25
Henry Pumphrey, 10

Bill Williams, 38
Hannah Williams, 42
John Williams, 6
John Williams, 13
*Samuel Clarke, 62
Joe Johnson, 1
Susan Pumphrey, 45
Maria Pumphrey, 17
Harriet Pumphrey, 7
Kitty Pumphrey, 8
George Williams, 4
Frances Williams, 48
Mary Williams, 48
Julia Ann Williams, 16
Robert Williams, 10
Rachel Williams, 68
Polly Johnson, 76
Moses Holland, 41
Matilda Williams, 42
Hilery Williams, 26
Pheby Green, 9
James Johnson, 9
Nancy Holland, 59
Ruth Dison, 40
John Dison, 19
Jacob Dyson, 16
Washington Dyson, 13
Samuel Dyson, 5
Rebecca Ann, 8 months
Mary Little, 22
Margaret Little,4
John Little, 2
Washington Little, 25
Nancy Little, 40
Abid Little, 65
Agnes Harden, 35
Betsy Harden, 14
Elijah Harden, 9
Thomas Harden, 6
Edward Harden, 2
Eliza Harden, 12
Polly Spurrier, 36
*Sally Spurrier, 16
Henry Gooden, 9
Mary Green, 8
William Green, 5
Edward Green, 3
Noble Boston, 19
Polly May, 30
Matilda Grinnage, 16
Daniel Savoy, 25
Anne Savoy, 21
Solomon Savoy, 1

Solomon Savoy, 35
Fanny Savoy, 50
Milly Shipley, 42
Hanson Shipley, 16
Rachel Shipley, 21
Thomas Shipley, 14
Maria Shipley, 12
Louisa, 10
Mary Shipley, 7
Samuel Dorsey, 40
Sophia Dorsey, 25
Nancy Dorsey, 4
Jane Matthews, 16
Ann Waters, 19
John Dorsey, 30
Kitty Dorsey, 6
Maria Dorsey, 4
William Dorsey, 2
Betsy Waters, 25
Rachel Waters, 2
Nelly Waters, 19
Henry Hardy, 5
Nicholas Jackson, 79
Philes Jackson, 70
Nacky Jackson, 13
Henry Jackson, 11
Samuel Jackson, 9
*Nicholas Jackson, 5
James Mays, 25
Mary Mays, 26
Jerry Mays, 10
Caroline Mays, 9
Matilda Mays, 7
Lewis Mays, 3 Mary Mays, 16
Lydia Mays, 2 months
George Brown, 35
Betsy Brown, 30
Isaiah Brown, 8
James Brown, 6
Thomas Bell, 50
Susan Bell, 30
Mary Ann Bell, 12
Thomas Bell, 9
Elizabeth Bell, 1
William Bell, 3
Susan Green, 11
Nancy Green, 50
Philip Howard, 60
Mary Scott, 36
Frank Scott, 34
Dick Scott, 8
Benjamin, 27
Ellen Ridgely, 25
Caroline Ridgely, 35

24

Anne Arundel County - 1832

Julia Ridgely, 5
Fanny Ridgely, 1
James Johnson, 9
Dinah Johnson, 30
Stephen Savoy, 39
Maria Savoy, 39
Joseph Savoy, 18
Henry Savoy, 14
Amos Savoy, 13
Becky Savoy, 9
Willy Savoy, 6
Mary Jane Savoy, 3
Sarah Savoy
William Savoy, 6
   months
Richard Boston, 70
Cassy, 70
Louisa Boston, 30
Jacob Hardy, 13
William Dyson, 45
Eliza Dyson, 19
Sally Dyson, 16
Julia Dyson, 14
Mary Dyson, 12
George Dyson, 10
Aohsah Dyson, 6
William Dyson, 4
Henry Dyson, 2
Jane, 1
Lucy Snell, 50
Kitty Snell, 35
Benjamin Snell, 8
Frank Scott, 50
Maria Scott, 10
Margaret Scott, 10
Daniel Scott, 8
Darky Bacon, 30
Isaac Bacon, 8
Bridget, 50
Vachel Waters, 22
Bill Williams, 22
Thomas Chambers,
   25
Jonathan Morris, 16
Sarah, 21
Benjamin Collins, 57
Betsy Harrison, 27
Josiah Harrison, 10
Sarah Harrison, 8
William Harrison, 3
*Elizabeth, 8 months
Jane Dorsey, 27
Kitty Dorsey, 6
William Dorsey, 2
Maria Dorsey, 1
Kitty Williams, 30

Anne Nelson, 30
Emily Nelson, 4
Jane Nelson, 8
   months
Henry Jackson, 64
Jacob Matthews, 25
Vachel, 12
Peggy, 12
William, 4
George, 3
Susan Sprigg, 49
Nancy Berry, 30
Edward Williams, 19
Thomas Williams, 40
Darkey Williams, 39
Jonathan, 26
Maria Diggs, 35
Emily Diggs, 1
Rebecca Anderson,
   45
William Flood, 30
Susan Roboson, 20
Amos Tyler, 35
Sarah Ann Jefferson,
   17
Maria Webster, 20
Wesley Foot, 12
Peggy Foot, 50
Mary Smith, 26
Samuel Bacon, 12
Mary Ann Bacon, 7
George A. Bacon, 5
Ellen Gardner, 17
Thomas Gardner, 40
Nacky Gardner, 36
*Kitty Gardner, 11
Barbury Gardner, 2
Ann Matthews, 22
Richard Matthews,
   35
William Creeks, 35
Florah Creeks, 28
Caroline Creeks, 4
Margaret Brown, 50
Abraham Haines, 50
Rachel Haines, 45
Jacob Haines, 13
Phoebe Haines, 9
Jonathan Dorsey, 14
Nancy Matthews, 30
Edward Matthews,
   11
Mary Matthews, 8
George Matthews, 5
Manala Matthews, 3

Hester Ann
   Matthews, 2
Rebecca Hall, 28
John Thomas Hall, 7
Susan Bailey, 22
Moses, 60
Darkey, 60
Selby, 60
David Boston, 30
Charlotte Boston, 19
Louis Boston, 6
   months,
Catherine Boston, 6
   months
John Hardy, 16
Harry Warfield, 40
Anthony Franklin,
   49
Caleb Jones, 18
Jane Warfield, 12
Louisa Warfield, 10
Ruth Ann Warfield, 8
Ephriem Warfield, 7
PerryWarfield, 4
*John Hamilton, 36
Ruth Hamilton, 35
Betsy Hamilton, 17
John Hamilton, 18
Sam Hamilton, 15
Green Hamilton, 12
William Hamilton, 7
Nancy Hamilton, 2
Harry Jones, 60
Chaney, 20
Lot Johnson, 50
Rachel Johnson, 40
Hamilton Johnson,
   16
Benjamin Johnson 14
Ellen Johnson, 12
Rachel Johnson, 12
Matilda Johnson, 10
Samuel Johnson 8
Joshua Johnson, 5
Branson, 2
Mary, 5
Ellen, 4
Solomon Hall, 13
James Hall, 5
Darky Jones, 37
Margaret Jones, 5
Kitty Jones, 3
Emily Jones, 3
   months
Maria Potts, 35
Susan Potts, 7

Free African Americans of Maryland - 1832

William Potts, 5
Clem Potts, 3
Benedict Potts, 2
Maria, 28
Henry, 3
Nelly, 1
Bill Williams, 35
Harriot Willliams, 40
*John Williams, 13
Reuben Williams, 6
Catherine Jackson, 40
Michael Jackson, 11
Bill Flood, 35
Edward Jensen, 70
Rachel, 40
Delilah Carr, 44
Robert Hopkins, 14

George M. Carr, 11
Kitty Ann Carr, 9
Isaac Carr, 4
Eliza Parker, 38
James Parker, 10
Joseph Parker, 8
Margaret Parker, 6
Henry Parker, 4
Henrietta Parker, 2
Margaret Topall, 36
Eliza Johnson, 30
Henry Strong, 30
Clem Watkins, 20
Peter Dorsey, 70
Hagar, 30
Rachel, 14
Levy, 25
Henny, 2

Richard, 1
John, 17
Nace, 12
Joe, 16
Mary, 9
Sophia, 7
Hester, 15
Horace, 4
Andrew, 7
*Eliza Ann, 5
John Henry, 14
_____, 35
Hager, 23
Kitty, 22
Henny, 13
Rachel, 5

****

MALE NAMES OF THE FREE PEOPLE OF COLOR IN CALVERT COUNTY, MARYLAND

Joseph Murry, 40
Events Murry, 14
Gustavus Murry, 17
Joseph Garry, 45
William Gurry, 25
Frisby Gross, 24
Thomas Gross, 40
Gideon Gross, 30
Harry Whittington, 25
James Willett, 40
____ Willett, 35
Adam Willett, 35
Phillip Dorsey, 45
William Coats, 80
George Jones, 25
Andrew Butler, 50
Thomas Dorsey, 80
Major Gross
William Reed, 23
Alfred Reed, 20
Isaac Jacks, 60
Jesse Mackall, 50
John Green, 80
Jacob Boots, 35
George Boots, 80
John Gross, 50
William Gross, 45

Christian Howard, 40
Andrew Gault, 54
Thomas Harwood, 30
Clement Harwood, 45
Joseph Moland, 30
Benjamin Mason, 13
Augustus Mason, 3
Joseph Mason, 60
Robert Norris, 71
Thomas Norris, 36
Sam Gross, 60
William Robertson, 70
Jerome Gross, 30
Henry Gross, 70
Samuel Fennel, 40
Charles Gross, 30
Jacob Gross, 20
Major Gross, 10
James Ireland, 45
Richard Rawlings, 70
Robert Johnson, 14
Richard Johnson, 12
Tobias Johnson, 20
Isaac Browne, 30
Peter Brooks, 40
James Travass, 70

Daniel Johnson, 40
John Brown, 2 months
Moses Gains, 56
John Gains, 20
Moses Gains, Jr, 18
*Levi Gains, 5
Bill Jefferson, 40
Samuel Blake, 45
John Blake, 24
George Blake, 20
Perry Blake, 10
Peter Blake, 12
Major Gross, 12
Robert Johnson, 14
Richard Johnson, 10
Caleb Batson, 50
Walter Lee, 40
George Buchanan, 80
Thomas Meekins, 20
Henry Ransom, 60
Jacob Meekins, 40
John Calendar, 10
Hezekiah Calendar, 11
Edward Brown, 40
William Barnes, 12 months
Robert Barnes, 3

Free African Americans of Maryland - 1832

William Cook, 3
Joseph Mason, 35
____ Batson, 50
____ Batson, 36
Daniel Batson, 222
William Batson, 17
Brice Batson, 12
Thomas Batson, 9
Gambril Batson, 6
George Buchanan, 5
Walter Lee, Jr, 30
George Anderson, 10
James Anderson, 6
John Calender Jr, 12
Eli Calender, 12
Jacob Meekins, 60
Nace Cooke, 30
Thomas Segal, 70
Allen Gibson, 26
Isaac White, 30
Edward Smothers,
    50
William Smith, 17
Abraham Smith, 11
John Smith, 6
Ceasar Harden, 60
Moses Ralph, 64
Pompy Butler, 65
John Jackson, 80
David Dorsey, 37
David Dorsey, Jr,30
Henry/Harry Dorsey,
    33
*Limas Dorsey, 19
Alexander Dors, 10
William Mason, 50
Isreal Mason, 3
Thomas Mason, 5
James Gray, 8
Joseph Gray, 50
Joseph Gray, jr, 30
George Gray, 28
William A. Gross, 2
Nace Murry, 10
Benjamin Jones, 35
Charles Jones, 7
Jackson Jones3
Isaac Reid, 30
Elijah Coats, 29
Abraham Jones, 565
William Jones, 49
Arthur Coats, 22
Henry Coats, 27
Hezakiah Cillas, 24
Nelson Cillas, 14
John Cillas, 13

Henry S___, 5
Levi Norris, 26
Orrange Bradley, 36
John Farland, 7
Elijah Farland, 8
Ezekial Gassaway,
    24
George Gassaway, 80
Elijah McCarty, 40
Benjamin Booth, 16
Jeremiah Gross, 40
Henry Moland, 8
Clement Moland, 6
Isaac Moland, 1
Richard Moland, 2
David Smith, 7
Edward Smith, 4
Joseph Mason, 50
Seasor Hardman, 50
Joseph Mason, jr, 18
Benjamin Mason, 12
Augustus Mason, 5
William Mason, 3
Lewis Mason, 2
Enoch Moland, 21
David Boone, 40
John Parran, 17
David Boone, jr, 35
John Miller, 30
Major Goodman, 35
Benjamin Banister,
    35
Alexander Brooks,
    13
Benjamin Brown, 50
Isaac Handman, 40
Basil Jones, 45
John Dorsey, 13
*James Dorsey, 12
David Handman, 12
Thomas Brown, 14
Nace Brown, 7
Patrick Gray, 13
Sam Stricknall, 30
David Lutheron, 20
Benjamin Locks, 29
Henry Dorsey, 14
Augustus Johnson, 7
Charles Hammon, 30
Isaac White, 30
Eli Rice, 40
William Hammon, 3
Charles Hammon1
John Badding
Wesley McKinsey, 10
Thomas Diggs, 30

Clem Shorter, 50
Peter Allen, 15
Charles Johnson, 13
George Allen, 3
Benjamin Hall, 4
John Mackall, 45
John Griffin, 35
Elijah Griffin, 16
____ Griffin, 14
*William Randal, 10
Benjamin Turner, 12
David Randal, 4
Jerry Fry, 60
Thomas Booth, 50
James Haace, 6
George Scrivener, 12
Hezekiah Brown, 53
Kinsey Brown, 16
Isaac Goddard, 45
Sampson Thomas,
    55
Jerry Gross, 30
Thomas Savoy, 26
John Smothers, 26
Richard Smothers, 9
David Byas, 30
James Weems, 6
John Weems, 5
John Dison, 15
William Dison, 12
Richard Dison, 10
Charles Dison, 2
Richard Guile, 35
Jacob Bowie, 6
Elijah Coats, 26
Samuel Green, 4
*William Green, 12
Richard W.
    Smothers, 1
Thomas Carter, 11
Kinsy Brown, 15
James D. Booth, 35
Kinsey Booth, 17
Samuel Booth, 7
Elijah Booth, 10
Stephen Mitchell, 70
John Jones, 19
Thomas Jones, 12
Samuel; Jones, 14
Elijah Jones, 10
George Jones, 6
Joseph Curtis, 35
Samuel Hardesty, 50
Samuel Harwood, 45
Michael, 60
Andrew Monk, 70

Calvert County, Maryland

Nace Barker, 60
M___ Cammel, 50
Prince Boone, 45
Everit Manner, 25
Seaser Brooks, 60
Thomas Mackall, 60
William Brown, 8
*John Wesley Brown, 4
John Brown, 7
___ Brown, 6
Jacob Guby, 45
William Hawwkins, 13
Henry Hawkins, 18
Ned Brown, 5
David Brown, 30
Henry Brown, 14
Isaac Brown, 10
William Brown, 7
T___ Hardman, 10
Thomas Hepbron, 6
Thomas Hardman, 40
Elisha Hardman, 12
David Taylor, 35
Frederick Hammon, 40
William Thomas, 14
Richard Boone, 14
Joseph Boone, 16
Richard Spaulding, 60
George Hawkins, 50
Jerry Gross, 26
Isaac Munk, 70
William Gross, 35
John Gross, 4
John Gross, 3 months
George Macks, 40
William Macks, 4
Henry Macks, 8
Plater Lee, 36
Joshua Sprauling, 18
Thomas Pinkney, 8 months
Sampson Baker, 28
Hillery Brown, 18
John Hardman, 2
Basil Boone, 70
Charles Parker, 45
Samuel Dorsey, 35
William Gross, 6 months

Andrew Gault, 50
Patrick Gault, 18
Thomas Norris, 25
James Robinson, 35
William Hood, 24
Edward Wood, 14
Major Butler, 6
Robert Butler, 1
John Butler, 16
Isaac Jackson, 1
John Green, 30
William Green, 6
Henry Brooks, 35
Ned Green, 60
Samuel Hardaker, 16
*John Handy, 7
Joseph Johnson, 5
Jesse Mackall, 40
William Gibson, 65
Littleton Peters, 40
Benjamin Foreman, 60
William Downs, 18
Anthony Downs, 20
John Parker, 10
Jack Green, 60
Basil Brown, 26
Amos Brown, 21
Charles Chambers, 31
Jacob Dike, 70
Samuel Brown, 10
Stephen Brown, 8
James Jones, 46
James Jones, Jr. 11
Isaac Reed, 7
Joseph Reed, 6
William Reed, 7
David Burk, 45
Thomas Burk, 18
John Burk, 14
Joseph Burk, 16
Richard Burk, 12
Samuel Gross, 60
William H. Gross, 1 month
Seasor Green, 60
Charles Johnson, 4
Benjamin Gross, 30
Major Gross, 10
Jacob Gross, 8
John Gross, 7
Levi Gross, 6
William Gross, 3
Joshua Weems, 30
James Burke, 45

Wesley Holland, 32
Major Fellen, 28
James Parran, 3
Henry Parren, 2
Mason Holland, 45
Robert Holland, 6
William Jones, 60
Ned Jones, 18
James Johnson, 16
William Johnson, 14
Major Comadors, 50
Samuel Fennel, 28
Major Fennel, 20
James Gurry, 50
William Gurry, 31
Samuel Jackson, 12
*John Jackson, 20
Leonard Jackson, 16
William Coats, 50
Henry Gross, 7
William Gross, 46
Jacob Gross, 6
Richard Gross, 3
Jeremiah Gross, 1 month
Henry Whittington, 26
Richard Whittington, 5
Richard Whittington, 5
Perry Whittington, 3
Thomas Gross, 70
William H. Skinner, 8 months
Phillip Dorsey, 40
Abraham Gross, 60
William, 23
William H. Butler, 2
Thomas Harttwood, 23
James Chase, 40
Young Chase, 16
Benjamin Gross, 26
Isaac Boone, 35
David Boone, 10
Thomas Boone, 8
Manuel Green, 14
Major Green, 18
Clement Ham___, 66
David Ham___, 20
Elijah Ham___, 30
Henry Deal, 18
Levi Deal, 12
Jeffrey Brown, 40
Nat Green, 18

28

Free African Americans of Maryland - 1832

William Gross, 35
William Gross, Jr. 5
David Ham___, Jr. 2
   months
Jasper Ham__, 16
Jacj Gross, 50
Thomas Gross, 6
David Gross, 17
William Hammons,
   28
Cournel Brown, 40
James Hammon, 28
Cournel Hammon, 3
Jesse Evans, 13
George Cooper, 12
James Cooper, 10
Gerral Gramby, 14
George Gramby, 10
Andrew Thomas, 50
Henry Dawkins, 30
George Gasaway, 50
Perry Naylor, 35
*William Brown, 12
Perry Brown, 10
Benjamin Quill, 45
Benjamin Quill, jr.
   20
Peter ____, 60
George Pinkney, 70
Isaac Gross, 35
Leven Norris, 25
Abraham Hanes, 25
Robert L. White, 62
Isaac White, 5

Joshua White, 4
David Boon, 5
Ned Taylor, 25
Thomas Wheeler, 6
William Wheeler, 3
William Alton, 25
James Gross, 30
Benjamin D___, 3
   months
James Chase, 7
   months
Tower Willet, 40
James White, 45
William Gross, 2
Richard Gross, 5
George W. Gray, 2
Isaac Reed, 26
Nathan Reed, 8
Isaac Reed, jr, 3
Jeremiah Reed, 9
   months
Samuel Johnson, 52
Peter Frazier, 60
Phillip Jones, 47
David King, 52
William Scrivener, 16
David Scrivener, 10
David Ennis, 23
Joshua Ennis, 19
Richard Ennis, 18
Thomas Ennis, 15
William Ennis, 13
Isaac Ennis, 11
Joseph Mackall, 15

Thomas Johnson, 50
Jesse Whittington,
   29
John McCarter, 80
Anthony Ennis, 25
Ned Wood, 3
Eleas Wood, 3
Major Brown, 5
Verzil Brown, 2
Isaac Hustron, 40
John Hawkins, 49
Jerry Harres, 9
William Brooks, 4
Benjamin Brooks, 1
Benjamin Cornelius,
   19
Major Coats, 20
James Gross, 8
Henry Gross, 3
Robert Gross, 4
   months
Thomas Gross, 15
Nelson Kyler, 15
John Kyler, jr. 12
Stephen Kyler, 5
John Harwood, 40
Lundon Coats, 40

No. of Males of the
   free people of
   Colour in Calvert
   County,
   Maryland } 520

FEMALE NAMES OF THE FREE PEOPLE OF COLOR IN CALVERT COUNTY, MARYLAND

Lyddy Willett, 40
   Jane Willett, 40
Lucy Willett, 45
Elizabeth Willett, 25
   Sarah Willet, 5
Ann Foot, 20
Sarah Foot, 2
Sarah Foot, Sr. 50
Hannah Gross, 50
Elizabeth Gross, 15
Roanny Gross, 20
Secelia Parker, 30
Mary LaCount, 40
Susan Jackson, 25
Mary Jackson, 20
Priscilla LaCount, 18
Nelly Reed, 32
Jane Gross, 50

Racheal Ward, 60
Mary Gross, 25
Susan Jacks, 20
Jane Gross, jr. 20
Sarah Givins, 73
Hannah Mackall, 60
Jane Wheeler, 32
Sarah Green, 60
Susan Green, 60
Mary Jones, 20
Sarah Pratt, 30
Randy Harwood, 32
Florah Jackson, 60
Grace Mason, 25
Eliza Mason, 18
Juliet Mason, 3
Everline Mason, 10
Hannah Mason, 12

Hannah Mason, Sr.
   40
Rosanne Mason, 16
Elenor Roberson, 50
Dinah Gross, 43
Grace Gross, 23
Ann Gross, 18
Hager Fennell, 30
Ann Fennell, 18
Elenor Fennell, 21
Anna__ Mason, 40
Mary Jackson, 14
Easter Cornelias, 50
Ann Gross, 40
Elizabeth Ireland, 50
Elizabeth Rawlings,
   50
Henny Johnson, 40

Calvert County, Maryland

Barbary Brooks, 30
Mahala Brown, 30
Caty Travass, 50
Hannah Gross, 90
Margaret Brooks, 10
Emeline Brooks, 6
Mary Brooks, 2
    months
Kizzai Brown, 60
*Hetty Brown, 6
Eliza Gains, 18
Margaret Gains, 10
Sophia Gains, 5
Terry Gains, 3
Silva Gains, 2
Nancy Gales, 20
Dianna Gales, 23
Dolly Gales, 23
Dolly Gales, 16
Margaret Gales, 90
Jane Gales, 3
Gaddy Blake, 26
Priscilla Blake, 16
Hanah Blake, 8
Eliza Blake, 5
Mary Blake, 2
Sarah Blake, 1
Dorcas Gross, 40
Hetty Travass, 25
Margaret Calendar,
    30
Anna Calendar, 16
Carolina Calendar,
    12
Letty Barnes, 25
Hanah Cook, 30
Margaret Cook, 12
Ailsa Cook, 7
Margaret Cook, 88
Adeline Batson,
Seana Buchanan, 30
Susan Lee, 38
Hetty Anderson, 30
Kitty Anderson, 2
Margaret Calendar,
    40
Ann Calendar, 17
Caroline Calendar, 8
Hannah Barnes, 6
Jane Gross, 40
Rode Ransome, 50
Caroline Moland, 30
Jane Wilson, 40
Jane Pruitt, 41
Mary Smith, 3
Sarah Bowen, 43

Sillar Bowen, 12
Fanny Harden, 60
Margaret Jackson,
    24
Alley Brooks, 50
Matilda Dorsey, 44
Sophia Dorsey, 24
Mary Dorsey, 15
Elizabeth Dorsey, 10
Jane Dorsey, 7
Mary Dorsey, 8
Elizabeth Mason, 56
Dinah Gray, 49
Jane Gray, 35
*Grace Cook, 31
Grace Butler, 64
Anaca Mason, 50
Ally Johnson, 40
Priscilla Gray, 30
Nelly Gray, 28
Sophia Gray, 27
Minty Gray, 26
Rebeca Gray, 18
Dary Gray, 20
Crisssey Gray, 26
Henny Gray, 18
Jane Johnson, 25
Rebeca Gray, 17
Caroline Murry, 18
Margaret Murry, 6
Lucy Taylor, 44
Margaret Chew, 18
Eliza Chew, 16
Sophia Brown, 17
Eliza Brown, 18
Henny Jones, 42
Lucy Jones, 25
Barbary Coats, 22
Elizabeth Jones, 13
Priscilla Jones, 12
Mary Jones, 7
Henny Jones, 3
Grace Reed, 7
Eliza Coats, 4
Milly Cellar, 30
Susan Cellar, 44
Ann Jones, 30
Mahala Freeland, 28
Harriet Freeland, 6
Rebecca Freeland, 5
Susan Jones, 40
Dorcas Jasby, 30
Patty Gross, 28
Jane Jasby, 60
Abby Jenny, 60
Mary Bowen, 5

Sara___ Bowen, 2
    months
Hannah Mason, Sr,
    46
Abby Mason, 6
Margaret Parran, 22
Drusilla Parran, 12
Harriet Parran, 19
Eliza Parran, 10
Abby Brook, Jr, 14
Jane Jackson, 40
Margaret Jackson,
    20
Chaney B___, 45
Dorcas Smith, 50
Dorcas Hardman, 40
Liddy Brown, 50
Susan Brown, 60
*Tilda Dorsey, 16
Lima Dorsey, 10
Lucy Dorsey, 8
Sarah Brown, 40
Kitty Brown, 20
Rachael Brown, 16
Sarah Brown, jr, 12
Nancy Brown, 7
Eliza Brook, 30
Elizabeth Brook, 5
Rebecca Brook, 3
Caroline Brook, 3
    months
Elizabeth Gurry, 45
Eliza Boon, 20
Sharlot Gray, 13
Lyddy Gray, 23
Eliza Gray, 2
Sealiah Stricknall, 4
Priscilla Johnson, 35
Diney Gray, 555
Ann Eliza Dorsey, 14
Rebecca Johnson, 8
Sophia Hammon, 25
Dinah Hammon, 5
Juliet McKinny, 8
Nelly, Soll, 40
Mary Ray, 34
Sarah Ray, 3
Minty Allen, 34
Minty A. Allen, 9
Nelly Hill, 31
Nelly Hill, jr, 9
Nelly Griffin, 30
Ann Griffin, 12
Harriet Washington,
    25

Free African Americans of Maryland - 1832

Anne Washington, 25
Ann Mariah Washington, 6
Mary Jane Washington, 5
Barbary Washington, 3
Mary Washington, 2
Sarah Griffin, 4
Nancy Dublinson, 45
Polly Bryan, 40
Dinny Hace, 30
Rebecca Whittington, 25
Rachel Hall, 32
Jane Hall, 30
Elender Hall, 25
Dorcas Pratt, 50
Elizabeth Hall, 30
Dianna Pillens, 60
Nelly Smith, 40
Juliet Smith, 13
Elen Smith, 7
Henry Smith, 4
Racheal Stewart, 62
Jane Stewart, 10
Sarah Waters, 52
Harriet Randall, 26
Mariah Fry, 57
Nelly Scrivener, 60
Mary Hall, 35
Jane Hall, 12
Polly Scrivener, 45
Sarah Stricknall, 20
Elender Stricknall, 18
Mary Offer, 25
Sarah Offer, 5
Ann Offer, 1
Ann Jones, 30
Frances Brown, 17
Sarah Woodard, 12
Rebecca Woodard, 10
Nelly Thomas, 48
Sarah Spriggs, 20
Elizabeth Spriggs, 7 months.
Sarah Woodard, Jr, 30
Margaret Woodard, 8
Drusilla Woodard, 2
Nancy Smith, 80
Susan Byas, 30
Margaret Byas, 20

Jane Downs, 40
Mary Hinson, 20
R. Susan Ray, 30
Hager Weems, 30
Elizabeth Weems, 15
Susan Ann Weems, 12
Ally Weems, 8
Chaneye, Weems, 32
Judy Anderson, 23
Sarah Dison, 10
Caroline Dison, 4
Susan Denton, 40
Elizabeth Johnson, 30
Susan Gray, 17
Nancy Gross, 10
Milly Gray, 8
Rebecca Green, 40
Margaret Bowie, 20
Elizabeth Bowie, 8
Ann Bowie, 4
Jane Brown, 40
Mary Hinson, 20
Barbary Coats, 20
Eliza Coats, 8
Dianah Mason, 20
Sarah Mason, 16
Ann Green, 20
Sarah Mainyard, 2
Elizabeth Green, 10
Mary Mainyard, 20
*Sarah Mainyard, 2
Charity Clinton, 30
Francis Smothers, 17
Eliza Booth, 31
Jane Booth, 11
Ann Booth, 10
Eliza Ann Booth
Jane Booth, Sr, 31
Margaret Booth, 8
Ann E. Booth, 6
Drusilla Booth, 4
Elender Booth, 55
Rachael Booth, 25
Mary Ellen Ennis, Ann Booth, 20
Drusilla Wicks, 10
Cate Jones, 35
Elizabeth Hartwood, 17
Rebecca Hartwood, 30 Sarah
Hogans, 50

Cassandra Biggers, 77
Sarah Hill, 50
Martha Hill, 50
Grace Scrivener, 48
Margaret Scrivener, 17
Hannah, 18
Sarah Ennis, 50
Nancy Ennis, 18
Susan Mackall, 50
Fanny Mackall, 35
Mary Mackall, 16
Susan Mackall, jr, 12
Dolly Mackall, 8
Rachael Mackall, 6
Henny Mackall, 4
Fanny Quill, 51
Hager Johnson, 47
Crissa Jones, 50
Sarah Jones, 47
Hadger MrCarty, 70
Pliner Gross, 18
Dafney Gross, 16
Alley Gross, 19
Mary Gross, 6
Margaret Gross, 16
Ann Gross, 4
Isabella Boone, 5
Derindy Boone, 3
Betty Henson, 40
Judy, 76
Jinny Gross, 25
Isabella Gross, 40
Chaniy Gross, 45
Rachael Locks, 35
Ally Murry, 40
Ally Macks, 30
Mary Lee, 25
Matilda Lee, 4
Rachael Lee, 3
Hannah Brown, 40
Hannah Brown
Ally Brown, 50
Mary Brown, 16
Ruthy Barker, 60
Flora Hardman, 35
Mary Gross, 35
Priscilla Butler, 30
Ally Gross, 25
Mary Lacount, 40
Priscilla Willet, 18
Lucy Willet, 16
Sarah Weed, 30
Rebecca Weed, 24

31

Calvert County, Maryland

Margaret Cammel, 40
Harriet Cammel, 6
Elizabeth Cammel, 20
Margaret Cammel. 18
Betty Brown, 35
Kitty Brown, 10
Sarah Booth, 50
Mary Brown, 25
Elizabeth Brown, 3
Lucy Mack, 60
Mary Ann Brown, 1
Caroline Brooks, 13
Milly Brooks, 16
Easter Brooks, 50
Milly Boone, 60
Mary Boone, 16
Jinny Gross, 25
Mary Boone, 16
Ally Mack, 10
Sharlotte Boone, 5
Catherine Boone, 25
Cassey Boone, 13
Margaret Pinkney, 20
Cassey Hardman, 19
Minah Hardman, 16
Rebecca Keemer, 13
Judy Sprawling, 45
Kitty Cammel, 6
Ann Cammel, 9
Frances Cammel, 1
Milly Gross, 2
Mary Wood, 26
Ann Wood, 16
Diney Boone, 25
Lucy Green, 60
Prissy Boone, 4
*Jane Boone, 2
____ Harrod, 50
Florah Johnson, 50
Henny Harrod, 25
Kissey Harrod, 5
Henny Spriggs, 50
Nancy Brown, 30
Betty Brown, 14
Milly Quill, 18
Dinnah Gross, 30
Priscilla Gross, 10
Susan Gross, 3
Hanah Harrod, 25
Julet Harrot, 16
Sarah Evans, 70

Mary Gross, 28
Frances A. Gross, 4
Sarah E. Gross, 2
Harriet Gross, 44
Rebecca Hammon, 24
Mary E. Hammon, 49
Ann Brown, 30
Mary Jackson, 50
Racheal Freeland, 23
Liddy Willet, 50
Ann Brown, jr, 9
Dinny Curry, 45
Susan Gramby, 17
Mary Whittington, 7
Jane Willet, 30
Chancy Gross, 40
Eliza Marsell, 20
Elizabeth Gross, 11
Minty Dorsey,40
Nancy Willet, 14
Sarah Whittington, 30
Susan Scott, 18
Sarah E. Whittington, 4 months
Elizabeth Whittington, 5 months
Rachael Green, 20
Caty Gross, 60
Elizabeth Gross, 15
Hannah Gross, 50
Crissey Gross, 8 months
Roanny Gross, 18
Barbary Jones, 24
Deney Groves, 40
Jane Dorsey, 8
Priscilla Dorsey, 6
Nancy Chase, 35
Alanda Butler, 1
Caroline Green, 22
Sarah Ann Green, 20
Mary Jones, 25
Ellen Fenell, 7
Lucy Johnson, 40
Martha Gross, 35
Nancy Gross,6 months
Mary Russell, 20
*Cecelia Russell, 3 months

Harriet Russell, 3 months
Mary Jones, jr, 7
Sarah Parran, 35
Sharlotte Parran, 17
Sarah Parran, jr, 16
Sinderilla Parran, 13
Polly Hollander, 23
Mary Blake, 20
Clancy Green, 10
Susan Green, 25
Elizabeth Green, 17
Sophia Green, 10
Rody Green, 8
Delindy Green, 26
Dianna Green, 23
Sarah an Mackall, 15
Caty Weems, 50
Rachael Green, 70
Grace Weems, 50
Caroline Weems, 20
Sarah Weems, 18
Sarah Jane Weems, 2
Dincy Brown, 4
Rachael A. Brown, 6
Nelly Brown, 4
Harriet Brown, 1
Sophia Jones, 30
Nancy Jones, 15
Jinny Freeman, 40
Dency Gross, 45
Dianer Jones, 6
Grace Gross3
Elen Jones, 8
Ann Fennell, 11
Mary Ann Butler, 30
Elizabeth Butler, 11
Sarah Ann Butler, 8
Elizabeth Gault, 13
Rachel Green, jr, 25
Sarah Green, 6
Emeline Green, 5
Milly Green, 2
Eliza Jackson, 20
Rachel Booth, 30
Betty Green, 30
Eliza Gross, 20
Mary Jones, 100
Rebecca Green, 1
Hannah Ann Jones, 3
Nancy Birk, 1
Rachel Brown, 50
Patterson Hawkins, 30

32

Free African Americans of Maryland - 1832

Susan Gross, 25
Sarah Green, 53
Nancy Hardy, 35
Sarah Hardy, 5
*Margaret Hardy, 2
Sarah Green, 25
Margaret A. Green, 10
Susan Johnson, 2
Elen Gibson, 40
Easter Green, 60
Elizabeth Thomas, 40
Hanah Bladen, 70
Jinney Gasaway, 70
Darkey Naylor, 30
Mary J. Naylor, 8
Caroline Naylor, 3
Mary Quill, 70
Rachel Quill, 38
Sarah Weems, 14
Sarah Laney, 50
Mary Johnson, 25
Emeline Johnson, , 7

Ann M. Johnson, 46
Sarah A. Johnson, 1
Letty Gross, 60
Sarah Barnes, 50
Elizabeth Barnes, 30
Juliet White, 7
Jinny Wheeler, 30
Dinny Green, 25
Sarah Green, 2
Judy Gross, 20
Diney Gross, 1
Margaret Down, 16
Elizabeth Down, 3
Hannah Jackson, 45
Anny Chase, 50
Issa Chase, 9
Bertha Ann G. Reed, 4
Milly White, 35
Jinney Willitt, 30
Susan Jones, 18
Elenor Jones, 20
_____ Gross, 30
Caroline Gray, 20

Mary Reed, 25
Milly Reed, 6
Hanah Taylor, 40
Elizabeth Gross, 8
Catherine Fennell, 25
Sophia Alton, 10
Darkey Brown, 30
_____ Mountain, 65
Rody Jones, 21
Martha Hardesty, 40
Sophia Gault, 30
___ Bailley, 59
Nelly Brooks, 25
Mary Brooks, 3
Alley Gross, 15
Margaret Chase, 12
Rosanna Chase, 40
Mary Chase, 14
Diney Chase, 8
Nelly Kyler, 35
Susan Kyler, 8

No of Females of Color in Calvert County, Md. – 572
August 13 1832
Henry L. Harrison, Sheriff.
Calvert County, Md.
To the Honorable Commisioners of the free people of color of the State of
Maryland.
Gentlemen
I herewith transmit to you a list of the free people of color no[1] residents of Calvert
County. The total amount of males and females is 1112. The first among the
foregoing list you will find to be the No. of males. And the second a list of the
females which I am in hope will meet your honors appreciation. I remain
Gentlemen your most obedient & humble servant to command.
    H. L. Harrison, Sheriff, Calvert County, Md.

---

[1] "no" meaning number

Caroline County

Nathan Roberts, 45
Susan Roberts, 35
William Roberts, 8
Moses Coker, 60
Grace Coker, 45
Isaac Coker, 22
Moses Coker, jr. 20
Henry Coker, 21
Catherine Coker, 15
Susan Coker, 13
Ellen Coker, 9
John Bantum, 20
Noah Grace, 9
Daniel Grace, 8
Henry Cooper, 15
Robert Cooper, 27
George Cooper
Charlotte Cooper, 10
John Cooper
William Cooper
Charles Cooper
H___ Goldsbourgh
Catherine
   Goldsbourgh
Lydia Goldsbourgh
Samuel Dickson
Jane Di___
Hezekiah Dawson,
   25
James Dawson, 6
Frances Dawson, 2
Rachel Mastin, 40
William Mastin, 22
John -----, 18
Esther Hawkins, 32
Elbert Hawkins, 13
Charles Hawkins, 11
William Hawkins, 10
Anderson Hawkins, 8
Mary Hawkins, 6
Caleb Hawkins, 4
Lydia Henry, 17
Dinah Dixon, 35
Joseph Matthews, 44
Ann Hawkins, 100
Henry Matthews, 25
Henry Miller, 22
Ann Matthews, 17
John Matthews, 13

Henrietta Matthews,
   11
Benedict Matthews,
   9
William Matthews, 6
Anderson Matthews,
   2
James Matthews, 1
Mary Matthews, 3
   months
Maria Miller, 25
Henry Johnson, 24
Mary Johnson, 20
Johnson Johnson,
   10 months
Elizabeth Bantum,
   28
Emory Green, 27
Ann Green, 34
Ann Green, jr. 16
Susan Green, 12
Perry Green, 6
Jane Green, 5
Benjamin Downs, 60
Margaret Downs, 45
William Miller, 7
Hannah Downs, 13
John Freeman, 39
Lucy Freeman, 44
Nancy Freeman, 14
Washington
   Freeman, 11
Emory ___, 24
Elizabeth Cooper, 30
Samuel Miller, 38
James Henry, 40
Thomas Henry, 50
John Murray, 73
Elizabeth Cooper, 20
James ____, 40
Lydia Callahan, 25
Elizabeth Stanford, 5
Lucy Stanford, 5
Henry Stanford, 15
Pompey Mattee, 36
Mary Mattee, 30
Rachel Mattee, 50
Susan Mattee, 6
___ Mattee, 3

Mary Mattee, 10
   months
Calab Dickson, 25
James Gibbs, 38
Lucretia Gibbs, 37
Fanny Price, 14
___ Gibbs, 10
John Dyer, 8
Hannah Gibbs, 3
William Gibbs, 2
John Turner, 36
Charles Turner, 23
Luke Walker, 46
Ann Walker, 35
Lucy Walker, 11
Thomas, Walker, 10
George Walker, 8
Mahaly Walker, 6
William Walker, 4
_____ Walker, 2
Joseph Walker, 1
Lydia Smith, 25
Edward B____, 26
Elizabeth B____, 55
Elizabeth B____, 30
___ Patchett
Martha Patchett
*Joseph Gibbs, 13
Perry Smith, 35
Josiah Smith, 30
Nathanial Smith, 21
Susan Smith, 16
Rachel Smith, 14
Benedict Wyatt, 27
Clementine Wyatt
Nathanial ___, 21
Elizabeth Wyatt, 35
James Wyatt, 35
Nancy Wyatt, 65
_____ Holmes, 25
Charles Beswick, 36
Mary Holmes, 1
Mahaly Beswick, 33
Mary Beswick, 12
Sarah Beswick, 1
William Wyatt, 35
Elizabeth Wyatt, 14
James Wyatt, 12
Mary Wyatt, 10
Caroline Wyatt, 8

34

Free African Americans of Maryland - 1832

William Wyatt, 6
_____ Wyatt, 3
John Wyatt, 6
   months
John Freeman, 39
Lotty Freeman, 44
Nancy Freeman, 14
Washington
   Freeman, 11
Emory _____, 26
Samuel Keller, 38
James Henry, 40
Margaret Henry, 50
John Kennard, 75
Daniel _____, 30
_____ ,
Thomas Murray, 10
Charles _____, 3
Harriet _____,1
Peter Hackins, 45
Samuel Cooper, 13
Luther Martin, 40
David Casson, 45
Samuel Sharp, 23
Aaron Foxwell, 55
David Grace, 55
Rachel Grace, 54
Ann Grace, 23
James Grace, 19
Sarah Lively, 20
Sarah Parker, 64
Joseph Parker, 64
Rachel Parker, 66
Isiah Harrison, 12
Charles ___, 50
Henry _____, 35
Charlotte ___, 28
Susan Benny, 25
Ann Lewis, 21
Nathanial ___, 17
John Wyatt, 41
Maria Wyatt, 43
Samuel Wyatt, 19
Ellen Wyatt, 17
John Wyatt Jr, 15
Henry Wyatt, 13
Maria Wyatt, 11
Adeline Wyatt, 8
Sarah Wyatt, 6
Charles Wyatt, 1
_____ Garner, 26
Clementine Garner,
   32
Mary A. Garner, 4
*Benjamin Garner, 3
Elizabeth Garner, 2

William Ward, 22
Eliza Ward, 25
Isaac Downs, 22
Harriett Downs, 33
John Willison, 60
Henry Willison, 55
*Benjamin Garner, 3
Elizabeth Garner, 2
William Ward, 22
Eliza Ward, 25
Isaac Downs, 32
Harris A Downs, 33
John Williams, 60
Henry Williams, 55
Lasalle _____, 21
Margaret ___, 18
Montgomery Downs,
   9
William Downs, 5
Elizabeth Downs, 2
Aaron Grace, 30
Mary Grace, 25
Abraham Grace, 5
Louisa Grace, 2
Rhoda Adams, 70
Martin Reason, 33
Mary Reason, 43
Henrietta Reason, 16
Alexander Thomas,
   27
Rachel Thomas, 21
   Mary Thomas, 1
Priscilla Thomas, 3
Jacob Woodland, 30
James Wickes, 26
John Frisby, 42
Mary Frisby, 31
James Frisby, 13
Mary Frisby, 9
Robert Tea _, 51
Robert Tea _, 22
John Tea _, 51
Stephen Tea _, 14
James Tea _, 5
William Tea _, 2
Esther Tea _, 40
Mary Tea _, 19
Elizabeth Tea _, 4
Jane Tea _, 1
Ellen Tea _, 1 month
Jacob Hammilton,
   42
Grace Hammilton,
   33
Rose Co ___, 40
Susan Co___, 28

Robert Rodrick, 56
Rachel Rodrick, 48
John Rodrick, 10
Jacob Lewis, 60
Mary Lewis, 51
John Hawkins, 32
Jacob Williams, 76
John Lewis, 16
James Lewis, 14
Mary Lewis, 10
Sarah Lewis, 8
Thomas B ___, 52
Albert B _____, 54
John B _____, 26
Thomas B ___, 20
Samuel B _____, 15
James B _____, 16
Thomas Fisher, 16
Ann Fisher,
John Fisher, 15
William Clayton, 35
Matilda Clayton, 57
Richard Dugans, 60
Nace D _____, 45
Mary Dugans, 46
Nancy Dunaway, 36
Margaret Beswicks,
   40
Margaret Beswicks,
   65
Isaac Baynard, 22
Ann Baynard, 31
*George Baynard, 6
Nathaniel Clarke, 28
Samuel H____, 65
Aaron _____, 25
Mary Adams, 25
Mary Jane Adams, 2
George Price, 63
___ Price, 65
Henry Price, 25
Mary Price, 21
L ___, Price, 16
A___ Price, 16
George Price, 13
Sarah Price, 11
John Price, 9
Rachel Price, 6
Elizabeth Price, 2
Mary Price
L___, 1
Ann Hawkins, 13
Thomas Freeman, 20
Matthew Harding, 35
Nancy Harding, 45

Caroline County

Ann Goldsbourgh, 23
Mary Goldsbourgh, 21
Jefferson Rideout, 20
___, Rideout, 16
Edward Caldwell, 35
___ Caldwell, 27
Washington Caldwell, 6
William H. Caldwell, 5
Ezekial Caldwell, 2
Samuel Fountain, 33
Henry Driver, 45
Thomas ___, 47
Richard Sharp, 24
Charlotte Sharp, 26
Jane Sharp, 14
*Emory Kirby, 35
Maria Kirby, 30
Phillip Kirby, 10
Elizabeth Kirby, 8
Eleanor Kirby, 5
James Thomas, 19
John Brooks, 16
John Rich, 9
Rachel Lockerman, 20
Samuel Thomas, 40
Susan Thomas, 30
Mary Ellen Thomas, 3
Ann Thomas, 32
Ann Thomas, 2
William H. Thomas, 1
James H. Wheeler, 15
Maria Wheeler, 2
John Baber, 41
Catherine Baber, 45
Elizabeth Baber, 20
Henrietta Baber, 18
James Baber, 21
Robert Baber, 19
Lucinda Black, 25
Edward Pendleton, 29
Mary Pendleton, 19
James _ Pendleton, 2
Jinnett Pendleton, 1
Mary Thomas, 22
Ann Emily Thomas, 7
Lucinda Black, 7

Henry Black, 6
Luther Black, 4
Louisa Black, 2
Stephen Potter, 65
Ann Emery, 24
Mary Johnson, 19
*Henrietta Rhodes, 10
P ___ Thomas, 48
Thomas H. Thomas, 6
Alexander Thomas, 2
Stephen Harper, 48
___ Harper, 38
Lafayette Harper, 9
Sidney Harper, 1
Mary Jane Eaton, 19
John Eaton, 2
Jane Hutson, 45
Sophia Hutson, 32
Sarah Hutson, 30
George W. Hutson, 20
Henrietta Hutson, 17
Adeline Hutson, 7
Hannah ___, 22
Mary Cottman, 11
Stephen ------, 45
Sophia Fountain, 37
Margaret Ruth, 21
___ Ruth, 27
John Henry, 30
Solomon Fisher, 10
Susan Vickers,
Phoebe Cottman, 56
Rebecca Cooper, 35
Joseph Driver, 55
___ Driver, 40
Eleanor Fountain, 27
Elizabeth Hutchins. 56
Martha Hutchins, 10
Solomon Hutchins, 11
Alexander Hutchins, 22
Resin Sutton, 35
Edward Clarke, 39
Amy Clarke, 33
H___ Jane Clarke, 6
Martha A. Clarke, 2
John Lockerman, 27
Sarah Lockerman, 27
Elizabeth A. Lockerman, 21

Rebecca Lockerman, 2
Elizabeth Ross, 28
Ann Maria Ross, 2
Catherine Nicols, 18
Catherine Black, 51
Lucretia Black, 55
Ailsey Black, 23
Frederick Black, 9
Celia Black, 4
Mary Black, 7
___ Black, 2
Obediah Bailey, 34
Henry Haines, 45
___ Haines, 40
Lloyd Haines, 21
Lewis Haines, 19
John Haines, 12
William Haines, 10
George W. Haines, 3
Mary Haines, 17
___ Haines, 5
Phillip Banks, 68
Priscilla Banks, 68
Levi Hawkins, 9
Peter Sullivan, 30
Adeline Sullivance, 12
Jacob Fisher, 15
Solomon Stanford, 14
Joseph Tilleton, 32
Eve Johnson, 51
Aaron Johnson, 23
Esther Johnson, 22
Samuel Johnson, 18
Mary Johnson, 16
Catherine Johnson, 12
James Johnson, 1
Joseph Howard, 10
Maria Howard, 9
Charlotte Grove, 37
Rachel Stanford, 15
Henry Stanford, 25
Solomon Stanford, 11
George Stanford, 10
Mary Stanford, 7
Stephen Stanford, 5
John H. Stanford, 4
Isaiah Stanford, 3
James H. Gross, 1
Stephen Dixon, 30
Nancy Dixon, 24
Mary Jane Brooks, 7

Free African Americans of Maryland - 1832

Catherine M. Brooks, 2
Elizabeth Brooks, 1
William Holland, 50
Catherine Holland, 45
John Holland, 3
Samuel Slaughter, 54
Martha Brown, 40
Lucretia Pennington, 41
Emmanuel Pennington, 18
William Whitely, 13
John Dyer, 35
Dianne Dyer, 35
Levi Dyer, 15
Esther Dyer, 12
Stephen Dyer, 10
Louisa Dyer, 7
John Dyer Jr, 5
Eve Dyer, 2
Richard Nichols, 45
Grace Nichols, 35
Jane Nichols, 16
Nancy Nichols, 12
Catherine Nichols, 10
Sarah Nichols, 7
Esther Nichols, 5
William Nichols, 2
Daniel Rich, 48
Lea_ Rich, 45
Hamilton Rich, 20
Marcelius Rich, 18
Joseph Rich, 15
Charles Rich, 15
Daniel Rich Jr, 7
Frederick Rich, 3
Henry Whiteley, 60
Esther Whiteley, 40
Joseph Shepherd, 57
Sarah Shepherd, 47
Henrietta Shepherd, 27
James H. Lockerman, 7
James Dixon, 65
Mary Dobson, 60
Judy Ann Hamilton, 15
Ann Boyer, 13
Harriett Fountain, 32
Mary E. Fountain, 6
Violet Maxwell, 60

Sarah Maxwell, 22
Mary Maxwell, 18
Elizabeth Maxwell, 14
Immanuel Taylor, 12
Flora ___, 75
George Wright, 58
Martha Wright, 40
Joseph Wright, 18
Alfred Wright, 15
Perry Wright, 13
Nathaniel Wright, 11
*James Wright, 9
Levi Wright, 8
Elizabeth Wright, 7
John Wright, 4
Henry Bias, 56
Esther Bias, 65
Joseph Bias, 14
Catherine Bias, 21
Sarah A. Bias, 20
___, Bias, 16
Daniel Downs, 60
Diana Downs, 64
David Robinson, 45
Margaret Robinson, 70
David Lockerman, 40
Lydia Robinson, 30
Sarah Robinson, 35
David Robinson JR, 20
Esther Wisher, 30
Frederick Wisher, 19
Edwin Wisher, 8
James Ringo, 16
Henry Atkinson, 12
Thomas Hines, 10
Harriett H.Hines, 30
Susan Dickerson, 28
Susan A. Dickerson, 7
Mary Dickerson, 11
Henrietta Born, 55
Simon Hines, 1
Allen Murray, 52
Lydia Murray, 45
Catherine Murray, 20
Mary Murray, 15
Emily A. Murray, 10
Rhonda Murrray, 9
Richard B. Murray, 6
Harriett Hemsley, 4
John W. Lockerman, 3

Levi Tilghman, 36
Rhoda Tilghman, 28
Sarah Tilghman, 11
Rachel Tilghman, 9
William H. Tilghman, 6
Perry N, Tilghman, 3
William Grace, 59
Dianna Grace, 60
C__ Grace, 17
G__ Grace, 12
Joshua Grace, 34
William Grace, 18
Sylvia Gorden, 1
Margaret Thomas, 49
John Thomas 11
Caroline Thomas, 6
A__ Gorden, 7
Henry Gorden, 3
Mary Gibson, 35
Peter Kennards, 70
Flora Kennards, 60
Elizabeth Grace, 24
Henry Grace, 23
Henry A. Grace, 1
Margaret Hammond, 17
Charlotte Lucas, 26
Nancy Thomas, 12
__ Hammond, 19
John Kennedy, 11
Elizabeth Hopkins, 4
Cato Casson, 18
Robert Casson, 15
Henrietta Jackson, 20
*Thaddeus Griffith, 58
Henrietta Griffith, 50
Fanny Sewell, 30
William L. Tillotson, 9
Henny Sewell, 4
Lucretia Sewell, 2
James Tillotson, 65
Eliza Mason, 25
Harrison Mason, 3
Elizabeth Mason, 9
Em__ Roy, 17
Jacob Smith, 35
Catherine Smith, 29
Anne Maria Smith, 7
Matilda Smith, 5
John Hicks, 27
Henrietta Hicks, 25
Emeline Hicks, 18

Caroline County

Esther Hicks, 50
D___ Hicks, 2
John Hicks, 6
Jennett Hicks, 14
James Mackey, 40
Lydia Mackey, 40
Montgomery Mackey, 19
Henry Mackey, 15
Annette Mackey, 10
Mary Mackey, 8
Adeline Mackey, 7
John Mackey, 4
Isaac Mackey, 1
Joseph Balden, 55
Rachel Balden, 45
___ Balden, 7
Sarah Ann Balden, 3
Maria Hute, 22
July A. Hute, 20
William Taylor, 25
Mary Ann Taylor, 2
Esther Cooper, 65
Mary Downs, 16
Eliza Roberts, 20
William Turner, 45
Loretta Turner, 14
William Turner Jr, 12
George Turner, 9
Eliza Ann Turner
Judy Fountain, 50
Jacob Fountain, 21
Benjamin Gray, 76
Robert Carter, 75
Benjamin Downs, 30
Sarah Downs, 30
Henry Goldsbourgh, 14
William Price, 30
Esther Roy, 60
Amelia Roy, 26
John Roy, 60
Mahaly Shepherd, 17
Martha A. Price, 6
Sarah A. Rich, 5
Frances A. Taylor, 4
Mary E. Rich, 3
John Done, 60
Catherine done, 45
Martha Mason, 30
Elizabeth L. Mason, 4
Thomas H. Mason, 1
Margaret P. Fountain, 25

Mary Done, 15
*William Done, 11
Francis Wayman, 49
Matilda Wayman, 45
John Wayman, 18
Joseph Wayman, 15
Alexander Wayman, 12
Benjamin Wayman, 9
William H. Wayman, 5
Robert Francis Wayman, 2
Ann James, 70
Eliza Fountain, 25
William Fountain, 65
Margaret Fountain, 45
William Fountain Jr, 25
Nicholas Fountain, 23
Margaret Fountain, 14
John Fountain, 9
Levi Fountain, 6
Anny Murray, 50
Philip Murray, 26
Elizabeth Murray, 24
Charlotte Murray, 18
William Murray, 12
Luther Murray, 10
James H___, 45
Sarah Anthony, 70
Aaron Berryman, 58
Rhoda Berryman, 55
Aaron Berryman Jr. 13
Flora Nichols, 30
Lucretia Nichols, 11
_____ Nichols, 9
John E. Nichols, 4
Nelson Allen, 38
Henrietta Allen, 30
Richard Allen, 6
Phoebe Hicks, 70
Solomon Potter, 28
James Warwick, 33
Harriett Warwick, 32
___ Jane Warwick, 8
William Whiteley, 14
Andrew W ____, 31
Emalis Rich, 18
Grace Pratt, 60
James Robinson, 17

Stephen Green, 50
Eva Green, 65
Joseph Green, 21
Alexander Green, 20
Stephen Green Jr, 17
Charles Green, 14
Rose Green, 7
Catherine Green, 5
Sarah A. Green, 3
Robert Green, 4
Levi Shepherd, 60
George Shepherd, 30
Lydia Shepherd, 31
Maria Shepherd, 20
Adeline Shepherd, 2
Elenor Shepherd, 1
James Hays, 10
James Harris, 35
Harriett Harrris, 30
Thomas Harris, 6
John Harris, 5
Ann Maria Harris, 3
Mary Ellen Harris, 1
M ___Driver, 67
Hester Driver, 55
Ailsey Ash, 19
Mary Ash, 17
Ann Ash, 2
*Ellen Ash, 1
David Lewis, 35
Martha Lewis, 22
Eliza Ann Lewis, 5
Nancy Johnson, 60
Samuel Black, 36
Margaret Black, 28
William Black, 9
James Black, 7
Sarah A. Black, 3
William Smith, 18
Charles Garner, 50
Rachel Garner, 48
Marcus Garner, 7
Mary Garner, 12
Daniel Rich, 22
Peregrine Cuff, 35
R___ Cuff, 32
Maria Lewis, 20
John Lewis, 5
William Brown, 70
Elizabeth Brown, 39
John Brown, 11
Alexander Brown, 8
___ Brown, 6
George Brown, 5
Thomas Grace, 25

Free African Americans of Maryland - 1832

___ Scott, 45
___ Scott, 9
Susan Scott, 5
Mary Ellen Scott, 1
J___ Scott, 14
Sarah A. Scott, 10
John Seth, 25
Charles Seth, 23
Jame Seth, 22
John Saulsbury, 49
William Saulsbury, 19
Henry Saulsbury, 15
Rachel Saulsbury, 14
G___ Saulsbury, 12
Amy Ann Saulsbury, 10
Louisa Saulsbury, 8
Standley Saulsbury, 7
Mary Ellen Saulsbury, 6
Sarah Jackson, 45
Lydia Boon, 40
Hannah Boon, 9
James Blake, 26
Rhoda Mitchell, 20
Henny Mitchell, 29
Noah Grove, 37
John Grinage, 70
Solomon Grinage, 28
Catherine Grinage, 25
John Buck, 65
Eli Buck, 24
Rebecca Buck, 20
William Buck, 19
Mary Buck, 17
Elizabeth Buck, 8
Catherine Buck, 4
Joshua Henry, 48
Lydia Henry, 45
Rhoda Henry, 7
Joshua Henry, 4
Richard White, 3
Violet White, 2
Hannah White, 5
H___ White, 4
*Caroline White, 9
Thomas White, 3
Susan White, 1
Emory Freeman, 23
Rebecca Knots, 60
Aaron Johnson, 63
Frisby Johnson, 11

Jacob Taylor, 38
Francis Burns, 12
Noah Black, 35
Ainey Black, 28
Susan A. Bowser, 8
Nancy Hiteh, 56
Charity Hiteh, 14
S___- Black, 30
Lucy Black, 28
Harrietta Black, 8
Luther Black, 5
Mary Black, 6
Julia Black, 3
Robert Black, 1
Susanna Grinage. 80
Elizabeth Satterfield, 36
Mary Ellen Satterfield, 10
___ Ann Satterfield, 7
G___ Satterfield, 5
Elizabeth Satterfield jr, 1
Esther Tilghman, 35
Mary Todd, 22
Lydia Stevens, 70
Perry Clarkson, 40
___ Clarkson, 35
John H. Clarkson, 4
James Clarkson, 1
David Wright, 36
Rachel Wright, 14
*Ann Wright, 11
Leveny Wright, 7
William Wright, 7
Mary Jane Wright 5
George Wright, 3
Susanna Wright, 20
Willoughby Wright, 46
___ White, 36
A___ A. White, 16
Maria White, 14
Mary White, 12
A___White, 10
Esther White, 8
Catherine White, 6
Sarah Ellen White, 4
Leance White, 70
Mary E King, 26
Thomas Smith, 11
James Babes, 30
Mahala Babes, 35
Ann Maria Babes, 3
Eliza Ellen Babes, 1

Ann Maria Clarke, 19
Sarah Ann Clarke, 1
Hache_ Boston, 55
Sarah Boston, 48
Margaret Boston, 14
Robert Boston, 10
Maria Boston, 8
Elishor Boston, 4
Sarah A. Boston, 2
William H. Boston, 6
Henry Adams, 40
___ Adams, 45
Eliza Adams, 18
*Rebecca Adams, 15
Nathan Cook, 46
Joseph Williams, 41
___ Williams, 38
Amy A. Williams, 14
Elizabeth Williams, 14
Louisa Williams, 7
Nathan Williams, 6
Joseph B. Williams, 4
Sophia Gasaway, 14
Garretson ___, 30
John Brown, 38
Lucretia Brown, 23
John Westley Brown, 4
Elizabeth Brown, 1
Ephriam Boston, 21
Elizabeth Boston, 18
James E. Boston, 1
Nancy Black, 27
Alexander Black, 7
Adeline Black, 5
Henry Stanford, 47
Nancy Stanford, 40
Thomas Stanford, 11
Lydia Stanford, 6
John H. Stanford, 5
Stephen Stanford, 4
Susan Stanford, 70
Thomas Stanford, 60
Jacob Cook, 47
Nancy Cook, 36
Elizabeth Cook, 15
Henry Cook, 9
William Mitchell Cook, 7
Elijah L. Cook
Henry Cook, 1
A___ Philips, 23
George W. Cook, 17

Caroline County

Washington Dennis, 11
___ Clark, 60
___, Clarke, 45
John Brooks, 10
Henry Price, 24
Esther Price, 24
Ellen Jane Price, 2
John Lewis Grove, 6
Sampson Satterfield, 41
Elizabeth Satterfield, 35
Mary Satterfield, 13
John Satterfield, 9
Elizabeth Satterfield, 7
Henry Satterfield, 5
D___ Satterfield, 3
Thomas _____, 37
Garretson Lewis, 25
William Steel, 17
Daniel Black, 39
Henry Fisher, 18
Mary M___, 16
Patience Thomas, 70
Emalls Causaway, 13
Lidia Causeaway, 40
Henrietta H___, 27
Ann Marie Camp, 1
William Johnson, 8
James Ash, 80
Jimmy Douglass, 70
___ James, 69
Elisabeth Murray, 3
Rachel Jenkins, 55
Violet Cooper, 50
Michael Lewis, 63
*Charity Dean, 67
Levi Dean, 4
___ Wright, 58
Jacob ___, 33
Mary Wright, 20
_____ Wright, 22
H. William H. Wright, 10 months
___Green, 28
Annette Green, 23
William Henry Green, 5
Samuel Green, 3
John ___Green, 3 months
Hester Thomas, 89
Hannah Thomas, 28

Mary Thomas, 28
Jane Thomas, 22
Betty Thomas, 20
Peter E. Foster, 5
Robert H___, 2
Emally Collins, 14
Henry Collins, 18
Elizabeth Dean, 7
Isaac Fountain, 50
Hager Fountain, 61
Henry Fountain , 17
Joseph Fountain, 14
John Smith, 46
Susan Smith, 35
Sarah R. Smith, 8
Josephine Smith, 6
Charity Smith, 5
A___ Mitchell, 60
Charles Downs, 45
Rachel Hooper, 33
William Downs, 19
E___ Downs, 16
Charles Downs, 10
___ Downs, 6
Susan Downs, 8
Henry Downs, 4
Nancy Downs, 8 months
Eli Harris, 43
Hannah Harris, 25
James W. Harris, 5
Elizabeth Harris, 3
Mary E. Harris, 3
Stephen Stanford, 27
___ Stanford, 30
William H. Stanford, 6
Mary E. Stanford, 4
Francis A. Stanford, 2
James F___
*___ Friend, 22
Lily Friend, 45
John Ross, 60
Esther Ross, 47
Enoch Ross, 6
Esther Ross, jr, 17
Rose Harris, 53
C___Harris, 45
Daniel Dutton, 13
H___ Ross, 21
Alfred Gross, 16
Joshua Downs 20
Eli Stanford, 23
Moses Hooper, 45
James Adams, 26

Fanny Pope, 32
Elizabeth Pope, 3
Joshua Adams, 19
E___ Adams, 8
William H. Adams, 24
Robert Emmets, 20
Washington Bre Kington, 20
Philip Philips, 42
Isaac Collins, 2 1
Gabriel Friend, 32
Henry Friend, 10
Hester Friend, 7
William Friend, 5
Elijah Friend, 3
Hannah Friend, 80
James Junson, 59
Margaret Junson, 45
William Junson, 8
William Friend, 8
William Sharp, 22
Elmer Sharp, 19
Grace Friend, 25
Henry Prattes, 34
Charles Prattes, 12
C___ Prattes, 22
James Prattes, 4
William H. Prattes, 2 months
Henry Johns, 16
Stanford Adams, 70
H___ Adams, 50
Elmer Sharp, 19
Grace Friend, 25
Henry Prattes, 34
C___ Prattes, 34
Charles Prattes, 12
James Prattes, 4
William H. Prattes, 2 months.
Henry Johns, 16
Stamford Adams, 70
Hancock Adams, 50
Julia Webb, 6
Joshua Webb, 10
Isaac Friend, 30
Sophia Friend, 30
Mary Friend, 10
James Friend, 7
July Ann Friend, 4
Ann Maria Friend, 3
Charles Prattes, 30
Nancy Prattes, 22
Mary Pratts, 8
James Prattes, 3

Free African Americans of Maryland - 1832

Delia Dean, 24
L__ Johns, 49
D__ Johns, 23
Mary Jane Johns, 22
Matthew U. Johns, 19
Henry L. Johns, 18
Hannah H. Johns, 14
N__ Jefferson Johns, 12
Eliza Ann Johns, 10
Catherine A. Johns, 8
Alexander Johns, 5
William F. Johns, 3
Asbury F. Johns, 8 months
Hester Willison
*Catherine Willison, 8
Caroline Willison, 4
George Adams, 58
Elizabeth Adams, 45
William Adams, 13
George Adams, 3
Dealy F__, 3
William Henry F__, 3
Eleanor Riggins, 14
John H. Hamilton, 60
Nelly Hamilton, 60
Abraham Webb, 25
Gallaway Webb, 2
Emily Jane Webb, 6 weeks
Ridgeway Wright, 24
Nancy Hill, 24
__ Adams, 36
Hannah Adams, 70
Jacob Burris, 25
Henry Burris 27
Thomas __ Butler, 14
Solomon Prattes, 2
Hester _ James, 36
Sarah Johnson, 8
Alexander Johnson, 8
William Johnson James, 19
James W__, 80
Rachel W__, 55
William Brian, 10
Isaac Wisher, 8

Alfonso Friend, 75
John Friend, 23
Ann Friend, 20
Nancy E. Friend, 8 months
John Alfred Brian, 15
James Henry Brian, 17
James Wolford, 21
Louisa Wolford, 20
John Chase, 15
Lambert Nichols, 72
Rachel Nichols, 60
Joshua Nichols, 14
Gallaway Webb, 40
Samuel Chase, 60
Mary Chase, 70
Ann Cephas, 15
Solomon Holmes, 36
July Ann Holmes, 31
Solomon M. Holmes, 7 months
Emelly Holmes, 5
John Boston, 17
Elizabeth Wolford, 35
Eleanor Wolford, 109
Mary Wolford, 12
Ann Wolford, 5
__ Brown, 63
Jane Hubbard, 66
Juda Hubbard, 65
Julia Hubbard, 17
Mary Ruffin, 18
Willison Hubbard, 14
Emily Jane Ruffin, 2
__ Hasket, 80
Eleanor Hasket, 55
Charles Adams, 32
Ann Adams, 28
Martha A. Adams, 7
*Hannah Adams, 2
Ann Francis Adams, 9 months
Ann Boston, 14
Joseph C. Webb, 11
Nancy Jackson, 27
A__ Jackson, 8
Harriet Jackson, 4
William Cooper, 26
Elizabeth Cooper, 19
William H. Cooper, 1
Harriet Tilghman, 35
Pere Farmer, 40
Mahala Farmer, 30

Mary Ann farmer, 6
Charles M. Farmer, 4
William Farmer, 2
Catherine Johnson, 22
Sarah Ann Johnson, 5
Hester Goldsbourgh, 25
Harriet Goldsbourgh, 7
William Goldsbourgh, 10
Daniel Adams
Mary Adams, 24
John Henry Adams, 2 months
Dafney Adams, 55
Perry Hubbard, 17
Eliza Collins, 22
Samuel __, 22
Joshua Webb, 17
Maria Dickerson, 18
Mary Conaway, 6
William C__, 17
Richard Hawkins, 15
Levin Eaton, 53
Sarah Eaton, 40
Owen Eaton, 21
Mary Ann Eaton, 17
George Eaton, 15
Henry Eaton, 9
Ann Eaton, 6
Caleb Eaton, 4
Sarah Eaton, 3
Elether Eaton, 2
Moody Jacobs, 70
Frank Jacobs, 60
Pompey Atkinson, 15
Henry B__, 26
Elizabeth Harris, 40
Eliza Harris, 17
Mary Burris, 60
William Pratt, 12
Jeremiah Batty, 36
Dida Johnson, 55
Mary Johnson, 23
Adam Wright, 22
Adam Sheppard, 45
Mary Sheppard, 35
Elizabeth Sheppard, 8
Louisa Sheppard, 6
Matilda Sheppard, 3
Eli Sheppard, 1
__ Thomas, 67

Caroline County

Nelson Thomas, 26
A__ Thomas, 18
Mary A. Thomas, 16
O__ Thomas, 15
John Thomas, 14
*Sarah Ann Thomas, 11
Curtis Thomas, 10
Mary Ann Thomas, 8
Rhoda Sheppard, 50
Mary Thomas, 20
Eve Sheppard, 31
John Chase, 5
John Camper, 2
Isaac Camper, 3 months
Lydia Prattes, 20
Ann Brown, 11
William J. Thomas, 3
Henry Clay Thomas, 5 months
Joseph Simpson, 26
William Simpson, 19
Nancy Simpson, 2
Adeline Simpson, 7
Margaret Simpson, 5
Elizabeth Simpson, 4
John H__ Simpson, 2
Jacob Sheppard, 45
Elmer Sheppard, 32
Sarah Pennington, 38
Eliza Sheppard, 15
John Henry Sheppard, 8
William B. Sheppard, 5
Elizabeth Sheppard, 3
Mary A. Sheppard, 6 months
Isaac Pratt, 40
C__ Pratt, 33
Rachel Pratt, 10
Stephen Pratt, 6
Tilghman Pratt, 8
William Pratt, 13
Henry __ Pratt, 4
Alexander Pratt, 3
Rachel Pratt, 63
Ann Pratt, 22
Thomas Riggs, 85
Mary C___, 40
Eliza Philips, 8
Madison Smith, 23
Prince Murray, 40

___ Murray, 35
Charlotte Murray, 18
Ann Murray, 17
William Murray, 1
Samuel Kinney, 61
Sarah Kinney, 70
___ Philips, 65
Mary Burris, 80
William Philips, 33
Mary Philips, 22
Christiana Philips, 9 months
Mary Philips, jr, 14
Eliza Philips, 33
William C. Philips, 10
___ Philips, 8
Ruth A. Philips, 6
Mary Thomas, 25
John F. Thomas, 4 days
Stphen Philips, 71
James Brown, 22
Ann Brown, 19
Lydia Pratt, 20
Joshua Betts, 30
*D___ Causeaway, 30
Nancy Brown, 19
Joshua Bell, 5
Elizabeth Bell, 3
Comfort Bell, 2
Charles Causeaway, 30
Rachel Causeaway, 32
L__ Causeaway, 10
Peter Causeaway, 6
Foster Causeaway, 5
Daniel Causeaway, 3
Mary Causeaway, 1
F__ Duggins, 40
Charlotte Duggins, 30
Solomon H. Duggins, 5
B__ Duggins, 7
Tom Duggins, 3
___ H. Duggins, 10 months
John Henry Friend, 24
Ann Friend, 18
Mary E. Friend, 2 months
Curtis Henry, 35
___ Ralter, 55

Henry Tilghman, 21
Jeremiah B. Bell, 4
Benjamin Tilghman, 3
Maria Jackson, 11
William Jackson, 13
John Pratt,9
Setter King, 90
Major King, 85
Joshua King, 7
Mary King, 17
Nancy James, 22
Daniel Collins, 50
Jeremiah West, 55
Darkey West, 50
Asbury Johns, 5
Rose Bias, 75
Rachel Turner, 40
James Chase, 39
Mary Chase, 38
Henry Chase, 16
Andrew Chase, 12
William Chase, 10
Lindley Chase, 8
Deborah E. Chase, 6
Josiah Chase, 3
Mary E. Chase, 6 months
Washington Adams, 60
J__ Adams, 38
Robert Adams, 14
William Adams, 11
Elisha Adams, 8
Sarah Adams, 4
Charles Adams, 6 months
Simon Wisher, 65
Moses Smith, 45
Fanny Smith, 35
Rachel Smith, 22
Eliza Smith, 17
Ruth Smith, 12
Benjamin Smith, 9
Rosetta Smith, 7
Charles H. Smith, 3
Moses Smith, 10
*Joseph Webb, 40
Henry Webb, 36
John Webb, 15
James Webb, 13
Joseph Webb, 11
Mary Webb, 9
Hester Webb, 7
William Webb, 5
Peter Webb, 3

Free African Americans of Maryland - 1832

Stephen Webb, 8 months
Samuel Chase, 60
Samuel Chase, jr, 30
Susan Chase, 22
Rosetta Chase, 9
George E. Chase, 8 months
Jinny Smallwood, 50
Rebecca Green, 4
Mary Jane Green, 3 months
Philip B__, 50
Clyde ___, 30
Mary Jackson, 45
Susan A. Jackson, 12
Jane Jackson, 3
John Wesley Jackson, 10 months
Mary Roberts 57
Henry King, 14
Elizabeth _ Smith, 5
George King, 11
John King, 9
C__ King, 8
Rebecca King, 12
Elizabeth King, 4
Levin G__, 45
William Green, 5
___ King, 70
James B ___, 66
Pompey New___, 55
D__ New__, 35

John Johnson, 11

___ New___, 7
Rhoda A. New___, 16 months
Rozette B__, 35
July Ann Br__, 7
Margart Johnson, 30
___ Johnson, 10
Maria Johnson, 6
Ann Gibson, 25
Mary E. Gibson, 7
George Washington Thomas, 9 months
John Cornish, 14
Peter Cornish, 25
Nelly Roberts, 46
Sarah A. Roberts, 8 months
Araminta Cornish, 13
D___ Cornish, 20
___ Bantum, 23
Rebecca Green, 25
William Green, 2 ½
Mary Jane Green, 8 months
Rebecca Webb, 70
Priscilla Webb, 60
Asbury Webb, 3
Elizabeth Ann Blay, 35
Hariett Bla_, 10
Agnes Bla__, 15
James Bla__, 5
___ Bla__4
John H. Bla__2
*Henry Holmes, 14

Mary A. Holmes, 13
___ Brewington, 45
A__ Ploughman, 50
Harrison Cephas, 30
Sarah Cephas, 20
Daniel Cephas, 5 months
Levin C__, 15
William R_-, 30
Nancy Russ__, 25
Henry Chase, 16
Abraham Chase, 33
Kitty Chase, 33
Washington Brewington, 19
Sarah A Satterfield, 14
Charles E__, 30
Philip Moore, 65
D__ Moore, 60
Jacob Richards, 85
Sarah Richards, 70
Margaret Richards, 7
James Steel, 30
John W. Steel, 9
Elizabeth Steel, 6
Levin Collins, 67
Mary Collins, 45
Levin Collins, jr, 14
Rebecca Collins, 12
Juliet Collins, 9
Mary Jane Collins, 7
Abraham Collins, 2
Henry Collins, 11 days
Mary Willson, 18 months.

■ ■

A LIST OF THE FREE NEGROES IN CECIL COUNTY

Anderson, John, 71
Anderson, Perry, 20
Anderson, Jacob, 47
Anderson, Wesley, 15
Anderson, Jacob, 2
Allen, Henry, 51
Anderson, Abe, 47
Anderson Isaih, 15
Anderson, Joseph, 56
Anderson, Infant
Anderson, Perry, 36

Anderson, Samuel, 9
Anderson, Christy, 1
Anderson, Mike, 28
Anderson, George, 40
Anderson, Ned, 10
Anderson, Steve, 8
Anderson, George, 4
Anderson, Alexander, 2
Anderson, Abe, 60
Anderson, Eli, 24
Anderson, John, 22

Anderson, Joe, 18
Anderson, George, 26
Allen, Benedict. 13
Ash, Charles, 26
Ash, Eliza, 5
Allen, Abe, 35
Aiken, Bill, 4
Anderson, Bill, 39
Ash, John , 27
*Ash, Tom, 5
Black, Jim, 65
Buck, Jim, 23

Cecil County

Black Hosea, 12
Buck, Amos, 2
Buck, Elisha, 17
Black, Jim, 6
Brown, George, 10
Berry, John, 50
Berry Willatson, 20
Berry, John, 18
Buck, George, 40
Berry, Dick, 17
Buck, Jacob, 20
Berry, Ellice, 13
Berry, Lewis, 8
Bladen, Dick, 43
Bladen, Dianna, 33
Bladen, Jack, 2
Brown, Levi, 28
Boddy, George, 50
Boddy, Ben, 22
Boddy, Jim, 13
Boddy, Bill, 12
Black, George, 20
Black, George, 1
Bashe, George, 8
Boulden, Isaac, 2
Bostic, John, 6
Bostic, Benjamin, 3
Brasch, Sidney, 10
Biles, Ben, 19
Butler, Tom, 55
Ball, John, 60
*Ball, Calob, 25
Ball, Abe, 6
Brady, James, 30
Brown, Tom, 1
Buck, Ned, 70
Bouser, James, 19
Bouser, Isaac, 17
Bouser, George, 13
Bond, Harry, 34
Black, Stephen, 23
Braton, Jim, 54
Braton, Tom, 9
Bradford, Jim. 8
Bradford, Flasky, 41
Bradford, John, 6
Brown, Jerry, 28
Brown, Bob, 35
Brown, George, 13
Bradford, George, 26
Berry, Abe, 30
Berry, John. 2
Bouldin, Robert, 65
Bouldin, Isaac, 15
Boyer, Reynard, 20
Boyd, Henry, 6

Boman, Michal, 35
Boman, Peter, 9
Boyer, Hephen, 44
Boyer, Sam, 48
Boyer, Steve, 11
Boyer, Jim, 6
Boyer, Ike, 5
Boyer, Bill, 3
Brown, Cyrus, 62
Bark, Lue, 4
Bostic, Cesar, 45
Bostic, Charles, 6
Bostic Cesar, 3
Boulden, Toby, 45
Bostic, Peter, 23
Bare, Joseph, 63
Brown, Jacob, 32
Busk, Natty, 60
Blackson, Jacob, 51
B___, Bill, 16
Bayard, Jim, 16
Bayard, Henry, 31
Bayard, Thomas, 72
Bayard, Perry, 9
Bealle, Bill, 34
Bealle, George, 7
Berry, Jim. 42
Berry, Henry, 45
Brown, Nace, 28
Brown, Jeremiah, 24
Bayard, Lewis, 26
Bayard, Perry, 2
Berry, Bill, 18
Berry, Sandy, 51
Berry, Bill, 28
Brooks, Jim, 35
Brooks, Sorrell, 12
Brooks, Robert, 8
Brooks, Samuel, 6
Brown, Levi, 3
Bayard, David, 27
Bayard, Henry, 1
Bayard, Harry, 23
Biggs, Joseph, 45
Biggs, Robert, 14
Bayard, Aaron, 7
Bayard, Levi, 25
Buck, Jacob, 3
Buck, George, 1
Bayard, Bob, 26
Bayard, Steve, 24
Bayard, Ike, 35
Bayard, Thomas, 61
Bayard, Jim, 23
Bayard, Bill, 17
Bayard, Aaron, 15

Bayard, Renard, 8
Bayard, Harry, 31
Bayard, Bill. 12
Bayard, Joseph, 14
Bayard, Charles, 1
Bayard, Thomas, 5
Bayard, Bill, __
Brading, Ned, 40
Brading, Edward, 14
Brading, Henry, 5
Bayard, Richard, 5
Benson, Jack, 37
Boulden, Levi, 4
Boulden, Aron, 2
Beardly, David, 22
Bakeman, Jonathan, 35
Bakeman, Henry, 18
Beakeman, John, 63
Beakeman, Bill, 7
Beakeman, Nace, 5
Beakman, Samuel, 3
Boyels, Benjamin, 40
Boyels, Amos, 22
Boyels, Ben, 14
Boyels, Jim, 15
Boyels, Bill, 9
Boyels, Alexander, 7
Byels, George, 2
Boyer, Reynard, 42
Boyer, Dan, 10
Bondly, Cyrus, 41
Bondly, Jim, 25
Boyer, Michal, 35
Bostic, Phillip, 40
Boyd, Freeman,
Boyd, Henry, 4
Brown, Henry, 64
Congo, Stephen, 55
Congo, John, 19
Congo, George, 11
Congo, Alfred, 10
Congo, Noah, 8
Congo, S__, 4
Cork, Abe, 37
Cork, Abe, 8
Cork, Bill, 6
Craig, Ben, 47
Craig, Dick, 13
Craig, Bill, 11
Craig, Joseph, 11
Carpenter, Charles, 50
Cato, Bill, 47
Caulk, Jacob, 39
Ciscoe, Bill, 60

Free African Americans of Maryland - 1832

Ciscoe, Perry, 29
Coppin, John, 18
Chew, Jack, 14
Chase, Prissa, 45
Chase, Henry, 16
Chase, Isaac, 12
Collins, Henry, 19
Cooper, Christopher, 1
Craig, Dick, 65
Craig, Dick, 4
*Craig, Ned, 4
Craig, _____, 1
Chambers, Perry, 1
Christmas, Adam, 50
Christmas, Solomon, 20
Christmas, Lewis, 16
Christmas, Adam, 6
Collan, Bill, 85
Clark, Jim, 47
Clark, Henry, 12
Clark, Jonathan, 10
Clark, Abraham, 8
Cornish, Samuel, 22
Cooper, John, 31
Cooper, Jim, 4
Cook, George, 35
Cato, Tom, 67
Cato, Lewis, 25
Cato, Bill, 22
Cato, George, 18
Cato Ruben, 12
Clark, Jacob, 45
Clark, Jacob, 14
Clark, Samuel, 33
Clark, Frederick, 10
Clark, Frederick, 10
Clark, Benjamin, 3
Craig, Cyrus, 49
Craig, Roman, 34
Craig, Joseph, 24
Craig, Jim, 22
Craig, Spencer, 21
Craig, Percy, 12
Craig, Hanson, 10
Craig, Benjamin, 43
Craig, Timmy, 17
Craig, Dick, 14
Craig, Bill, 10
Craig, ___, 8
Craig, Joseph, 3
Cook, William, 25
Cook, Elias, 12
Clarkson, Levi, 30
Collins, Vick, 40

Collins, Vick, 48
Coper, Bill, 4
Collins, Augustene, 18
Collins, Joe, 4
Casper, Sam, 2
Collins, Dennis, 2
Ciscoe, John, 40
Collins, Jim, 18
Collins, Jerry, 14
Collins, Ike, 29
Dawson, Charles, 15
Dennis, Charles, 27
Droh, James, 65
Dudley, Albert, 9
Danby, Dick, 38
Danby, Thomas, 11
Danby, Joseph, 10
Danby, Ned, 80
Danby, Bill,
Dumpson, Thomas,
  Dumpson,
  Dambe,
Dennis, Abe,
Doman, John
Disney, Harry, 39
Disney, George, 7
Disney, Richard, 3
Disney, Jim, 4
Disney, Joe, 65
Deanham, George, 41
Demby, Peter, 80
Delany, Bill, 14
Delany, Henry, 48
Dunmoore, Squire, 55
Dunmoore, Ned, 25
Dunmoore, Ned, 25
Dunmoore, Issac, 21
Dickson, Sampy, 2
Dorsey, John, 10
Dorsey, John, 70
Elias, Emory, 27
Fisher, Solomon, 22
Fisher, Saul, 28
Fisher, Jacob, 43
Fisher, Anthony, 14
Fisher, George, 10
Fisher, Jim, 8
Fisher, Bill, 3
Freeman, George, 38
Freeman, James, 17
Freeman, Isaac, 9
Freeman, Ned, 7
Freeman, Ben, 5

Ford, Daniel, 37
Ford, John, 28
Faumar, James, 35
Ford, Samuel, 40
Fish, George, 28
Fish, Samuel, 2
Fisher, Jake, 48
Fisher, Autone, 15
Fisher, George, 6
Fisher, Bill, 4
Fountain, Jacob, 45
Fountain, Peter, 11
Fields, Isaac, 42
Forgewell, Wesley, 22
Forgewell, Thomas, 9
Fields, Thomas, 2
Fox, Thomas, 48
Fox, Thomas, 48
Ford, Jake, 51
Furl, James, 25
Fish, Cato, 28
Guison, Jake, 51
Gray, Jerry, 35
Granderson, Charles, 26
George, James, 45
Graves, Thomas, 4
Garnett, Samuel, 50
Garnett, Adam, 43
Garnett, Joe, 61
Green, Jerry, 28
Gale, Joseph, 31
Gale, Jim, 6
Gale, Joseph, 4
Gale, Robert, 2
Gale, John, 1
Garrett, Charles, 4
Green, Keazy, 40
Garrett, Joseph, 80
Green, Bill, 3
Gibbings, John 16
Garrott, Henry, 20
Gasby, Abe, 23
Gasby, Bill, 1
Garrott, Leonard, 28
Garrott, Mike, 6
Garrott, Bob, 4
Garrott, George, 3
Gibbings, Charles, 35
Gibson, Levi, 36
Glover, George, 23
Glover, Joseph, 46
Glover, Jacob, 20
Glover, Bill
Glover, Joseph, 12

45

Cecil County

Glover, Samuel, 12
Glover, John, 8
Glover, Robert, 6
Glover, James, 2
Gale, Littleton, 32
Gorden, Ike, 14
Gorden, Samuel, 23
Givings, Charles, 45
Grant, Ike, 33
Grant, John, 7
Grant, James, 1
Griffy, Ben, 25
Givens, Charles, 49
, Leonard, 40
, Michael, 5
, Robert, 3
Garrett, Levi, 80
Graves, Natty, 60
Hartshorn, Moses,
45
Hartshorn, Samuel,
16
Hartshorn, George,
14
Hartshorn, Moses,
12
Hartshorn, Ellis, 10
Hartshorn, Jim, 8
Hopkins, Jack, 40
Hopkins, Jim, 15
Hopkins, John, 13
Hopkins, George, 11
Hopkins, Lewis, 2
Hall, Isaac, 33
Hartshorn, Peter, 80
Hawkins, Francis, 25
Hawkins, Samuel, 15
Hawkins, David, 1
Hawkins, George, 2
Hawkins, Samuel, 62
Hawkins, Jim, 35
Hawkins, Robert, 39
Hewes, Henry, 85
Hand, Emery, 35
Hand, Emery, 7
Hand, Asbury, 5
Henderson, Jack, 60
Hand, Josep, 65
Hollingsworth, Isaac,
52
Hamond, James, 43
Henderson, David,
Henderson, Bill
Henderson, Absalam,
15
Henderson, David, 6

Henderson, Israel,
21
*Hackett, Benjamin,
35
Harding, James, 40
Harding, John, 18
Harding, Henry, 5
Holland, Bill, 35
Henry , Bill, 5
Hackinson, Dick, 5
Hall, John, 8
Hall, Charles, 1
Hall, Mike, 2
Harris, Isaac, 34
Hogan, ___, 43
Hogan, Jerry, 15
Hogan, John, 7
Hogan, Noble, 2
Hogan, Jim, 3
Hughs, George, 5
Hughs, Henry, 3
Hughs, Henry, 31
Harris, Samuel, 43
Hasmon, Tom, 35
Hogan, Andrew, 38
Hogan, Bill, 22
Hogan, David, 17
Hogan, Andrew, 11
Hogan, William, 6
Hogan Thomas, 42
Hogan, Levi, 19
Hall, Washington, 16
Huchinson, Andrew,
57
Huchinson, Andrew,
18
Huchinson,
Augustas, 22
Huchinson, Daniel,
18
Hutchinson, Perry,
16
Holland, Jim, 32
Holland, George, 7
Holland, Bill, 29
Hawkins, John, 41
Hall, Perry, 20
Holland, Jim, 34
Holland, Charles, 5
Hall, Jim, 40
Holland, Frederick, 8
Hall, Ike, 28
Henderson, Harry,
50
Hall, Morgan, 33

Henderson, Asbury,
18
Henson, Perry, 54
Henderson, Harmon,
16
Henderson, George,
10
Henderson, Thomas,
8
Henderson, Jim, 7
Huson, Perry, 42
Henderson, Henry,
65
Huison, Perry, 42
Hayes, Dennis, 35
Huison, John, 20
Huison, James, 33
Jackson, James, 36
Jues, Frances, 40
Jiles, Kessa, 8
Jorden, Bill, 40
Jorden, Perry, 45
Jorden, Bitha, 5
Johnson, Ned, 63
Jackson, Samuel, 20
Johns, Elias, 35
Johns, Elias, 25
Johns, John, 2
Johnson, Mike, 30
Johnson, Jack, 11
Johnson, Bill, 9
Johnson, Nace, 3
Johnson, Mike, 1
Jeff, Mike, 35
Jeff, Jake, 5
Johnson, Dick, 50
Jackson,
Washington, 39
Johns, Eliza, 28
Johns, John, 8
Johns, Samuel, 6
Johns, George, 4
Jorden, Bill, 38
Jeff, Dicj, 33
Jones, Richard, 63
Jones, George, 11
Jones, John, 5
Jones, Bill, 3
_____, Henry, 25
_____, Isaac, 57
_____, Jake, 56
_____, Bill, 26
Johnson, Abraham,
51
Johnson, Ned, 20

Free African Americans of Maryland - 1832

Johnson, 22
Johnson, Robert, 21
Johnson Isaac, 18
Johnson, Henry, 8
James, Ned, 25
James, Robert, 6
James Nicholas, 1
Johnson, Ned, 51
Johnson, Ben, 32
Johnson, George, 27
Jackson, Phillip, 28
Jackson, Charles, 57
Jackson, Charles, 21
Jacobs, Levi, 35
Jacobs, Adam, 6
Jacobs, Allen2
Jacobs, Isaac, 22
Jay, Jarrott, 25
Jay, Jonah, 50
Jay, Bennett, 18
Jay, Randle, 14
Jay, Jim, 11
Johnson, Benjamin, 28
Jones, Theophilis, 30
Jones, George, 60
*Jones, Horace, 17
Jones, Samuel, 6
Jones, Maryland, 6
Johnson, Charles, 39
Knoxen, Benjamin, 19
Kell, Abraham, 80
Kinsolo, Nathan, 31
Kinsolo, Robert, 33
Kinsolo, James, 18
Kinsolo, John, 8
Kinsolo, Charles, 4
Kinsolo. Bill, 2
Kinsolo, Robert, 16
Kinsolo, Thomas, 33
Kinnard, Thomas, 49
Lee, Nathan, 35
Lee, Pat, 13
Lee, Charles, 9
Lee, William, 5
Lum, Cook, 49
Limbo, Benjamin, 49
Limbo, Benjamin, 7
Limbo, David, 3
Lewis, Robert, 52
Lewis, Abe, 5
Lewis, Harry, 10
Long, Bill, 18
Long, Richard, 45
Long, Bill, 18

Long, Samauel, 15
Long, Dick, 8
Long, Aaron, 3
___, John, 35
Lusby, Nathan, 36
Lee, Moses, 14
Lee, George
___, Thomas, 40
___, John, 18
___, Emory, 2
___, Elias, 1
___, Sandy,
___, Emory, 20
___, Bill, 7
Lawson, Daniel, 39
Lawson, John, 29
Lee, Levi, 8
Lum, Pompey, 45
Lum, Thomas
Lum, Bill, 18
Lum, Dick, 16
Lum, Samuel, 47
Lum, Sam, 14
Lee, Bick, 10
Lee, Bill, 17
Lee, James, 40
Lee, ___, 43
L__, Ike, 12
Miller, Cesar, 43
Milburn, Peter, 35
Milburn, Joseph, 13
Milburn, Washington, 11
Milburn, Levi, 6
Milburn, Peter, 3
Milburn, Bill, 1
Mills, Richard, 54
Martain, Perry, 46
Miller, Levi, 19
Miller, David, 7
Mongomery, Bill, 31
Monsall, Benedict, 7
Muller, Lewis, 45
Mullin, Whitman, 1
Moore, Bill, 26
Moore, Samuel, 1
Moulton, Samauel, 35
Moulton, Bill, 6
Moulton, George, 2
Moulton, Ellis, 8
McCabe, John, 30
McCabe, Joseph, 5
McCabe, Jack, 7
McCabe, ___, 2
McCabe, ___, 4

McCabe, Charles, 1
Mount, ___, 28[2]
Mathews, Tom, 7
Moore, John, 57
Moore, James, 15
Moore, Samuel, 11
Moore, Moses, 9
Moore, Jacob, 2
Middleton, Bill, 25
Mercer, George, 60
Moore, John, 4
Moore, Samuel, 30
Nooris, Charles, 42
Naudini, Dick, 42
Negro, Isaac, 29
Nichols, Harry, 55
Nichols, Levi, 22
Nichols, Samuel, 10
Nichols, John, 6
Nelson, George, 28
Nelson, George, 33
Nelson, Jim, 40
Nelson, August, 10
Owens, Jacob, 43
Owens, Steve, 14
Owens, Poladore, 42
Owens,Thomas, 59
Owens, Cook, 30
Owens, Jim, 10
Owens, Steve, 8
Owens, Thomas, 4
Parker, Thomas, 65
Pennington, Elias, 6
_____, Robert, 34
_____, Isaac, 9
Penae, Jim, 7
Paken, Samuel, 45
Penae, ___, 70
Penae, Daniel, 25
Penae, John, 20
Penae, Bill, 50
Parker, John,36
Parker, Bill, 9
Parker, John, 7
Peters, Josiah, 17
Peters, Ally, 11
Peters, John, 9
Parris, Grace, 19
Philips, Jim, 49
Philips, Jake, 9
Philips, Jarret, 8

---

[2] The balance of this page is torn and illegible.

Cecil County

Phillips, Jim, 6
Plemeth, Ben, 30
Plementh, Joshua, 1
Parker, Philip
Palmore, Jake, 45
Palmore, George, 15
Powell, Abe, 70
Pinow, George, 8
Price, James, 71
Price, Larry, 25
Price, Bill, 9
Price, Jerry , 4
Parrott, Stephen, 25
Parrott, John, 42
Peck, Jim, 21
Prig, William, 2
Prig, Sam, 1
Parker, Nace, 29
Rickett, William, 39
Rickett, James, 4
Riceman, Iseral, 35
Reading, Ned, 40
Reading, George, 22
Rider, John, 29
Rouse, Richard, 4
Roberts, John, 35
Richerson, Moses, 28
Richerson,
   Benjamin, 30
Richerson, Bill, 2
Read, Andrew, 29
Ridgely, Isreal, 15
Read, John, 23
Read, Empson, 18
Read, William, 21
Read Dafanny, 15
Read, James,
   Roberts,
   Alexander, 5
Reading, Ned, 14
Reading, George, 22
Riden, John, 29
Richerson, Moses
Richerson,
   Benjiamion, 30
Richerson, Bill, 2
Read, Andrew, 29
Ridgely, Andrew, 29
Read, John, 23
Read, Empson, 18
Read, William, 21
Read, Daffanny , 15
Read, James, 11
Roberts, Alexander,
   5
Reading, Ned, 14

Smith, Perry, 20
Smith, John, 20
Sprig, Jacob, 34
Simpers, Isaac, 45
Sanders, Bill, 43
Sanders, James, 12
Sampson, Henry, 4
Sasol, James, 35
Sasol, Jim, 1
Stevenson, Bill,
Shaw, Linkin
Shaw, Moses
Simpson, Daniel
Simpson, James
Sulamin, James
Sulamin, Ned
Sulamin, Bill
Salten, Washington,
   17
Shields, George, 29
Shields, Henry, 28
Shields, George, 14
Shields, Wesly, 12
Smith, Bill, 27
Smith, Bill, 4
Smith, thot, 2
Shain, Peter, 22
Smith, George, 32
Simpers, March, 32
Simpers, March, 33
Simpers, John, 5
Sewall, Benjamin, 33
Sewall, Henry, 27
Sewall, Ike, 14
Sewall, John, 8
Sewall, Ned, 5
Sanders, Jim, 2
Starlin, Harry, 40
Stevenson, Bill, 70
Stevenson, Daniel,
   40
Stevenson, Thomas,
   38
Stevenson, John, 21
Stevenson, Nicholas,
   19
Stevenson, Wesley, 7
Sea, James, 18
Steward, Henry, 56
Steward, Henry, 15
Steward, Stephen,
   12
Sparrow, ____, 47
Sparrow, Jim, 1
Sears, John, 3
Sears, Samuel, 9

Sears, Bill, 14
Sears, Henry, 19
Sears, Jake, 24
Sears, Jim, 25
Stevens, John, 71
Torby, Daffany, 47
Tue, Wilmer, 2
Thomas, Edward, 2
Thompson, Samuel,
   35
Thompson, Samuel,
   2
Thompson, James, 1
Thompson, Terry, 19
Thompson, Barney,
   28
Thompson, John, 9
Thompson, James, 7
Thompson, Perry, 5
Trusty, John, 29
Thompson,
   Abraham, 49
Thompson, Perry, 15
Trager, Mike, 12
Thompson, Steven,
   38
Trusty, Nace, 18
Thompson, Steve, 44
Thompson, Mike, 34
Thomas, Bill, 2
Thomas, John, 1
Thomas, Daniel, 28
Thomas, George, 1
Thomas, Bill, 49
Thomas, Samuel, 41
Thomas, Perry, 14
Thomas, David, 12
Thomas, Frederick,
   46
Torbey, George, 32
Turner, Jefferson, 56
Taylor, Solomon
Taylor, James
Taylor, ____
*Taylor, Infant
Torby, Charles, 3
Torbert, Paul, 55
Torbert, John, 10
Torbert, Jim, 5
Thompson, Harry, 1
Thompson, James,
   24
Thompson, Abe, 10
Thompson, Guy, 6
Veal, Harry, 10
Veal, ____, 31

Free African Americans of Maryland - 1832

Veasey, John, 40
Veasey, Jim, 4
Veal, Jim, 2
Veal, Sidney, 1
Veasey, Tom, 40
Wright, Samuel
Williams, Jake, 37
Willis, John, 35
Worthington,
    John, 32
    George, 22
Williams, Levi, 7
    George, 5
    Bill, 3
Williams, Robert,
    38
    George, 36
    John, 34
    James, 30
Wilson, Mark, 23
Williams, John,
    30
    Joseph, 4
    Bill, 2
    Bill, 40
    Sewall, 8
Wilson, Isaac, 13
Williams, Loyd,
    22
Webster, Amos, 40
Wabes, Isaac, 30
Webster, Tom, 11
Wabes, Issac, 5
Wallace, James, 2
Williams, Bill, 43
Williams, Suwall, 7
Williams, Abraham,
    35
Warner, Noah, 27
White, Jacob, 40
White, Christopher,
    9
White, Robert, 7
White, Thomas, 5
White, Blackburn, 4
Wright, Joshua, 24
Wright, Bill, 5
Wright, Ned, 33
Wilson, Abe, 28
Wallace, James, 40
Wilson, Steven, 41
Washington, George,
    30
Waters, Henry, 37
Waters, Samuel, 3
Waters, Emery, 1

Wilson, Bill, 3
Wilson, Joshua, 17
Wills, Joseph, 65
Wesley, Isaac, 8
Williams, Steven, 50
Washington, George,
    35
*Wey, Jacob, 34
Wey, Samuel, 56
Wey, Frances, 4
Wey, James, 14
Walls, Jacob, 52
Walls, Jake, 5
Warner, Jim, 7
Warner, Thomas, 5
Wright, Poladore, 45
Wright, Bill, 21
Wright, Charles, 24
Ward, Perry, 39
Ward, Nathan, 19
Wright Emery, 35
Wright, M___, 37
Wright, Isiah, 7
Wright, Henry, 3
Wright, alphus, 2
Wright, Anthony, 2
Wright, Steve, 1
WatersHenry, 37
York, Benjamin, 66
Young, Samuel, 53
Young, John, 10
Young, James, 7
Young, Levi, 4
Young, Isaac, 3
Young, Bill, 16
Young, Samuel, 11
Yawkin, Samuel, 11
Yawkin, Aaron, 6
Yawkin, Henry, 4
Yawkin, James, 1
Young, George, 27
York, Samuel, 20
York, Jeremiah, 40
Young, Frances, 39
Young, Kirk, 12
Young, Jim, 10
Young, Steve, 6
Young, Nace, 4
Yaken, Samuel, 34
Yaken, Jim, 12
Young, Jerry, 4
Young, Harry, 24
Yaken, Harry, 24
Yaken, Aaron, 4
Young, Jeremiah, 40
Young, Samuel, 40

York, Samuel, 40
York, David, 20
York, David, 2
York, Amos, 19
York, Aaron, 17
York, Jeremiah, 15
York, Samuel, 10
Young, Steven, 59
Young, Adam, 20
Young, Amos, 17
Young, Joseph, 13
Young, Daniel, 9
Young, Steve, 5
Yorken, Soll, 20
York, George, 3
Anderson, Dinah, 47
Anderson, Hariet, 79
Anderson, Eliza, 17
Anderson, Lucretia,
    13
Anderson, Caroline,
    11
Anderson, Philis, 55
Allen, Becky, 62
Anderson, Philis, 40
Anderson, Elizabeth,
    12
Anderson, Maria, 14
Anderson, Dinah, 51
Anderson, Hariet, 28
Anderson, Nancy, 25
Anderson, Elizabeth,
    3
Anderson, Hariet, 38
Anderson, Betsy, 5
Anderson, Ruth, 25
Anderson Salt, 4
Anderson, Eliza, 19
Anderson, Jane, 1
Anderson, Mary, 60
Allen, Sarah, 19
Allen, Emily, 9
Ash
, Mary, 25
Ash, Hanah, 50
Adams, Mary, 21
Allen Rebacca, 30
Ash, Mary, 24
Alexander, Lydia, 30
Buck, Dinah
Buck, Jane
Buck, Sarah
Buck, Susan, 10
Black, Hannah, 14
Black, Ann, 30
Black, Marsha, 18

49

Cecil County

Black, Mary, 9
Black, Amy, 6
Black, Hannah, 70
Black, Ann, 33
Black, Martha, 18
Black, Mary, 23
Brown, Hannah, 60
Brown, Jule, 60
Brown, Jane, 27
Brown, Milly, 16
Brown, Ann, 9
Black, Amy, 40
Black, Hannah, 65
Black, D__, 18
Black, Hannah, 4
Black, Caroline, 20
Bini, Ann, 65
Bouser, Charity, 35
Boulden, Jane, 80
Bayard, Sophia, 1
Bayard, Martha, 17
Black, Caroline, 20
Bine, Ann, 65
Bouser, Charity, 35
Boulden, Jane, 80
Bayard, Sophia, 1
Bayard, Martha, 17
Brown, Matilda, 21
Bond, Susan, 33
Bond, Becky, 5
Bond, Jane, 2
Boulden, Hariet, 23
Brown, Daffany, 27
Brown, Eliza, 1
Black, Cassy, 25
Black, Hariet, 1
Bantor, Kitty, 36
Bradford, Martha, 31
Boyer, Dinah, 50
Bradford, Betsy, 2
Brown, Debby, 32
Brown, Sally, 17
Brown, __, 15
Brown, Susan, 11
Boyer, Ann, 5
Boyer, Kitty, 62
Berry, Matilda, 28
Boulden, Milly, 52
Boyer, Mita, 27
Boyer, Milly, 3
Bowen, Priscilla, 30
Bour, Philis, 5
Bour, Libby, 4
Bour, Rachel, 2
Boyer, Mary, 30
Boyer, Ann, 14

Boyer, Louisa, 12
Boulden, Mary, 21
*Brown, Nance, 54
Bouserm Jane, 45
Bostic, Kitty, 40
Bostic, Dian, 16
Bostic, Araminta, 14
Bostic, Mary, 12
Bostic, Rachel, 10
Bostic, Caty, 3
Bouserm Darkey, 25
Bayard, Mary, 18
Boulden, Violet, 40
Boulden, Sarah, 8
Boulden, Maria, 10
Boulden, Araminta,
 6
Boulden, __, 4
Bostic, Darkey, 21
Bostic, Sall, 3
Bostic, Rachel, 1
Bayard, Fanny, 65
Bayard, Nell, 11
Bush, Henly, 55
Blackson, Sarah, 42
Bayard, Kitty, 24
Bayard, Ann, 3
Bayard, Ally, 1
Bayard, Mary, 28
Bayard, Nelly, 6
Bayard, Fanny, 53
Bayard, Louisa, 13
Bondly, Beckey, 45
Beatte, Eliza, 31
Beatte, Hannah, 14
Beatte, Ellen, 4
Beatte, Isabella, 2
Berry, Hariet, 5
Brown, Lucinda, 33
Brown, Susan, 1
Bery, Bell, 25
Brooks, Philis, 32
Brooks, Peg, 4
Brooks, Ann, 2
Berry, Ally, 35
Berry, Hannah, 2
Berry, Eliza, 4
Brown, Mary, 5
Bayard, Nance, 22
Bayard, Mary, 70
Bayard, Mary, 2
Bayard, Minty, 21
Brigs, Betsy, 41
Briggs, Kitty, 17
Bayard, Hariet, 25
Buck, Susan, 25

Buck, Mary, 5
Brown, Maria, 35
Bayard, Betsy, 37
Bayard, Maria, 5
Bayard, Martha, 9
Bayard, Minty, 3
Bayard, Beckey, 1
Bayard, Martha, 31
Bayard, Elizabeth, 1
Berry, Betsy, 23
Boulden, Lydia, 24
Boulden, Martha, 7
Brown, Rachel, 21
Bakeman, Ann, 39
Bakeman, Betsy, 15
Bakeman, Peg, 1
*Boyles, Ann, 42
Bayard, Eliza, 10
Boyles, Mary, 12
Bayard,Margo, 7
Bayard, M__, 41
Bayard, Rachel, 2
Boyer, Nance, 2
Boulden, Mary, 30
Boulden, Margaret, 5
Bostic, Dina, 35
Butler, Filles, 50
Ball, Sally, 50
Boyer, Fanny, 30
Brown, Eliza, 23
Beatle, Becky, 13
Buck, Rachel, 60
Boyd, Prissa, 5
Boyd, Amanda, 2
Brown, Jane, 81
Blackson, Jane, 15
Bayard, Fanny, 58
Cornish, Ann, 19
Clark, Rachel, 35
Clark, Ricy, 42
Clark Araminta, 1
Clark, Darkey, 12
Clark, Margaret, 8
Craig, Lucretia, 50
Craig, Lutitia, 50
Craig, Sarah, 9
Craig, Ann, 35
Craig, Eliza, 19
Craig, Reany, 20
Craig, Martha, 19
Clinton, Moll, 28
Congo, Mary, 14
Congo, Maria, 43
Clarkson, Betsy, 59
Cork, Susan, 42
Cooper, Rainy, 20

Free African Americans of Maryland - 1832

Craig, Nancy, 35
Craig, Eliza, 17
Craig, ___, 15
Craig, Becky, 9
Carpenter, ___, 45
Carly, Peg, 20
Carly, Louisa, 1
Ciscoe, Maria, 65
Ciscoe, Susan, 22
Copper, Ann, 15
Chase, Margaret, 18
Chase, B___, 12
Collins, Hariet, 34
Cooper, Lauvina, 42
Craig, Becky, 4
Chambers,
    Araminta, 42
Chambers, Mary, 24
Chambers, Eliza, 16
Christmas, Fanny,
    42
Christmas, Libby, 14
Christmas, Jane, 12
Cole, Mary, 40
Cole, Betsy, 3
Cole Philis, 11
Cole, Mary, 6
Clark, Flora, 37
Clark, Sophia, 6
*Clark, Isaabella, 4
Crouch, Martha, 12
Coatman, Sharlott,
    27
Cose, Mary, 25
Cornish, Sophia, 18
Coat, Mary, 4
Collins, Becky, 65
Cooper, Sall, 25
Cook, Nancy, 29
Clark, Sarah, 27
Cato, Hannah, 47
Cato, Maria, 20
Cato, Lyd, 15
Cato, Emeline, 3
Conrad, Sarah, 60
Collins, Angelina, 23
Collins, Dealia, 18
Collins, Ann, 23
Collins, L___, 15
Cook, Sarah, 22
Cook, Sharlott, 6
Cook, Ellen,
 Cook, Hariet, 39
Cook, Jane, 14
Cook, Milly, 10
Douglass, Nancy, 50

Dudly, Patience, 50
Dudly, Hester, 12
Demby, Eliza, 36
Demby, Ann, 18
Demby, Mary, 12
Dumpson, Patty, 41
Dumpson, Hester, 45
Dumpson, Ann, 14
Duff, Sharlot, 27
Delany, Margaret, 51
Dason, Nelly, 22
Disney, Beckey, 58
Disney, Mary, 22
Disney, Narbery, 15
Disney, Amy, 2
Disney, Ann, 1
Disney, Prissy, 62
Dawson, Nancy,43
Dunmoor, Hariet, 7
Dunmore, Phoebe,
    25
Dunmoore, Sarah,
    14
Dulen, Ann, 17
Duckett, Nancy, 30
Dawsey, Betsy, 20
Dawsey, Hannah, 18
Dorsey, Lydia, 8
Dover, Nelly, 55
Dison, Nancy, 21
Dunmoore, Sarah,
    51
Dunmoore, Susan, 5
Dumpson, Hannah,
    18
Ellens, Sarah, 22
English, Nelly, 50
Fields, Mat, 23
F___, Mat, 23
Fountain, Rebecca,
    30
Fountain, Hannah, 8
Fountain, Anna, 2
Fields, Betsy, 35
Forgewell, Betty, 56
Tilghman, Peg, 51
Furl, Poll, 35
Furl, Maria, 6
Furl, Mary, 3
Furl, Lotty, 1
Forman, Rachel, 367
Fish, Peggy, 25
Fisher, Betsy, 88
Fax, Rachel, 14
Fisher, Sarah, 21
Fisher, Ann, 19

Fox, Debby, 27
Fisher, Minty, 18
Fax, Sarah,
Fisher, Ann. 16
Fisher, Minty, 12
Freeman, Martha, 45
Furman, Sarah, 12
Ford, Rachel, 60
Furl, ___, 24
Fader, Sally, 20
Fader, Nancy, 2
Fader, Ann, 1
Fish, Jane, 25
Fish, Jane, 19
Givens, Dian, 28
Givens, Philis, 11
Gasby, Rachel, 26
Givens, Cady, 9
Givens, Eliza, 7
Garrott, Pall, 36
George, Race, 38
George, Mary, 8
Glover, Sarah, 40
Glover, Sarah, 18
Glover, Sophia, 10
Gale, Margaret, 22
Gorden, Maria, 19
Garden, Susan, 12
Gorden, Flora, 42
Gover, Susan, 2
Gorden, Flora, 42
Gover, Susan, 2
Givens, Philis, 15
Givens, Kitty, 13
Givens, Mary, 9
Grant, Eliza, 30
Grant, Jane, 9
Grant, Emily, 5
Grant, Catherine, 3
Granderson, Libby,
    18
Granderson,
    Permiilia,1
Graves, Mary, 28
G___, Rachel, 31
Green, Eliza, 25
Garnet, Judy, 54
Green, Eliza,, 1
Green, Ann, 24
Gibb, Nancy, 23
Gale, Rachel, 25
Gale, Sibby, 1
Gary, Sall, 15
Garrrott, Mary, 26
Gibbings, Dinah, 31
Gibbings, Philis, 10

Cecil County

Gibbings, Kitty, 8
Gibbings, Mary, 6
Gorden, Hariet, 1
Gray, Elizabeth, 26
Garrot, Lotty, 36
Garrot, Milly, 5
Garrot, Mary, 1
Green, Ann, 41
Hinson, Agnes, 51
Harris, Debby, 30
Harris, Minty, 61
Harding, Hester, 43
Harding, Ann, 5
Harding, Sarah, 1
Harding, Tempy, 35
Harding, Ann, 6
Hutchinson, Fanny, 26
Holland, Matilda, 35
Hart, Mary, 46
Hinson, Jane, 35
Hinson, Cousi, 9
Hinson, Jane, 7
Hollis, Jane, 72
Hogans, Mary, 9
Hogans,Racy, 34
Hogans, Betsy, 4
Hughs, Betsy, 2
Hogans, Hannah, 28
Holland, Kitty, 4
Hogans, Margaret, 24
Hogans, Kitty, 41
Hogans, Nancy, 15
Hogans, Sarah, 18
Hogans, Kitty, 19
Hogans, Mary, 12
Hogans, Betsy, 21
Hogans, Susan, 38
Huchinson, Debby, 48
Huchinson, Martha, 14
Huchinson, Susan, 12
Holland, Hannah, 48
Holland, Hannah, 12
Hogans, Mary, 10
Henderson, Minty, 48
Henderson, Betsy, 3
Hawkins, Jane, 35
Hawkins, Sophia, 5
Hawkins, Deleana, 60
Hawkins, Mary, 14

Hawkins, Nancy, 27
Hawkins, Dafffany, 5
Hawkins, Caroline, 2
Hawkins, Emeline, 2
Howard, July, 27
Howe, Sally, 13
Hewes, Betty, 54
Hawkins, Dane, 28
Hill, Hannah, 62
Hall, Emenoual, 25
Hawkins, El;iza, 22
Hill, Milly, 42
Hill, Kitty, 12
Hill, Millison. 9
Hill, Sarah, 7
HowardMary, 50
Howard, Kitty, 40
Howard, Rosetta, 6
Hand, Mary, 31
Hand, Peg, 11
Hawkins, Hannah, 27
Hand, Caroline, 9
Hand, Jane, 7
Henderson, Susan, 60
Howard, Ann, 46
Hussan, Mary, 33
Howard, Eveline, 11
Henderson, Dian, 45
Henderson, Devanna
Howard, Ann
Henderson, Nance, 14
Henderson, Nelly, 12
Henderson, Sarah, 9
Hill, Betsy, 23
Hartshorn, Dina, 35
Hopkins, W___, 35
Hill, Amy, 70
Hill, Nancy, 22
Henderson, Nance, 20
Harding, Mary, 2
Holland, Ann, 4
JohnsonKelly, 10
Johnson, Hariett, 12
Johnson, Milly, 34
James, Minty, 75
Jacobs, Melinda, 25
Jacobs, Mary, 4
Juery, Mary, 20
Juery, Poll, 4
Johnson, Nancy, 49
Johnson, Mary, 13
Johnson, Cassy, 11

James, Melice, 36
James, May, 7
James, Nancy, 6
Johnson, May, 17
Johnson, Nancy, 27
Johnson, Betsy, 48
Johnson, Phillis, 36
Johnson, Phillis, 40
Johnson, Nell, 76
Jackson, Susan, 50
Jackson, Ellen, 19
Juery, Mary, 18
Jackson, Ann, 16
Jay, Cassy, 20
Johnson, Nancy, 26
Johnson, Jane, 3
Jiles, Sarah, 30

_____,
Jiles, Ann, 4
Jiles, Sarah, 1
Johnson, Minty, 52
Jenkins, Susan, 24
Jenkins, Mary, 9
Jenkins, Jane, 7
Jenkins, Peg, 4
Johnson, Tempy, 38
Johns, Minty, 3
Johns, Elvina, 4
Johnson, Lucy, 33
Johnson, Jane, 7
Johnson, Pall, 5
Jeff, Minty, 34
Jeff, Peg, 3
Johnson, Muinty, 54
Jorden Mary
Johnson, Minty, 14
Juery, Sarah, 20
Jeff, Minty, 29
Jones, Sarah, 5
Juery, Sarah, 64
Jones, Ann, 55
Juery, Hannah, 6
Jones, Sarah, 5
Juery, ___, 38
Jones, Susan, 24
Jenkins, Nell, 28
Johnson, ellen, 34
Johnson, Ann, 20
Jorden, Darky, 40
Knossien, Jane, 1
Knossien, Sharlott, 15
King, Jane, 50
Kinsolo, Emily, 26
Kinsolo, Ann, 38
Kinsolo, Philis, 16

Free African Americans of Maryland - 1832

_____, Sharlott, 11
_____, Rachel
Kinsolo, Mary, 11
Kinsolo, Frances, 15
Kennard, Sarah, 62
Kinsolo, Polly, 17
Kell, Hannah, 80
Knoxen, Fanny, 45
Knoxen, Adeline, 16
Knoxen, Ann, 11
Knoxen, Sarah, 9
Lum, Betsy, 38
Lum, Eliza, 23
Lum, Mary, 19
Lun, Sarah, 15
Lum, Milly, 13
Lum, Philis, 10
Lias, Elizabeth, 70
Lawson, Mary, 3
Lawson, Rachel, 23
Lasal, Betsey, 25
Lasal, Catherine, 3
Lusby, Philis, 41
Lias, Betsy, 61
Lee, Iran, 52
Lee, Cass, 45
Lee, Rachel, 9
Lee, Delia, 6
Lee, Sylvia, 11
Lum, Precella, 50
Little, Patty, 85
Lynch, Susan, 18
Lawyer, Philis, 28
Ly__, Judy, 65
Limbo, Hannah, 44
Limbo, Mary, 8
Lewis, Martha, 45
Lewis, Maria, 12
Lewis, Sarah, 45
Long, Betsy, 41
Long, Hannah, 13
Long, Mary, 11
Long, Betsy, 5
Lawman, Eliza, 23
Lee, Jane, 39
Lee, Maria, 12
Lee, Rosey, 8
Lee, Ruth, 6
Lee, Ann, 25
Lee, Sarah, 3
Lee, Mary, 10
Lawson, Hareit, 4
Mount, Luticia, 29
Morgan, Violet, 45
Morgan, Maria, 12
Morgan, Minty, 30

Morgan, Mary, 4
McDaniel, Mary, 60
Moore, Sarah, 3
McHurd, Zena, 31
McHurd, Judy, 13
McHurd, Kitty, 7
McHurd, ___, 5
McHurd, Vilet, 3
McHurd, Maria, 23
McHurd, Vilet, 1
McHurd, Peg, 19
McHurd, Betsy, 19
McHurd, Sarah, 28
Mucer, Judy, 51
Miller, Gracy, 36
Morris, Sophia, 35
Morris, Judy, 1
Miller, Sarah, 23
Matthews, July, 17
Matthews, Jinny
Moore, Mary
Moore, Rachel, 16
Moore, Ann, 7
Moore, Sarah, 5
Miller, Sharlot, 35
Miller, Carolina, 63
Miller, Mary, 11
Miller, Hariet, 9
Miller, Eliza, 7
Mills, Flora, 48
Mills, Lydia,
Miller, Julia, 28
McGloven, Mary, 20
Miller, Hariet, 16
Monsura, Ruth, 14
Myers, Hannah, 35
Miller, Mary, 28
Miller, Eliza, 7
Miller, Harriet, 18
Martain, Sall, 26
Moulton, Luisa, 28
Moulton, Mary, 3
Magher, Rachel, 58
Moore, Ellen, 88
McCabe, Milly, 27
Milburn, July, 8
Morgan, Ann, 12
Morgan, Maria, 5
Moore, Hannah, 23
Moore, Louisa, 3
Morgan, Sarah, 4
Moore, Jane, 10
Moore, Susan, 8
Moore, Lydia, 4
Flora, 28
Dolly, 60

Mary, 4
Rebeca, 15
Nichols, Ruth, 57
Nichols, Mary, 20
Nichols, Rachel, 18
Nichols, Levina, 12
Nichols, Cassy, 8
Nelson, Hannah, 2
Norris, Hareit, 37
Nelson, Debby, 20
Nelson, Philes, 18
Nelson, Jane, 11
Nelson, Flora, 14
Nelson, Hannah, 10
Nelson, Cassy, 2
Owens, Lucy, 38
Owens, Emeline, 36
Owens, Ann, 11
Owens, Libby, 7
Owens, Jane, 8
Owens, Jane, 7
Owens, Sarah, 40
Penae, Sall, 16
Penae, Ann, 11
Penae, Minty, 6
Penae, Malinda, 4
Penae, Jane, 1
Parker, Sarah, 43
Parker, Rachel, 17
Promus, Dolly, 60
Penae, Elizabeth, 24
Penae, Mary, 17
Peters, Hannah, 30
Peters, Susan, 15
Peters, Caroline, 13
Peters, Hannah, 40
Peters, Hannah, 48
Philips, Peg, 13
Plemeth, Pall, 25
Plemeth, Susan
Plemeth, Mary, 3
Palmer, Caroline, 41
Penae, Milly, 16
Powell, Nell, 70
Pennington, Milly, 25
Pinor, Jane, 40
Piner, Betsy, 3
Piner, Susan, 1
Price, Rainey, 62
Parker, Hannah, 26
Porter, Dealy, 12
Porter, Jane, 10
Porter, Infant
Price, Darkey, 21
Price, Hariet, 3
Pearce, Hannah, 54

Cecil County

Parrott, Patt, 41
Parker, Clary, 65
Parker, Elizabeth, 8
Penae, Sally, 16
Parker, Ann, 3
Parker, Coe, 39
Parker, Sally, 5
Parker, Hariet, 3
Rice, Susan, 2
Roberts, July, 32
Reid, Dinah, 45
Richardson, Sarah, 21
Reece, Ann, 40
Reece, Adeline, 45
Reece, Martha, 60
Reece, Jane, 4
Ringgold, Betsy, 55
Ringgold, Betsy, 45
Ringgold, Melvina, 13
Roy, Jane, 23
Roy, Bets, 4
Roy, Jane, 1
Reid, Amy, 49
Reid, Sarah, 14
Reid, Hannah, 9
Reid, Catherine, 5
Reid, Caroline, 3
Reid, Ann, 4
Ringgold, Sarah, 45
Ringgold, Kitty, 5
Ringgold, Judy, 3
Reading, Ann, 36
Reading, Hannah, 18
Reading, Ann, 7
Sears, Maria, 31
Smith, Martha, 10
Simpson, Hariet, 40
Simpson, Sophia, 19
Starch, Eliza, 32
Smith, Betsy, 65
Satten, Racy, 16
Satten, Racy, 14
Shortts, Eliza
Smith, Elizabeth, 55
Smith, Easter, 25
Sims, Dinah, 35
Shain, Cassy, 39
Shain, Hannah, 15
Shain, Jane, 2
Shain, ___, 27
Sheridin, Ann, 17
Sheridin, Kesiah, 8
Sherididn, Mary, 7
Sears, Ann, 29

Sear, Susan
Sears, Betsy
Sears, Pall, 22
Sears, Ann, 20
Sears, Jane, 13
Sears, Eliza, 7
Sears, Caroline, 5
Sears, Infant
Severson, Betsy, 7
Severson, Mary, 3
Severson, Peg, 20
Severson, Maria, 6
Sanders, Jane, 4
Shaifer, Nancy, 31
Smith, Sarah, 3
Smith, Julia, 1
Smith, Minty, 28
Sharer, Mary, 25
S___, Betsy, 40
Shockley, Betsy, 40
Shockley, Julia, 35
Shockley, Mary, 7
Shields, Patty, 51
Shields, Mary, 19
Shields, Susan, 3
Shain, Jane, 12
Shain, Ellen, 10
Smith, July, 28
Smith, Sarah, 31
Stevenson, ___, 61
Stevenson, Daffany, 36
Stevenson, Ann, 19
Stevenson,
Sarah, 31
Infant, female,
Sims, Arabella, 3
_____, 14
Savin, Martha, 25
Shain, Jane, 23
Simpers, Hetty, 41
Simpers, Eliza, 7
Stewart, Judy, 38
Steward, Maria, 18
Steward, Elizabeth, 16
Steward, Julian, 14
Steward, Jane, 12
Steward, Debby, 10
Steward, Ann, 1
Simmons, Minty, 44
Simmons, J__, 24
Sterlin, Rachel, 35
Stevenson, Dafanny, 36
Stevenson, Ann, 19

Stevenson, Sarah, 2
Stevenson, Infant
Spencer, Hannah, 32
Spencer, Mary, 19
Steward, Becky, 27
Steward, Rachel, 56
Steward, Libby, 29
Smith, Isabela, 29
Smith, Rachel, 3
Smith, Hetty
Starks, Becky, 3
Smith, Ruth, 60
Smith, Dinah, 40
Smith, Hariet, 18
Smith, Emeline, 10
Spry, Betsy, 22
Sprig, Mary
Simpers, Libby, 15
Simpers, Dian, 4
Simpers, Sarah, 28
Savin, Mary, 7
Smith, Jane, 40
Thompson, Ann, 6
Thompson, Caroline, 8
Thompson, Mary, 12
Thompson, Milly, 34
Tilghman, Hannah, 36
Thomas, Sophia, 23
Thomas, Philis, 35
Thomas, Clarrasa, 35
Thomas, Ann, 35
Thomas, Jane, 3
Thomas, Elizabeth,
Turman,
Rebecca, 30
Tue, Margaret, 40
Tue, Ann, 8
Tue, Ann, Frances, 3
Tillotson, Rosanna, 21
Tillotson, Ann, 17
Thomas, Eliza, 36
Thomas, Ann, 13
Thomas, Elizabeth, 6
Thomas, Susan, 30
Thomas, Martha, 3
Trusty, Peg, 5
Thomas, Betsy, 80
Thompson, Dolly, 25
Trusty, Fanny, 25
Trusty, Minty, 1
Thompson, ___, 72
Teger, Hannah, 35

Free African Americans of Maryland - 1832

T___, Minty, 38
Teage, July, 2
Thompson, Ann, 37
Thomas, Rachel, 38
Thomas, Hariet, 34
Thomas, Kissy, 8
Thomas, Harriet, 38
Thomas, Sarah, 51
Williams, Mary, 2
Williams, Ann, 32
Ward, Anna, 1
Ward, Mary, 3
Ward, Livennia, 11
Ward, Rachel, 13
Ward, Nancy, 15
Williams, Hannah,
    25
Williams, Elizabeth,
    10
Williams, R__, 17
Williams, Mary, 24
Williams, Sarah, 29
Wallace, Mary, 25
Wallace, Julyann, 16
Wallace, Rachel, 5
Wallace, Ann, 1
Webster, Alsey, 25
Williams, Ann, 30
Williams, Mary, 2
Williams, Eliza, 30

Williams, Ann35
Wilson, Patty, 51
Washington, Ann, 30
Wallace, Milly, 57
Warner, Sharlott, 20
White, Hester, 41
Wills, Jane, 60
White, Jane, 92
Williams, Jane
Wilmer, Mary, 4
White, Araminta, 11
White, Adeline, 2
Williams, Mary, 11
White, Ann, 27
Wright, Julia, 32
Wright, Jane, 8
Wright, Sarah, 20
Wilmer, Sharlott, 45
Webster, Mary, 20
Webster,Susan, 28
Webster, Jane, 10
Williams, Ann, 60
Wilmer, Emeline, 6
York, Debory, 61
Young, Rachel, 31
Young, Ann, 14
Young, Hannah, 9
Young, Sarah, 7
Young, Maria, 4
Young, Hosanna, 1

Yakin, Nance, 33
Yakin, Susan
Yakin, Matilda
York, Dinah
York Abigal
Young, Sharlot
Young, H___
Young, ___Yaken,
    Sarah, 5
Yaken, Anna, 3
Yaken, Jane
Young, Isabella
Young, Debby, 9
Young, Jane, 5
Young, Ann, 3
York,
Sarah, 25
York, Ann, 8
York, Jane, 5
York, Sall

To the Honorable
Board of
Commissioners.
   I hereby certify
that the above and
foregoing list of

names and ages are a just and true list of the names and ages of the free Negroes

Cecil County as far as there could be ascertained by me or those employed by me
to do so.

   George McCulloh
      Sheriff
Of Cecil County
Elkton, Maryland
September 1 1832.

■■

A List of the Free People of Color in Charles County

Edward Green, 58
Henry Day, 15
Susan Day, 10
Ned Day, 14
Mary Ann Corner, 60
Mary Corner, 35
John Corner, 25
Ann Corner, 12
Henry Corner, 8
Mary Ellen Corner, 4

Grayson Corner, 2
Anthony Butler, 30
Clem Thomas, 49
Charles Lucas, 46
Eliza Queen, 35
Jane Queen, 13
Susan Queen, 12
Charles H. Queen,
    10
Eliza A. Queen, 11

James Queen, 9
John Queen, 7
Julian Harkey, 19
James Hill, 55
John Hill, 25
James Hill, jr, 23
Ellen Hill, 21
William Hill, 19
Ann Hill, 17
George Hill, 8

Charles County

Samuel Swann, 46
Robert Ledlow, 32
Billy Day, 32
Martha _ Day, 25
Washington Day, 22
Eliza A. Day, 11
Henry Clark, 25
Ellen Jackson, 45
Nelly Jackson, 31
Elizabeth Jackson,
18
Th__ Jackson, 14
Edward Jackson, 13
Child
Illegible name, 30
Martha Beale, 40
Ann Beale, 21
Mary Beale, 18
Sarah Beale, 16
Robert Beale, 14
Nelly Beale, 11
___ Beale, 6
Child
William Day, 30
Thomas Day, 26
Billy Corner, 35
Thomas Corner, 5
Andrew ___ Corner, 2
John Robertson, 38
Nelly Robertson, 28
Alex Robertson, 11\
Al__ Robertson, 8
James Swann, 38
Chloe Swann, 36
___ B. Swann, 17
James Swann, jr, 15
Elizabeth Swann, 13
Emeline Swann, 11
Aletha Swann, 3
Child
Ignatius Washington,
58
Mary Washington, 46
Francis Washington
*Hezekiah Butler, 35
Elizabeth Butler, 45
Rebecca Butler, 9
James Henry Butler,
5
Child, 11 months
John Butler, 26
Ellen Butler, 18
Ann Butler, 2
Eliza Butler, 9
months
Simon Butler, 27

Benny Day, 23
___ Day, 8
___ Day, 5
Madison Day, 5
William Day, 5
Child,
John Hagen, 55
Andrew ___ 45
Nacy Hanson, 56
Harriet Hanson, 29
William Hanson, 25
Andrew Hanson, 32
John Hanson, 4
George Tubman, 50
Charity Tubman, 46
Robert Tubman, 33
John Tubman, 18
Mary Tubman, 18
___ Tubman, 13
Samuel Tubman, 11
George Mankins, 25
Dolly Hanson, 48
Alfred Cook, 32
Samuel Handson, 18
Joseph Handson, 12
William Hanson, 12
Sarah Mankins, 30
Jane Mankins, 16
William Mankins, 12
Richard Mankins, 9
Mary Mankins, 6
Ann Mankins, 4
Sarah Mankins, 2
Grace Sanders, 28
James Sanders, 7
Robert Sanders, 5
A__ Sanders, 2
Jane ___, 38
James Dent, 18
Nelly Dent, 15
Ignatius Dent, 8
Nancy Perry, 34
Abraham Posey, 18
Nelly James, 16
Lubenda James, 14
Eliza Perry, 8
Rebecca Perry, 7
Daniel Perry, 5
Henry Perry, 2
James H. Perry
James Graves, 58
Malinda Graves, 55
John Mankins, 26
Molly Mankins, 20
Chloe Mankins, 60
Mary Day, 6

Henry Mankins, 4
Elizabeth Mankins, 2
Ann Penny, 5
Ann Penny Jr, 12
Jane Penny, 55
Eliza Penny, 30
Harriet Ann Penny, 6
Sarah Penny, 4
Mary Penny, 1
Betsy Penny, 18
Chloe Ann Penny, 13
Joseph Swann, 55
Eleanor Swann, 44
William Swann, 30
Nancy Swann, 38
Charles, Mollison, 24
John Butler, 35
Benjamin Butler, 28
John Tarman, 17
John Butler, 4
John Ross, 6
David ___, 40
Joseph ___, 11
Henry Butler, 19
William Butler, 14
Samuel Butler, 13
Nesby Butler, 10
Old Peter, 80
Sally Bedder, 36
Billy Marbury, 55
Mary Proctor, 2
Adam Proctor, 23
Sally Wiseman, 35
Elizabeth Wiseman
Kitty Wuseman, 7
Dabney ___, 40
Hannah Butler, 30
Jane Butler, 28
Elizabeth Butler, 3
Ellen Butler, 6
Sarah Ford, 25
Polly Semmes, 31
Mary Semmes, 67
Jacob Butler, 70
Peter Short 42
___ Thompson, 45
Joseph Adams, 25
George Watson, 35
Mary Ann Mason, 18
James Howard, 35
Pamelia Howard, 30
Elizabeth Mason, 45
James Mason, 8
Rebecca Mason, 10
Child, 1
Joseph Butler, 65

Free African Americans of Maryland - 1832

Henny Massey, 70
Susan ___, 30
Elizabeth
   Washington, 30
Ann Washington, 8
Maria Washington,
   33
Ignatius Washington,
   10
Joseph Washington,
   8
James Swann, 23
Susan Swann, 22
William H. Swann, 1
Mary Swann, 20
Elizabeth Massey, 30
Stephen Massey, 8
Edward Day, 15
William Shorter, 20
Lucinda Penny, 18
Caroline Hailey, 22
Eleanor Shorter, 25
Henrietta Butler, 60
Nancy Shorter, 38
John Shorter, 17
Sarah Shorter, 19
Rachel Shorter, 13
Nelly Shorter, 15
Thomas Shorter, 5
Sophia Butler, 35
Matilda Butler, 18
Thomas Butler, 14
Sharon Butler, 13
*Samuel Butler, 10
Bill Butler75
Lucy Dorsey, 22
John Dorsey, 2
Aquala Swann, 54
Elizabeth Swann, 40
Ann Swann, 18
M___ Swann
Henny Swann, 16
Elizabeth Swann, 12
William Swann, 12
Lucinda Swann, 8
Frances Swann, 6
Aquala Swann, 1
Nancy Butler, 75
M___ Butler, 27
Nancy Butler, 10
Thomas Butler, 7
Elizabeth Butler, 4
Susannah Butler, 1
Ignatius Butler, 45
A___ Butler, 24
Agnes Butler, 24

William G___ Butler,
   2
Elizabeth Day, 16
Illegible name, 36
___ Wiseman, 60
Aqualla Proctor, 43
_____ Proctor, 31
Thomas Carter, 30
Jane Ford, 80
Catherine Ford, 40
Mary Ford, 8
Philip Ford, 3
Thomas Ford, 27
Philip Ford, 24
Sarah W___, 44
Amanda W___, 21
Nancy W___, 19
B___ W___, 15
Charles W___, 1
B___ W___, 15
Charles Butler Jr, 36
Nace Green, 90
Sophia Green, 45
Charles Thompson,
   30
John Butler, 30
Eliza Butler, 25
James ___, 36
Mary ___, 40
____ Thomas, 70
____ Thomas, 24
Walter Thomas, 22
John Shorter, 28
Elizabeth Ford, 17
Richard Thomas, 33
Cecelia Thomas, 25
John Thomas, 40
Harriet Thomas, 25
Mary Thomas, 11
Wesley Neale, 35
Elizabeth Neale, 28
Mary Thomas, 30
John Thomas, 14
Samuel Thomas, 12
Columbus Thomas, 6
Eleanor Thomas, 4
Francis Thomas, 2
Lily Thomas, 38
Joseph Thomas, 20
Margaret Thomas, 8
Cornelius Thomas,
   12
Letty Thomas, 8
Richard Thomas, 6
Henrietta Thomas, 4
Walter Thomas, 3

Betty Hall, 62
Ann Hall, 20
Betty Hall, 30
Ann Hall, 10
Susanah Adams, 80
Mary Adams
Ruth Adams, 50
Hariett Adams, 25
Mary Adams, 23
Hezekiah Adams, 12
Jacob Adams, 10
Henry Adams, 8
Eleanor Adams, 7
John Adams, 5
Elizabeth Adams, 4
Jane Adams, 4
Charles Adams, 2
George Adams, 1
Mary Adams, 35
William Adams, 6
Joseph Adams, 3
Isaac Proctor, 70
Elizabeth Proctor, 69
John Proctor, 37
Polly Proctor, 27
Alexander Proctor,
   16
Matilda Proctor, 15
Mary Proctor, 13
___ Proctor, 11
Isaac Proctor, 7
George Proctor, 7
Washington Proctor,
   4
Sylvester Proctor, 2
Henry Proctor, 9
A___ Proctor, 9
Henry Proctor, 15
Patrick Booth, 25
John Harley, 27
Tim Harley, 27
George Harley, 7
Elizabeth Harley, 8
John B. L. Harley, 6
Richard Harley, 3
William Harley, 1
John Newman, 35
___ Newman, 35
Maria Newman, 17
Frances Newman, 12
Wesley Newman, 12
Wesley Newman, 10
Rosetta Newman, 8
Julian Newman, 5
___ Newman, 2
Lydia Humphries, 75

Charles County

Letty Scroggin, 27
Henny Walker, 25
John Dixon, 22
Joseph Gray, 38
Nelly Gray, 30
Lucy Gray, 30
Dick Gray, 10
Chloe Gray, 5
William Gray, 3
Martha Gray, 1
James Hall, 30
Nace Jenkins, 65
Michael ___, 25
Jane Scrogins, 18
___ Proctor, 40
Susan Proctor, 30
Maria Proctor, 14
Charles Proctor, 12
Miley Proctor, 10
John Francis
    Proctor, 7
Christiana Proctor, 6
Henry _ Proctor, 4
A____, 24
Louisa _____, 20
Frank ___, 24
Mary Savoy, 56
John Savoy, 13
Alex Savoy, 18
Gustavius Savoy, 15
D___ Savoy, 7
Jacob Butler, 50
Eliza Butler, 50
John Butler, 25
Josias Butler, 23
Sally Butler, 20
Kitty Butler, 18
A___ Ann Butler, 1
ThomasProctor, 34
Eliza Proctor, 27
A___ Proctor, 2
John Butler, 65
Elizabeth Butler, 70
Henny Butler, 33
Jane Butler, 32
James Butler, 10
Mary Butler, 8
Thomas Butler, 6
Matilda Butler, 4
Louisa Butler, 1
___ T. Butler, 26
Matilda Butler, 26
Thomas Butler, 5
Elizabeth Butler, 3
Julian Butler, 2
Henry Proctor, 37

Mary Proctor, 37
Kitty Proctor, 15
John Proctor, 12
Henry Thomas
    Proctor, 10
Josiah Proctor, 8
Sarah Ann Proctor, 4
Elizabeth Proctor, 2
Stanislaus Boddow,
    22
Hasker Garner, 16
Ann Booth, 16
Mary Shorter, 40
Henry Shorter, 18
Adison Shorter 15
Adaline Shorter, 10
Alex Shorter, 9
John Shorter, 5
John Lamb, 5
Henry Shorter, 1
Sarah Mar__, 70
Wallis Jackson, 37
Sophia Jackson, 25
Martha Ann
    Jackson, 17
William Jackson, 7
Mary Jackson, 5
Jane Jackson, 3
John Jackson, 1
Isaac Whitlow, 63
Fanny Whitlow, 57
James Whitlow, 19
David Whitlow, 12
John Laurence, 25
Caroline Laurence,
    23
Joseph Laurence, 11
Sarah Laurence,
Nathaniel
    Whitlow, 35
Ann Whitlow, 22
Isaac Whitlow, 4
Matilda Whitlow, 1
Amanuel Gilbert, 60
James Butler, 22
Charles Butler, 26
Sarah Butler, 40
Julian Butler 15
Chloe Ann Butler, 14
William Henry Butler
    12
Elizabeth, 8
John Butler, 5
Janus Hodges, 32
Adeline Hodges, 28
Mary Hodges, 7

Mason Hodges, 3
Caroline Hodges, 1
William Gray, 30
___ Gray, 28
Offy Gray, 20
Milly Gray, 40
John Henry Gray, 5
William Gray, 3
Emeline Gray, 1
Lucenda Turner, 45
Dolly Turner, 30
G___ Turner, 25
Jeremiah Turner, 20
Sarah Turner, 18
Ann Maria Turner,
    16
Sophia Turner, 14
Lucinda Turner, 12
Mary Turner, 8
Jne Turner, 4
Nelly Day, 60
Nancy ___, 65
Rose Day, 35
Nelly Day, 33
Thomas Day, 24
Henry Day, 22
Maria Day, 7
Caroline Day, 5
Julia Chaney, 35
Thomas Channey, 7
Ann Channey, 5
Eliza Channey, 3
Child
Sarah Day, 28
Eliza Day, 10
Mary Day, 6
Thomas Day, 6
___ Day, 4
Margaret Day, 3
Thomas Day, 8
    months
Mary Gray, 40
Edward Gray, 17
John Gray, 15
Sarah Ann Gray, 14
James Gray, 11
Louisa Gray, 9
--- Gray, 7
Mary Gray, jr, 4
Ossy Gray, 2
John Penny, 25
Thomas Day, 50
Jinney Day, 70
Riley Swann, 60
Sarah Timmans, 40

Free African Americans of Maryland - 1832

Elizabeth Timmans, 20
Mary Timmons, 13
James Timmons, 10
Francis Timmons, 4
Henry Jenkins, 24
___ Jenkins, 22
Ann Jenkins, 20
Elizabeth, 17
___ Jenkins, 11
Jane Jenkins, 1
Charles Day, 70
Jane Day, 69
L___ McConchie, 40
Mary McConchie, 18
Jake McConchie, 7
George McConchie, 4
Child, 1
Ben Campbell, 14
Sidney Rays, 50
Aaron Rays, 64
Ann Rays, 50
Sarah Penny, 45
Jane Penny, 18
Mary Penny, 15
Sarah Ann Penny, 12
___ Penny, 7
___ H. Penny, 3
Harriet Swann, 45
William Swann, 20
John Swann, 16
Walter Swann, 14
John Butler, 45
Charles Butler, 40
Edward Butler 18
___ Butler, 16
Harriet Butler, 14
William Butler, 12
Francis Butler, 10
Ann Butler, 7
Mary Hart, 22
Henny Hart, 25
Mary Hart, jr, 6
Solomon Hart, 1
John Hart, 5 months
Nancy Jones, 24
John Jones, 12
William Jones, 10
Joseph Jones, 10
A___ Jones, 8
___ Jones, 3
George Jones, 2
___ Jones, 8
Wiliam Holt, 10
John Holt, 8
Henry Woodland, 30

Jefferson Ford, 25
Henry Lock, 22
Robert Booth, 22
William Thompson, 40
Thomas Thompson, 35
___, 42
___ Thompson, 30
Janus Thompson, 28
William Thompson, 12
Henry Thompson, 14
Alex Proctor, 60
Elizabeth Jones, 34
Mary Jones, 7
Catherine Jones, 2
Ann Read, 30
Mary Thompson, 65
___ Holt, 12
Peggy Thompson, 35
Ann Murphy, 26
___ Murphy, 16
Ann Proctor, 30
___ Proctor, 14
Cely Thompson, 16
Dorothy Thompson, 16
James Thompson, 6
Ada Thompson, 30
Aley Ford, 58
Jane Simms, 5
Ann Simms, 2
Jane Rush, 30
Mary Rush, 15
Sally Rush, 5
John Proctor, 29
William Proctor, 25
Washington Proctor, 25
Washington Proctor, 20
Thomas Thompson, 7
John Thompson, 7
James Thompson, 1
John Bush, 40
John Bush, 11
Ignatius Bush, 7
Child Bush, 2
Washington Carter, 28
Janus Carter, 30
Henry Grendle, 25
Henry Woodland, 28
Charles Mollison, 30

Miller Proctor, 22
Charles Proctor, 21
John Proctor, 28
Henry Proctor, 80
___ Proctor, 7
Francis Proctor, 5
Robert Proctor, 45
___ Butler, 4
Charles Butler, 1
Henry Laurence, 36
A__ Laurence, 23
Mary Laurence, 1
C__ Day, 56
___ Day, 22
___ Day, 30
Jake Day, 24
___ Jones, 44
Stephen Briscoe, 36
Theopolis ___, 45
Eliza Penny, 14
Illegible Name, 12
Theophilos ___, 10
Henry Day, 38
Sally Day, 26
Mary Day, 4
___ Day, 2
Ann Day, 1
___ Butler, 65
James ___, 40
___ Jackson, 55
Jane Jackson, 38
___ Jackson, 16
Matilda Jackson, 10
Mary Jackson,
Harriet Jackson, 4
Thomas Jackson, 2
Peter Swann, 45
Ignatius Hawkins, 72
Catherine Penny, 27
Joseph N ___, 35
Peter ___, 75
Flora ___, 40
Sarah ___, 18
Basil ___, 15
Illegible name, 13
George Brooks, 11
Susan Brooks, 9
Mary Brooks, 7
Matilda Brooks, 4
Elizabeth Brooks, 1
Charles Adams, 40
Nancy Adams, 26
Elizabeth Adams, 12
Ann Adams, 8
Sarah ___, 15
Nancy C___, 55

Charles County

Betsy Colten, 54
Menny Jane Collins, 28
William Collins, 26
Thomas Collins, 24
___ Collins, 32

Samuel Collins, 24
Ale__ Collins
Ann Collins, 13
Caroline Collins
John Bond
Dick Swann

Joseph Proctor
Mary Procotor
Joseph Proctor, 4
___ Proctor, 2

Thomas Perry, Sheriff of Charles County.

■■

Free African Americans of Dorchester County

State of Maryland, Dorchester County to wit,
In Compliance with the act of Assembly passed
December Session 1831. Entitled "an act relating to
The people of color in this State," the following
are registered this 20th. August 1832.

William Hughes, 63
Eben Hughes, 25
Denwood Hughes, 20
William Hughes jr, 20
Joseph Hughes, 12
Robert Hughes, 9
Joseph Waters, 15
Henry Pinder, 9
Henry Cephas, 15
Thomas Smart, 65
Josiah Ennels, 7
William H. Ennels, 4
Charles Cole, 80
David Banks, 35
Cuffin Haywood, 70
Phill Hodson, 35
Daniel Hodson, 5
James Hodson, 3
Josiah Hodson, 1
Daniel Hodson, 67
Edmond Hodson, 25
Levin Hodson, 22
Lemuel Hodson, 15
Denwood Hodson, 13
Charles Robinson, 35
Richard Robinson, 7
Henry Griffith, 60
William Griffith, 16
Robinson Hill, 35
William Hill, 4
Aaron Hill, 12
Clement See, 7
Moses Harris, 14

Levin Cole, 9
Tobias Byus, 70
Moses Byus, 16
Tobias Byus, 12
Noah Byus, 8
Stephen Byus, 4
Shadrac Cromwell, 45
George Robinson, 7
*James Blake, 63
Edward Blake, 55
Henry Blake, 13
Robert Blake, 58
Joseph Roles, 58
Henry Roles, 33
Levin Roles, 27
Joseph Roles, 22
William Roles, 5
Levin Robinson, 35
Isaac Roles, 2
Levin Robinson, 6
Joseph Roles, 1
Moses Blake, 30
James Blake, 5
Josiah Blake, 2
Peter Fletcher, 50
Peter Fletcher, 7
Henry Dickerson, 30
Garritson Stanley, 24
James H. Stanley, 1
Josiah Stanley, 5
Jacob Gusty, 60
John Cornish, 35

William H. Cornish, 12
David Cornish. 13
Charles Stanley, 35
Josiah Blake, 5
John Chew, 23
Edward Jew, 21
Hooper Jew, 16
William Jew, 7
Aaron Jew, 3
John Jew, 1
Chamberly Bowley, 30
Henry Bowley, 5
Washington Johnson, 21
Charles Chamberlain, 25
Robert Stanley, 25
Henry Stanley, 8
Jeremiah Stanley, 30
Edward Stanley, 35
Solomon Humby, 80
William Hughes, 56
George Robertson, 16
John Roles, 1
William Hughes, 7
*Levin Hughes, 5
Henry Hughes, 10
Perry Jackson, 55
Peter Jackson, 19
Perry Jackson Jr, 17
James Jackson, 15
Moses Jackson, 10

Free African Americans of Maryland - 1832

Joseph Hollen, 60
Charles Hollen, 6
Josiah Hall, 2
Dansey Foster, 56
William Foster, 1
James Kinse, 90
Harry Holiday, 35
Harry Molock, 13
Henry Griffin, 6
George Adams, 35
Harry Stanley, 52
James Stanley, 15
John Stanley, 10
Joseph Stanley, 7
Moses Stanley, 3
Robert Cook, 32
Henry Cook, 5
Nat Cook, 3
Robert Cook, 2
Aaron Cook 1
Manoky Toadvine, 90
Samuel Waters, 60
Phil Prices, 55
James Jolly, 21
William Jolly, 2
Thomas Sharp, 60
Eli Woolford, 36
Willis Woolford, 14
John Morris, 11
Harry Morris, 16
Danish Stanley, 23
Jane Stanley, 25
Jacob Gibson, 40
Thomas Clash, 33
John Clash, 7
James Clash, 42
Denswood Clash, 15
James Clash, 13
John Clash, 11
Arch Clash, 8
*Durum Clash, 5
William Johnson, 4
Darius Johnson, 1
John Hughes, 3
Peter Ben, 70
Edward Ben, 26
John Hughes, 11
Henry Hill, 10
Peter Camper, 6
William Smart, 18
John Smart, 10
Thomas Smart, 7
William Simson, 5
Henry Smart, 5
Samuel Molock, 60
Levin Molock, 17

James Molock, 12
Richard Molock, 7
William Chase, 45
Levin Bryant, 24
John Camper, 4
Allen Green, 57
Samuel Wilson, 17
Kennard Coleman, 3
Jacob Cephas, 50
Josiah Cephas, 10
John Cephas, 4
Little Hutson, 19
Joshua Stanley, 55
Green Stanley, 17
Elise Stanley, 14
Joshua Stanley, 12
James Stanley, 1
Matthew Pinder, 50
Denwood Pinder, 15
James W. Pinder, 14
Thomas Pinder, 18
Matthew Pinder, 12
John C. Pinder, 2
James Thompson,
   35
James Thompson,
   14
Jefferson Thompson,
   13
John Waters, 30
Little Molock, 25
___ Ennalls, 17
Henry Molock, 1
*Dennis Pinder, 35
Draper Pinder, 70
Richard Pinder, 2
Draper Lee, 40
 Washington Lee, 16
Denwood Lee, 9
Elisha Pinder, 65
Noah Pinder, 35
John Caros, 11
Dennis Brooks, 65
William Hollins, 14
Edwain Hollins
Darius Baltimore, 14
Shadrack Perry, 55
Major Perry, 9
John Perry, 5
Elijah Perry, 2
Eli Pinder, 34
William Pinder, 4
Robert Pinder, 3
Elijah Jones, 35
John Jones, 10
Richard Molock, 56

Abram Molock, 50
Henry Stiles, 18
Major Molock, 16
George Molock, 14
John Busnis, 11
Ephraim Molock, 26
Emory Molock, 11
Abram Molock, 4
John Molock, 3
Isaac Molock, 1
Ralph Mitchell, 45
Lot Brown, 80
Charles James, 5
Epharim Pinder, 40
Moses Jones, 60
Moses Jones Jr. 28
Kenny Jones, 25
Stephen Jones, 19
Major Jones, 4
William Wilson, 14
Joseph Stanley, 55
Joseph Stanley Jr.
   25
Steven Stanley, 20
Bob Stanley, 19
John Stanley, 17
William Stanley, 14
Henry Stanley, 2
Enoch Wilson, 409
Charles A. Wilson, 2
Abraham Stanley, 6
James Fisher, 6
Josiah Fisher, 3
Dick Weaver, 70
Pompy Strawberry,
   60
Noah Strawberry, 24
Edward Strawberry,
   3
Stephen Glasgan, 21
Nace Bapst, 70
Dick Pinder, 60
Washington Pinder,
   9
Wesley Pinder, 5
Mitchell Pinder, 1
Moses James, 27
William Stanley, 24
Thomas Hollan, 1
James Jones, 30
James Pinder, 65
James Pinder Jr. 21
Washington Pinder,
   13
Charles Earle, 30
Arch Ennells, 36

Dorchester County

Nicholas Lee, 5
William Lee, 1
Henry T. Lee, 58
John Thompson, 15
Henry Thompson, 8
James Thompson, 6
Bos Pinder, 10
Richard Pinder, 1
Washington
    Baltimore, 21
William Sampson, 10
Joseph Pinder, 5
Charles Pinder, 3
Matthew Pinder, 1
Joseph Cephas, 80
Moses Stanley, 55
Jeffery Woolford, 68
Emory Woolford, 18
Little Woolford, 33
Bat Woolford, 2
Levin Oney, 1
Jeffrey Woolford, 1
Josiah Cephas, 6
John Cephas, 13
Abram Coleman, 35
John McGlotten, 3
Daniel McGlotten, 1
Anthony Robinson,
    70
Alexander Robinson,
    9
John Robinson, 19
Ezekial Stanley, 57
James Stanley, 9
Josiah Stanley, 4
Anthony Stanley, 28
Gabriel Stanley, 1
Daniel Denwood, 50
Jeremiah Jackson, 1
Ben Jackson, 50
Thomas Cooper, 56
John Cephas, 19
Jacob Longtask, 12
Jacob Todd, 30
Virgin Nichols, 6
James Nichols, 3
William Williams, 3
Thomas Keene, 1
John N. Camper, 5
Levin H. Camper, 4
Alfred I Stiles, 1
Levin Young, 5
Hugh Young, 9
Moses Young, 8
James Young, 6
Alfred Young, 5

Elijah Horsey, 55
Elbert Horsey, 20
Major Horsey, 5
George Horsey, 2
Robert Stanley, 70
Izanel Stanley, 11
Charles Stanley, 30
Renbin Stanley, 6
John Stanley, 5
Charles Stanley, 2
Joseph Brison, 15
William Brison, 15
Charles Bead, 65
John Jackson, 30
John Stanley, 1
James Camper, 30
Ezekial Stanley, 60
Robert Stanley, 22
Eben Stanley, 19
Levin Stanley, 18
Peter Young, 69
Elisha Young, 36
____ Gainby, 86
Emory Dobson, 10
John Kiah, 25
Charles Dobson, 30
John King, 20
Edward Wheatley, 31
Henry Barnes, 40
Harry Maser, 50
Daniel Dickerson, 30
Noah Woolford, 32
Algy Woolford, 7
James Wheatley, 45
John Wheatley, 5
Washington
    Dickerson, 25
Thomas Jackson, 21
John Jackson 3
John Brown, 45
John Brown Jr, 5
Aaron Banks, 50
John Thomas, 27
Ezekial Stanley, 50
James Cole, 22
Job Smith, 20
George Dobson, 8
John Williams, 7
Joseph Williams, 11
Henry Williams, 6
James Cole, 22
Ezekiel Stanley, 55
Dennis Neild, 20
Isaac Neild, 7
*Joshua Johnson, 35
Levin Thomas, 8

Isaac Brown, 40
Stephen Hunt, 25
Jack Neild, 60
William Banks, 60
Josiah Barnes, 2
Littleton Banks, 14
Joseph Thomas, 65
David Murray, 50
Joseph Murray, 31
William Murray, 27
Thomas Dutton, 5
William Dutton, 5
George Dutton, 7
Charles Dutton, 5
Hunt Nutter, 80
Charles Kiah, 2
Charles Kiah, 50
Isaac Parker, 50
Arthur Hayward, 51
Robert Hayward, 9
John Hayward, 6
Solomon Jackson,
    40
Peter Jackson, 17
Robert Jackson, 14
Solomon Jackson, 6
Levin Winder, 50
Stephen Jackson, 50
Moses Cephas, 75
Samuel Brietlain, 65
Job McCollester, 65
Joseph Holt, 70
Stephen Parker, 12
Laurence Dutton, 19
David Jolley, 7
John Jolley, 5
William B___, 30
Arch Chace, 12
James Chace, 1
Elisha Jolley, 1
*Jesse Nace, 70
George W. Fisher, 8
William H. Fisher, 4
Levin Woolford, 9
George Parker, 60
Ben Burrows, 40
Thomas Jackson, 22
Thomas Jolley, 85
Baccus, 90
Charles Camper, 90
Simon Jolley, 40
Simon Jolley, 17
Elisha Jolley, 7
Henry Hughes, 10
Thomas Hughes, 18
Peter Burrows, 18

Free African Americans of Maryland - 1832

George Burrows, 12
Levin Rideout, 12
Robert Rideout, 14
Thomas Atkinson, 45
Easter Jolley, 8
H_ Austin, 49
___ Austin, 12
George Austin, 1
Isaac Camper, 55
Isaac Camper Jr. 16
William Camper, 9
Levin Camper, 9
James Camper, 7
John Camper, 4
James Nichols Jr, 25
James Nichols, 54
James Kiah, 45
Samuel Mitchell, 7
Darius Kiah, 4
William Kiah, 1
Sandy Rideout, 50
Ellick Rideout, 10
Jesse Woolford
Elick Woolford, 1
Abram Waters, 60
James Nichols, 6
Isaac Nichols, 4
Levin Nichols, 2
Levin Camper, 60
William Jolly, 7
Levin Jolly, 4
Hooper Jolly, 2
Samuel Hill, 30
James Thompson, 2
Levin Pinder, 2
Richard Barnett, 7
John Barnett, 9
Jacob Young, 14
Samuel Young, 10
Joseph Young, 22
Evan Hill, 21
John Farrow, 30
Robert Parker, 42
Levin Parker, 7
Wesley Parker, 5
Robert Parker, 3
Charles Sye, 28
James Sye, 2
Joseph Sye, 7
Edward Sye, 5
Edward Sye JR, 15
Levin Johnson, 4
James Young, 60
Ellick Harry, 1
Algy Pinket, 12
Levin Pinkett, 7

James Tilman, 7
Ben Johnson, 56
Washington
  Johnson, 24
Ben Johnson Jr, 14
Darius Johnson, 5
John Johnson, 1
Henry Brooks, 45
James Brooks, 7
Wesley Brooks, 4
Thomas Waters, 4
Abram Stiles, 30
Damon ___, 55
James Hughes, 40
Robert Hughes, 8
Joseph Hughes, 7
James Hughes, 4
Charles Gray, 12
James Gray, 10
Levin McGlotten, 2
Jacob Wing, 60
David Wing, 14
William Wing, 18
Benjamin Wing, 1
Nero Kirkman, 70
Patrick Callaway, 80
Ben Cannon, 60
Denwood Cannon,
  16
Levin Cannon, 6
Tom Jackson, 50
Isaac Moore, 50
Jim Tarpin, 50
Jim Collins, 50
Jim Collins Jr. 20
Jefferson Hubbard,
  29
Isaac Hubbard, 8
Sol Hubbard, 4
Charles Tilman Jr.
  16
Charles Tilman, 45
Willis Tilman, 8
Bayard Tilman, 6
Bill Butler, 30
Nevil Neild, 50
Isah Neild, 10
Charles Neild, 9
George Neild, 4
Andrew Neild, 2
Littleton Hubbard,
  28
Washington
  Hubbard, 9
Greentree Hubbard,
  3

Harick Hubbard, 1
Risden Webb, 50
John Webb, 21
Peter Webb, 12
Harritson Webb, 10
James Webb, 8
Edward Dodran, 26
Isiah Dodran, 3
Bill Butler Jr. 3
Josiah Button, 3
Edward Dodran, 2
Phinalls Phillips, 6
Phillip Phillips, 3
James Butter, 2
Bob Wright, 45
Charles Sims, 60
Gus Hammond, 20
Tom Hammond, 16
Bill Hammond, 12
Bob Hammond, 10
Paul Hammond, 10
Silas Hammond, 6
John Camper, 6
Josiah Camper, 4
Adam Land, 47
Reubin Land, 22
John Land, 17
George Johnson, 35
Washington
  Johnson, 8
Matthew Johns, 2
Henry Johns, 11
Bill Johns, 19
Bob Johns, 23
Roger Fletcher, 10
Charles Dickerson,
  50
Ennalls Dickerson,
  28
Cyrus Dickerson, 24
Charles Dickerson
  Jr. 17
Bob Dickerson, 8
Jim Dickerson, 6
George Woolford, 40
Wesley Murray, 21
Vance Murray, 12
Dick Cephas, 20
Joe Cephas, 14
Levin Cephas, 12
Will Johnson, 20
Charles Hurlock, 25
Silas Johnson, 14
Joe Dickerson, 12
Charles Johns, 3
*Charles Camper, 30

Dorchester County

Will Cornish, 60
Hugh McGlotten, 25
Will McGlotten, 28
Daniel Coleman, 60
Daniel Hill, 60
Evan Hill, 22
Dan Hill, 17
Hill Hill, 15
Jim Hill, 13
Joe Sampson, 4
Jim Sampson, 2
Joe Sampson, 23
Wesley Sampson, 12
Jake Sampson, 33
William Sampson, 4
Daniel Sampson, 28
Henry Sampson, 35
Gabriel Sampson, 12
Wash Sampson, 10
Major Sampson, 8
John Sampson, 3
Jim Hollin, 22
Sam Hollin, 20
John Hollin, 17
Nathan Kennard, 60
Daniel Thompson, 35
Jim Thompson, 3
Bob Sampson, 11
Mitchell Sampson,
    Tom Brumwell,
    35
Jim Brumwell, 4
Adam Davis, 3
John Davis, 35
Peter Cornish, 63
Tom Hollis, 12
Will Cornish, 7
Moses Cornish, 14
Jim Cornish, 8
John Sampson, 12
Adam Davis, 1
Aaron Harris, 45
Tom Harris, 4
Jim Harris, 18
Aaron Harris Jr. 16
Alfred Hollis, 20
Nevill Hollis, 18
Levin Bayard, 45
Will Bayard, 14
Hooper Baynam, 13
Moses Coleman, 50
Jim Coleman, 25
Jim Coleman, 1
Daniel Coleman, 6
Josiah Coleman, 4
Wesley Brumwell, 12

Will Roberts, 45
George Chamberlain,
    6
Sam Sephas, 4
Gilda Ray, 50
Hooper Ray, 23
Nat Ray, 21
John Haynes, 18
Tilman Younge, 16
Wash Hanes, 10
Major Hanes, 8
Jim Tilman, 11
Sam Cephas, 70
Joe Cephas, 16
Will Cephas, 13
Mitchell Neild, 30
Jim Neild, 6
Mitchell Neild, 1
Jack Thompson, 60
Levin Thompson, 30
Will Thompson, 25
Star Thompson, 22
Henry Thompson, 15
Tom Holiday, 55
Harrison Willis, 23
Levin Simpson, 8
John Allen, 1
Jim Thompson, 58
Harrison Willis, 19
Levin Simpson, 8
John Allen, 1
Jim Thompson, 58
Harritson Cornish,
    19
John Camper, 13
Draper Camper, 11
Denwood Camper, 2
Will Cornish, 10
*Sam Cornish, 7
Jake Cornish, 5
Charles Cornish, 5
Jim Cornish, 3
John Cornish, 1
Tom Mitchell, 10
Major Mitchell, 2
Batt Jinkins, 35
Dave Jinkins, 12
Joe Jinkins, 10
John Jinkins, 8
Bill Jinkins, 7
Ratio Jinkins, 6
John Bantum, 10
Bill Hopkins,22
George Johnson, 5
John Johnson, 7
Joe Harry, 6

Ezekial Small, 57
Thomas Holiday, 12
John Holiday, 14
Joe Thompson, 30
Draper Thompson,
    55
John Thompson, 17
William Thompson,
    11
Harry Thompson, 6
Harry Thomas, 50
Harry Thomas, 1
George Harris, 8
Peter Dickerson, 30
Harry Jones, 45
Dickens Jones, 18
Bat Jones, 17
Emery Jones, 13
Hugh Jones, 8
Littleton Jones, 1
George Johnson, 3
James Johnson, 18
Harrison Young, 3
Edmond Roberts, 60
Levin Jinkins, 30
James Jinkins, 2
Bill Jinkins, 1
Hooper Lee, 6
Peter Gladden, 80
Joe Hodson, 65
Tom Gye, 65
Levin Pinkett, 8
Horace Standford, 10
Jacob Quntons, 60
Charles Bayle, 10
George Bayle, 8
Jacob Farrar, 35
John Farrar, 5
Moses Farrar, 2
Sol Emery, 45
Charles Thompson,
    80
Abram Jinkins, 262
John Pinkett, 20
Josiah Pinkett, 10
Ben LeCompte, 60
Ben Jinkins, 35
Moses Jinkins, 20
John Jinkins, 6
Levin Jinkins, 5
Abram Jinkins, 3
Solomon Smart, 30
Tom Mitchell, 16
Cyrus Mitchell, 14
Charles Aldridge, 45
Dennard Bryan, 5

Free African Americans of Maryland - 1832

Tom Cye, 18
Isaac Cye, 23
HooperCye, 12
Charles Cye, 1
George Nutter, 55
Hooper Nutter, 25
John Austin, 6
John Danley, 17
Charles Fletcher, 1
Charles Fletcher, 28
Goldsborough
    Stanley, 30
Adam Woolford, 50
Sam Woolford, 4
George Woolford, 3
Charles Fletcher, 35
Madison Fletcher, 1
Bob Fletcher, 43
Charles Dickerson,
    60
Ennalls Dickerson,
    28
Cyrus Dickerson, 28
Charles Dickerson,
    20
Joe Dickerson, 15
Wesley Dickerson, 13
James Dickerson, 6
Bob Dickerson, 10
Sam McDonald, 60
Levin Simpson, 70
Joe Nutter, 70
Will Carr, 60
Moses Carr, 14
Charles Pinket, 30
Daniel Pincket, 4
Hugh Boss, 50
John Boss, 16
___ Boss, 14
Washington Boss, 12
Allen Green, 55
Sampson Young, 55
G___ Stanley, 38
Josiah Stanley, 15
Henry Stanley, 5
Moses Lee, 37
Harry Lee, 50
John Lee, 25
Robert Lee, 23
Richard Lee, 18
Wash Lee, 17
Will Lee, 13
Levin Lee, 27
Washington Lee, 3
Jim Stanley, 55
Eben Stanley, 20

Alford Stanley, 8
Bill Banks, 55
Tom Cornish, 8
William Dickerson,
    10
Joseph Lee, 30
Moses Lee, 8
William Lee, 1
Moses Horner, 45
William Horner, 20
Eben Horner, 21
George Coleman, 40
Harritson Johnson,
    18
Dick Johnson, 40
Stephen Johnson, 17

William Johnson, 12
Josiah Johnson, 5
George Johnson, 2
John Stanley, 63
Ennalls Stanley, 18
Danish Inglish, 50
Kely Frazier, 22
William Frazier, 21
Clem Frazier, 26
Jim Inglish, 12
Joe Inglish, 7
Bill David, 28
Levin Dent, 12
Isaac James, 80
Tom Glanden, 70
Saul Stanley, 40
Will Smith, 80
Bangilia Lake, 55
John Lake, 11
Eben Horner, 18
Jeffrey Henry, 55
George Johnson, 2
Thomas Holiday, 13
Bill Holiday, 2
John Holiday, 9
John Noir, 45
Jacob Bowdle, 48
Henry Brown, 43
John Brown, 3
Bill Mitchell, 22
Will Cornish, 67
Sam Cephas, 65
Charles Camper, 30
Albert Hollis, 21
Nevitt Hollis, 19
Bill Hollis, 15
Eben Hollis, 11
John Buley, 18
John Franklin, 32

Charles Jackson, 22
Thomas Jackson, 16
*Draper Jackson, 12
Isaac Jackson, 20
Daniel Jackson, 8
Abraham Jinkins, 25
John Jackson, 20
Charles Pinket, 30
Adam Davis, 35
John Davis, 3
Dick Davis, 1
Henry Davis, 10
Levin Fletcher, 29
Will Fletcher, 10
Charles Fletcher, 3
Elias Fletcher, 1
Charles Fletcher, 25
Madison Fletcher, 1
James Benson, 35
Albert Bohan, 3
James Washman, 10
Peter Hubbard, 25
Foster Hubbard, 6
Wright Hubbard, 5
Gabriel Baley, 33
Samuel McDonald,
    60
Joe Nutter, 60
Joe Fletcher, 35
John Fletcher, 3
Thomas Jackson, 60
David Jackson, 21
Sam Cornish, 69
Curtis Cornish, 33
Roger Cornish, 28
Will Cornish, 9
Jacob Cornish, 2
Jim Cornish, 4
Bill Horner, 17
Josiah Fletcher, 2
Jefferson Stanley, 30
George Woolford, 30
Stephen Simpson, 55
Nevitt Young, 25
Bill Bradley, 25
Moses Johnson, 35
Stephen Johnson, 16
Nevitt Young, 25
Bill Bradley, 25
Moses Johnson, 35
Stephen Johnson, 16
Benjamin Hopkins,
    12
Joe Bryan, 30
John Bryan, 8
Charles Bryan, 3

Dorchester County

Charles Bryan, 50
Angus Bryan, 40
Jim Stanley, 55
Eben Stanley, 24
Alfred Stanley, 10
David Stanley, 55
Joe Stanley, 8
Bill Stanley, 6
Charles Stanley, 4
Stokely Morris, 55
John Griffith, 56
Thomas Griffith, 8
Joseph Walton, 70
John Lake, 50
Samuel Lake, 37
Joe Lake, 47
Silas Todd, 2
Moses Todd, 5
Aaron Thomas, 32
Zachariah Todd, 45
John Todd, 11
Silas Travens, 24
Draper Travens, 59
Stephen Keene, 27
Obediah Lake, 53
George Thomas, 6
John W. Thomas, 2
William Todd, 60
Manuel Mister, 37
Obediah Baskley, 26
Sheppard Baskley, 13
Edward Foster, 8
John Pattison, 14
Joseph Brown, 13
Edward Mister, 5
William McNamara, 50
Nathan Willey, 50
Emanuel Griffin, 25
John Griffin, 19
Robert Hooper, 9
Andrew Tyler, 60
Charles Elliot, 14
James Elliot, 12
John Elliot, 10
Jacob Elliot, 9
Robert Elliot, 6
John Elliot Sr. 50
William Willing, 35
Aaron Wrotten, 40
Jessey Wrotten, 37
William Fish, 30
Levin Griffith, 16
John Nevit, 51
Edward Nevit, 1

Joseph Vaughn, 5
John Vaughn, 4
Moses Banks, 50
Robert Reah, 42
Abram Lee, 27
David Lee, 8
Major Bright, 32
James Bright, 12
Major W. Bright, 4
Frances C. Bright, 2
Jacob Bayley, 65
Jacob Bishop, 18
Isaac Bishop, 4
Titus Cornish, 55
Thomas Meekins, 10
Samuel Evans, 28
David Evans, 19
Alexander Evans, 14
Mingo Evans, 60
Harry Thomas, 38
Moses Harris, 3
Adam Muir, 67
Charles Moore, 12
Sipes Banner, 62
Charles Kune, 45
Robert Pokety, 4
James M___, 8
John Cornish, 2
James Cook 32
Daniel Hopkins, 56
John Muir, 16
William Hopkins, 15
Thomas J Hopkins, 3
Daniel Stanley, 30
Daniel Foster, 55
William W. Foster, 2
John H. Harris, 9
Joshua Harris, 45
Abram Harris, 12
George Harris, 9
Dennis Harris, 2
Isaac Macer, 54
John Jackson, 27
Enock Goden, 52
Howan Matthews, 11
John Newman, 33
Charles Macer, 10
Robert Newman, 10
Moses Driver, 46
Moses Driver Jr. 10
Edward Driver, 5
Anthony Driver, 1
Charles Sanders, 30
John Driver, 68
Anthony Driver, 27
Joseph Ennalls, 18

Stephen Brown, 18
Richard Willis, 10
Jacob Henry, 50
Levin Kennard, 13
John Henry, 10
Doblin White, 66
Jerry Marien, 50
Jerry Marien Jr. 21
Richard Marien, 19
Noble Marien, 15
Josiah Marien, 13
Frank Drake, 60
Isaac Harris, 23
Thomas Harris, 60
Matthew Dixon, 45
Roger Hacket, 5
John H. Dixon, 6
George Dixon, 3
Joseph Atkins, 20
Keel Atkins, 15
Robert Atkins, 12
James Atkins, 10
Charles Atkins, 7
Eben Hughes, 2
Littleton Hughes, 30
Joseph Brown, 33
Edward Scott, 21
George Wilson, 32
Joseph Chaplain, 11
William Hitt, 19
Jacob Atkins, 65
James Shintons, 33
Joseph Johnson, 40
Henny Griffin, 65
Isaac Griffin, 35
Levin H. Griffin, 7
Isaac Bayley, 30
William Bayley, 4
John Henry, 6
Isaac Bayley, 2
John Molock, 30
Charles Camper, 22
Washington Griffin, 28
Ezekiel Stanley, 40
Sovran Stanley, 4
Jacob Harris, 26
Thomas Brusset, 10
Charles Brusset, 8
Solomon Woolford, 30
Jacob Small, 50
William Giles, 27
George W. W. Keene, 5
Samuel H. Keene, 4

Free African Americans of Maryland - 1832

John Denwood, 27
Abraham Bishop, 23
Anthony Brown, 31
Job Brown, 28
Joseph Brown, 28
Isaac Driver, 9
Edward Driver, 7
William Vaughn, 31
John Driver, 3
Charles Sanders, 10
James Mongomary, 22
Elijah Mongomary, 17
John Mongomary, 2
Josiah Mongomary, 5
James Mongomary, 4
William D. Mongomary, 1
John H. Dixon, 4
George W.W. Dixon, 1
Matthew Dixon, 32
Jerry Driver, 5
Nathan Brown, 40
Zachariah Nevit, 10
William Harrison, 3
Major Jones, 57
Thomas Thomas, 18
Samuel Thomas, 22
Gabriel Griffin, 40
Ezekial Stanley, 36
Harklis, LeCompte, 61
Henry LeCompte, 40
Righteous LeCompte, 6
Edward LeCompte, 5
Harrisons LeCompte, 3
Thomas Radin, 65
Harris Jackson, 27
Henry Jackson, 5
Allen Smith, 35
William Johnson, 83
Joseph Marien, 47
Richard Marien, 4
John E. Marien, 2
Joseph Marien, 9
Samuel Harris, 34
Thomas Harris, 32
Edward Dunnack, 48
Samuel I. T. I. Thomas, 10
Wesley P.Furrow, 5

John Cooper, 9
John Bayard, 52
John H. Cornish, 10
Alexander Cornish, 8
Abraham Cornish, 50
Joseph Atkins, 20
Keel Atkins, 15
Robert Atkins, 12
James Atkins, 10
Charles Atkins, 7
Henry Hughes, 6
Eben Hughes, 2
Littleton Hughes, 30
Joseph Brown, 33
Edward Scott, 21
George Wilson, 32
Joseph Chaplain, 11
William Hitt, 19
*Jacob Atkins, 65
James Stantons, 33
Joseph Johnson, 40
Henry Griffin, 65
Isaac Griffin, 35
Levin H. Griffin, 7
Isaac Bavley, 30
William Bayley, 4
John Henry, 6
Isaac Bayley, 2
John Molock, 30
Charles Camper, 22
Washington Griffin, 28
Ezekiel Stanley, 40
Sovran Stanley, 4
Jacob Harris, 26
Thomas Brussett, 10
Charles Brusset, 8
Solomon Woolford, 30
Jacob Small, 50
William Giles, 27
George W. W. Keene, 5
Samuel H. Keene, 4
John Denwood, 27
Abraham Bishop, 23
Anthony Brown, 31
Jos. Brown, 28
Isaac Driver, 9
Edward Driver, 7
William Vaughn, 31
John Driver, 3
*Daniel Parker, 50
Sarah Singleton, 21
Solomon Hinson, 22

Josiah Hinson, 13
James Wheatley, 22
Isaac Gibson, 50
Junipher Holland ,4
James Holland, 3
David Dickerson, 15
Charles Dickerson, 11
Thomas Dickerson, 1
Henry Washington, 11
Uriah Johns, 18
Solomon Quash, 5
Edward Kier, 25
Jeremiah Kier, 6
Edward Kier, 5
Francis Kier, 1
Simon Brown, 38
Josiah Brown, 6
John Brown, 4
Edward Blake, 33
John King, 50
John Kier, 55
Stephen Camper, 16
George G___, 57
John Hooper, 17
Isaac Banks, 6
Jacob McGloten, 22
William McGloten, 12
Stephen McGloten, 17
Thomas Manokey, 53
Emanuel Jackson, 50
Charles Jackson, 17
James Jackson, 12
Benjamin Jackson, 5
Stephen Kier, 40
Josiah Kier, 14
Major Lee, 37
James Lee, 1
Foster Adams, 60
Abraham Camper, 45
Francis Cromwell, 13
Samuel H. Cromwell, 4
Price Smith, 46
Jacob Mcglotin, 5
William Nichols, 21
John Jackson, 26
John Anthony, 7
Samuel Jackson, 30
John Jackson, 55
Draper Jackson, 16

67

Dorchester County

Charles Jackson, 22
William Jackson, 18

John Jackson, 6
Mingo Edmondson,
60
Joseph Stafford, 36
David Stafford, 10
Josiah Stafford, 7
John W. Stafford, 1
Charles Wing, 5
David Haskins, 1
Joseph Jenkins, 56
Charles Wing, 68
Joseph Richardson,
32
Moses Pennington,
73
Jasper Jenkins, 60
Jacob Payne, 55
Darius Stevens, 5
Alfred Stevens, 3
Stephen Long, 32
James Ward, 70
Elizabeth Warfield,
18
Ralph Wheatley, 55
Jacob Wheatley, 17
John Wheatley, 13
Augustus Wheatley,
9
Daniel Wheatley, 7
David Gannons, 38
Perry Gannons, 13
William Gannons, 7
Noble Gannons, 11
Charles Warfield, 48
Charles Gibson, 8
Francis Brannock,
42
Stephen Bombary,
45
Lin Cook 60
James Cook, 21
Lin Cook Jr. 18
Levin Cook, 17
*Moses Cook, 7
Ralph Tubman, 51
Thomas Camper, 50
Juby Pokety, 25
Jacob Camper, 10
Abel Cromwell, 48
Loyd Cromwell, 5
John Cromwell, 2
John Bryan, 52
Jacob Light, 52

Cyrus Hooper, 10
Moses Driver, 51

John Cornish, 58
Arnay Cornish, 3
Hezekiah Cornish, 3
Job Boley, 71
James Henry, 47
Henry Johnson, 60
Macall Brickle, 66
Josiah Brickle, 12
John Brickle, 8
Isaia Brickle, 67
Shadrick Brown, 19
Henry Brown, 9
Mark Brown, 4
Mark Cook, 50
Richard Jinkins, 30
Alexander Jinkins, 9
Jacob Macer, 68
Francis Jinkins, 48
Daniel Holland, 50
Nathaniel Brickle, 69
Joseph Wheatley, 3
John Mills, 3
Stephen McGaulin,
17
Washington Brickle,
35
John Brickle, 4
Nat Brickle, 2
Peter Plater, 45
David LeCompte, 65
Joseph Boley, 8
Edward Dixon, 36
Alfred Green, 4
Curtis Brooks, 35
John Brooks, 6
Henry Brooks, 1
John Cornish, 35
Ezekial Woolford, 71
Job Williams, 75
Charles Elbert, 60
John Cromwell, 2
Peter Mitchell, 60
George Mitchell, 12
John Mitchell, 8
Thomas Cooper, 12
John Cooper, 10
William Cooper, 8
Samuel Cooper, 1
Tobias Bind, 50
Peter Dickinson, 32
Jacob Barnett, 50
Zachariah Barnett,
11

Washington Barnett,
2
William Barnett, 30
Cyrus Boley, 49
William Boley, 24
Joseph Boley, 21
Cyrus Boley Jr. 18
Richard Boley, 16
Henry B. Boley, 7
James Banks, 21
William Banks, 17
David Banks, 14
Moses Bright, 40
James Bright, 16
Moses A. Bright, 9
John W. Bright, 7
Dennis Bright, 1
Thomas C. Cornish,
12
Drue Colston, 52
Tubman Tubman, 10
Daniel Keene, 35
James Keene, 10
Murray Keene 7
Daniel Keene, 7
Abraham Bishop, 25
*Shadrick Henry, 25
Garalson Bright, 35
Draper Keene, 50
Draper Keene Jr. 10
Terry Todd, 6
Samuel Todd, 35
John W. Henry, 8
Epharim Henry, 20
Robert Keene, 21
Thomas Cornish, 18
Charles Woolford, 40
Summer Cornish, 30
John Bell, 12
Matthew Dixon, 55
David Linthicum, 23
Thomas Linthicum, 2
John Henry, 39,
Jonas V. Henry, 5
John W. Henry, 12
Abram Stiles, 12
Jonathan Stiles, 12
Thomas Retta, 5
Parris Green, 8
James, 16
Levin, 10
Jerry Reed, 17
Job Slater, 83
Ignatious Driver, 40
William Hythe, 24

Free African Americans of Maryland - 1832

James Green, 25
James LeCompte, 30

George Ward, 21
James Ward, 18
Joseph Chaplain, 9
James Hythe, 1
Thomas Torook, 7
Robert Mansey, 65
Charles Gibson, 10
Phener Ennalls, 40
James Henry, 8
George Buley, 76
George Buley Jr. 4
Oliver Buley, 2
Emanuel Bennett, 45
Jacob Bennet, 13
William Bennet, 9
Joshua Lockerman,
    50
Thomas Lockerman,
    20
George Lockerman,
    18
David Lockerman, 11
Robert Lockerman, 8
Daniel Hythe, 20
Edmond Brown, 50
William Miller, 18
Adam Banks, 45
Charles Edwards, 67
Jacob C. Edwards, 7
John Travers, 40
Samuel Pattison, 42
Geen Pattison, 7
Charles Pattison, 6
Domanick Bright, 61
John Pattison, 67
Jack Pattison, 25
Joseph Lee, 57
Francis Travers, 46
Jacob Hooper, 35
Epharaim Travers,
    10
Jacob Travers, 49
Richard Travers, 27
Joseph Travers, 17
Jacob Travers, 12
John Travers, 10
Christopher Pattison,
    50
Jacob Gamby, 50
Jacob Gamby, 59
Lawrenceon Gamby,
    4
Loyed Gamby, 1

James Dean, 10
Draper Creighton, 57

Jacob Johnson, 41
John Johns, 10
Isaac S. Johnson, 4
Moses Harress, 60
*Moses Haress, 22
Henry Green, 45
Jessey Harress, 22
Monk LeCompte, 57
James Stanley, 50
John Ellis, 50
Garrison Ellis, 19
John J. Ellis, 13
Fountain Ellis, 10
Adam Ellis, 5
John Gaines, 22
Stewart Gaines, 20
Noah Gaines, 15
George Cornish, 24
Stewart Cornish, 18
Jeremiah Cornish,
    14
Thomas Travers, 48
Levin Ellis, 40
George Ellis, 28
Caleb Ellis, 22
Thomas Ellis, 52
Isaac Dawson, 58
Isaac Dawson, 26
Jacob Dawson, 21
Matthew Dawson, 20
David Baughn, 5
John C. Tubman, 15
Henry Hooper, 50
George Jones, 53
Joel Jones, 25
George Jone, 16
John Jones, 14
Dennis Jones, 11
Morgan Jones, 6
Thomas Bishop, 72
Hicks Bishop, 37
Travers Bishop, 23
Major Bishop, 22
Stephen Lane, 70
Marmaduke Dove, 19
Joseph Wilson, 8
James Wilson, 5
George Bennett, 15
David Bennett, 11
Noah Bennett, 7
William Bennett, 3
Benjamin Buck, 60
Benjamin Buck, 30

Henry Ross, 55
Jacob Petrkin, 60

John E. Jones, 3
John Johnson, 10
Abraham Johnson, 7
Isaac Bishop, 58
Mial Hooper, 70
Samuel Hooper, 18
Henry Hooper, 11
Joseph Hooper, 8
Robert Hooper, 8
William Hooper, 5
Joseph Creighton, 14
John E. Creighton, 5
Frank Branock, 78
Thomas Bishop, 13
Jacob Gaines, 65
Evins Gaines, 24
Jacob Wilson, 73
Daniel Wilson, 70
Gabriel Bishop, 11
Stephen Ennalls, 3
Anthony Gaines, 6
Samuel Keene, 40
Summer Thompson,
    53
Washington Bayley,
    28
Solomon Barnes, 78
Jacob Parker, 31
Robert Shapes, 60
Evens Tubb, 40
James Hensley, 35
Jacob Jackson, 33
Samuel Thomas, 23
Dennis Camper, 65
Levin Camper, 31
Dennis Camper, 17
Andrew Camper, 10
George Camper, 6
Noah Camper, 4
Jacob Sanders, 65
Hutson Sanders, 18
Jacob Camper, 55
Jacob Wilson, 38
Charles Manoky, 65
Michael Manoky, 15
George Manoky, 7
Lazius Fish, 49
John Tubman, 38
Benjamin Pattison,
    61
Jube Pattison, 36
Matthew Dixon, 61
Jube Ennalls, 40

Dorchester County

James Ennalls, 8
Henry Ennalls, 5

Charles Ennalls, 13
Jacob Dixon, 41
Mary Brown, 35
*Sally Brown, 7
Mary Brown, 6
Maria Brown, 4
Ritty Cornish, 60
Eliza Cornish, 20
Mahalia Camper, 24
Sarah Hollis, 43
Rachel Cephus, 50
Mary Stanley, 18
Lydia Hollis, 9
Betsy Hollis, 50
Mary Bayley, 21
Sopha Bayley, 15
Mary Jackson, 45
Sally Jackson, 24
Rachel Jackson, 18
Nancy Jackson, 13
Mary Jackson, 6
Betty Banks, 17
Leah Bird, 26
Mary Davis, 6
Rachel Davis, 5
Lue Fletcher, 25
Sally Fletcher, 11
Resy Fletcher, 4
Mary Fletcher, 3
Henny Fletcher, 20
Hester Washman, 25
Susan Washman, 3
Sue Washman, 2
Harriet Washman, 1
Nancy McDonald, 55
Crecy McDonald, 6
Emily Brown, 12
Mary Dye, 20
Mahala Hubbard, 32
Margaret Hubbard, 15
Mary Hubbard, 9
Ann Hubbard, 14
Ann Buley, 24
Margaret Buley, 10
Eliza Buley, 8
*Betsy Buley, 6
Harriet Buley, 4
Mary Buley, 1
Louisa Harress, 25
Sarah Jackson, 30
Margaret Cornish, 26
Ann Cornish, 22

___ Cornish, 4
Leah Roberts, 48

Eliza Roberts, 22
Lotty Dennis, 40
Leah Dennis, 12
Nancy Dennis, 8
Milley Dennis, 3
Hetty Collins, 18
Betty Collins, 16
Tabby Simpson, 55
Rachel Chopper, 55
Mary Hubbard, 26
Ainey Hubbard, 6
Patience Tilman, 40
Mary Tilman, 17
Ritty Tilman, 10
Mary Butler, 23
Ann Butler, 4
Nancy Neild, 13
Eliza Neild, 13
Pricilla Hubbard, 30
Adeline Hubbard, 7
Cassey Hubbard, 5
Hester Webb, 45
Mary Webb, 18
Nancy Webb, 16
Hester Webb, 4
Mary Dodson, 27
Cassey Dodson, 1
Mary Dodson, 23
Ann Dodson, 17
Chloe Dodson, 16
Elizabeth Dodson, 12
Harriet Dodson, 8
Leah Fletcher, 25
Araminta Johnson, 1
Dirana Phillips, 30
Sidney Johnson, 30
Mary Butter, 30
Maria Butter, 4
Sarah Phillips, 50
Mary Hammond, 11
Becky Hammond, 22
Elizabeth Hammond, 8
Sarah Fletcher, 25
Eliza Fletcher, 23
Minta Camper, 50
Susan Camper, 25
Nancy Camper, 2
Gracy Lord, 38
Rhoda Lord, 18
Mary Lord, 2
Betty Lord, 12
Ann Lord, 9

Jane Johnson, 10
Rachel Johnson, 6

Deborah Johns, 37
Mary Johns, 25
Ann Johns, 1
Ann Johns, 12
Ann Dickinson, 20
Jane Dickinson, 16
Minta Dickinson, 12
Mary Dickinson, 10
Leah Murray, 40
Sopha Murray, 23
Sarah Murray, 6
Leah Murray, 2
Ann Murray, 22
Harriet Murray, 14
Emely Murray, 16
Dinah Matthews, 42
Hannah Williams, 22
Mahala Camper, 30
Mary Camper, 13
Emeline Johns, 20
Ritty Cornish, 45
Eliza Cornish, 20
Elsy McGlotten, 25
Milly McGlotten, 26
Eliza McGlotten, 4
Betsy Barronet, 40
Henny Coleman, 50
Betsy Coleman, 24
Nancy Coleman, 19
Lucy Coleman, 17
Lilly Coleman, 25
Beck Sampson, 2
Milly Sampson, 28
Beck Sampson, 8
Mary Sampson, 4
Sally Sampson, 25
Elizabeth Sampson, 5
Margaret Sampson, 2
Nancy Sampson, 35
Ann Sampson, 16
Mary Sampson, 14
Harriet Sampson, 15
Henny Hollis, 45
Silva Hollis, 18
Lilly Hollis, 9
Ann Hollis, 6
Eliza Thompson, 30
Eliza Thompson, 8
Sally Thompson, 6
Mary Thompson, 3

Free African Americans of Maryland - 1832

Margaret Thompson, 1
Letty Young, 45
Maria Young, 11
Ann Young, 8
Mary Hill, 6
James Hill, 1
Nancy Brumwell, 25
Rachel Brumwell, 6
Lucy Brumwell, 2
Ann Brumwell, 1
Mary Davis, 5
Fanny Hill, 55
Ann Hill, 25
Margaret Hill, 23
Rachel Hill, 11
Debby Clarr, 14
Lettice Clarr, 50
Cassey Harris
Rachel Harris, 8
Sarah Hollis, 40
Lydia Hollis, 6
Sylvia Bayman, 30
Mary Bayman, 14
Ann Bayman, 1
Rhoda Coleman, 45
Mary Coleman, 25
Maria Coleman, 8
Leah Coleman, 3
Ester Chamberlain, 40
Mary Cephus, 25
Eliza Cephus, 7
Rachel Cephus, 6
Caroline Roy, 12
Milly Roy, 14
Eliza Roy, 16
Maria Johnson, 17
Rachel Cephus, 55
Harriet Cephus, 19
Henry Cephus, 12
Nancy Neild, 25
Ann Neild, 9
Susan Thompson, 22
Mary Thompson, 20
Sally Thompson, 15
Susan Thompson, 10
Mary Thompson, 1
Henrietta,
    Thompson, 4
Maria Johnson, 60
Pheby Johnson, 80
Ester Roberts, 70
Sally Roberts, 13
Eve Roberts, 6
Ann Roberts, 6

Ann Roberts, 16
Eliza Cornish, 25
Fanny Christmas, 70
Lydia Willis, 55
Sarah Simpson, 40
Rachel Bryan, 75
Iby Simpson, 16
Mahala Allen, 45
Ritty Allen, 14
Leah Allen, 12
Mary Cornish, 32
Eliza Cornish, 14
Jane Cornish, 12
Entrenett Cornish, 8
Mary Cornish, 5
Milly Cornish, 30
Ritty Cornish, 16
Julia Cornish, 14
Sarah Cornish, 9
Elizania Cornish, 8
Henrietta Cornish, 3
Ritty Cornish, 35
Mary Camper, 11
Leah Camper, 9
Sue Camper, 7
Margaret Cornish, 32
Ann Cornish, 25
Eliza Cornish, 8
Maria Mitchell, 35
Sally Mitchell, 8
Eliza Mitchell, 22
Leah Jinkins, 40
Lucy Jinkins, 14
Mary Jinkins, 11
Ann Jinkins, 8
Catherine Jinkins, 5
Leah Jinkins, 4
Sarah Bantom, 35
Emily Bantom, 8
Maria Bantom, 7
Sidney Johnson, 35
Ann Johnson, 8
Hannah Evans, 75
Mahala Hary, 30
Ann Henry, 2
Mahala Henry, 1
Aleny Roseberry, 60
Mary Thompson, 30
Rachel Thompson, 1
Elizabeth Thompson, 46
Affie Thompson, 15
Mary Thompson, 8
Maria Thomas, 26
Delia Thomas, 4
Ann Thomas, 3

Rachel Harris, 30
Mahala Jones, 35
Maria Jones, 16

Mary Jones, 12
Lacy Jones, 10
Debby Jones, 8
Maria Jones, 35
Eliza Mitchell, 18
Mary Mitchell, 16
Sally Mitchell, 12
Harriet Mitchell, 4
Sally Johnson, 28
Mary Johnson, 4
Polly Lee, 30
Annetta Lee, 5
Rachel Johnson, 17
Linah Banks, 30
Rachel Gladden, 70
Kitty Gladden, 15
Ann Pinkett, 25
Ann Pinkett, 9
Mary Pinkett, 3
Eliza Pinkett, 2
Ann Pinkett, 25
Catherine Pinkett, 4
Minty Pinkett, 3
Ritty Pinkett, 27
Harriet Pinkett, 2
Maria Pinkett, 1
Sally Jinkins, 25
Rhod Stanford, 30
Leah Quinton, 50
Ann Bowdle, 30
Sofa Farars, 25
Ann Farars, 4
Margaret Emory, 35
Rachel Thompson, 45
*Silva Dutton, 24
Mary Jackson, 40
Rhoda LeCompte, 60
Tempy Elbert, 40
Ann Jackson, 30
Leah Jinkins, 25
Mary Jinkins, 20
Sofa Jinkins, 14
Milly Jinkins, 13
Rhoda Jinkins, 9
Nancy Bryan, 30
Sally Aldridge, 12
Linah Cye, 40
Betne Cye, 15
Nancy Cye, 8
Violet Austin, 28
Ann Austin, 3

71

Dorchester County

Harriet Fletcher, 9
Jane Fletcher, 8
Adeline Fletcher, 1
Emely Fletcher, 6
Rhoda Woolford
Henny Fletcher, 28
Hetty Dickinson, 15
Mary Diet, 39
Nancy McDonald, 50
Crecy McDonald, 14
Emely McDonald, 10
Rhoda Simpson, 40
Jane Simpson, 4
Mary Boss, 40
Eliza Boss, 18
Mary Boss, 8
Darky Boss, 6
Leah Pinkett, 30
Ann Pinkett, 8
Mary Stanley, 35
Ann Stanley, 18
Rosy Stanley, 16
Mary Stanley, 8
Eliza Stanley, 4
Lacy Stanley, 2
___ Lee, 50
Sophia Lee, 8
Polly Lee, 23
Margaret Lee, 2
Mary Stanley, 16
Betty Guy, 60
Sarah Banks, 50
Patty Guy, 17
Ann M. Banks, 4
Matilda Banks, 25
Ritty Cornish, 6
Mary Dickinson, 45
Cassy Lake, 38
Barbary Lee, 30
Rosey Lee, 10
Polly Horner, 40
Sally Horner, 17
Milly Horner, 13
Mary Johnson, 35
Jane Johnson, 10
Sally Stanley, 60
Harriet Inglish, 25
Jane Inglish, 12
Nicy Frazier, 20
Rachel Banks, 60
Beck Greenwood, 30
Gracy Cornish, 70
Arietta Lake, 9
Levinah Lake, 5
Eliza Lake, 4
Linah Greenwood, 40

Maria Greenwood, 3
July A. Lake, 2
Nancy L. Ledam, 35
*Mary Ledam, 5
Comfort Henry, 50
Julia Johnson, 25
Sally Thompson, 8
Eliza Holiday, 35
Ann Holiday, 15
Margaret Holiday, 7
Lucy Holiday, 5
Gracy Simpson, 50
Ann Simpson, 10
Rachel Dickenson, 60
Mary Porgety, 25
Ann Porgety, 9
Ann Simpson, 25
Jane Turner, 50
Sarah Young, 50
Rosey Dodson, 23
Phillis Smart, 60
Dinah Bagly, 45
Prissy Bryan, 30
Harriet Bryan, 6
Harriet Strawberry, 20
Mary Stanley, 18
Ann Stanley, 45
Julia Stanley, 13
Margaret Stanley, 10
Mary Dent, 8
Sally Dent, 6
Ann Dent, 2
Charity Young, 50
Hetty Stanley, 45
Rachel Gainby, 70
Grace Human, 60
Maria Dobson, 22
Harriet Dobson, 23
Ianty Woolford, 25
Mary A. Woolford, 2
Julian Woolford, 1
Margaret Brown, 16
Leah Brown, 12
Cloe Brown, 10
Lilly Brown, 45
Mileah Jackson, 22
Mary A. Jackson, 1
Delia Dobson, 45
Caroline Dobson, 4
Mary Williams, 30
Rhody Murray, 45
Rebecca Neild, 40
Lina Johnson, 35
Henny Thomas, 35

Ann Thomas, 17
Maria Johnson, 6
Henny Johnson, 25
Charity Barnes, 26
Eliza Barnes, 9
Rhoda Barnes, 5
Mary Thomas, 70
Mary Hughes, 45
Lilley Hughes, 16
Sophia Hughes, 14
Mary A. Hughes, 12
Patience Hughes, 10
Sally Robertson, 65
Siby Possum, 60
Rachel Smart, 70
Rachel Steele, 48
Mahala Ennalls, 35
Mary A. Jackson, 16
Hannah Cole, 80
Jane Haywood, 60
Sophia Haywood, 30
Nancy Hodson, 35
Nancy A. Hodson, 10
Henrietta Hodson, 6
Louisa Dickerson, 40
Eliza Robinson, 33
Mary Robinson, 19
Mary Hodson, 19
Dido Banks, 60
Martha Griffith, 55
Liddy Denwood, 33
Eliza Denwood, 14
Nancy Denwood, 10
Lovy Blake, 7
Ester Blake, 21
Mary Blake, 30
*Eliza Blake, 10
Sophia Blake, 6
Hester Blake, 1
Sally Roles, 60
Mary Roles, 20
Nicey Robinson, 30
Sally Robinson, 1
Ann Maria Denwood, 13
Mary7 Stanley, 19
Mary Stanley, 12
Sally Roles, 7
Rebecca Blake, 25
Any Fletcher, 25
Mary A. Fletcher, 8
Lydia Dickenson, 23
Leah Stanley, 30
Hester A. Stanley, 7
Liney Gusty, 80
Selance Jackson, 70

Free African Americans of Maryland - 1832

Phillis Jackson, 40
Mary A. Jackson, 8
June Jackson, 4
Harriet Blake, 35
Polly Blake, 40
Milly Jew, 30
May A. Jew, 3
Maria Jew, 12
Asiley Morris, 60
Dinah Bowley, 45
Cassa Bowley, 17
Nancy Bowley, 1
Eliza Lee, 21
Henrietta Bryan, 15
Rachel Stanley, 27
Leah Stanley, 45
Lotty Jackson, 30
Ann M. Jackson, 12
Harriet Jackson, 5
Sarah A. Jackson, 1
Sarah Dickinson, 42
Ianty Humby, 70
Ianty Holiday, 10
Dolly Holiday, 6
Nancy Bromwell, 30
Sally Hughes, 40
Maria Hughes, 18
Eliza Hughes, 16
Sally Hughes, 15
Matilda Hughes, 13
Leah Hughes, 10
Betty Hughes, 32
Milly Hughes, 13
Prissey Ross, 60
Adeline Jackson, 5
Harriet Jackson, 3
Prissy Hollan, 45
Rachel Hollan, 20
Nicy Cooper, 22
Margaret Blake, 16
Rebecca Foster, 27
Elizabeth Blake, 6
Rebecca Foster, 4
Hinny Clash, 60
Nelly Kier, 29
Eliza Griffith, 33
Sopia Griffith, 5
Eliza Stanley, 16
Mahala Johnson, 3
Rachel Adams, 65
Maria Stanley, 19
Sophia Stanley, 17
Rose Stanley, 14
Rachel Stanley, 13

Mary Stanley, 8
Abigal Stanley, 1
Rose Cook, 30
Eliza Cook, 9
Rose Cook, 8
Polly Ennalls, 30
Prissy Stanley, 45
Susan Price, 38
Nancy Jolly, 40
Hester A. Jolly, 16
Eliza Hollan, 9
Ritty Woolford, 30
*Nelly Henry, 45
Margaret Henry, 6
Mary Stanley, 18
Eliza Stanley, 23
Polly Gibson, 40
Harriet Clash, 20
Mary Clash, 2
Siner Hill, 30
Caroline Smart, 14
Julian Smart Hill, 6
Sally Hill, 4
Matilda Benson, 16
Jane Benson, 14
Nancy Kier, 30
Pleasant Kier, 40
Mahala Clash, 35
Sally Johnson, 30
Grace Hughes, 25
Rhody Bain, 42
Illegible
Sally Bowlin, 16
Sophy Hooper, 60
Eliza Smart, 23
Sophia Smart, 19
Ann Smart, 16
Mary A. Smart, 1
Leah Molock, 40
Milly Molock, 11
Caroline Molock, 6
Henny Chace, 40
Mary A. Chace, 11
Charlotte Chace, 2
Nancy Nutter, 40
Rachel Camper, 30
Jane Camper, 6
Matilda Waters, 25
Caroline Cephus, 15
Nancy Camper, 37
Ann M. Coleman, 8
Lina Cephus, 50
Mary Cephus, 27
Eliza A. Cephus, 9
Betsy A. Cephus, 2

Prissy Hutson, 60
Rose Hutson, 16
Cloe Hutson, 15
Dolly Hutson 17
Ann Stanley, 33
Ann Stanley, 21
Hester A. Mitchell,
    19
Emeline Mitchell, 5
Jane Mitchell, 3
Maria Pinder, 40
Fanny Pinder, 21
Nelly Pinder, 21
Ann M. Pinder, 8
Mary Stanley, 19
Virginia Pinder, 4
Annett Pinder, 2
Milly Thompson, 30
Jane Thompson, 16
Betsy Griffith, 15
Nancy Griffith, 12
Mary Possum, 18
Harriet Hill, 30
Margaret Hill, 1
Maria Hill, 9
Jane Thompson, 35
Araminta Thompson,
    10
Betsy Thompson, 6
Lettia Lee, 14
Silvy Lee, 12
Rose McGlotten, 22
Nancy Cole, 40
Ann Cole, 14
Rebecca Mitchell, 5
Sophia Byus, 45
Charity Byus, 8
Eliza Cromwell, 30
Liny Cromwell, 70
Caroline Cromwell, 4
Liny Cromwell, 2
Rachel Molock, 27
Rose Stanley, 9
Lacey Pinder, 27
Mary A. Pinder, 9
Lotty Pinder, 4
*Mary Lee, 25
Ann Stanley, 15
Ann M. Lee, 4
Sophia Lee, 3
Charlotte Lee, 1
Fanny Lee, 60
Fanny Pinder, 42
Mary Brooks, 70
Arthur Perry, 40

Dorchester County

Delila Perry, 16
Maria Perry, 15
Eliza Perry, 10
Sophia Perry, 6
Jane Perry, 1
Rachel Pinder, 25
Milly Pinder, 3
Lucy Pinder, 2
Emeline Jones, 30
Betsy Grace, 28
Marietta Grace, 9
Milly Grace, 4
Tamer Molock, 58
Leah Molock, 17
Mary Johnson, 13
Henrietta Molock, 12
Lacy Molock, 25
Dido Kemp, 70
Rhoda Ennalls, 35
Mary Pinder, 30
Milly James, 30
Hannah James, 14
Eliza James, 4
Aley James, 1
Camford Jones, 50
Matilda Jones, 17
Betsy Jones, 16
Maria Jones, 13
Milly Jones, 12
Marissa Jones, 6
Sarah Farrah, 70
Nelly Wilson, 30
Jane Stanley, 25
Ibby Stanley, 50
Sophia Stanley, 17
Mahala Wilson, 18
Nancy Fisher, 26
Mary Fisher, 8
Henrietta Fisher, 1
Polly Strawberry, 40
Ann Clash, 19
Loisa Woolford, 16
Leah Strawberry, 14
Aley Bassil, 65
Henny Pinder, 55
Ann Pinder, 16
Maria Pinder, 17
Sally Hollan, 24
Dolly Davis, 5
Nancy Stanley, 24
Kitty Pinder, 60
Hannah Pinder, 17
Ester Pinder, 50
Mary Pinder, 5
Minta Nash, 50

Dido Pinder, 100
Tamay Johnson, 28
Silvy Thompson, 53
Emma Thompson,
    20
Henrietta Thompson,
    17
Eliza Ennalls, 27
Rhoda Pinder, 21
Leah Baltimore, 53
Rachel Pinder, 37
Mary Pinder, 8
Susan Jinkins, 16
Lydia Benson, 40
Aley Woolford, 60
Mary Woolford, 34
Lucy Woolford, 7
Mahala Nash, 11
Jane Nichols, 10
Lucy Woolford, 21
Lina Oney, 19
Jane Camper, 6
Fanny Cephus, 70
Sophia Cephus, 40
Ritty Cephus, 12
Sophia Cephus, 7
*Rose McGlotten, 35
Sarah McGlotten, 5
Leah Waters, 30
Mazy Grace, 22
Fanny Robertson, 40
Ann Robertson, 26
Sophia Robinson, 5
Emeline Robinson, 3
Mary Hughes, 22
Lilly Robertson, 21
Mary Stanley, 29
Eliza A. Stanley, 1
Charlotte Stanley, 30
Elizabeth Stanley, 4
Diner Denwood, 40
Ross Denwood, 22
Polly Denwood, 13
Henny Denwood, 6
Tamer Jackson, 50
Sarah Cooper, 56
Mary Cooper, 16
Mary Ross, 33
Margaret Adams, 15
Jane Keene, 5
Araminta Rikeens, 3
Ann Ross, 20
Priscilla Hardcastle,
    3
Mary Camper, 35

Harriet Camper, 13
Lucinda Camper, 10
Ann M. Camper, 2
Sarah Stiles, 23
Sarah Young, 46
Mary Young, 25
Caroline Young, 16
Mary Young, 16
Elizabeth Young, 1
Lucy Young, 60
Eliza Horsey, 50
Milly Horsey, 23
Mary Horsey, 16
Ailey Stanley, 60
Ailey Stanley, 16
Mary Stanley, 14
Leah Stanley, 10
Prissilla Stanley, 1
Katy Stanley, 25
*Lucy Brisons, 50
Mary Jackson, 25
Eliza Stanley, 19
Mary Stanley, 3
Sally Camper, 25
Katy Murray, 50
Adeline Dutton, 19
Charlotte Murray, 16
Harriet Jolly, 21
Ann M. Jolly, 3
Sarah J. Jolly
Leah Nutter, 60
Susan Murray, 25
Milly Kiah, 37
Sarah Kiah, 11
Adeline Kiah, 4
Jane Kiah, 3
Prissy Haywood, 36
Peggy Haywood, 14
Mary Haywood, 12
Sally Haywood, 7
Violet Haywood, 3
Rebecca Jackson, 35
Milly Jackson, 13
Easter Horsey, 24
Harriet Wrider, 33
Dasha Molock, 13
Ann Molock, 6
Jane Rideout, 2
Elizabeth Rideout, 1
Nancy Jackson, 22
Mary Brittain, 20
Dasha Nichols, 65
Martha Cephus, 70
Fanny Jackson, 80
Minta Woolford, 28

Free African Americans of Maryland - 1832

Nelly Woolford, 34
Harriet Jackson, 21
Ann McColloster, 40
Philis Hall, 65
Ritty Jolly, 24
Ritty Jolly, 2
Ann Price,70
Milcah Chace, 35
Matilda Chace, 5
Milcah Chace
Jinny Cephus, 23
Matilda Cephus, 13
Mary J. Cephus, 10
Milly Brittain, 22
Catherine Brittain, 6
Nancy Human, 30
Nelly Human, 2
Rhoda Molock, 60
Nancy Jolly, 22
Ibby Brittain, 17
Ester Camper, 10
Milly Jolly, 35
Rhoda Jolly, 18
Leah Jolly, 8
Milly Jolly, 4
Ritty Jolly, 1
Sally Hughes, 40
Mary Hughes, 18
Eliza Hughes, 14
Milly Jolly, 25
Susan Jolly, 1
Prissey Parker, 20
Polly Camper
Jane Camper, 20
Elizabeth Camper, 2
Lydia Austin, 30
Harriet Austin, 9
Ally Camper, 50
Ally Camper, 14
Tamer Camper, 14
Hannah Hughes, 70
Minty Sulivane, 45
Rachel Cornish, 35
Lovy Cornish, 16
Mary Cornish, 6
Judy Nichols, 62
Rosetta Nichols, 19
John Thompson, 5
Mary Meir, 40
Louisa Baltimore, 12
Elizabeth Meir, 2
Lovy Perry, 65
Nancy Rideout, 45
Mary A. Rideout, 6
Ann U. Rideout

Ritty Woolford, 30
Effy Woolford, 5
Sissy Ennalls, 60
Prissy Lockerman,
   10
Rhoda Nichols, 25
Emeline Nichols, 8
Matilda Camper, 25
Rachel Cornish, 8
Maria Cornish, 5
Isaac Camper, 1
Mary Camper, 26
Prissy Camper, 60
Judy Jolly, 37
Polly Teacle, 41
Hester A Teacle, 17
Rosetta Teacle, 14
Eliza Pinder, 7
Linea Pinder, 23
Linea Pinder, 30
Mary Barnet, 14
Betsy Barnett, 13
Hannah Barnet, 1
Margaret Barnet, 30
Elizabeth Young, 17
Ritty Homes, 30
Katy Robertson, 50
Affey Sys, 26
Betty Sye
Sarah Sye, 5
Judy Thompson, 7
Tilly Farrow, 30
Milly Farrow, 13
Fanny Sye, 25
Lilly Sye, 6
Mary Sye, 5
Louisa Sys, 25
Milly Sye, 3
Leah Johnson, 45
Silvy Denby, 25
Margaret Young, 60
Maria Stewart, 30
Nancy Pinket, 35
Adeline Henry, 25
Julian Pinkett, 19
Sally Pinkett, 5
Sarah Pinkett, 55
Mary Pinkett, 17
Hannah Young, 55
Nancy Matthews, 45
Siny Waters, 60
Clacy Tilman, 22
Mary J. Tilman, 3
Margery Pinder, 12
Sally Johnson, 44

Eliza Cornish, 22
Ann Johnson, 17
Mary Johnson, 16
Sally Johnson, 7
Emeline Johnson, 4
Elizabeth Johnson, 3
Mary J. Cornish, 2
Margaret Brooks, 35
Sally A. Brooks, 2
Sarah Stanley, 40
Ann Stanley, 8
Prissy Stanley, 15
Sarah Matthews, 30
Sidney Matthews, 5
Violet Hughes, 28
Nancy Hughes, 1
Milky Hughes, 70
Ann McGlotten, 35
Betsy Gray, 35
Sarah A. McGlotten,
   12
Ann M. McGlotten,
   16
Nancy Gray, 4
Louisa Cornish, 4
Pleasant Wing, 40
Emely Wing, 9
Maria J. Wing, 6
Sarah, 40
Rachel Griffin, 18
Phillis Fallin, 65
Charity Todd, 25
Matilda Todd, 40
Matilda Todd, 1
Rachel Todd, 14
Mary Todd, 14
Catherine Travers,
   20
Sally Banks, 50
Maria Travers, 48
Nelly Travers, 24
Rachel Travers, 22
Jane Slocum, 75
Ritty Thomas, 25
Mary Thomas, 4
Dyanner Todd, 60
Margaret Barkley, 10
Margaret Barkley, 45
Phillis Foster, 53
Racchel Foster, 11
Eliza Foster, 19
Jane Meekins, 55
Jane Meekins, 12
Rebecca Todd, 75
Aney Todd, 30

Dorchester County

Mary Todd, 11
Maria Todd, 6
Sarah Todd, 2
Elizabeth Todd, 1
*Selah Brown, 45
Mary Brown, 3
Elizabeth Brown, 7
Darah Mister, 34
Rachel Mister, 40
Ester Griffin, 35
Henny, 30
Susan Griffin, 32
Letty Griffin, 8
Mary Griffin, 15
Jane Sanders, 35
Rachel Todd, 9
Mary Johnson, 25
Catherine Hosper, 40
Eliza Elliott, 8
Hanner Elliott, 7
Nicy Elliott, 5
Phillis Elliott, 1
Rachel Elliott, 35
Zippora Willey, 25
James Willey, 50
Mary Keene, 40
Ritty Griffin, 45
Maria Griffin, 14
Rachel Griffith, 6
Mary Griffith, 16
Matilda Cornish, 45
Phillis Parker, 44
Hester A. Parker, 14
Sarah Parker, 9
James Parker, 4
Mary Hinson, 50
Susan Hinson, 17
Elizabeth Hollan, 25
Mary Hollan, 1
Mary Dickinson, 35
Nancy Dickinson, 13
Mary A. Dickinson, 3
Liddy Elsey, 25
Rosey Bennett, 35
Alecy Camper, 47
Minta Hinson, 45
Ester Bolin, 60
Sarah Johns, 65
Mary Johns, 16
Alcey Johns, 50
Rebecca Quash, 22
Sally Quash, 20
Leah Quash, 14
Mahala Kier, 28
Araminta Kier, 3

Rachel Brown, 37
Rose Kier, 37
Rose Kier, 41
Margaret Blake, 23
Any wing, 50
Nancy Hooper, 25
Ester James, 75
Milly Moore, 20
Sewsy Stevens, 63
Rosey Tripp, 82
Ann Hooper, 24
Mary A. Hooper, 4
Minta Maglaulin, 50
Kitty Manokey, 51
Hannah Jackson, 47
Mary Jackson, 14
Maria Kier, 35
Mahala Lee, 22
Caroline Lee, 4
Eliza Johnson, 25
Jane Kier, 65
Rachel Camper, 53
Jane Phillips, 17
Juda Adams, 65
Rose Cromwell, 33
Elizabeth Cromwell, 16
Dianna Smith, 46
Margaret Anthony, 25
Louisa Anthony, 23
Mary A. Anthony, 20
Henrietta, 19
Eliza Ann Mcgllin, 3
Caroline Anthony, 2
Sarah Anthony, 32
Ann Anthony, 11
Fanny Anthony, 9
Fanny Jackson, 50
Maria Jackson, 12
Eliza Jackson, 12
Priscilla Edmonson, 48
Mahala Stafford, 34
Mary Ann Stafford, 5
Emeline Stafford, 3
Rose Haskins, 27
Susan Wing, 8
Willey Jinkins, 40
Rosey Wing, 58
Charlotte Cornish, 45
Ann Cornish, 1
Eve Fletcher, 87
Susan Walls, 35
Maria Waters, 1

Mary Pennington, 22
Rachel Gather, 50
Harriet LeCompte, 25
Sarah Waters, 25
Jane Stephens, 39
Mary Ann Stephens, 1
Lilley Ward, 65
Nancy Ward, 30
Affey Ward, 25
Dianna Wheatley, 42
Ann Wheatley, 20
Susan Wheatley, 15
Rachel Gannon, 27
Aney Gibson, 40
Caroline Gibson, 14
Elizabeth Gibson, 10
Harriet Gibson, 1
Bender Cook, 50
Mary Cook, 15
Jane Cook, 13
Martha Cook, 3
Margaret Tubman, 45
Jane Camper, 48
Pricilla Allen, 38
Margaret Anthony, 27
Aley Cromwell, 40
Mary Cromwell, 14
Seina Cromwell, 12
Adeline Cromwell, 9
July A. Cromwell, 6
Elizabeth Bayard, 58
Sarah Cooper, 13
Priscilla Hooper, 36
Eliza Hooper, 14
Sally Ann Hooper, 5
Sopha Hooper, 1
Juda Hooper, 11
Lovey Pennington, 40
Caroline Cornish, 30
Jane Cornish, 8
Fanny Cornish, 2
Dorithy Henry, 40
Sarah Boley, 114
Judy Johnson, 60
Sarah Brickle, 22
Harriet Brickle, 19
Mary Brickle, 17
Elizabeth Brickle, 65
Eliza Anthony, 28
Lewey Brown, 40
Elizabeth Brown, 14

Free African Americans of Maryland - 1832

Priscilla Brown, 12
July A. Brown, 6
Rager Cook, 40
Priscilla Brooks, 20
Polly Jinkins, 40
Ann Phillips, 38
Mary Phillips, 20
Amely Phillips, 14
Dafney Macer, 60
Lewey Jinkins, 40
Virginia Jackson, 4
Mary Ann Jackson, 2
Lavander Jinkins, 1
Rachel Nancy, 60
Mazey Nancy, 25
Elizabeth Nancy, 23
Sarah Wilson, 20
Rachel Brickle, 35
Margaret Brickle, 5
Mary Ann Brickle, 3
Elizabeth Brickle, 1
Milly Plater, 42
*Silvy LeCompte, 45
Mary LeCompte, 14
Patience Dixon, 36
Dianna Holland, 8
Liday J. Holland, 4
Harriet Green, 22
Mary Brooks, 25
Sarah Brooks, 7
Sarah Cooper, 30
Ann Maria, 3
Rosey Woolford, 75
Delia Elbert, 60
Mary Cromwell, 30
Eliza Cromwell, 1
Henrietta Mitchell, 55
Hester Mitchell, 22
Harriet Mitchell, 2
Milly Lincos, 58
Susan Lincos, 10
Dinah Cooper, 30
Dafney Dickenson, 50
Hester Foreman, 2
Rosey Barnet, 40
Eliza A. Barnet, 18
Mary I. Barnet, 6
Jane Boley, 50
Jane Banks, 50
Jane Banks, 19
Priscilla Banks, 12
Maria Bright, 36
Silvey Cornish, 31
Selvy Colston, 47

Sophia Keene, 26
Mary A. Keene, 5
Eliza A. Keene, 5
Leene Bishop, 18
Aley Henry, 20
Sarah Bright, 30
Frances C. Henry, 3
Kitty Jane Henry, 2
Elizabeth Henry, 13
Rachel Keene, 30
Rosa A. Keene, 12
Jane Henry, 35
Elizabeth Henry, 18
Hannah Henry, 15
Mary Henry, 25
Affey Cornish, 20
Tish Bell, 35
Elizabeth Dixon, 10
Hester Small, 60
Maria Linthicum, 17
Elizabeth Dixon, 40
Hannah Meekins, 21
Emely Linthicum, 1
Mary Henry, 32
Emeline Henry, 13
Cynta A. Henry, 11
Lucinda J. Henry, 9
Matilda S. Henry, 7
Melvine S. Henry, 6
Caroline D. Henry, 1
Mary A. Henry, 35
Child, 9 months
Hannah Stanley, 32
Rachel Slacum, 35
Elizabeth Retta,32
Margaret Retta, 9
Linars Retta, 8
Elizabeth Retta, 4
Rachel A. B. Retta, 2
Hester Green, 45
Hester A. Green, 10
Eliza Tall, 13
Rachel Keene, 25
Mary Chaplain, 35
Hester Chaplain, 12
Sophia Chaplain, 7
Jane Chaplain, 1
Maria Hythe, 20
Sarah Brooks, 46
Susan Brooks, 15
Roseanna Brooks, 15
Ellen Brooks, 11
*Sophia Mamsey, 15
Harriet Ward, 5
Mary Ward, 3
Elizabeth Ward, 1

Sidney Henry, 48
Loisa Henry, 13
Ann Henry, 3
Gracey Buley, 34
Leah Cornish, 8
Minta Bennet, 30
Rosey Bennet, 11
Rachel Bennet, 7
Minta Bennet, 3
Susan Lockerman, 50
Eliza Lockerman, 23
Silvy Lockerman, 14
Anny Lockerman, 75
Lina Hithe, 75
Grace Hopkins, 55
Milly Camper, 36
Mary Hooper, 17
Eliza J. Keene, 1
Susan Pattison, 22
Barthang Peterkin, 6
Jane Edwards, 25
Dafney Pattison, 49
Lise Pattison, 13
Sarah Pattison, 70
Roseann Lee, 20
Elizabeth Lee, 18
Rennes Travers, 38
Lewinitetia Travers, 17
Mary Travers, 40
Elenor Travers, 30
Lewinitia Travers, 22
Susan Travers, 17
Mary Travers, 4
Amey Creighton, 31
Jane Ross, 44
Lovey Gamby, 44
Hager Gamby, 12
Hester Gamby, 7
*Leah Oglesby, 50
Mary Canady, 5
Emely A. Canady, 2
Mary E. Canady, 1
Taney Johnson, 16
Ann Johnson, 31
Priscilla Johnson, 6
Ann Johnson, 1
Kisiah Johnson, 25
Julian Harress, 18
Easter Stanley, 30
Sophia Stanley, 26
Rachel Stanley, 24
Kisiah Stanley, 22
Jane Stanley, 18
Lovey Gaines, 42

Dorchester County

Elizabeth Gaines, 15
Mary A. Gaines, 11
Lovey A. Gaines, 1
Mary Marine, 12
Betsy Ellis, 25
Flora Ellis, 35
Rhoda Keene, 45
Elizabeth Travers, 23
Emily Broughn, 3
Mary A. Travers, 17
Lillen Tubman, 50
Elizabeth, 25
Mary Gaines, 28
Emely Gaines, 8
Henny Gaines, 5
Margaret Gaines, 2
Tenny Gaines, 5
Margaret Gaines, 2
Tenny Jones, 35
Susan Jones, 21
Elizabeth Jones, 14
Mary Travers, 12
Diner Travers, 9
Caroline Travers, 7
Emeline Travers, 6
Nancy Travers, 4
*Lucretia Travers, 2
Nancy Bishop, 27
Tenny Bishop, 18

Polly Bishop, 16
Tenny Lane, 50
Rachel Lane, 6
Nancy Wilson, 30
Nicey Wilson, 13
Ruth Bennet, 55
Maria Bennet, 16
Vilet Bennet, 27
Elizabeth Bennet, 12
Rosan Buck, 45
Nancy Buck, 18
Sarah Buck, 16
Hannah Buck, 16
Ann Johnson, 28
Delia Peterkin, 18
Christian Hooper, 34
Lewinititia Hooper, 15
Christian Hooper, 8
Mary Hooper, 7
Killey Creighton, 55
Susan Colston, 24
Nancy Colston, 15
Roe Lee, 16
Grace Lee, 48
Tamon Gaines, 55
Fanny Gaines, 25
Sarah Gaines, 23
Ritty Keene, 32

Mahala Ennalls, 30
Mary Ennalls, 5
Lovey Bagly, 29
Hannah Douglass, 50
Sarah Tubb, 76
Hannah Cornish, 21
Anney Cornish, 18
Sophia Cornish, 7
Susan Cornish, 3
Dinar Beli, 29
Ritty Slacum, 65
Mary Marine, 29
Mary A. Marine, 6
Milly Camper, 36
Aley Camper, 28
Rosey Camper, 22
Rachel Camper, 14
Fortin Camper, 12
Tarissa Camper, 1
Minty Sanders, 63
Ritta Camper, 25
Rachel Manoky, 40
Eliza Lane, 18
Ardilly Manokey, 4
Rachel Starkes, 1
Mary Fish, 38
Susan Ennalls, 40
Sarah Ennals, 4

Amount of Females – 1413
Amount of Males – 1478
Total – 2891

Dorchester County to wit
I hereby certify that the foregoing register is a true account of the free People of Colour of County aforesaid as far as they came to my sight and knowledge
August 21 1832 Reuben Tall, Sheriff
■■

Free African Americans of Maryland - 1832

FREDERICK COUNTY

John Matthews, 23
Lynard Towns, 90
William Jones, 60
Jesse Stout, 60
Abraham Stout, 11
John Bell, 9
William Brown, 12
George Brown, 4
Marcus Brown, 3
Augas Fieds, 5
   months
Charles Smith, 39
Absolum Barton, 48
James Barton, 48
James Warren, 45
Henry Thomas 7
Daniel Thomas, 2
Edward Thomas, 4
James Jones, 12
Alexander Jones, 25
Joseph Warren, 10
Joseph Garner, 44
Hiram Hill, 8
Francis Davis, 47
William Tilghman, 16
George J. Thompson,
   6
Mary Stout, 43
Nelly Fields, 43
Tamor Bell, 17
Ellen Bell, 11
Fanny Fields, 34
Charlotte Prout, 22
Linny Barton, 38
Caroline Boman, 11
Angeline Levus, 19
Sarah Thomas, 32
Peggy Goings, 43
Easter Brooks, 75
Catherine Fergerson,
   45
Mary Warren, 25
Rebecca Hill, 28
Marie Warren, 8
Christina Davis, 35
Kitty Krane, 76
Betsy Tilghman, 58
Peggy Ford, 50
Lucy Ford, 6
Rosetta Ford, 3
Rebecca Walker, 30
Lucy Ann Walker,
Catherine Prout, 4

George Goodman, 4
Robert Ford, 7
Adam Watkins, 3
Robert Prout, 12
James Prout, 14
John Prout, 9
Joseph Armstrong, 4
James Armstrong, 1
Jacob Armstrong, 55
Charles Armstrong, 9
William Armstrong, 6
Absolum Goings, 24
George Briscoe, 27
Charles Booth, 26
Alexander Harper, 21
Frederick Hill, 2
Horace Thorn, 8
James W. Thorn, 6
   Limon Thorn, 28
Nathan Williams, 30
Tom Gordon, 32
John Watson, 13
William H. Gordon, 2
John Boon, 10
Tom Boon, 8
Jacob Boon, 1
David Boon, 5
   months
Henry Bladen, 9
William Turbutt, 40
Upton Lee, 4
Sally Prout, 5
Elizabeth Prout, 4
Mackey Smith, 55
Susan Armstrong, 28
Nacky Combs, 35
Mary L. Combs, 7
Ruth Booth, 28
Matilda Thorn, 30
Mary Hill, 16
Matilda Thorn, 16
Catherine Butler, 21
Levina Butler, 60
Mary Gross, 35
Liddy Gross, 17
Lucy Gordon, 38
Catherine Toogood,
   27
Rebecca Watson, 15
Isabella Toogood, 4
Hannah Boon, 25
Nancy Boon, 17
Mary Bladen, 33

Sarah E. Bladen, 33
Mary Tarbutton, 25
Sarah A. Barton, 7
Nelly Lee, 34
Hariet Lee, 7
Miscilla Brown, 29
Mary A. Brown, 8
Henny Brown, 12
Milla Brown, 50
Hariet Brown, 2
Frances Lee, 2
John Brown, 4
Frederick Brown, 2
   months
Nace Jones, 76
William Brown, 10
Marshy Dorsey, 2
Tobert Proby, 12
Ned Galaway, 53
Samuel Tomson, 61
William Prout, 51
William Prout, 3
William Little, 39
Isaac Brown, 22
George Brown, 25
John Gant, 22
Guy Robinson, 75
William Robinson, 23
Robert Cromwell, 12
Thomas Hines, 45
John Riggs, 35
Joseph Murdock, 4
Robert Murdock, 3
Samuel Hammond,
   40
Otho Hammond, 5
Eli Hammond, 3
   Phillip Galaway,
   14
Samuel Neil, 35
Jospeh Neil, 12
Samuel Neil, 3
John H. Williams, 3
Joseph Williams, 30
Harriet Dorsey, 40
Sally Dorsey, 16
Margaret Boon, 7
Mary Boon, 4
Angeline Proby, 16
Sally Wright, 45
Rebecca Galaway, 48
Harriet Galaway, 18
Sally Prout, 47

Kent County

Ann Thompson, 70
*Polly Chase, 33
Kitty Gasaway. 40
Hinny Gasaway, 5
Martha Gasaway, 4
Betsy Gasaway, 8
Nelly Martin, 35
Mary Hawkins, 20
Matilda Hawkins, 4
Rebecca Hawkins, 1
Polly Prout, 26
Harriet Prout, 6
Henrietta, 3
William Rix, 11
Frederick Brown, 3
Thomas Richardson, 3
William Butler, 8
Frank Diggins, 26
Lem Thomas, 45
John Brown, 26
Frederick McGruder, 36
Dennis Myers, 14
Lloyd Myers, 8
James Prout, 38
Jacob Harris, 35
John Thomas, 35
Jesse Comb, 27
James Prout, 35
Charles Jones, 2
Peter Jones, 4 months
John Bowens, 31
John Davis, 58
Thomas Boon, 45
Bill Bently, 40
John Clark, 35
Robert Campbell, 26
Cornelius Campbell, 3
Richard Bender, 80
David Cromwell, 3
Alexander Cromwell, 6
Edward Cromwell, 2
William Higgins, 40
Bill Warren, 15
Jane Prout, 19
Sarah J. Prout, 1 month
Elizabeth Hammond, 50
Molly Hammond, 50
Louisa Wayman, 22
Maria Wayman, 10

Susan Myers, 22
Mary Myers, 20
Airy Myers, 15
Lydia Twogood, 36
Kitty Butler, 74
Eliza Addison, 16
Mary Hammond, 16
Rutha Hopp, 30
Rathel Hall, 35
Becca Cook, 37
Frawny Cook, 7
Aly Peters, 15
Mary J. Conner, 14
Catherine Somson, 24
Catherine Williams, 26
*Kitty Clark, 46
Maria B____, 17
Eliza Weems, 12
Cass A. Thomson, 10
Rachel Jackson, 35
Sarah A, Jackson, 3
Sarah Briscoe, 50
George Davis, 31
Robert Tilghman, 80
Thomas Larkins, 62
Joseph Lewes, 27
William J. ___, 6
John H. ___, 3
Samuel Weeks, 40
William Gaither, 40
Abraham Gaither, 1
Levin Thomas, 40
Daniel Thomas, 11
George Thomas, 2 months
Benjamin Smith, 23
George Williams, 34
John Murdock, 34
John Brown, 33
Phillip Nelson, 19
William Neely, 28
William, Bucks, 25
Samuel Neil, 34
Joseph Neil, 8
Ben Brown, 35
Robert ____, 11
John Watson, 10
William Higins, 50
Allen Watkins, 2
Ezekial Rine, 25
Perry Rideout, 9
Daniel Dorsey, 28
Henry Clark, 26
John Chambers, 12

Nancy Briscoe, 23
Maria Briscoe, 22
Mary Harper, 41
Joice Norris, 80
Maria Chester, 40
Linda Gaither, 11
Alice Harper, 50
Margaret Gray, 23
Maria Hillery, 2
Sarah Briscoe, 55
Maria Briscoe, 25
Maria Armstrong, 30
Mary James, 5
Susan Perdy, 35
Rachel Tyler, 35
Nancy Ford, 17
Ann Prout, 21
Harriet Castle, 25
Jane Williams, 10
Mary Holiday, 75
Kitty Jones, 30
Cassa Mitchell, 40
Elizabeth Thomson, 13
Fanny Gross, 55
Araminta Brooks, 30
*Charlotte Campbell, 26
Caroline Campbell, 9
Cassa Campbell, 5
Nelly Campbell, 7
Catherine Campbell, 1
Betty Cromwell, 29
Thomas Ford, 10
Henry Ford, 15
Dick Job, 70
William Brown, 10
Marcus Brown, 3
George Brown, 8
Levi Rideout, 19
George Davis, 31
John Prout, 22
Henry Spriggs, 50
Samuel Deal, 67
Thomas Jones, 35
John Goodman, 30
John Thomas, 25
Isaac Saint, 12
Alexander Jones, 21
James Saint, 44
Moses Saint, 5
John Saint, 7
Joseph Saint, 2
Isaac Prout, 28
Abraham Adam, 22

Free African Americans of Maryland - 1832

Samuel Contee, 23
Samuel Jocks, 24
Jim Weems, 8
John Weems, 1
Jim Weems, 35
Eliza Brown, 23
Thomas Richardson, 50
William H. Barnes, 4
Harriet Cromwell, 1
Polly Grass, 32
Milla Turner, 35
Isabella Toogood, 3
Lilly Carroll, 3
Jane Redden, 19
Lilly Tilghman, 88
Rachel Larkins, 47
Phebe Severes, 19
Sophia Severe, 8 months
Esther Severes, 75
Rebecca Gaither, 38
Charlotte Thomas, 35
Maria Williams, 23
Judy Luber, 30
Jane Addison, 17
Becca Smith, 45
Jane Bowens, 18
Anna Boon, 30
Cecillia Brown, 22
Sally Dorsey, 17
Rachel Hall, 13
Kitty Toogood, 25
Else Ritchie, 26
Sarah Richardson, 25
Amelia Back, 60
Mary Russell, 26
*Jane Taylor, 30
Nancy Pinkney, 50
Jane Higgins, 40
Becca Watkins, 24
Harry Burgess, 30
Nelson Davis, 25
Jim Bolen, 25
Lewis Brown, 2
Isaac Carr, 8
Lloyd Goodman, 23
Harry Butler, 35
Ephraim Herd, 19
John Butler, 23
Mason Booth, 22
Henry Butler, 30
Richard Goodman, 35

Joseph Goodman, 2
Joshua Brooks, 40
Sampson Gross, 56
Ben James, 25
Wilson Riggs, 18
James Harper, 47
Ely Butler, 10
John Butler, 7
Augustus Butler, 4
Zack Briscoe, 62
Caleb Lawson, 45
Edward Robinson, 1
William H. Lawson, 2
John Riggs, 26
William Riggs, 29
Hanson Riggs, 10
George Riggs, 20
Lucy Watkins, 6
Mary Armstrong, 26
Mary Campbell, 35
Kitty Goiigs, 22
Minta Culbert, 35
Lethy A. Martin, 18
Nancy Ford, 19
Fanny Jonson, 2
Fanny Fields, 35
Matilda Smith, 40
Mary Smith, 17
Tamor Spriggs, 50
Jane Deal, 60
Polly Goodman, 37
Margaret Goodman, 8
Ellen Thomas, 23
Sarah A. Pierson, 25
Elizabeth Saint, 34
Indiana Saint, 4
Margaret Goings, 14
Charity Prout, 30
Rachel Gaither, 8
Anna Contee, 17
Lavina Jacks, 24
Eliza Jacks, 2
Caroline Jacks, 1
Mary Goings, 16
Betsy Weems, 60
Dina Weems, 35
Ann Weems, 9
Leka Jackson, 35
*John Riggs, 6
Edward Miles, 27
Josiah Cook, 40
Josiah Cook, 4
Joseph Holmes, 70
Bill Younger, 40
Jeffry Younger, 60

Thomas Boon, 30
Stephen Smith, 50
___ Russell, 18
James Russell, 13
John Smith, 8
Helton Dutton, 27
James Roades, 55
Henry Spriggs, 60
James Spriggs, 45
James Noland, 30
Harry Noland, 35
Rice, Norman, 75
John Locks, 3
Joseph Bett, 8
Robert Camel, 30
John Camel, 13
Wilson Camel, 8
Levy Mahomet, 35
Isaiah Mahomet, 8
Edward Mahomet, 3
Robert Bush, 40
Dina M. Jackson, 7
Mary J. Jackson, 9
Jane ___, 40
Ann Richardson, 60
Norah Barnes, 28
Rachel Barnes, 8
Susan Barnes, 40
Ann Brown, 9
Ellen Brown, 7
Margaret Galaway, 20
Maria Galaway, 2
Debby Jackson, 42
Sarah A. Jackson, 8
Ellen Jackson, 1
Amia Goodman, 35
Rachel Brooks, 20
Margaret Boon, 8
Minta Harper, 50
Linna Butler, 35
Mary A. Butler, 14
Betty Butler, 3
Cecelia Butler, 6
Elizabeth Butler, 4
Ellen Ledwick, 25
Anna Ledgewick, 2
Linna Norris, 12
Betty Briscoe, 65
Cecilla Butler, 10
Rochall Lawson, 4
Sam Weeks, 30
Len Nairs, 45
William Nairs, 10
*Ben Malone, 24
Charles Bell, 24

Kent County

Lewis Bell, 2
John Leekins, 25
Peter Leekins, 60
Henry Bell, 19
Robert Bishop, 30
Anthony Bishop, 50
Frank Bowen, 33
Nace Gibbs, 29
Enoch Jenkins, 15
Edward Penn, 4
Henry Jenkins, 1
James Fuly, 80
Joshua Clark, 28
Enoch Little, 40
R. James Liles, 19
P. James Liles, 17
Elijah Liles, 13
Nelson Liles, 12
Samuel Lewes, 43
Jacob Lewes, 35
William Long, 6
William Devan, 76
Evan Devan, 20
Benjamin Devan, 14
Wesley Devan, 8
John Swan, 44
Hariet Lawson, 38
Cassa Robinson, 33
Amy Riggs, 13
Betsy Riggs, 21
Eliza Riggs, 24
Eliza Riggs, 28
Mary A. Riggs, 4
Caroline Riggs, 2
Margaret Cook, 19
Esther Holmes, 55
Betsy Boon, 35
Levia Smith, 45
Harriet Duton, 18
Detsy Roades, 60
Rachel Norman, 25
Lydia Locks, 30
Julia Locks, 6
Alice Belt, 24
Eliza Belt, 14
Barbara Campbell, 30
Amy Campbell, 10
Barbara Campbell, 1
Charlotte Norris, 23
Sylva Rick_, 100
Rose Whitton. 70
Nahomy Whitton, 35
Serena Mahomet, 28
Margaret Mahomet, 6

Jane Mahomet, 5
Mary Mahomet, 1
Jerry Majors, 54
Lloyd Myers, 17
John Myers, 11
William Myers, 9
Mashack Myers, 6
*Abraham Cole, 23
James Coles, 2
Nathan Miles, 36
John Corsy, 40
John Miles, 8
Cyrus Waters, 3
Benjamin Males, 10
Wesley Waters, 6
William Waters, 2
Thomas Day, 60
Henry Day, 32
Samuel Brown, 33
James Davis, 10
Samuel Lewis, 45
William Davis, 40
Nathaniel Cosly, 4
William Cosly, 2
Simon Busher, 60
Richard Todd, 20
James Lax, 29
Owen Todd, 20
Dennis Todd, 23
Dennis Lax, 3
Richard Lax, 3
Joseph Waters, 47
Stephen Anthony, 50
Susan Ennis, 60
Rachael Bishop, 65
Betsy Weeks, 30
Jane Ramsay, 65
Sophia Ramsey, 60
Sasan Laws, 40
*Henrietta Malone, 24
Ellenor Bell, 22
Amira Leekins, 10
Henny Leakins, 60
Susan Williams, 80
Charity Johnson, 45
Lena Jenkins, 19
Mary Jenkins, 19
Charity Roberts, 2
Eliza Tub, 50
Maria Dickerson, 39
Ann Todd, 2
Rachel Little, 39
Caroline Liles, 11
Louisa Liles, 10
Emily Little, 3

Ann L. Little, 2
Lydia Bowens, 80
Martha Liles, 7
Esther Anthony, 56
Ann Lewis, 34
Kitty Lewis, 25
Eliza Lewis, 16
Peter Swales, 2
James Swales, 2
James Davidson, 35
James Garret, 28
Robert Johnson, 60
John Lawrence , 44
James Lawrence, 12
*_____ Bias, 40
Israel Bias, 12
_____ Bias, 7
Edward Bias, 4
Tom Bias, 1
James Emmett, 60
Abram Coale, 50
Phillip Burgess, 48
Samuel Washington, 55
Benjamin Matthews, 40
Benjamin James, 4
Samuel Thomas, 26
Solomon Penn, 24
John Valentine, 54
Emanuel Valentine, 2
Harrison Cosley, 6
Isreal Cosley, 2
_____ Davis, 11
James Buchanan, 5
James Howard, 3
David Hill, 38
James Hill, 5
Mary James, 9
Eliza James, 1
Emily James, 2
Ann Penn, 2
Lydia De____, 50
Mary De___, 10
Margaret Swan, 38
Sarah Swan, 18
Martha Swan, 17
Eliza Swan, 8
Margaret Swan, 1
Sarah Myers, 15
Eliza Myers, 14
___ Myers, 6
Harriet Grace, 17
Caty Corsey, 80
Ann Price, 40

Free African Americans of Maryland - 1832

Elizabeth Miles, 12
Kitty Miles, 3
Laura Waters, 33
Kity Waters, 8
J Waters, 5
Susan Waters, 1
Katy Day, 76
Maranda Brown, 22
Dolly Johnson, 20
Martha Johnson, 1
Susan Davis, 32
Sarah Davis, 10
John Tubman, 54
Liza Tubman, 23
James Tubman, 18
William Tubman, 7
George Mulberry, 20
Jerry Mulberry, 15
Sam Armstrong, 41
Bill Chambers, 8
Sam Chambers, 4
David Fergerson, 11
Elias Fergerson, 9
Otho Fergerson, 7
Anthony Hill, 84
John Hill, 40
Lewis Hill, 38
William Hill, 33
Anthony Hill, 26
___ Hill, 24
Joshua Bennett, 3
_____ Hill, 5
Sam ___, 45
Elias George, 25
Acox James, 16
Thomas Jones, 3
James H. Jones, 3
Bennett Fletcher, 20
Cato ___, 44
Bernard Brown, 75
Tom Fletcher, 70
Charles Fletcher, 70
Jane Davis, 8
Eliza Davis, 6
Ann Davis
Mary Roberts, 12
Lydia Davis, 38
Susan Coates, 19
Minta Davis, 21
___ Warfield, 30
Ann Cosley, 27
Rebecca Cosley, 6
_____ Todd, 60
Henrietta Todd, 23
Hager Waters, 48
___ Armstrong, 60

___ Hill, 33
Anthony Hill, 26
Stephen Hill, 24
Joshua Bennett, 3
___ Hill, 5
Tom ___, 45
Elias George, 25
____ James, 16
Thomas Jones, 3
James H. Jones, 3
Bennett Fletcher, 20
Cato ___, 44
Bernard Brown, 75
Tom Fletcher, 70
Charles Fletcher, 70
Jane Davis, 8
Eliza Davis, 6
Henny Davis, 40
Ann Davis
Mary Roberts, 12
Lydia Davis, 38
Susan Waters, 19
Minta Davis, 21
Katy Warfield, 30
Ann Cosley, 27
Rebecca Cosley, 6
Mary ___, 19
____ Todd, 6
Henrietta Todd, 23
Hager Waters, 18
Illegible
Illegible
Illegible
Illegible
*Maria Cosley, 40
Mary Johnson, 45
Kitty Johnson, 12
Caroline Johnson, 8
Ann Johnson, 4
Eliza Lawrence, 35
Ann Lawrence, 4
___ Lawrence, 8
Hager Lawrence, 59
James Brown, 2
Tom Brown, 12
John Brown, 6
Samuel ___, 11
Leonard Davis, 35
Jim Howard, 45
Phillip Howard, 5
Charles Hall, 62
Elijah Hopewell, 50
William ___, 20
Jack Johnson, 37
John Lee, 38
John Lee, 9

___ Lee, 6
___ James, 35
Isaac Johnson, 40
___ Johnson, 4
Charles ___, 22
John H. Johnson, 5
Charles H. Jones, 10
Henry ___, 18
Illegible
___ Sparks, 48
___ Sparks, 7
___ Sparks, 4
Perry Sparks, 25
Tom George, 25
Benjamin Miller, 25
Robert Brown, 55
Emeline Brown, 2
Sam Walker, 38
Eleanor ___, 37
___ Bennett, 45
Mary ___, 24
Ann ___
Harriet ___, 9
Ester Matthews, 45
Eliza ___, 60
Eliza ___, 22
Eliza Cr___, 25
Ester Ann Larkins, 9
Charlotte Denn, 4
Eliza Cosley, 4
Ann Buchanan, 2
Bety Hill, 55
Mary Hill, 7
Ann Hill, 4
Maria Hill, 1
___ Fraling, 38
Mary Fraling, 2
Harriet Fraling, 3
Elizabeth Fraling, 8
Martha Fraling, 5
Maria Fraling, 18
Hannah Mulberry, 43
Eliza Mulberry, 22
Sarah Mulberry, 12
Elizabeth Mulberry, 1
Rebecca Armstrong, 39
Sarah Chambers, 6
Mary Chambers, 2
Rebecca Stewart, 7
E_ Walker, 35
George Molone, 18
John Harrison, 44
Robert Johnson, 35

83

Kent County

James Thompson, 22
Lewes Thompson, 18
James Thompson, 8
John Thompson, 3
Lewis Stevens, 21
Leo Addison, 11
William Orm, 25
John Riggs, 26
Thomas Buckingham, 15
William Buckingham, 16
William Devan, 26
James Devan, 16
Daniel Devan, 28
Nelson Devan, 24
Benjamin Swan, 34
Paul Williams, 46
Affy Williams, 48
Stephen Rodes, 7
Mary Rodes, 5
John Toogood, 2
Abram Shriver, 14
Jacob Black, 27
Joseph Hanna, 55
Joseph Hanna, 5
George Jackson, 16
Emanuel H___, 22
William Harper, 54
Margaret Fergerson, 40
*Josephine Freeman, 99
Mary Fergerson, 6
Illegible
Anna ___, 1
Nelly Barrett, 45
Mary Hill, 74
Mary Hill, 31
Priscilla Hill, 28
Mary ___, 7
_____ Rideout, 2
Harriet Hill, 25
Mary Hill, 3
Illegible
Catherine ___, 38
Dolly Jones, 45
Mary Jones, 15
S___ Jones, 12
Catherine Jones, 14
_____ Jones, 10
Mary Jones, 8
___ Jones, 5
___, Jones, 2
Diana Jones, 40

___ Bell, 40
___ Bell, 14
___ Ward, 55
Sarah Fletcher, 69
Nelly ___, 11
Pricilla Brown, 5
Elizabeth Brown, 1
Ann ___, 45
Rizza Myers, 7
Susan Lawrence, 40
Catherine Howard, 3
Maria Lee, 22
A___ Lee
Minta Johnson, 39
Caroline Johnson, 5
Laura Johnson, 3
Elender Jones, 8
Rachel ___, 45
Ann ___, 2
Maria Joice, 8
Henrieta Goins, 33
Malinda ___, 13
Elander Brown, 55
Mary Brown, 25
Jenett Harrison, 46
Ann Harrison, 26
Betsy ____, 40
Mary Ann Thompson, 17
Henrietta Thompson, 10
Affey Thompson, 12
Artha _ Thompson, 7
Lucy Rollings, 24
Serena Devan, 27
Mary A Devan, 3
Elizabeth Devan, 3
Elizabeth Swann, 7
Nancy Brooks, 35
Mary Toogood, 28
Sally Good, 5
Susan Ott, 12
Sarah Ott, 5
Lucinda Black, 20
Eliza Black, 2
Elizabeth Black, 55
Hannah Ott, 45
Lydia Brooks, 16
Bal Selimer, 17
Sarah Curtis, 18
Elizabeth Harper, 53
Dennis Harper, 17
Lucy A. Harper, 13
Joseph Harper, 60
Henry Harper, 56
Jacob Wayman, 45

Clarissa Wayman, 46
Polly Rollings, 27
Maria Jane, 4
Henry Rollings, 1 month
Edward Rocker, 27
George Goings, 42
Susan Goings, 35
Ellen Goings, 16
Hillery Goings, 15
Caroline Goings, 14
Caroline Goings, 13
Robert Goings, 11
James Goings, 8
Robert Goings, 6
Mary Goings, 5
Ruth Goings, 2
Godfrey Swan, 70
Henry Shorter, 42
Rodian Shorter, 25
John William Shorter, 9
Benjamin Henry, 5
James Henry, 3
William Ormes, 23
Wesley Dunn, 15
Sam Plumer, 14
Reuben Johnson, 15
Nicholas Rubson, 10
John Green, 25
Clarissa Only, 55
Elizabeth Only, 13
Stephen Only, 15
Fender Smith, 50
July Francis, 52
Margaret L. Snyder, 14
Rachel Goings, 45
Elizabeth Scott, 22
Jane Plater, 75
Lucy Daffin, 37
Mary E. Daffin, 9
William H. Daffin, 4
Nancy A. Ring, 27
Caroline Francis, 11
Julian Ring, 6
James Ring, 4
Francis Wheter, 44
Mary Wheter, 32
Jim Wheter, 14
Harriet Wheter, 13
Mary A. Wheter, 11
Caroline Wheter, 8
John F. Wheter, 5
Samuel Wheter, 3

Free African Americans of Maryland - 1832

Harris Wheter, 6
Eliza Porter, 30
Ann Porter, 14
Harrison, 8
Lewis Porter, 6
Cornelia Porter, 4
Malinda Porter, 3
Philis Hopewell, 60
William Baker, 52
Eleisa Baker, 50
Tom Gale, 74
Susan Walker, 20
Sam Walker, 25
Anna Walker, 1
Sam Overlton, 58
Lucy Overlton, 35
William Overlton, 23
Sally A, Ovelton, 18
Caleb Ovelton, 16
John H. Ovelton, 14
Sam E. Mole, 12
Mary E. Mole, 9
Jim P. Mole, 4
Nelly D. Brooks, 35
Hanny Dorsey, 22
Henry Dorsey, 23
Charlotte A. Dorsey,
     6 months
Adelia Brooks, 13
Margaret Brooks, 8
Susan Brooks, 5
Liza Brooks, 6
     months
Jim Mole, 20
Lucy Black, 32
Pol Brooks, 17
Henry Brooks, 15
Lucy Nicholson, 23
Sam Lasker, 24
Charles Bell, 25
Clenda Bell, 22
Lewes Bell, 1
Henson Johnson, 7
Henry Bell, 18
John Bell, 14
Robert Smothers, 40
Polly Smothers, 35
Henson Smothers7
William Smothers, 7
Mary Smothers, 6
Robert Smothers, 4
John Smothers, 3
Lemanda Smothers,
     2
Jacob Smothers, 1
William Goings, 30

Mariah Goings, 21
Lewes Goings, 1
Charles Bell, 40
Charles Jones, 41
Tom Bucker, 65
Nathan Rosiar, 22
Benn Russale, 28
Sam Lasker, 23
:Louisa Nichols, 23
Anthony Bowens, 67
Agnes Bowens, 60
Henrietta Bowens,
     22
Andrew Bowens, 24
Lidia Bowens, 20
Gabriel Briscoe, 45
Clarissa Briscoe, 39
William Briscoe, 14
Sebastian, Briscoe,
     11
Ann Briscoe, 9
James Briscoe, 7
*Minta ___, 15
Nancy Savoy, 13
Missa Peach, 37
Mary Peach, 14
Susan Peach, 9
Debby Peach, 7
Hannah Peach, 3
___ Mitchell, 45
Emeline Mitchell, 16
Lydia Mitchell, 11
Illegible
___ Slater, 2
Thomas Simpson, 2
William Dorsey, 45
William Dorsey, 7
Isaac Dodson, 50
___ Toogood, 25
Benjamin Toogood,
     45
Augustus Toogood,
     12
John Howard, 55
__ Mason, 22
Bob ___, 35
Elias Davis, 40
Grafton Davis, 4
Perry ___, 18
Edward Howard, 60
Joshua Howard, 25
Henry Thomas, 30
Ephriam Hill, 11
Samuel Hill, 7
Otho Jenkins, 25
John Green, 14

Elias Green, 16
Edward Pearman, 23
Eliza Thomas, 22
Elizabeth A. Thomas,
     1
Ruth Jones, 35
Esther Fisher, 45
Maria Fisher
Betsy Harris, 35
Katy Harris, 12
Illegible, 20
Harriet Slater, 21
Millie Slater, 22
Margaret Simpson,
     25
_____ Simpson, 6
Harriet Simpson, 4
Polly Jones, 60
Katy Jones, 60
Susy Richardson, 50
Mary Dorsey, 12
Caroline Dorsey, 8
Susy Dorsey, 3
Jane Toogood, 45
Nelly Howard, 50
Eliza Mason, 35
Eliza Mason, 2
James Waters, 41
John Waters, 14
James Waters, 1
John _____, 33
Thomas Buchanan,
     50
Jeremiah Slater, 50
Richard Mason, 16
Richard Thomas, 4
H ___ Slater, 8
Edward Matthews,
     26
Philip Matthews, 2
Tom Waters, 7
Dennis Waters, 5
Illegible
Amos Valentine, 12
_____ Valentine, 2
Richard Dorsey, 41
Elisha Hall, 30
Nace Stewart, 30
Samuel Brown, 60
Edward Brown, 33
John Brown, 24
Rachel ___, 25
Ann _____, 2
Jane Davis, 35
Mary A. Davis, 1
Mary Howard, 55

Kent County

Hester Howard, 30
Charlotte Travers, 25
___ Travers, 5
Rachel Hill, 35
Mary Ann Hill, 4
William Hill, 5
Mary Jones, 100
Drusilla Green, 38
Louisa Green, 8
Marianna Pearman, 22
Marietta Waters, 30
Mary ___, 28
Martha Matthews, 28
Elizabeth Waters, 4
M Juricks, 6
Margaret Juricks, 2
Ann Valentine, 30
Rachel Dorsey, 40
Mary Dorsey, 11
Ruth Dorsey, 9
Susan Dorsey, 4
Milton Edwards, 10
James Edwards, 1
Samuel ___, 65
David ___, 15
Jerry Fisher, 45
Samuel Johnson, 35
William Frances, 35
John Howard, 50
Greenberry Barton, 55
James Barton, 18
William Williams, 6
Cato Adams, 60
Adam Adams, 16
Mathias Carroll, 36
Samuel Carroll, 12
Braxton Carroll, 14
William Snowden, 43
Perry Snowden, 16
Samuel Snowden, 13
Richard Snowden, 7
___ Snowden, 1
Thomas Jones, 43
David Jones, 28
Charles Thomas, 40
Perry Thomas 12
___ Stewart, 50
Temperance Brown, 50
___ Brown, 31
Susan Brown, 28
Ann Brown, 28
Henny Edwards, 40
Susan Edwards, 7

Mary Edwards, 2
Milla ___, 55
Charlotte Fisher, 52
Rachel Fisher, 9
Ann Thomas, 40
Judy Howard, 45
Fanny Howard, 70
Betsy Howard, 40
Harriet Barton, 25
B__ Quicks, 21
Rachel Gaither, 11
Lucy Adams, 55
Miranda Adams, 14
Lucy Carole, 33
Louisa Carroll, 5
Helen Carrol, 1
Eliza Snowden, 32
Charlotte James, 32
Francis Gant, 55
William Gant, 7
Edward Gant, 5
George Cook, 60
Issac Lansel, 23
Lamuel Lansel, 1
John Lansel, 2
Thomas Dunmark, 45
H__ Dunmark, 7
Sappington Dunmark, 3
Henry Butler, 75
Jerry Butler, 25
John Butler, 25
Henry Butler, 30
Ben Johnson, 50
Minerva Jones, 13
Deborah Jones, 11
Fancy Jones, 8
Eliza Jones, 1
Elizabeth Jones, 3
Rebecca Holmes, 50
Lydia Thomas, 33
Louisa Thomas, 16
Eliza Thomas, 14
Nancy Thomas, 15
Debby Edwards, 50
Lydia Rice, 11
Susan Tyler, 33
Nancy Gant, 50
Esther Tyler, 58
Harriet Gant, 33
Ara Lansel, 20
Maria Dunmark, 32
Rachel Dunmark, 13
Maria Dunmark, 11
Koellen Dunmark, 3

Fanny Dunmark, 1
Caty Butler, 55
Millie Coats, 37
Harriet Coats, 45
Charlatta Johnson, 35
James Matthews, 35
Charles Pearman, 50
Edward Pearman, 5
Richard H. Pearman, 52
Grafton Coleman, 22
Isaac Stewart, 30
Moses Stewart, 8
John Stewart, 2
Samuel ___, 25
John ___, 25
Illegible
Charles T__, 63
Robert ___, 20
Jacob ___, 22
Charles ___, 14
Thomas ___, 6
William Russell, 7
Peter Jackson, 45
John Armstrong, 60
Perry Jackson, 18
Henry Jackson, 14
Washington Jackson 5
Charles A. Jackson, 2
William Carroll, 35
Thomas ___, 68
Henry Smith, 45
Sarah Pearman, 45
Sarah Ann Pearman, 18
Elizabeth Pearman, 10
Harriet Calowill, 18
Martha Callowill, 1
Rachel Procter, 14
Tobetha Proctor, 4
Sarah Stevenson, 30
Sophia Stevenson, 10
Darcus Stevenson, 6
Milenda Stevenson, 4
Elizabeth Cromwell, 50
Maria Mander, 20
Ann Mander, 17
Eliza Mander, 14
Cassa Mander, 60
Marissa Tilman, 23

Free African Americans of Maryland - 1832

Pegga Tilman, 22
Adelia Tilman, 18
Caroline Tilman
Betty ___, 60
Jenny Jackson, 30
Elizabeth Jackson, 15
Mary Jackson, 8
Emeline Jackson, 5
Henrietta Jackson, 4
Polly Jackson, 30
Thomas Forman, 30
Lewis Bond, 25
William Dorsey, 25
Nace Hopkins, 40
James Lucas, 43
William Lucas, 5
Arthur Solomon, 25
Clem Chaney, 57
William Maritt, 60
Nathan Maritt
Alexander Barbour, 3
Joseph Barber, 2
___ Norris, 49
Benjamin Jones, 28
Joseph James, 4
Abram L___, 55
George Laine, 10
Thomas Norris, 35
Thomas Norris, 2
John Hubbard, 1
Thomas Graham, 7
Robert Warner, 50
Illegible
Thomas Adams, 18
John Addison, 13
Ann Carroll, 2
Henry Johnson, 40
Nancy Green, 5
Rachel Solomon, 35
Susan Smith, 51
Sarah M Pearman, 8
Lucy Marritt, 50
Susan Marritt, 28
Henrietta Jones, 25
Mary Deane, 33
Susan Lawson, 45
Jane Norris, 30
Jane Humbird, 30
Susan Jones, 22
Margaret Jones, 1
Polly Prout, 40
Ellen Graham, 4
Mary Graham, 3
Patty Graham, 2

Ann Graham, 12
Hetty Farmer, 38
Amelia Farmer, 28
Priscilla Farmer, 10
Harry Hardman, 45
Thomas ___, 18
Jacob Waters, 65
Jonas Cromwell, 35
George Gowings, 41
John Goings, 13
Robert Gowings, 9
James W. Goings, 7
John Goings, 53
George W. Goings, 1
Thomas Gasaway, 53
Robert Gasaway, 11
Alfred Gasaway, 9
James Gasaway, 5
Godfrey Swan, 70
John Swan, 35
*Ben Swan, 28
Jacob Swan, 24
John Swan, 7
Ben Swan, 5
John Lee, 18
Alexander Jackson, 11
Perry Jackson, 9
George Jackson, 5
Henry Jackson, 2
Henry Shorter, 35
Sophia Li___, 30
Cassandra Norman, 55
Elizabeth Gull, 17
Henry Jones, 6
Emeline Jones, 6
Elizabeth Addison, 19
Nancy Addison, 21
Louisa Hardman, 38
Mary A. Goings, 7
Maria Robinson, 40
Nancy Cromwell, 25
___ Goings, 52
Martha Goings, 17
Caroline A. Goings, 11
Mary E. Goings, 5
Ruth A. Goings, 2
Elizabeth Goings, 28
Elisabeth Goings, 3
Mary Goings, 5
Closy Gasaway, 35
Caroline Gasaway, 39

Polly Swan, 75
Rody Swan, 17
Ellen Jackson, 33
Hannah Jackson, 7
George Scott, 37
Ben Brown, 27
James Goodwin, 25
Thomas Martin, 22
Henry Duffin, 3
James King, 4
Henry Rollins, 1
Thomas Aires, 53
William Gross, 7
Charles Gross, 5
Enoch Aires, 25
Thomas Aires, 25
John Aires, 13
William Aires, 1
Mason Aires, 11
Basil Duffin, 38
Jacob Scroggins, 50
Nelson Scroggons, 22
Joshua Scroggins, 19
John Contes, 26
Henry Contes, 2
Thomas Diggs, 9
James Diggs, 6
Wesley Diggs, 1
Betsy Scott, 24
Nancy Scott, 1
Lucy Duffin, 36
Nancy King, 27
Polly Rollins, 27
Mary Duffin, 7
Caroline King, 13
Judy King, 7
Maria Rollins, 4
Polly Gross, 36
Clara Aires, 45
Eliza Duffin, 23
Patience Aires, 17
Ellen Aires, 5
Sarah Duffin, 1
Rachel Scroggins, 45
Susan Contes, 30
Eliza Scroggins, 19
Martha Scroggins, 1
Darcus Diggs, 38
Betsy Coates, 3
Lydia Everett, 75
Serena Runnels, 57
Charles Scroggins, 68
Hannah Scroggins, 61

Kent County

Peter Clark, 42
Sally Clark, 35
Susan Clark, 11
Mary Clark, 9
Lucy Clark, 7
Phillip Clark, 3
Ann Clark, 2
Julia Matthews, 18
James Coates, 45
Polly Coates, 46
John Coates, 18
Augusta Coates, 16
Thomas Coates, 12
Badel Coates, 8
Mary Brown, 7
William Watson, 32
Lucy Watson, 19
John Hopkins, 45
Polly Hopkins, 58
Mary Hopkins, 15
Nathan Colbert, 33
Maria Colbert, 27
Susan Colbert, 2
Lewes Hill, 50
Susan Hill, 50
Agnes Hill, 11
Isaac Sandes, 39
Lucy Sandes, 25
Peter Butler, 55
Matthew Brister, 54
Elizabeth Brister, 25
William Smith, 12
Hester Smith, 10
Joshua Jenifer, 58
Matilda Jenifer, 51
John Coale, 51
Prissa Coale, 42
Tom Coale, 10
Margaret Coale, 8
David Sedan, 45
Rachel Sedan, 45
John Sedan, 17
Jesse Sedan, 14
David Sedan, 10
William Sedan, 8
Sarah Sedan, 6
Mary Sedan, 4
John Green, 42
Betsy Green, 68
William Green, 10
David Brin, 76
William Brin, 13
Sarah A, Brin, 8
Sussanna Brin, 3
Elias Robinson, 3

Charlotte Tilghman, 33
Ann Cook, 25
Amos Butler, 40
Mary Butler, 24
Cassa Black, 45
Eli Scott, 48
Henry Matthews, 33
Ellen Matthews, 51
Jacob Lightner, 38
Betsy Howard, 18
Harriett Brin, 36
James Brin, 38
George Corsey, 80
Mary Corsey, 42
Simpson Williams, 30
Betsy Laway, 44
Maria Laway, 10
William Laway, 8
Eliza Jobes, 37
George Jobes, 15
Ellen Jobes, 13
William Jobes, 11
Charles Jobes, 9
Margaret Jobes, 7
Jerry Jobes, 3
Nicholas Jobes, 1
Betty Jones, 36
Louisa Mathews, 30
James Mathews, 28
Ben Mathews, 40
Nicholas Mathews, 27
Jerry Mathews, 21
Henry Mathews, 19
*Richard Hall, 22
Sam Mathews, 17
Louisa Mathews, 14
Elizabeth Mathews, 17
Dennis Mathews, 3
Jemina Mathews, 2
William H. Mathews, 1
Charlotte White, 33
Charles Pye, 36
Eliza Pye, 26
Rachael Pye, 22
Nicholas White, 40
Charity White, 30
Sarah J. White, 5
Edward Brown, 55
Rebecca Brown, 36
Ephraim Brown, 8
Susan Brown, 6

Mary Brown, 4
James Brown, 2
Lloyd Moles, 48
Macky Moles, 40
Jenny Moles, 7
Patrick Moles, 5
John Moles, 3
John Brooks, 50
Ann Brooks, 45
David Woodyear, 33
Dan Woodyear, 24
Isaac Bruce, 28
Miranda Bruce, 26
Alfred Bruce, 24
Uriah Bruce, 2
Sarah A. Bruce, 6
Hezekiah Griffith, 35
Lenia Griffith, 33
John Griffith, 12
Susan Griffith, 8
Jerry Matthews, 27
Samuel Key, 64
Mass Key, 63
James Engram, 12
Charity Engram,48
Sam Engram, 16
Mary Engram, 6
Eliza Engram, 30
Lydia Engram, 29
Solomon Walker, 38
James Walker, 30
Eliza Walker, 12
James Waters, 40
Eliza Walker, 12
Dennis Waters, 40
Sally Waters, 35
Dennis Waters, 12
Barbara Waters, 7
Betty Jane Waters, 4
Sally Slater, 51
Abram Brown, 30
Roseann Brown, 27
Henry Tompson, 50
___ Tompson, 60
Sarah H___, 57
Gabriel Biggs, 42
Betsy Biggs, 45
Hercules Heinz, 40
Ann Heinz, 36
Harriet Woodard, 21
William Hill, 40
Nancy Hill, 36
Peter Clark, 50
James _____, 23
Illegible
Cato ___, 23

Free African Americans of Maryland - 1832

John Murdock, 27
Cato McPike, 22
Hannah Queen, 61
Rachel Brine, 36
___ Wood, 48
Ann Wood, 47
Ann Smith, 25
Bob Squire, 21
George Dark, 45
Phillip Brown, 40
James Freeman, 47
Charles Watkins, 60
David Briscoe, 24
George Breede, 28
Hannah Breede, 25
Eliza Breede, 24
Amos Brewer, 1
William H. Myers, 7
Abraham White, 4
John White, 2
Ann W___, 13
Darky ___, 64
Sally ___, 40
Mercella Key, 29
Henry Whatkins, 60
Sophia Whatkins, 60
George Whatkins, 6
Joseph Whatkins, 31
George Whaley, 29
Ben Jefferson, 50
Mary Jefferson, 31
Peter Boyer, 60
Ann Boyer, 48
Harriet Bowen, 28
Mary Bowen, 26
Lydia Bowen, 24
Catherine Bowen, 20
William Bowen, 10
Sally Bowen, 8
Easter ___, 43
Ruth ___, 22
___ Owings, 21
Sarah Owings, 31
Nicholas ___, 49
Katy ___, 44
Katy Corsey, 20
Henry Fisher, 28
Betty Roberts, 29
Elizabeth Roberts, 23
Rachel Parker, 23
Augustus W. Jackson, 30
Anthony Jackson, 33
Polly Jackson, 28
Ann Jackson, 9

Laura Jackson, 2
Francis B___, 38
Jane B___, 29
Emanuel Bowen, 9
William Bowen, 7
Juliann Bowen, 5
Malinda Brooks, 27
Mary Brooks, 27
Moses Jones, 58
Mariah Jones, 31
Joe Brooks, 27
Ann Jones, 18
Thomas Jones, 20
Mary Jones, 10
Susan Jones, 8
Ben Jones, 8
Ann Jones, 4
Milla Williams, 19
Susan Gross, 36
Cassa Roberts, 50
Stephen Roberts, 40
Moses Roberts, 44
Hannah Roberts, 29
Polly Barnes, 58
Henry Mazer, 28
Lucy Smith, 30
William Byers, 43
Hager Byers, 38
Isreal Byers, 15
Moses Byers, 8
John Byers, 4
William Byers,
Timothy Saunders, 50
Ann Saunders, 60
James Saunders, 28
Polly Saunders, 26
Maria Saunders, 24
Harriet Saunders, 23
Issick Saunders, 20
George Saunders, 10
Abby Saunders, 12
Enoch Saunders, 5
Ann Hill, 24
Louisa Cook, 24
Ann Cook, 23
John Johnston, 61
Caty Johnson, 52
Ephraim Johnson, 29
___ Johnson, 26
Gracey Johnson, 23
Allen Johnson, 15
Ben Johnson, 12
John Johnson, 10
Charity Johnson, 6

Jack Jones, 29
James Cook, 30
John Key, 37
Mary ___, 25
Frank Key, 57
Caty Key, 74
Ceasar Keenes, 41
Bessa Keenes, 29
John Keenes, 8
Tom Keenes, 5
James Keenes, 3
Maria Beach, 34
Nicholas Cosley, 28
B___ Cosley, 23
Oscar Black, 40
George H Cosley, 1
Mary Cosley, 2
Jerry Myers, 28
Hannah Myers, 18
Anna Cook, 40
Susan Scroggins, 17
Caty Mathews, 21
John Richards, 36
Henry Buhards, 38
Hannah Buhards, 18
James Hahn, 14
Perry Jones, 34
Hannah Jones, 33
Lydia Jones, 2
Allen T___, 27
Mary Cook, 32
David Black, 25
George Black, 23

Total: 2117.

89

A Census
of the Free Negroes and Mulattoes
in Kent County. State of
Maryland

Nathan Laddy, 72
Frances Laddy, 60
Moses, Laddy, 28
Henny Laddy, 22
Rachel Laddy, 20
Samuel Berryman, 26
Eliza Pervine, 7
Frances Narvijo
  Berryman, 2
Peregrine Murray, 44
Mary Murray, 30
Benjamin Hynson, 36
James Wright, 50
William Reed, 45
Peregrine Chambers, 25
Peter Tilghman, 35
Mary Welcome, 30
William Coursey, 26
Samuel Shealds, 58
Samuel Dudley, 19
Charles Wolley, 45
Francina Turner, 45
Mary Turner, 15
Louisa Turner, 13
Pere Turner, 10
Julianna Turner, 4
Samuel Graves, 23
Samuel Wright, 60
Frank Ward, 28
Charles Berryman, 85
Sarah Berryman, 78
Abe Freeman, 46
Minty Freeman, 48
Julianna Freeman, 2
Anna Maria
  Freeman, 4
Emeline Scott, 21
Frederick Munson, 38
Moses Hopkins, 49
Fanny Hopkins, 48
Maria Wall, 16
Teney Kennard, 55
Hannah Jones, 20
Francis Jones, 4
Henrietta Jones, 2
Louisa Ann Jones, 3
  months.
Thomas Ricaud, 13

John Berryman, 7
Emory Chase, 28
Peter Hudson, 54
Cezar Scott, 48
Sarah Scott, 50
Sophia Bowers, 25
Richard Lyles, 29
Ann Lyles, 27
Abe Lyles, 6 months
Sarah Ann Bowers, 5
*Maria Elizabeth Bowers,
  9 months
Henry Jones, 59
John Jones, 12
Amoy Tower, 56
Elizabeth Dudley, 47
Nathan Dudley, 17
Joseph Hynson, 7
John Dudley, 3
Chloe Tilghman, 70
Edward Bryam, 40
Francis Byram, 45
Samuel Johnson, 60
Sarah Scott, 28
Emeline Scott, 28
Samuel Scott, 6
Sarah Jane Scott, 4
Anna Maria Scott, 9
  months
William Cole, 5
Joseph Warren, 22
Abraham Shields, 33
Harriett Shields, 24
Araminta Shields, 4Sarah
  Elizabeth Shields
Henry Miers, 20
Peter Glenn, 53
David Johnson, 35
Samuel Goulden, 41
Dina D. Goulden, 49
Louisa Course, 9
Maria Kendal, 29
James Byram, 76
Sarah Byram, 65
Sarah Jones, 28
James Jones, 25
James Jones, 4
John Johns, 2

Milly Jones, 8 month
Sarah Blake, 11
Gilbert Hamilton, 45
Venus Hodges, 41
William Saunders, 4
James Pearce, 36
Henry Pearce, 24
Richard Pearce 8
Lemuel Pearce, 4
William Pearce, 2
John Pearce, 6
Hester Ann Pearce, 5
  months
Robert Wright, 45
Robert Ward, 47
Rebecca Freeman, 1
Hester Freeman, 9
Hannah Browne, 52
*Harriet Riley, 35
Sarah Jane Lyles, 23
John Lyles, 24
Henrietta Browne, 8
Sarah Rebecca Riley
Hannah Taylor, 54
Toney White, 40
David Blake, 41
Harriet Blake, 42
Lemuel Blake, 4
Nathan Blake, 2
John Blake, 3 month
Mary Browne, 29
William Browne, 9
James Browne, 6
John Browne, 2
William Wright, 56
Sarah Chambers, 44
William Chambers, 8
Frances Chambers,
Mary Ann Chambers
  months
Charles Wolley, 44
Samuel Dudley, 29
Sarah Reed, 23
Rachel Boyer, 50
Cyrus Dover, 45
Priscilla Dover, 40
Charles Berryman,
Philip Williams, 31

Free African Americans of Maryland - 1832

Benjamin Hollis, 18
Darkey Thomas, 19
Alexander Ward, 40
Joseph McComas, 53
John Demby, 27
Sidney Demby, 25
Ann Elizabeth Demby, 4
William Henry Demby, 2
Mary Jane Demby, 1
Sarah Rebecca Demby, 2
  weeks.
Harriet McComas, 19
Rebecca McComas, 4
Sarah, McComas, 1
Moses Nichols, 67
Daphne Nicols, 70
James Browne, 25
Hannah Frisby, 65
Samuel Cotton, 29
Samuel Lively, 29
Pere Boyer, 14
Samuel Coy, 40
Benjamin Wilkins, 44
Shadrick Demby, 2
Esther Minigan, 47
Harry Phillingham, 66
Grace Tilghman, 59
Jacob Beswick, 27
Peter Wickes, 44
Darkey Wickes, 45
Frances Wickes, 22
Elizabeth Wickes, 14
Peter Wickes, 12
Elenor Wickes, 9
Lydia Wickes, 7
Martha Wickes, 5
Alphonsa Wickes, 2
James Browne, 10
Amelia Brooks, 22
Siner Sanders, 67
Joshua Wright, 51
Caroline Wright, 25
Joseph Wright, 6
Rachel Wright, 3
Henry Wright, 1
Isaac Brice, 48
Charlotte Brice, 35
James Brice, 6
Nathan Brice, 4
Daniel Brice, 2
Jane Brice, 2 months
Joseph Hynson, 45
Ann Hynson, 38
Mary Ann Hynson, 1
Anthony Duvall, 50
Maria Duvall, 45
Mary Demby, 52
William Moore, 61

George Merritt, 50
Daniel Gresham, 40
Charles Berryman, 11
Rachel Freeman, 19
William James Freeman,
  11
Grace Graves, 11
Eliza Lewis, 30
Mary Lewis, 14
Elijah Lewis, 4
Peter Stater, 51
Jane Brooks, 50
Samuel Brooks, 8
Richard Brooks, 6
Henry Fountain, 45
Hester Fountain, 6
Prince Hodges, 36
Daniel Murray, 39
Latitia Murray, 32
Frances Ann Murray, 14
Cornelius Murray, 12
Amanda Melvina Murray,
  9
Isaac Murray, 6
Maria Louisa Murray, 4
Cornelia Murray, 9
  months
Linty Russell, 47
Eliza Russell, 12
William Browne, 43
Sarah Browne, 8
Joseph Briscoe, 31
Willamina Luscow, 31
Hark Brooks, 23
James Munsen, 9
Lucy Murray, 65
Henrietta Hynson, 19
Rasa Wright, 60
Mary Berryman, 40
Hannah Berryman, 17
Jeff Berryman, 17
Richard Berryman, 8
Mary Berryman, 4
Jane Louisa Berryman, 2
Samuel Bowers, 19
Mary Kennard, 20
Amanda Kennard, 1
Lisbon Bordley, 72
Rachel Bordley, 65
Catherine Freeman, 31
Minty Freeman, 10
Francine Freeman, 9
Catherine Freeman, 7
Fanny Freeman, 6
Hetty Mims, 61
Philis Tilghman, 50
Sylvia Wright, 49
Isaac Browne, 30

Joseph Cudja, 58
Dinah Munsur, 46
Eliza Munsur, 22
Mary Munsur, 15
Thomas Dunn, 69
Ddinah Dunn, 58
Ann Page, 36
Jacob Bowers, 23
Nathaniel Scott, 44
Thomas Scott, 8
Benjamin Scott, 6
Nathaniel Scott, 4
Sarah Ann Scott, 3
Mary Scott, 5 months
Isaac Boyer, 26
Alexander Scott, 31
Thomas Wyncoop, 27
Mary Ann Anderson, 33
Welthy Page, 17
*Henry Holland, 18
D___ Graves, 22
Abraham Browne, 45
Mary Browne, 40
Louisa Browne, 14
Henry Browne, 14
Frances Browne, 10
Letetia Browne, 7
Benjamin Ringgold, 50
Hannah Wright, 16
Rachel Starling, 14
James Smith, 10
Frisby Jones, 8
Thomas Sewell, 8
Charlotte Jenkins, 43
Nathaniel Jenkins, 41
James Jenkins, 1
Elizabeth Jenkins, 7
Grace Jenkins, 1
Trilus Stuart, 54
Rachel Stuart, 52
Lydia Wright, 13
Martha Browne, 3
  months
James Nichols, 50
Henry Walker, 26
Eliza Walker, 26
Horace Graves, 10
Henry Walker, 6
Mary Ann Walker, 1
Jane Oliver, 50
Frank Brooks, 25
Nathan Page, 7
Charles Benson, 16
Pere Turner, 30
Shadrack Browne, 16
George Wilson, 59
Ann Mitchell, 37
Pere Jenkins, 3

Kent County

Lydia Jenkins, 2 weeks
William Johnson, 35
Averilla Johnson, 31
William Johnson, 11
John Johnson, 13
Isaac Johnson, 8
Deborah Johnson, 5
Frances Beswick, 23
Jacob Swift, 35
Arthur Jenkins, 17
David Derry, 8
George Yorkes, 16
Emory Sheaf, 16
Frisby Taylor, 14
Wesley Taylor, 14
Henny Walker, 65
*John Williams
Margaret Shears, 50
Ann Shears, 30
Samuel Derry, 6
Joseph Johnson, 60
Manuel Taylor, 20
James Derry, 7
Matthias Derry, 2
Manuel Derry, 1
Elizabeth Derry, 7
Milcah Derry, 45
Pere Shears, 40
Julia Walker, 13
Samauel Derry, 12
Henrietta Derry, 11
Joseph Graves, 12
Darkey Ringgold, 30
David Miller, 50
Lucy Brooks, 20
Jacob Beswick, 60
Didnah Beswick, 65
Jane Reise, 3
Frank Reise, 1
Frank Beswick, 30
Pere Johnson, 24
Philips Philips, 24
*James Derry, 30
Alexander Johnson, 25
Robert Philips, 55
Caroline Phillips, 25
Henry Philips, 6
Isaiah Lively, 25
Maria Lively, 29
Stephen Yorkes, 16
Mary Yorkes, 12
Maria Yorkes, 9
Jeremiah Yorkes, 4
Isaiah Lively, 1
Hannah Gilbert, 24
Ann Gilbert, 4
Eliza Derry, 26
Joseph Dublin, 21

James Dublin, 33
Catherine Dublin, 18
Jane Dublin, 16
Elizabeth Dublin, 14
Richard Dublin, 12
Sidney Dublin, 9
Sarah Ann Matilda
    Dublin, 3
Rebecca Snow, 15
James McComas, 25
*Solomon Cox, 36
Ann Cox, 31
Maria Cox, 11
Sarah Cox, 4
Solomon Cox, 2
James Samuel Cox, 3
    months
Catherine Taylor, 55
Deborah Taylor, 9
Solomon Cox, 5
John Broadway, 23
Rachel Gale, 61
Nancy Beswick, 36
Ann Derry, 17
Louisa Beswick, 3
Elizabeth Beswick, 1
Millison Snow, 2
Robert Wilson, 15
Mary Wilson, 13
Jonathan Wilson, 9
Eliza Wilson, 7
Richard Wilson, 5
Ann Wilson, 1
Joseph L. Derry, 38
Henrietta Derry, 35
Elizabeth Derry, 15
Samuel Derry, 12
Henny Derry, 10
Hester Derry, 6
Mary Derry, 4
James Derry, 2
Susan Derry, 10 months
Lydia Johnson, 42
Catherine Perkins, 27
Catherine Ward, 8
Hannah Ann Perkins, 2
Catherine Perkins, 5
    · months
Stephen Graves, 41
Hannah Graves, 33
Jane Graves, 15
Mary E. Graves, 5
Emeline Graves, 3
Charlotte Graves, 10
    months
Henry Graves, , 56
Jeremiah Miller, 30
Elizabeth Miller 28

Mary Ann Miller, 2
James Gilbert, 54
Teney Gilbert, 52
Elizabeth Gilbert, 12
Alford Richardson, 6
Jacob Wright, 51
*Eliza Houston, 24
William Henry Houston, 7
James Washington
    Houston, 3
John Johnson, 30
Mary Johnson, 31
Samuel Johnson, 10
Pere Johnson, 4
Edwin Johnson, 10
    months
Ann Johnson, 19
Edwin Johnson, 21
Benjamin Gibson, 56
Margaret Gibson, 54
Richard Gale, 38
Hannah Gale, 32
Julianna Gale, 15
Susan Gale, 13
Cornelia Gale, 7
Esther Gale, 5
Harriett Gale, 10months
Henry Staten, 33
Rainey, 70
Henry Sullivan, 22
Joseph Gordon, 44
Pere Gidley, 21
Elizabeth Jamison, 20
Charles Jacobs, 29
Henry Graves, 22
*Levi Snow, 21
Jacob Page, 16
Emeline Tilghman, 32
Ann Warner, 36
Sarah Warner, 11
Ann Warner, 9
Benjamin Warner, 7
David Warner, 5
Elizabeth Warner, 2
James Ellis, 45
Maria Ellis, 24
Hester Ellis, 2
George Griffith, 29
Thomas Johnson, 23
Daniel Young, 63
Sarah Moore, 36
Milcah Graves, 64
Charles Johnson, 35
Maria Johnson, 36
Selina Johnson, 10
Henry Johnson, 7
Rachel Johnson, 3
Lucy Johnson, 8 months

ree African Americans of Maryland - 1832

lizabeth Warren, 60
ane Houston, 40
arriett Houston, 12
Joseph Houston, 4
enry Graves, 55
ebecca Graves, 40
lizabeth Shears. 12
nn Eliza Murray, 11
nn Bordley, 38
arah Bordley, 11
lizabeth Bordley, 9
enjamin Bordley, 7
lary Ann Bordley, 5
tephen Miller, 55
avid Miers, 18
ames Jones, 15
'illiam Graves, 28
arriett, Graves, 24
lary Jane Graves, 2
enry Graves, 63
enny Graves, 55
meline Graves, 16
amuel Johnson, 10
ames Johnson, 8
tephen Bowser, 40
ere Hodges, 40
udy Yeates, 50
imon Derry, 35
rail Yates, 12
orace Derry, 10
nn Rebecca Bordley, 2
eremiah Gale, 9
harles Boyer, 30
nn Brookins, 35
ichard Graves, 48
lary Ann Turner, 6
raminta Shealds, 5
emperance Shealds, 4
arriett Shealds, 4
homas Jenkins, 29
ere Cotton, 60
lizabeth Cotton, 56
ulia Tawner, 25
eorge Johnson, 65
xford Martin, 51
osephine Wright, 8
laria Worrell, 6
laria Lloyd, 35
'illiam Tilghman, 27
'illiam Lloyd, 2
ichard Clever, 67
lary Blake, 20
lartha Giles, 34
braham Gleaves, 45
liza Gleaves, 35
lary Gleaves, 8
lartha Gleaves, 7
arah Gleaves, 6

Thomas Gleaves, 5
Ann Gleaves, 1
Alexander Jones, 48
Rebecca Jones, 7
Sarah Jones, 30
Alexander Jones, 4
Ann Jones, 2
Emeline Vickers, 35
Albert Vickers, 11
Rebecca Vickers, 8
Elizabeth Vickers, 4
Mary Vickers, 2
Pere Johnson, 35
Henry Jones, 45
Julia Jones, 30
James Gidley, 35
Thomas Bowser, 60
Pere Munson, 30
John Sudler, 60
George Paca, 30
Frank Gordon, 14
Samuel Pratt, 40
Araminta Pratt, 30
*Eliza Pratt, 16
Julia Pratt, 12
Ann Pratt, 8
Samuel Pratt, 3
William Johnson, 25
Thomas Gordon, 30
Ashberry Frisby, 45
Catherine Pearce, 10
Mary Pearce, 12
George Washisngton, 45
Ann Washington, 35
Sarah Hanson, 30
George Hanson, 4]
Hanson Johnson, 2
Zachariah Munsun, 50
Sarah Munsun, 35
Martha Munsun, 17
Eliza Munsun, 15
Sarah Munsun, 14
Zacharia Munsun, 6
Mary Munsun, 5
John Blake, 35
Elizabeth Frisby, 50
Hannah Blake, 30
Eliza Blake, 15
Henrietta Blake, 12
Elizabeth Blake, 7
Richard Blake, 40
*Catherine Pearce, 30
James Pearce, 18
Henrietta Pearce, 15
James Pearce, 18
Henrietta Pearce, 15
Jane Pearce, 10
Elizabeth Pearce, 6

John Blake, 55
Araminta Blake 30
Ann Blake, 35
Rachel Shears, 52
Lingo Couvaiden, 60
George Rasin, 45
Darkey Green, 35
William Johnson, 18
Robert Browne, 14
Thomas Browne, 19
Samuel Tilghman, 19
Rufus Bayard, 16
Pere Wolly, 13
Margaret Frisby, 13
William Wright, 15
Charles, 10
Mingo Garrettson, 40
Rachel Garretson, 40
Dolly Tilghman, 30
James Wilson, 35
George Hanson, 28
Hannah Pines, 55
George Denning, 15
James Butler, 65
Milicent Butler, 36
Mary Butler, 16
Elizabeth Butler, 19
George Butler, 14
Ann Butler, 10
Robert Butler, 8
Hannah Ann Butler, 5
Edward Butler, 3
James Butler, 2
George Phillips, 45
Letty Phillips, 30
George Phillips, 5
James Phillips, 3
Garrett Phillips, 1
Joseph Rasin, 33
George Wilson, 15
Chester Bowser, 12
Elizabeth Hynson, 12
Peregrine Frisby, 3
George Hance, 70
Rebecca Hanson, 55
Sarah Cruickshanks, 17
Harriett Savoy, 29
John H. Savoy, 10
Jasmes Savoy, 4
Clara Ann Savoy, 4
Catherine Savoy, 1
Robert Wilson, 1
Jacob Weaver, 55
*Elizabeth Weaver, 35
Mary Weaver, 15
Hosanna Weaver, 9
Clarissa Weaver, 2
Nathanial Johnson, 37

93

Kent County

Darius Grooms, 55
Margaret Dorsey, 35
Millicent Dorsey, 16
Maria Dorsey, 12
Aaron Dorsey, 10
James Dorsey, 7
Benjamin Hynson, 27
Pompy Butler, 70
William Seamy, 40
Deborah Seamy, 35
Arthur Seamy, 7
Sarah Rebecca Seamy, 5
Moses Riley, 55
Dinah Riley, 60
Jacob Riley, 57
Rebecca Price, 55
Jacob Riley Jr. , 17
Yorick Betts, 50
Delia Betts, 45
Mary Betts, 16
Jane Betts, 14
Benjamin Betts, 11
Harriett Betts, 13
*Paul Gale, 70
Rachel Rasin, 45
John Stuart, 55
Daphne Stuart, 50
Catherine Nailor, 55
John Nailor, 28
James Nailor, 20
Mary Nailor, 25
Benjamin Nailor, 12
Samauael Nailor, 5
Phebe Nailor, 3
Louisa Waller, 30
Ann Louisa Walker, 6
Editha Maria Walker, 4
John Wm. Stuart Walker, 2
William Walker, 35
Joseph Ringgold, 22
Ann Tilghman, 14
Benmjamin Lamb, 30
Catherine Nailor, 11
Lavinia Nailor, 26
Elizabeth Nailor, 6
Rachel Nailor, 4
Sampson Nailor, 65
Jacob Trusty, 70
Susan Weaver, 10
Theodore Johnson, 35
*Rosetta Johnson, 30
Mary Rosetta Nailor, 2
Vincent Nailor, 5
James Berry, 90
Rebecca Berry, 70
Louis Linton, 17

William Henry James
  Berry, 4
Hannah Ann Berry, 2
Joseph Burgin, 36
William Peacock, 70
Catherine Anderson, 23
John Pearce, 29
William Spencer, 30
Margaret Brooks, 68
Sarah Brooks, 28
Thomas Brooks, 21
Anthony Hynson Brooks, 16
Henry Spencer, 3
Christopher Brice, 37
William Linggo
David Linggo, 37
Simon Wilmer, 38
Anthony Hynson, 51
Matilda Hynson, 37
Thomas Hynson, 15
Ann Wilson, 16
Grace Tilghman, 90
*Benjamin Frisby, 37
Ann Frisby, 30
Moses Hynson, 40
Abraham Redding, 45
Catherine Redding, 45
Maria Redding, 30
Sarah Redding, 17
Catherine Redding, 15
Abraham Redding, 12
Benjamin Wilkins, 35
Rachel Wilkins, 30
Mary Ann Pearce, 9
Margaret Wilkins, 4
Alexander Ford, 2
Aaron Ringgold
Pere Harper, 34
Joseph Wilmer, 58
Rebecca Wilmer, 55
Samuel Wilmer, 18
Henry Wilmer, 15
Esther Wilmer, 13
Chester Wilmer, 10
Mary Jane Wilmer, 8
Jacob Wilmer, 55
Araminta Wilmer, 40
Peregrine Wilmer, 9
John Henry Wilmer, 5
*Maria Wilmer 2
George Tiller, 40
David Bowers, 42
Mary Bowers, 11
Harriett Matilda Bowers, 6
Sarah Elizabeth Bowers, 4

David Henry Bowers, 1
Elenor Hynson, 73
Nelly Hynson, 20
Araminta Clayton, 7
John Henry Thomas, 1
Jacob Anderson, 55
Elizabeth Anderson, 14
George Anderson, 12
Phillip Anderson, 5
James Pearce, 2
Peregrine Johnson, 28
Samuel Hamilton, 35
Alice Hamilton, 35
George Martin, 19
Gustavus Sanderson, 2
Daniel Warner, 37
James Frisby, 45
Casander Frisby, 55
*Lewis Frisby, 7
Emory Stout, 19
Peregrine Wright, 54
Hannah Wright, 50
William Wright, 20
Wilson Wright, 20
Elizabeth Wright, 12
Peregrine Wright, 10
Sarah Rebecca Wright,
David Green, 42
Margaret Green, 28
Benjamin Anderson, 4
Margaret Anderson, 65
George Browne, 36
Hester Browne, 34
Mary Browne, 14
Maria Browne, 10
William H. Browne, 7
George Browne, 5
John Wesley Browne,
Catherine Browne, 1
James Chany, 13
Rosamond Raisin, 75
Sophia Calder, 15
Daniel Jones, 28
Aaron Gibbs, 15
Caroline Pearce, 17
Matilda Tillotson, 30
James Tillotson, 12
Elizabeth Tillotson, 9
Peregrine Tillotson, 6
William Tillotson, 2
Richard Barroll, 43
Araminta Barroll, 39
Harriett Barroll, 22
Esther Maria Chany,
Harriett Matilda Chan
Alexander Chany, 36
Charlotte Chany, 30
Abraham Price, 11

llicent Forman, 15
xander Ford, 25
omas Wolly, 27
regrine Stoops, 37
ary Wright, 8
ancis Ringgold, 55
zabeth White, 28
cob Ford, 73
atilda Ford, 39
aac Ford, 27
encer Ford, 23
lliam Ford, 21
cob Ford, 17
bert Ford, 12
ichard Ford, 8
seph Ford, 6
ster Ann Ford, 1
orge Mingo, 72
an Stout, 80
arah Stout, 30
artha Ann Stout, 9
nty Stout, 12
llicent Stout, 16
hn Stout, 8
an Stout, 1
ses Wright, 23
mes Hynson, 28
win Chany, 29
arah Chany, 23
an Maria Chany, 1
ther Lamb, 60
ephen Johnson, 45
annah Freeman, 18
ster Ann Freeman, 2
cob Houston, 45
cy Houston, 42
annah Houston, 3
ly Ann Houston, 1
ephen Trusty, 55
olet Trusty 36
aminta Richardson, 17
och George Trusty, 1
nry Worrell, 63
an E. Worrell, 33
ary Denning, 45
aminta Denning, 8
omas Wilmer, 45
an Rasin, 55
bert Wilson, 27
illicent Wilson, 23
bert Wilson, 3
ary Champ, 24
artha Ann Champ, 3
mes Holly, 45
aminta Holly, 37
aac Holly, 18
arriett Holly, 16
exander Holly, 16

Thomas Holly, 14
Elizabeth Holly, 12
James Holly, 14
John Holly, 8
Standsbury Holly, 6
Araminta Holly 2
Sarah Cotton, 60
Mary Cotton, 27
David Cotton, 27
*James Demby, 28
Thjomas Chany, 70
Charity Tilden, 55
Mary Chany, 3
James Chany, 1
Charlotte Chany, 9
Elizabeth Chany, 6
Ezekial Chany, 31
Aaron Chany, 24
James Chany, 22
Cudjo Rasin, 55
Ann Rasin 41
Sarah Elizabeth Rasin, 18
Harriett Rasin, 16
Warner Rasin, 12
George Rasin, 10
Susan Rasin, 8
Benjamin Rasin, 6
Wesley Rasin, 4
Martha Hall, 2
Thomas Anderson, 5
Trusty Johnson, 56
Michael Jackson, 45
Benjamin Wilmer, 21
Millicent Hanson, 36
Alexander Wilson, 22
Peregrine Hansdn, 40
*Philis Redding, 26
Margaret Redding 8
Nehemiah Redding 6
Joseph Redding, 3
Margaret Johnson, 20
Mary Trusty, 25
Pere Trusty, 2
Abraham Scott, 12
Henry Thomas, 73
George Washington Stuart, 10
David Worrell, 35
Joseph Richardson, 28
Harriett Thompson, 40
Rebecca Pearce, 13
Emma Garrettson, 19
Samuel Chase, 20
Nathanial Tilghman, 48
Tene Tilghman, 40
Henry Tilghman, 5
Ann Tilghman, 3

Mary Jane Tilghman, 1
Maria Johnson, 34
Samuel Rasin, 31
Louisa Rasin, 16
Maria Rasin, 9
Allen Warner, 33
William Johnson, 31
Ann Johnson, 28
Ann Johnson, 4
James Johnson, 2
James Ringgold, 12
Darcus Gale, 15
Aaron Miller, 16
Henry Ford, 17
Chester Bowser, 65
Matilda Bowser, 25
Delia Bowser, 4
Samuel Rosier, 42
Rachel Rosier, 37
Robert Rosier, 7
Richard Rosier, 1
Rebecca Rosier, 3
Henry Stuart, 12
Jacob Walker, 10
Darcas Graves, 70
John Blake, 35
Ann Blake, 32
Henry Blake, 12
James Blake, 7
Margaret Ann Blake, 3
Jane M. Blake, 1
Thomas Jones, 18
Benjamin Snow, 45
Mary Snow, 34
James Berry, 8
Harriett Snow, 6
Alexander Turner, 24
Rebecca Turner, 25
James Bowser, 30
Daniel Gadis, 35
Charles Hynson, 43
Joicy Hynson, 37
Grace Barroll, 50
James Mansfield, 38
Orange Young, 23
Hetty Frisby, 24
Darius Groom, 40
James L. Wilmer, 9
Edward Pearce, 28
Henry Tilghman, 28
Hannah Wilmer, 45
David English, 40
Henry Walker, 40
Ann Walker, 55
James Jones, 19
Charles Jones, 17
Joseph Rasin, 40
Lewis Holly, 37

95

Kent County

Susan Wormsley, 18
Dolly Copper, 70
William Rasin, 67
Darcus Rasin, 60
Issac Rasin, 35
Richard Barroll, 45
Pere Tillotson, 35
Rosamond Rasin, 42
Rachel Rasin, 25
Maria Chambers, 12
Richard Rasin, 3
Harriett Johnson, 37
Eve Scott, 45
Willamina Scott, 13
Sarah Ann Scott, 10
William Henry Scott, 8
Frances Elizabeth Scott, 5
John Wesley Scott, 3
Rebecca Scott, 16
Amanda Scott, 1
Maria Chambers, 55
Ann Browne, 16
Margaret Lamb, 24
Minty Lamb, 14
John Lamb, 12
Sarah Lamb, 9
Elizabeth Lamb, 1
Jemima Simmons, 42
Violet Warner, 30
James Frisby, 36
Abraham Adams, 13
Henry Spencer, 16
Jacob Trusty, 38
Jacob Wright, 25
Margaret Hollis,55
Abraham Scott, 40
James Carroll, 32
Mary Rasin, 25
James Rasin, 32
Joseph Rasin, 6
Ann Maria Rasin, 2
Samuel Rasin, 1
William Johnson, 10
Elizabeth Johnson
Violet Miller, 60
Francis Steel, 65
Phillis Harris, 30
Hannah Hynson, 14
Teney Hynson, 65
Jacob Trusty, 39
Henrietta Trusty, 35
Harriet Trusty, 5
John Trusty, 3
Thomas Wright, 28
Alexander Brooks, 38
Caroline Brooks, 25
Marshall Jones, 5

Daniel Brooks, 1
Noah Corke, 24
Noah Chambers, 36
Willamenia Chambers, 24
Alexander Chambers, 6
John Chambers, 3
Mary Ann Chambers, 2
Isaac Cotton, 33
Loucretia Cotton, 31
Eliza Ann Cotton, 11
Elizabeth Cotton, 8
Louisa Cotton, 7
Hannah Blethia Cotton 4
Joseph Cotton, 45
Rachel Cotton, 45
Rachel Cotton, 40
Isaac Cotton, 14
Pere Cotton, 14
Emory Cotton, 10
Rachel Cotton, 5
Araminta Trusty, 15
George Barroll, 55
Sarah Barroll, 55
George Washington
   Wright, 8
Jacob Dorsey, 44
*Rachel Dorsey, 57
Eliza Johnson, 23
Rebecca Tillotson, 80
Samuel Jackson, 41
Lewis Holly, 36
Abraham Hindman, 23
Mary Garrett, 27
Robert Sewell, 31
Daniel Harvey, 54
Alnut Sewell, 13
Mary Augustus, 27
Dolly Henry, 48
Hark Gaddis, 60
Ann Gaddis, 57
Edward Gaddis, 24
Henry Cotton, 15
Rebecca Gaddis, 19
Pere Trusty, 40
Editha Trusty, 35
Elizabeth Cork, 19
Fanny Johnson, 55
Lewis Hailes, 13
Rachel Hands, 65
George Johnson, 30
David Browne, 27
Emory Rasin, 41
Henry Ringgold, 19
*Eben Posey, 9
Mary Posey, 35
Edward Posey, 7
Alford Posey, 5
Elizabeth Posey, 3

Araminta Bankiston, 57
Joshua Corke, 46
Martha Corke, 35
Margaret Ann Corke, 15
Isaac Corke, 13
Elizabeth Cork, 11
Temperance Levina Cork 9
Joshua Thomas Cork, 7
Albert James Cork, 3
Jacob Corke, 1
James Chambers, 34
Henrietta Chambers, 33
Sarah Etta Chambers, 3
Ellen Maria Chambers, 1
George Anderson, 35
Sarah Anderson, 27
Sarah Elizabeth Jones, 5
Amos Jones, 31
Ann Jones, 36
William Elbert Jones, 11
Charles Wesley Jones, 6
Marshall James Jones, 4
Mary Jane Elizabeth
   Jones, 1
Mary Elizabeth Elbert, 1
Mary Ringgold, 27
Eliza Ann Ringgold, 5
James Henry Ringgold, 2
Priscilla Palmer, 40
Tamasina Palmer, 11
Adeline Palmer, 6
William Jackson Palmer, 4
Pere Maltimore Palmer, 1
William White, 22
Richard Wright, 50
Sarah Wright, 52
Pere Wright, 16
Sarah Maria Wright, 14
James Henry Wright, 2
George Rasin, 5
Abraham Butler, 28
Ann Butler, 25
Teney Wilson, 22
Ann Ringgold, 18
Sarah Ringgold, 40
Araminta Ringgold, 13
Mary Ann Ringgold, 12
Hannah Ringgold, 11
Sarah Ann Ringgold, 9
Cynthia Elizabeth
   Ringgold, 7
*James White, 24
Hester Ann Ringgold , 3
Henrietta Ringgold, 4
Angelina Ringgold, 3
Alexander Ringgold, 3

9

ree African Americans of Maryland - 1832

Rachel Palmer, 13
Henry Cotton, 17
Caroline Davis, 18
Thomas Jones, 48
Harriett Jones, 40
Harriett Jones, 21
Sarah Ann Jones, 17
Abraham Jones, 14
James Jones, 10
Pere Jones, 5
Jane Jones, 2
Sarah Pearce, 71
William Jones, 72
William Jones, 74
Rebecca Jones, 50
Ann Jones, 39
Mary Jones, 16
Araminta Jones, 13
Samuel Jones, 12
Josiah Jones, 10
William Jones, 7
Rebecca Woodland, 6
Jeff Elwood Woodland, 1
Sophia Comegys, 37
John Hall, 38
Catherine Carroll, 52
Joseph Miller, 10
Mary Riley, 16
Joseph Miers, 45
Tricy Miers, 38
George Miers, 6
John Henry Miers, 1
Joseph James Miers, 1
Sarah Scott, 13
Judy Fox, 72
Rachel Wiggins, 69
William Gleaves, 32
Michael Trusty, 45
Elizabeth Trusty, 40
Catherine Trusty, 9
Thomas Wilson, 55
Eliza Wilson, 40
Charles Bordley, 57
Henry Sullivan, 22
Mary Tilghman, 35
Mary Snow, 17
Eliza Chaney, 20
Richard Gibbs, 40
Rebecca Gibbs, 30
Caroline Standsbury, 19
David Jones, 31
Martha Jones, 25
Sarah Ann Jones, 11
Araminta Berry, 27
Susan Ann Berry, 2
Samuel Rogers, 40
Judy Rogers, 35
William Rogers, 17

Caroline Standsbury, 19
David Jones, 31
Martha Jones, 25
Sarah Ann Jones, 11
Araminta Berry, 27
Susan Ann Berry, 2
Samuel Rogers, 40
Judy Rogers, 35
William Rogers, 17
Vincent Roberson, 49
Hannah Roberson, 11
Hannah Roberson, 48
Jane Roberson, 6
Thomas Cuff, 60
Pere Gustus, 38
Milicent Gustus, 37
Elender Gustus, 12
Philis Legar, 4
Deborah Legar, 4
Catherine Salter, 1
Emory Woodland, 24
Pere Thompson, 42
Eliza Thompson, 45
James Thompson, 6
Rachel Boyer, 37
Levi Boyer, 7
Elizabeth Boyer, 5
Benjamin Boyer, 2
Henrietta Berry, 80
Lucy Walker, 40
Elizabeth Walker, 17
Mary Ann Walker, 11
Henrietta Walker, 10
Ann Rebecca Frisby, 4
Elizabeth Sudler, 70
John Salter, 64
Catherine Salter, 49
Joseph Lloyd, 55
Martha Lloyd, 40
Harriet Wright, 25
Henry Wright, 7
Mary Elizabeth Wright, 2
Thomas Smith, 21
Louisa Green, 11
Pere Chambers, 30
Jane Chambers, 20
Pere Chambers, 9
Ann Chambers, 6
Jacob Chambers, 3
Pere Rabough, 35
*Nathan Wilson, 40
Phillip Jones, 40
Catherine Jones, 40
Maria Jones, 3
Margaret Jones, 1
Arthur Glenn, 28
James Jones, 29
Ann Jones, 29

Temperence Jones, 2
William Jones, 1
David Morgan, 14
John Jones, 16
Fanny Blake, 13
Selina Page, 18
Mary Ward, 8
James Riley, 6
William Smith, 56
Mary Smith, 48
Caroline Smith, 20
Mary Ann Smith, 1
James Miller, 6
William Frisby Miller, 1
Francis Ward, 80
Molly Hazzard, 100
Maria Corse, 37
Thomas Murray, 35
Daniel Dorsey, 14
James Mechanic, 60
Jane Mechanic, 55
Maria Jane Chambers, 10
Mary Pearce, 5
Araminta Pearce, 3
George Stephen Pearce, 1
Susan Goulden, 61
Hannah Jones, 62
John Jones, 26
Samuel Perkins, 33
Sarah Elizabeth Perkins,
    19
William Perkins, 12
Louisa Jane Elizabeth
    Perkins, 1
Simon Sheppard, 45
Elizabeth Sheppard, 39
*Eveline Sheppard, 24
Simon Sheppard, 12
Benjamin Sheppard, 9
Hannah Ann Sheppard, 6
Harriet Jones, 35
John Goulden, 18
Charles Henry Martin, 10
Charlotte Young, 12
Rebecca Wickes, 60
Mary, 16
Isaac Anderson, 45
Henrietta Anderson, 34
Isaac Anderson Jr, 14
Rachel Anderson, 15
Eliza Lias, 35
Henrietta Lias, 5
Limas Turner, 70
Rebecca Turner, 60
James Oliver, 25
Edward Boyer, 7
Candis Boyer, 60
Jane Fray, 80

Kent County

Joseph Landsman, 10
John Barrett, 25
Mary Barrett, 22
James Barrett, 6 months
*William Blake, 13
Harriett Blake, 13
Eliza Berry, 30
Harriett Berry, 30
Charlotte Berry, 1
Eliza Jones, 30
Eliza Smith, 28
Mary Smith, 27
William H. Smith, 7
Edward H. Smith, 5
Ann Leatherbury, 25
Ann Elizabeth
    Leatherbury, 2
Emory Bowers, 43
Elizabeth Bowers, 21
Emory Bowers, 5
Rebecca Bowers, 3
William Bowers, 2
Moses Richardson, 40
Temperance Richardson,
    37
Eliza Richardson, 2
Shadrach Browne, 42
Darkey Browne, 50
Henry Browne, 19
Thomas Brown, 13
Horace Brown, 11
William Gale, 18
*James Murray, 30
John Hawkins, 40
Rasa Hawkins, 45
Charles Oliver, 35
Darkey Oliver, 34
Charles Oliver Jr. , 6
Isaac Oliver, 3
Anna Maria Oliver, 1
Mary Jane Chambers, 8
Esther Gidley, 52
William Gidley, 15
David Gidley, 12
Moses Thomas, 56
Mary Thomas , 47
Harriett Thomas, 9
Simon Blake, 5
Louisa Blake, 65
Araminta Shaffley, 50
Samuel Burgess, 29
Jacob Shaffley, 27
Lydia Graves, 17
Samuel Burgess, 15
Betsy Graves, 14
Ann Matilda Sheppard,
    13
James Warwick, 35

*Teaney Warrwick, 40
Selina Warrwick, 16
Samuel Chambers, 32
Harriett Chambers, 30
Rebecca Brown, 4
Teney Coy, 50
Joseph Coy, 45
William Coy, 40
Eben Perkins, 4
Dolly Walker, 70
Rebecca Bordley, 30
Kitty Bordley, 11
William Bordley, 4
Charles Bordley, 3
James Hartshorn, 50
Alphy Hartshorn, 50
Minty Spencer, 15
Kitty Gordon, 7
Henry Anderson, 30
Charlotte Anderson, 25
Henry Anderson, 26
Harriet Anderson, 2
Arthur Anderson, 9
Richard Homely, 35
Ann Homely, 25
James Homely, 1
Jane Homely, 9
Rachel Bowser, 40
James Bowser, 23
*Hannah Sheppard, 15
James Grooms, 55
Hester Grooms, 35
Tempy Grooms, 15
Henry Grooms, 13
Emory Grooms, 9
Jane Grooms, 7
Mary Grooms, 5
Caroline Grooms, 2
John Boyer, 40
Ann Boyer, 40
David Boyer, 4
Hester Boyer, 5
William Boyer, 1
Mary Grooms, 40
Susan Grooms, 9
Thomas Grooms, 2
Ruth Grooms, 4
Dianna Hall, 70
Pompey Smith, 60
Milly Lyas, 27
Henry Corse, 28
Eliza Page, 42
James Corse, 9
Anna Maria Corse, 8
Pere Bolten, 4
Dyer Gleaves, 45
Anna Maria Gleaves, 40
Kitty Morgan, 35

*William Gleaves, 10
Charles Gleaves, 6
Ann Gleaves, 4
John Grooms, 2
Caroline Grooms, 30
Mary Grooms, 7
Joseph Hynson, 40
Betty Hynson, 40
Henrietta Hynson, 12
Matilda Hynson, 8
Mary Hynson, 5
Harriett Ward, 30
George Ward, 5
Philis Ward, 3
Fanny Jordon, 50
Teany Vandike, 12
Henrietta Joiner, 36
Henry Miers, 45
Ann Miers, 18
Margaret Bordley, 45
James Kendle, 28
Maria Guy, 45
William Briscoe, 19
Stepney Jones, 50
William Sanders, 37
Eliza Tooney, 24
Mary Ann Tooney, 4
Abraham Wilcox, 54
Vincent Green, 50
*Elizabeth Jane Duckery,
    9
Sewell Thomas, 13
Phillis Fields, 12
Thomas Peaker, 28
James Morgen, 37
Pere Moody, 30
Joseph Rhodes, 11
Norris Miller, 10
Daniel Harris, 27
Thomas Mander Bowers,
    20
Eby Scott, 25
Samuel Scott, 3
Rachel Kennard, 45
Ann Morgan, 40
Isaac Hopkins, 22
Robert Davis, 17
Julia Ringgold, 40
Stephen Kennard, 37
Margaret Kennard, 36
Araminta Kennard, 11
Isaac Kennard, 10
Stephen Kennard, 6
William Kennard, 5
Deborah Kennard, 3
Hester Kennard, 1
James Pearce, 37
Edward Jenkins, 47

ree African Americans of Maryland - 1832

achel Jenkins, 55
o__ Chew, 45
nn Demby, 54
ashington Demby, 17
ames Butler, 54
hilis Butler, 45
ames Butler Jr, 17
usan Butler, 15
atherine Tilghman, 13
ester Anderson, 41
ere Anderson, 19
ary Anderson, 17
illiam Anderson, 13
nn Maria Anderson, 9
arah Williams, 60
usan Gray, 27
tephen Roberts, 36
llen Roberts, 40
ary Bordley, 11
lement Hackett, 50
lizabeth Hackett, 54
nna Maria Thompson, 15
harles Thompson, 30
achel Thompson, 18
ebecca Thompson, 13
atherine Pines, 33
ilicent Freeman, 34
arah Ann Freeman, 7
lexander Freeman, 14
assa Freeman, 2
Rebecca Freeman, 2
illiam Spencer, 26
eorge Johnson, 36
raminta Forman, 36
braham Forman, 1
enry Forman, 6
ere Turner, 27
illiam Davis, 19
empy Jackson, 40
liza Barroll, 35
ohn Barroll, 6
nn Johnson, 50
hade Thompson, 24
ohn Boyer, 13
esley Boyer, 19
illiam Bazell, 40
nn Lingo, 35
ere Carville, 30
amuel Wilson, 80
ohn Hynson, 30
uff Geddis, 65
hilis Lockerman, 30
charles Lockerman, 6
annah Ann Lockerman, 9 months
aria Nicholson, 8
ere Hackett, 14

Adam Simms, 35
Stephen Barroll, 54
*Samuel Scott, 24
Mary Scott, 20
Catherine Barroll, 13
Emeline Parker, 18
Enoch Leverson, 26
Hannah Bradshaw, 50
Mary Gaddis, 36
Harriett Chambers, 40
Linda Cartwright, 2
Abraham Cartwright, 2
Isaac Cartwright, 1
Ezekial Chambers, 31
Joseph Rasin, 70
Darcus Comegys, 31
Maria Comegys, 2
William Green, 41
Jane Green Peaker, 31
Richard Peaker, 9
Stephen Peaker, 7
Susan Haylent, 40
Jonathon Cornelius Holylent, 1
Phebe Chambers, 34
Joseph James Chambers, 3
Alford Chambers, 4 months
Elizabeth Thompson, 25
Henry Savin, 4
Eliza Ann Snow, 1
Milicent Lewison, 20
*Mary Ann Sevin, 4
Emeline Severson, 3 months
Martha Savin, 21
Sarah Hynson, 47
Jacob Hackett, 18
Eliza Jane Peaker, 13
Ann Harris, 54
Charlotte Riley, 38
Abraham Riley, 6
Mary Bowser, 7
Eliza Hackett, 40
James Henry Hackett, 7
Matilda Hackett, 5
Ann E. Hackett, 4
Hannah Ann Hackett, 3
George Morocco, 60
Phebe Morocco, 60
Henrietta Lockerman, 3
William Butcher, 32
Maria Burns, 35
Eliza Burns, 6
Samuel Burns, 4
William Chase, 38
Sophia Chase, 28

Ann Maria Chase, 9
Samuel Chase, 70
Phillip Jordon, 40
*Rachel Thompson, 40
Rachel Thompson Jr, 10
Shade Thompson, 9
Mary Richardson, 22
Isaac Spencer, 73
Darcus Browne, 50
Pere Brown, 12
Martha Ann Carville, 7
Mary Maria Carville, 3
Rebecca Carville, 25
John Browne, 32
Eben Browne, 22
Isaac Browne, 24
Agnes Browne, 33
Martha Blackiston, 60
Ann Blackistone, 24
Rasa Jane Wright, 4
Priscilla Miller, 40
Washington Miller, 9
Charles Miller, 17
Sarah Grimes, 53
Pere Bordley, 7
Moses Young, Jr, 28
Ann Young, 24
Spencer Young, 5
Mary Ann Young, 3
Abraham Young Jr. 26
Elizabeth, 27
Pere Young, 3
*Caroline Young, 2
Abraham Young, 58
William Grindage, 36
Eliza Grindage, 35
Jonathon Grindage 15
Mary Grindage, 17
James Grindage, 7
Araminta Grindage, 2
James Riley, 25
George Belican, 14
Elizabeth Thompson, 60
Zachariah Thompson, 32
Ezekial Thompson, 30
Richard Thompson, 22
Caroline Thompson, 34
James Salisbury, 5
Adam Norris, 40
Ritta Norris, 38
John A. Norris, 8
Daniel Norris, 6
William Norris, 3
Joseph Norris, 1
Caroline Norris, 15
Alethia Norris, 13
Sarah Norris, 9
Amy Wilmer, 42

99

Kent County

Samuel Young Dyer Wilmer, 12
Isaac Wilmer, 8
Simon Wilmer, 5
*Tempy Young, 45
Thomas Young Hall, 16
Pere Rhodes, 50
William Rhodes, 13
Caroline Rhodes, 8
Janaett Rhodes, 6
Jacob Rhodes, 4
Hannah Wilmer, 58
Carson Wilson, 60
Araminta Wilson, 49
Frederick Wilson, 17
Samuel Wilson, 23
Peter Perkins, 50
Daniel Moore, 54
Rachel Wright, 60
Ann Blackiston, 28
Louisa Blackistone, 12
Dianna Blackistone, 6
Mary E. Blackistone, 3
Jacob Jackson, 30
Ezekial Browne, 32
Henry Chase, 35
Mary Chase, 23
Gassaway Chase, 21
Sarah Ann Chase, 19
*Lambert Chase, 17
Eliza Case, 15
Pere Miller, 4
Samuel Black, 18
Daniel Doman, 62
Elizabeth Doman, 56
Abraham Doman, 23
Isaac Doman, 22
Samuel, Doman, 18
John Henry Doman, 16
Rachel Doman, 17
Mary Jane Doman, 13
George Washington Doman, 9
Joseph Doman, 6
Hannah Doman, 4
Dianna Stout, 56
Abraham Mann, 65
Grace Mann, 63
Jane Miller, 26
Mary Jane Mann, 7
Julia Emily Miller, 18 months
Ann Mann, 2
Thomas Potts, 44
Amy Potts, 40
William Potts, 16
James Potts, 14
Bina Potts, 13

Rebecca Potts, 4
*Christopher Belican Jr, 6
William Chambers, 60
Cynthia Belican, 5
Rosetta Belican, 13
Phileman Belican, 10
Christopher Belican, 53
Mary Belican, 40
Ann Chambers, 40
Louisa Chambers, 10
Pere Benson, 50
Ann Benson, 38
Jane Hatcheson, 35
Henry Hatcheson, 6
Catherine Hatcheson, 2
Willy Hynson, 25
Catherine Hynson, 18 months
William Dudley Bishop, 12
Stephen Kennard, 12
Charlotte Dudley, 9
William Rochester, 40
Anna Rochester, 35
Alexander Kennard, 11
Mary Ann Bishop, 14
Fanny Dudley, 7
Jenny Cacy, 45
Henry Massey, 40
Phillip Thomas, 20
*Jacob Bell, 45
Mary Bell, 35
Maria Gibbs, 35
Julia Ann Gibbs, 8
Rachel Anderson, 50
Charlotte Rochester, 9
Jane Rochester, 7
William Henry Rochester, 4
Benjamin Franklin Rochester, 3
Hannah Riley, 35
William Spencer, 7
William Gibbs Jr, 20
John Ringgold, 19
Phillip Browne, 12
Lewis Davis, 12
Jeff Hales, 40
Joseph Doman, 56
Temperance Doman, 60
Elizabeth Doman, 25
Joseph Doman Jr, 22
James Doman, 19
Samuel George Doman, 16
Thomas Boyer, 16
Daniel Doman Jr, 32

Elizabeth Doman, 26
James Doman, 7
Hannah Doman, 4
*Josiah Doman, 3
Temperance Doman, 3 days
William Jones, 70
Josiah Doman, 3
Temperance Doman, 3 days
William Jones, 70
Rebecca Jones, 65
Ann Woodland Jones, 38
Rebecca Jones, 18
Sarah Jones, 25
Emeline Jones, 22
Elizabeth Jones, 20
Kitty Minty Jones, 12
Samuel Jones, 10
William Jones, 7
Washington Jones, 3 months
Daniel Henry, 60
Mary Henry, 50
Mary Elbert, 32
Isaac Elbert, 32
Elijah Elbert, 26
Hinsley Jackson, 18
Joseph Elbert, 6
Margaret Elbert , 3
Elizabeth Elbert, 11 months
Henry Jackson, 14
James Elbert, 12
Matilda Elbert, 8
Darius Jackson, 8
Pere Trusty, 45
Edy Trusty, 42
*Fanny Trusty, 63
Betsey Caulk, 25
William Caulk, 4
John Henry Caulk, 3
Milly Rasin, 40
Charles Rasin, 35
Rebecca Rasin, 13
Elizabeth Rasin, 10
Rasin Rasin, 3
Editha, 11
Daniel Gaddis, 33
William Ringgold, 12
Joseph Rasin, 5
Emeline Browne, 35
George Browne, 6
Thomas Brown, 1
Elizabeth Freeman, 32
James Rasin Freeman, 6
Elizabeth Nicholson, 35
Mary Jane Nicholson, 3

ree African Americans of Maryland - 1832

achel Bowser, 20	James Boyer, 4 months	Lavinia Scott, 17
re Thompson, 22	Rebecca Boyer, 2	Abt Polly, 21
ames Grindage, 36	William Wilson, 75	James Tilghman, 3
ohn Thompson, 19	Hannah Wilson, 60	Peter Gooding, 45
re Corse, 33	Prissy Whittington, 57	Benjamin Scott, 18
amuel Brown56	Lewis Wilmer, 7	Pere Thompson, 40
an Brown, 16	*Pere Dawson, 40	Arthur Thompson, 50
arriett Ann Brown, 6	Matilda Dawson, 54	Lavinia Munson, 9
rances Ann Brown, 3	Hannah Browne, 29	Pere Munson, 8
ebecca Ann Brown, 2	Charles Brownqe, 30	Philis ____, 79
re Brown, 3 months	Eliza Browne, 16	Rachel Massey, 34
ephen Parker, 50	Pere Brown, 4	Anthony Granger, 70
achel Parker, 45	Charles Brown Jr. , 20	Grace Granger, 74
ouisa Parker, 7	Sharper Brown	Grace Granger, 9
anny Henry, 26	Jacob Jones, 73	Anthony Granger, 1
ne Freeman, 32	Letty Jones, 72	George Tillotson, 40
arah Johnson, 35	Caty Mander, 17	James Cudge, 45
aria Johnson, 9	Samuel Scott, 43	*Welthy Cudge, 63
mily Johnson, 4	*Pere Dawson, 40	Richard Cudge, 21
ancy Johnson, 2	Matilda Dawson, 54	Rosetta Witman, 30
athanial Frisby, 24	Hannah Brown, 29	Ann Granger, 30
estel Wright, 19	Charles Brown, 30	Louisa Warner, 12
raham Thompson, 27	Eliza Brown, 16	Ann Warner, 45
lia Ann Thompson, 20	Pere Brown, 4	Samuel Warner, 20
annah Bishop, 80	Charles Brown Jr. , 20	Jonathan Warner, 14
hn Browne, 35	Sharper Brown, 10	Levi Warner, 10
argaret Ashley, 33	months	Emeline Warner, 1
dward Thompson, 24	Jacob Jones, 73	Judy Warner, 21
hn Murray, 50	Letty Jones, 1	Rainey Moody, 23
omas Griffith, 33	Caty Mander, 17	Julia Ann Moody, 12
njamin Riley, 24	Samuel Scott, 43	Cuff Tillotson, 33
arriett Griffith, 33	William Doman, 37	Augusta Hall, 79
omas Griffith, 18	Debby Lusby, 20	Rebecca Hall, 75
months	Rachel Thompson, 7	Thomas Duckery, 47
raham Maxwell, 43	Ann Lusby, 4	Ann Duckery, 41
be Ricketts, 15	Isaac Lusby, 1	Patty Ann Duckery, 12
hn Geddis, 40	Nat Lusby, 32	Mary Duckery, 8
nny Geddis, 45	Joseph Thompson, 40	Henry Duckery, 5
izabeth Barroll, 21	Milcah Thompson, 45	Pere Duckery, 4
ebecca Grindage, 12	Hannah Wallis, 13	Eliza Duckery, 3
re Bryan, 12	Rebecca Salisbury, 35	Ruth Duckery, 3 months
orge Pruitt, 50	Harriett E. Salisbury, 1	Sarah Hopkins, 34
ter Smith, 80	Arthur Salisbury, 6	Hannah Hall, 60
ron Warner, 40	Mary Viere, 40	Tobias Hall, 25
nry Thompson, 17	Phillip Browne, 50	John Hall, 22
wis Cooper, 15	Elizabeth Brown, 48	Sophia Hall, 25
nry Woodland, 12	Emory Brown18	*Robert Hall, 5
mes Blackiston, 56	Jane Brown, 9	Eliza Ann Hall, 3
rah Blackiston, 56	Horace, 11	Mary Ann Hall, 2
nrietta Blackiston, 7	Martin Wilson, 43	John Hall, 4 months
atilda Blackiston, 10	Darkey Wilson, 46	Frisby Hall, 18
ary Warner, 30	Pere Granger Jr, 15	Daniel Mingo, 18
lliam Warner, 2	Noble Festus, 50	Perry Veasy, 39
ron Warner Jr, 6	Lucy Offett, 65	Roseq Gumm, 35
months	Mary Hackett, 26	James Warner, 55
nnah Wilmer, 50	Ann Mander, 18	Thomas Mander, 35
nny Vallow, 29	William Jordan, 29	William Hurtt, 26
argaret Vallow Boyer, 3	Rebecca Scott, 40	Thomas Browne, 60

Kent County

Henrietta Brown, 60
Sewell Greenwood, 9
Henry Mingo, 13
Stephen Harden, 60
Araminta Harden, 32
Stephen Jr. 4
Rachel Harden,7
Ann Harden, 10
Sarah Ann Barroll, 7
Michael Allen, 35
Louisa Allen, 21
Michael Allen, 21
Rachel Jones, 18
James Graves, 41
Henry Helms, 50
Susan Poolman, 30
Caroline Poolman, 11
*Charles Poolman, 4
Ezekial Warner, 30
Elizabeth Salisbury, 27
Pere Salisbury, 26
Stephen Salisbury, 3
Charles Salisburyq, 2
Araminta Salisbury, 1
Aino Browne, 35
Rosetta Brown40
William Henry Brown, 7
James Wesley Brown, 4
Arnold E. Naudain, 3
James Tillotson, 56
Rainey Tillotson, 50
Mary Tillotson, 30
Emory Harris, 2
Jacob Black, 60
Judy Black, 61
Pere Brown, 12
Rachel Ricketts, 35
Thomas Ricketts, 12
Ann Ricketts, 10
Rebecca Hynson, 30
William Cuff, 38
Ann Cuff, 40
John Duckery, 16
Daniel Shugling, 19
David Kennard, 37
Mary Kennard, 30
*Stephen Kennard Jr.
    12
Mary L. Kennard, 8
David Kennard, 6
Eliza Kennard, 3
John Kennard, 1
Milcah Graves, 35
Sarah Ann Graves, 5
John Graves, 2
William Thompson, 50
Mary Thompson, 34
Isaac Mason, 38

Jane Mason, 40
Ann Louise Mason, 2
Araminta Mason, 5
    months
Sarah E. Mason, 3
Isaac Seegar, 56
Araminta Seegar, 50
Margaret Spearman, 70
Ann Brinkley, 4
Pere Dudley, 40
Abraham Wilmer, 50
Sarah Dudley, 45
Ann Whittington, 100
Isaac Hynson, 45
Ruth Hynson, 47
Elizabeth Wilmer, 17
Eliza Lamb, 40
Richard _____, 35
Stephen Simmons, 45
Maria Simmons, 35
George Simmons, 6
Eliza Simmons, 3
Caroline Simmons, 4
Charlotte Wilson, 30
P__ Purnell, 50
Ann Ayres, 25
William Ayres, 3
Edward T. Ayres, 4
    months
Ann Wilson, 12
Martha Ayres, 6
Abraham Simons, 50
Ezekial Chambers, 37
Susan Chambers, 19
James Chambers, 10
Samuel Chambers, 7
Ccharlotte Willis, 27
Ann Maria Willis, 1
Charlotte A. Browne, 5
Jacob Riley, 68
Zene Riley, 58
Joseph Waltham, 8
Letetia Walker, 11
___Ann Butcher, 30
Elizabeth Rideout, 23
*Elizabeth Gibbs, 15
Thomas Henry Rideout, 5
Emely Jane Rideout, 3
Amanda Levinia Rideout,
    4 Months
Jeremiah Joseph Gibbs,
    1 month
Samuel Frazier, 40
*Elizabeth Gibbs, 15
Thomas Henry Rideout, 5
Emely Jane Rideout, 3
Amanda Levina Rideout,
    4 months

Jeremiah Joseph Gibbs,
    1 month
Samuel Frazier, 40
Matilda Dawson, 40
Emory Green, 12
William Rasin, 40
Margaret Rasin, 40
William Henry Rasin, 1
Rachel Lamb, 58
Martha Doman, 28
Rachel Ann Doman, 5
Thomas Butcher, 9
Sarah Bayard, 40
John Thompson, 9
William Bayard, 3
Samuel Bayard, 1
Jemina Piper, 60
Frederick Piper, 18
Hannah Rasin, 45
Ann Little, 55
Jacob Rasin, 17
Ann Gilbert, 16
Alethia Browne, 40
Rachel Nailor, 60
Moses Allen, 45
Eliza Allen, 45
Jonas Rasin, 35
Samuel Ward, 15
Dolly Frisby, 35
Abraham Ward, 39
Ann Ward, 30
Rachel Ward, 13
Rebecca Ann Ward, 12
Harriett Ward, 11
Abraham Ward, 4
Sarah Jane Ward, 12
Alexander Benson, 62
Alexander Benson Jr. 26
Alexander Smith, 14
Daniel Roberts, 40
Stephen Wilmer, 33
Hester Wilmer, 23
Isaac Hynson Wilmer, 5
Catherine Ann Wilmer, 7
    months
Stephen Woodland, 60
*Rachel Woodland, 53
Temperance Wright, 42
Julian Wright, 7
Milcah Wright, 12
Martha Chambers, 16
Margaret Carmichael, 55
Lydia Hurtt, 15
Sarah Hurtt, 13
Moses Mann, 4
Araminta Butcher, 50
Julia Butcher, 28
Peregrine Butcher, 21

Richard Ridgely, 40
John Ridgely, 10
Mary Ann Ridgely, 7
Elizabeth Ridgely, 5
Augustine Ridgely, 2
Moses Hardesty
Dinah Mackall
R___ Hall, 10
Theophilus Mackall
Thomas Brooks, 70
Fanny Brooks, 7
A___ Rowe
Elizabeth Rowe
Amelia Laws
John Bowens
Milly Forman
Mary Jane Forman
Margart Ann Forman
William Warren
Forman
Joseph ___
Nace Nevit
Milly Nevit
William Nevit
James Nevit
Henry Key
Joseph Briscoe
Charlotte Briscoe
Anna Adams
_____ Adams, 8
Caroline Adams, 6
U___ Adams, 3
William H. Adams, 1
Alexander Adams, 1
Eleanor___
Charlotte Scott, 60
Christina L___, 26
Mary Ann Gassaway
Caesar L____
Fanny L___
Richard Robertson,
45
Kitty Robertson, 40
Henry Robertson, 17
Mary Ellen
Robertson, 16
Robert Robertson, 12
Charity Culver, 60
Peter Culver, 4
Sarah Culver, 2
Rachel Russell, 7
Polly ___
Charles Jones, 60
Ann Jones, 49
George Jones, 19

Cassy Jones, 23
Edward Jones, 10
Samuel Jones, 5
Mary Ray, 25
William Allen, 5
Eli Ray, 2
Harriet Ann Ray, 1
William Bowen, 31
Julian Ann Bowen,
11
Rosetta Bowen, 9
William John Bowen,
7
John Boswell, 6
Ann Mariah Bacon
Ann Mariah Bacon, 3
days
Jeremiah Johnson,
63
Nancy John, 56
Jeremiah Johnson
Jr. 25
Rachel Johnson, 23
Benjamin Johnson,
21
Grafton Johnson, 20
Garrison Johnson,
20
Mary Ann Johnson,
14
Martha Maranda
Johnson, 12
Eleanor Lancaster,
35
Caleb Adams, 61
Nacky Adams, 43
Elizabeth Adams, 16
Middleton Adams, 13
Kitty Adams, 7
Linda Adams, 5
Lucy Ann Adams,
Charlotte Lancaster,
38
Lila Lancaster, 13
William Lancaster,
10
George Lancaster, 8
Benjamin Lancaster,
6
Richard Lancaster, 4
Rachel Lancaster, 2
Caesar Plummer
James Prater
Susan Ross, 55
Edward Ross, 45

Samuel ___, 7
Susan Letton,
Samuel Jones, 22
William Jones, 21
Elick Adams, 40
Kitty Nichols, 60
___ Boswell, 30
Susan Watts, 28
Kitty Watts, 14
Betty Watts, 12
___ Watts, 8
Louis Watts, 10
V __ Ann Watts, 5
Modecai Bellow, 61
___ Bellows, 45
Cassy Adams, 22
Kitty Bellows, 6
____ Bellows, 11
Isaac Bellows, 33
Priscilla Bellows, 25
Mordecai Bellows Jr.
33
Nancy Ann Bellows,
6
Mary Bellows, 11
months
Cephas Hall, 52
Jane Hall, 38
Cassandra Hall, 13
Kitty Hall, 10
Joseph Hall, 8
Louisa Hall, 5
Sarah Bacon, 40
Eliza Bacon, 16
Barbara Bacon, 12
Otho Bacon, 9
months
James Barrett, 57
Edward Adams, 52
Harriett Boswell, 38
Sarah Bacon Jr. 26
William Brown, 18
Nelly ___, 13
Andrew Boswell, 10
Nancy Boswell, 9
Jane Adams, 18
Thomas Boston, 21
William Shipley, 22
Lewes Jackson, 53
Lutetia Davis, 28
James Henry Davis,
10
Mahala Davis, 7
Mary Ann Davis, 7
Charlotte Davis

Montgomery County

A List of the Free People of Color In Montgomery County As Enumerated by William O'Neale Jr, Sheriff in the year 1832.

Peter Hopkins, 35
Samuel Stephens, 44
James Carter, 46
Robert A___, 26
M___ Plummer, 24
Elijah Plummerq, 3
Greenberry
    Plummer, 7
    months
James Butler, 33
Nancy Fitzhugh, 16
Tobias Snell, 40
Caloy Dixon, 50
Alice Jane Dixon, 3
Alfred Dixon, 6
    months
Easter Coates, 60
Nelly King, 35
Sally Howard, 20
John King, 12
Henry King, 6
George King, 1
___ Howard, 1
Ruth Dickens, 14
John Freeman, 62
Candass Freeman,
    69
Elijah ___, 23
Samuel Riggs, 40
John Mills, 42
Rachel Wotton, 45
Leonard Jackson, 53
Susan Gray, 13
Jeremiah B. Adams,
    40
Monica Adams, 35
Nelson __ Adams, 6
Lucy Ann Gaither, 4
Edward Norris, 51
Nancy ___, 69
Philomon ___
Charles Norris
Julia ___ ___
Ruth Only, 98
Caty Only, 64
Henry Only, 38
___ Spriggs, 50
Elizabeth Spriggs, 9
James H___, 5
___Snowden, 26

John Snowden, 6
Samuel Snowden, 4
Leucretia Snowden
    18 months
Polly ___, 60
Phoebe Coates, 55
Lydia Weems, 21
Jerry Weems, 3
Mary Weems, 18
    months
Vachel Snowden, 65
Emily Snowden, 6
Joseph Tyler, 3
Clary Lyles, 22
___ Disney, 70
Crissy ___
___ Hawkins, 34
Elisa Hawkins, 2
    months
Charles Brent, 13
Henry Johnson, 11
Harrison King, 3
Darius King, 4
    months
Maria ___, 6 months
Ann Holland, 40
Catherine Isabella
    Holland, 4
_____, 50
William Bowie, 23
Nelly Bowie, 23
H___ Bowie, 19
Caroline Bowie, 18
Margaret Bowie, 16
Dory Bowie, 12
Evan Bowie, 8
Angeline Bowie, 2
William Henry Bowie,
    3 days
Lucy ___, 70
___ Prather, 48
Sarah ___, 48
John Robert ___, 7
Samuel Thomas ___,
    5
Susan Rebecca ___,
    2
Thomas Brown, 40
Samuel Coates, 55

George Thompson,
    40
Edward Holland, 65
Nancy Hammond, 5
Ruth Lyles, 45
Robert _ Lyles, 29
Thomas Lyles, 24
___ Lyles, 12
Jesse Lyles, 7
Henry Lyles, 18
A___ Lyles. 15
Ann Lyles, 21
Lydia Ann Frasier, 4
Ruth Ann Frasier, 2
Gabriel Hopkins, 9
Samuel Hopkins, 10
Elizabeth Maria
    Lyles, 8
___Hall Dorsey, 9
___ Hammond, 25
Louisa Belt, 6
John Bell, 4
William Hammond, 1
___ Hammond, 21
Mary Ann Diggs, 6
Elizabeth Diggs, 5
Clarasy Diggs
Israel Diggs, 14 days
Otho Hammond, 15
___ Gutter, 50
Rebecca Gutter, 18
Hester Ann Rogers
    Gutter, 16
Mary Gutter, 12
Margaret Ann
    Hopkins Gutter,
    9
Thomas Dover Jones
    Gutter, 8
Benjamin Wilkinson
    Davis, 1
Edward Welsh, 39
Nancy Welch, 32
Rashel Ann Welsh, 6
William Henry
    Welsh, 4
Matilda Ann Welsh,
    18 months
Betsy Adams, 65
Mariah Davis, 62

Free African Americans of Maryland - 1832

Jemina King, 16
Warner Stapelton, 14
___ Magruder, 36
Judy Bowman, 39
Vachel Bowman, 7
Ann Bowman, 3
Cassy Bowman, 4
Alfred Johnson, 24
Rachel Carroll, 39
George Brown, 20
Eliza Brown, 19
Sara C. Brown, 9
Hamilton Hall, 16
William Miles, 10
Charles Miles, 12
Jaret Hopkins, 43
___ Hood, 16
Harriet Fisher, 14
Esther Bowie, 36
Eliza Ann Bowie, 17
Catherine Bowie, 12
Rachel Ann Bowie, 10
George Williams, 40
Milly Snowden, 60
___ Hamilton, 10
Basil Bond, 31
Betsy Bond, 25
William Bond, 10
Daniel; Bond, 8
John Bond, 7
Uriah Bond, 4
___ Bond, 2
Betsy Jones, 16
Nathaniel ___, 28
George Edward
    Matthews, 19
Dolly Countee, 44
Angelia Countee, 10
Richard Countee, 8
Mary Ann Countee, 18
Jane Countee, 16
Joseph Nuggent, 36
Harriet Nuggent, 30
John Henry Nuggent, 9
Sarah Nuggent, 7
Rebecca Nuggent, 5
Granville Nuggent, 3
Joseph Nuggent, 5
    months
Mary Ellen Bond, 15
Caesar Williams, 42
Nancy Bowen, 47

John Cyrus Bowen, 21
Ary Scott Dorsey, 48
Ruth Ann Dorsey, 11
___ Dorsey, 14
Daniel ___, 44
Minta Budd, 36
George Washington
    Budd, 6
Caroline Elizabeth
    Budd, 3
Elizabeth Jane
    Woodward, 16
___ Redman, 16
Cecelia Dorsey, 67
Rachel Richardson, 60
Warner I. Dorsey, 4
Matilda Williams, 28
John Williams, 11
Robert Williams, 4
Gusty Williams, 2
L___ Williams, 7
    months, 7
    months
Rachel Marbury, 27
Maria E. Marbury, 7
John Marbury, 6
Celia Marbury, 4
Eliza Marbury, 2
George W. Thomas, 2
Lydia Clement, 15
John Clement, 11
Eliza Ann Clement, 9
___ Clement, 5
Isabella Clement, 3
Joseph Clement, 9
    months
Mary Fisher, 14
Mary Jane Green, 5
Nathan Green, 3
Margaret Mackall, 50
Illegible
Lucinda M___, 31
Sarah Johnson, 28
Mary Elizabeth
    Johnson, 13
Eliza Ann Johnson, 11
Greenberry Johnson, 8
John Edward
    Johnson, 3
Lucinda Johnson, 3
    months
Henry Mackall, 15

Caroline Mackall, 10
Martha Mackall, 8
Jacob Mackall, 8
L___ Manuel, 2
Margaret Ann
    Manuel, 12
Matilda Mackall, 18
Mary Ann Mackall, 2
Illegible
Leonard Hamilton, 36
Mary Ann Hamilton, 33
James William
    Hamilton, 7
Adolphus Hamilton, 5
Rosetta Hamilton,
Priscilla Matthews, 31
James Matthews, 37
Elizabeth Jane
    Matthews, 7
Joseph Matthews, 6
Flora Waters, 3
Kitty Waters, 46
Patience ___, 10
Eliza Ann ___, 8
Betsy ___, 5
John Martin ___, 3
    months
Elizabeth Thomas, 55
Alfred Thomas, 55
Mariah Thomas,, 20
Lydia Clements, 29
William Henry
    Clements, 4
Sarah Thomas, 4
Jeremiah Brooks, 15
Hanson Hill, 18
Remus Hill, 18
Hannah C. Powell, 19
Thomas Williams, 15
Alfred Graham, 9
Sarah Ann Snell, 13
Rachel Bright, 42
Robert Bright, 10
William Bright, 14
Mary Ann Bright, 12
Rachel Elizabeth
    Bright, 6
John Wesley ___, 8
Samuel Thomas
    Snowden, 6

Montgomery County

Martha Lucretia Snowden, 4
Rachel Weems, 37
John William Weems, 1
Phil Gray, 70
Katy Gray, 55
Joseph Shriver, 7
Old Grace, 83
Ruth Williams, 52
David Williams, 26
Elizabeth Williams, 25
George Williams, 4
John Williams, 3
Angeline Williams, 2
Mary Elizabeth Williams, 1
Lydia Ann Stanton, 10
William Gibbons, 9
Lydia Magruder, 60
___ King, 65
Benjamin Foreman, 26
Cecil Richardson, 23
Charles Powell, 29
George Thomas, 17
Peter Hopkins, 38
Eliza Frederick, 5
Mary Bowen, 15
Mary Frederick, 1
Henry Toody, 87
___ Carn, 95
Peggy Carn, 70
Harry Clowden, 90
Nelly Clowden, 80
Robert Slater, 30
Betsy Fisher, 12
Mary Fisher, 18
Hassey Fisher, 21
Gabriel Tyler, 27
Richard Snowden, 23
William Dent, 6
Jane Dent, 40
Hanson Dent, 6
Susan Dent, 3
Wesley Brown, 34
James Madison, 21
Joseph Stone, 14
Lot Davis, 60
India Nelson, 50
John Nelson ___, 26
Ann Nelson, 20
Mary Benson, 40

Mary Jane Benson, 6
Kitty Benson, 8
Harriet Benson, 1
Charles Davis, 65
Sophia Bright, 29
William Sloane, 29
Eliza Thomas, 4
Fanny Ann Thomas, 2
George Thomas, 2
Fanny Clarke, 40
Ann Clarke, 9
Betsy Clarke, 2
William Chase, 55
Tricia Chase, 48
Charity Chase, 7
Rezin Johnson, 40
Edward King, 19
James Plummer, 20
Henry Plummer, 17
Dick King, 15
Serna King, 13
Washington King, 11
Lucy King, 9
John ___, 40
Harry ___, 49
Ned Lyles, 64
Anny Lyles, 40
Robert Dorsey, 40
Harriet Lucas, 38
Ann Lucas, 6
Davy Beall, 4
Jerry Beall, 66
Harriet Beall, 66
Ann Beall, 66
Harriet Green, 32
Jim Spencer, 16
William Johnson, 38
Margery Lee, 35
Sandy Lee, 13
Becky Lee, 8
Polly Lee, 6
Eliza Lee, 3
Jenny Diggs, 80
John Diggs, 8
Eliza Jason, 27
Bill Jason, 3
John Jason, 3
Richard Jason, 2
Emily Smith, 21
Sarah Smith, 3
Rachel ___, 14
Hester Green, 44
Joseph Nailor, 30
Stephen Burke, 51
Jack Burke, 52

Nelly Burke, 52
Sarah Burke, 18
Henny Burke, 16
Irvin Gaither, 11
John Davis, 2
Nathan Nailer, 20
Nelly Nailer, 15
Adam Nailer, 12
Ned Bowen, 20
Henny Addison, 47
Elizabeth Addison, 79
Esther Addison, 29
Ellen Addison, 74
Lidda Addison, 17
Rosella Addison, 16
Rozetta Addison, 15
Frances Addison, 8
Jane Addison, 6
Washington Addison, 4
Thomas Hamilton, ___
Sally Hamilton, 30
Peggy Hamilton, 24
William Hamilton, 20
Nelly Hamiltonq, 19
Ann Hamilton, 17
Margaret Washington, 6
___ Freeland, 3
Ned Norris, 50
Ann Norris, 48
Nathan Norris, 22
Philimon Norris, 18
Charles Norris, 16
Julia Ann Norris, 13
Caty Spriggs, 50
Elizabeth Spriggs, 8
Hester Plummer, 40
Peggy Plummer, 22
Rachel Plummer, 15
Benjamin Plummer, 13
John Plummer, 9
Harriet Ann Plummer, 5
William Plummer, 4
John Plummer Jr, 2
John Tillison, 6
Sarah Tillison, 10
Lydia Spencer, 56
Phillip Spencer, 26
Mary Spencer, 28
William Spencer, 24
Rachel Spencer, 22
George Spencer, 4

Free African Americans of Maryland - 1832

Jim Spencer, 3
Thomas Spencer, 3
Mary Spencer, 1
Lucy Bettis, 28
William Bettis, 7
Cassandra Bettis, 2
Sarah Bettis, 1
John Magill, 1
William Wornar, 19
Louisa Jenkins, 23
John Jenkins, 1
Simon Rice, 28
Richard Burguion, 27
Charles Clarke, 37
Henry Chubb (alias King), 26
Judson Chubb (alias King), 1
Matilda Sanders, 2-
James Bowman, 61
Isaac Carrington, 34
Beverly H___, 34
Netty Carrington, 40
Isaac Carrington Jr. 3
James Banks, 50
Sabra Banks, 50
Louise Carr, 27
John Lee, 80
Hannah Lee, 31`
Betsy Lee, 80
Betsy Lee, 37
Robert Lee, 35
Vatch Robertson, 55
Easter Robertson, 40
Betsy Robertson, 21
John Robertson, 19
Eliza Robertson, 15
Lucinda Robinson, 14
E___ Robinson, 9
Jessie Robinson, 6
Richard Thomas, 28
Mary Thomas, 25
Alexander Thomas, 5
Elizabeth Thomas, 6
Mary Thomas Jr. 5 months
Eliza Bond, 18
Mary Bond, 18
John Webster, 19
Caroline Contee, 1
Jacob Willson, 33
Ann Willson, 30

Julia Ann Willson, 10
Mary Ann Willson, 9
Susan Rebecca Willson, 9 months
John Thomas, 31
Minty Thomas, 28
Joseph Thomas, 7
William Thomas, 5
Samuel Thomas, 4
George Washington Thomas, 11 months
Jacob Dorsey, 25
Silas Webster, 60
Samuel Bowen, 44
Juliet Bowen, 42
Samuel Bowen Jr. 19
James Bowen, 17
Amelia Bowen, 74
Rebecca Bowen, 10
Cyrus Bowen, 12
Edward Bowen, 8
Cornelious Bowen, 6
Henry Bowen, 4
Matilda, 9
Abetha Adams, 21
John Detter, 45
Frederick Detter, 43
Dina Detter, 25
Joseph Detter, 7
William Thomas Russell, 2
L___ Russell, 1
Henry Johnson, 10
Peter Johnson, 11
Jacob Hardester, 22
Fanny Hardester, 68
Mary Hardester, 24
Margaret Hardester, 6
Ann Rebecca Hardester, 2 months
James Cooter, 28
Susanne Cooter, 34
Ruth Patterson, 14
Hannah C. Bowen, 19
Samuel Bowen, 1
Samuel Bowen, 1
___ Uncles, 7
Stephen Robertson, 50

Elizabeth Robertson, 26
Caleb R. Robertson, 7
Joshua Robertson, 5
Sarah Ann Robertson, 4
Stephen Robertson Jr. 2
Julia Ann Robertson, 5 months
Mary Robertson, 60
___ Bowen, 45
Elizabeth Bowen, 36
Martha Ann Bowen, 10
Elizabeth Bowen, 7
Marshall Bowen, 2
Moses Lynn, 47
Easter Lynn, 54
Remus Lynn, 15
Mary Lynn, 15
Moses Lynn Jr. 13
George Lynn, 9
Eliza Allen, 13
Patience Allen, 11
Paul Edmondston, 45
Abigale Rosier, 60
Charles Rosier, 20
Nace Rosier, 22
Joseph Rosier, 17
Susan Cole, 50
Julia Cole, 14
Samuel Cole, 12
Elizabeth Cole, 10
John Cole, 8
Abigale Cole, 6
Nace Rosier Sr. 60
Richard Edmondson, 65
Joan Contee, 36
Eliza Contee, 11
Richard Contee, 9
Lucinda Contee, 7
Jessy Contee, 3
Rezin Contee, 11
Dark Johnson, 47
Henry Joppy, 36
Maria Joppy
Harriet Joppy, 11
Mary Joppy, 10
Elias Joppy, 7
Louisa Joppy,,5
William Joppy, 1
Greenbury Joppy, 60

Montgomery County

Charles Tyler, 22
Washington Hodges, 25
Mary Ann Hodges, 23
James Edward Hodges, 2 months
Sarah Ellen Hodges, 9
Hannah Matilda Hodges, 6
Letty ___, 90
Elizabeth Russell, 30
Caroline Russell, 4
Priscilla Lyles, 17
Henry ___, 30
Henry Davis, 16
Ann Cook, 24
Susan Cook, 22
Polly Cook, 16
Ann Thomas
Kitty Bowie, 16
Rachel Thomas, 16
Reuben Thomas, 2
Mary ___ 16
Hester____, 75
Solomon Davis, 15
Hillary Dorsey, 10
Hester Smith, 40
Margaret Locker, 23
Nathaniel Smith, 45
Richard Mason, 22
Henry Tarlton, 35
Jessy Martin, 75
Molly Martin, 60
Massy Martin, 3
7
Mary Martin, 23
Betsy Martin, 21
Thomas Martin, 18
Robert Martin, 17
Jessy Martin Jr. 12
John Martin, 4
Kitty Ann Martin, 2
Ellen Martin
Robert Martin, 1
Samuel Allen, 60
Mary Allen, 40
John Allen, 15
H___ Campbell, 40
Molly Ferrell, 80
Dick Bowie, 45
Mary Summers, 45
F___ Joye, 18
Sally Butler, 50

Henny Martin, 45
James Jones (Dead), 80
Samuel Martin, 55
Eleanor Martin, 50
Jenny Henderson, 60
Milly Offett, 35
Hannah Green, 70
Tom Gittings, 23
Michael Martin, 50
Adeline Martin, 24
Artelia Martin, 10
Hanson Martin, 4
Octavia Martin, 2
Samuel Martin Jr. 28
Nathan Martin, 27
Michael Martin Jr. 8
Maranda Hepburn, 26
Nelly Martin, 35
Elizabeth Devinia Martin, 7 months
Sarah Eleanor Ann Martin, 6
Liley Tarlton, 35
Mary Ann Tarlton, 5
Mary Butler, 31
Caroline Pace, 10
Elizabeth Pointer, 40
Milly Bowman, 24
James Smith, 12
Willie Smith, 20
Sarah Bowman, 3
James Henry Hepburn, 1
Priscilla Lyles, 17
Henry Summerville, 30
Lydia Gross, 68
Jerry Gross, 70
___ Snowden, 65
Betsy Brooks, 30
Eliza Brooks, 6
Eliza Murray, 6
Eliza Higgins, 32
Letty Higgins, 30
Harriett Jackson, 30
John Jackson, 1
John Clagett, 22
Sarah Patrick, 40
William Norman, 18
Susan Norman, 20
William Norman Jr. 4
Robert Norman, 2

Jenny Tyler, 60
Henny Norman , 50
Lucy Warren, 25
Mariah Warren, 4
Rachel Warren, 2
Dinah Cook, 50
Massy Martin, 20
Ellick Martin, 3
Robert Martin, 2
Julia Cook, 40
Sophia Cook, 10
Margery Campbell, 60
Henry Lamar, 60
Betsy Lamar, 50
Jenny Stewart, 50
Richard Bowman, 60
Mary Carter, 8
William Sewell, 25
Rose Childs, 75
Jenny Burton, 60
Kitty Cook, 70
William Buchanan, 50
Eliza Edwards, 50
William Edwards, 2
Jacob Edwards, 69
Margaret Edwards, Kitty Cook, 70
William Brashears, 50
Eliza Edwards, 4
William Edwards, 2
Sarah Edwards, 69
Margaret Edwards, 80
___ Edwards, 40
Ned Edwards, 30
Isaac Sewell, 50
___ Sewell, 50
Rachel Cole, 70
Elliott Mason, 6
Mary Mason, 12
Charity Mason, 50
Carlton Mason, 31
Ellen Mason, 18
Polly Sewell, 22
William Sewell, 4
Betty Tasker, 60
Benjamin Tasker, 60
John Hamilton, 40
Philis Hamilton, 40
Barney Hamilton, 15
John Hamilton Jr. 10
Nicholas Hamilton, 3

Free African Americans of Maryland - 1832

Sarah Hamilton, 1
Rene Mitchell, 34
Rachel Mitchell, 8
Harriett Mitchell, 6
Elizabeth Mitchell, 5
Hezekiah Mitchell, 2
Hannah Brashears, 4
Perry Butler, 60
Rachel Butler, 60
Jane Wood, 10
Henry Wood, 4
Harriet Bowen, 8
John Bowen, 5
Cyrus Bowen, 50
Liley Bowen, 30
Margaret Harris, 8
Charles Harris, 2
Benjamin Richardson, 25
India Richardson, 20
___ Green, 35
Margaret Green, 5
John Green, 2
Phebe Chase, 50
Eliza Chase, 30
George Chase, 10
Mariah Chase, 8
Matilda Chase, 4
Caroline Chase, 1
Henry Somerville, 30
Mary Somerville, 25
Mariah Brion, 30
Matilda Williams, 20
Louis Williams, 3
Margaret Brion, 2
Elizabeth Brion, 7
Mary Shorter, 8
William Shorter, 2
Abraham Shorter, 40
Lewis Shorter, 15
Rachel Shorter, 13
Betsy Brashears, 50
William Brashears, 25
Mary Ann Brashears, 19
Sally Brashears, 17
Sarah Edwards, 10
Nancy Culbert, 65
Alfred Hodge, 21
Jacob Willson, 35
Ann Willson, 50
Mary Ann Willson, 6

Susan Rebecca Willson, 9 months
George Boston, 16
Elizabeth ___, 13
Thomas Nevit, 22
Sarah Ann Nevit, 20
Hazel Hill, 60
Mary Ann Hill
Charles Hill, 14
Martha Hill, 13
Lorenzo Thomas, 8
James Dorsey, 5
James Lynn, 40
Lavinia Lynn, 45
Stephen Matthews, 18
Eliza Matthews, 20
Wesley Lynn, 16
James Lynn, 14
Rebecca Ann Lynn, 8
Virginia Dorsey, 4
Ignatius Ross, 47
Harriet Ann Ross, 56
Kitty Ann Ross, 18
Ada Ross, 15
Richard K. Taylor, 17
Charles Grandison, 15
William Webster, 13
Louis Budd, 10
Thomas Budd, 8
Milly Naylor, 60
Rachel Brown, 4
William Brown, 3
Mary Brown
___ Brown,
Charlotte Brown, 9
Rachel Berry, 55
Elijah Webster, 9
Henry Webster, 6
H___ Webster, 34
Franklin Webster, 14
Deborah Webster
Tom Webster, 9
Mary Ann Webster, 7
Elizabeth Webster, 2
James Webster, 1
Samuel Powell
Flora Powell
Basil Powell, 17
Ann Denny, 9
William Henry Powell, 4
George Franklin
Rachel Franklin

Nancy Franklin
Kitty Franklin
___ Thomas
Ellen Thomas, 45
Otho Gantt
Henrietta Gantt
Thomas Brown
Priscilla Brown
Isaac Brown
Susan Matthews
Betsy Brown
Rebecca Matthews, 16
Richard Matthews, 14
Clement Matthews, 8
Susanna Matthews, 6
Sarah Elizabeth Matthews, 3
Martha Ann Bowen
Jonathan Bowen
Richard Bowen
Benjamin Ray
Richard Ridgely, 40
John Ridgely, 10
Mary Ann Ridgely, 7
Elizabeth Ridgely, 5
Augustine Ridgely, 2
Moses Hardesty
Dinah Mackall
R___ Hall, 10
Theophilus Mackall
Thomas Brooks, 70
Fanny Brooks, 7
A___ Rowe
Elizabeth Rowe
Amelia Laws
John Bowens
Milly Forman
Mary Jane Forman
Margart Ann Forman
William Warren Forman
Joseph ___
Nace Nevit
Milly Nevit
William Nevit
James Nevit
Henry Key
Joseph Briscoe
Charlotte Briscoe
Anna Adams
_____ Adams, 8
Caroline Adams, 6
U___ Adams, 3

Montgomery County

William H. Adams, 1
Alexander Adams, 1
Eleanor___
Charlotte Scott, 60
Christina L___, 26
Mary Ann Gassaway
Caesar L___
Fanny L___
Richard Robertson, 45
Kitty Robertson, 40
Henry Robertson, 17
Mary Ellen Robertson, 16
Robert Robertson, 12
Charity Culver, 60
Peter Culver, 4
Sarah Culver, 2
Rachel Russell, 7
Polly ___
Charles Jones, 60
Ann Jones, 49
George Jones, 19
Cassy Jones, 23
Edward Jones, 10
Samuel Jones, 5
Mary Ray, 25
William Allen, 5
Eli Ray, 2
Harriet Ann Ray, 1
William Bowen, 31
Julian Ann Bowen, 11
Rosetta Bowen, 9
William John Bowen, 7
John Boswell, 6
Ann Mariah Bacon
Ann Mariah Bacon, 3 days
Jeremiah Johnson, 63
Nancy Johnson, 56
Jeremiah Johnson Jr. 25
Rachel Johnson, 23
Benjamin Johnson, 21
Grafton Johnson, 20
Garrison Johnson, 20
Mary Ann Johnson, 14
Martha Maranda Johnson, 12

Eleanor Lancaster, 35
Caleb Adams, 61
Nacky Adams, 43
Elizabeth Adams, 16
Middleton Adams, 13
Kitty Adams, 7
Linda Adams, 5
Lucy Ann Adams,
Charlotte Lancaster, 38
Lila Lancaster, 13
William Lancaster, 10
George Lancaster, 8
Benjamin Lancaster, 6
Richard Lancaster, 4
Rachel Lancaster, 2
Caesar Plummer
James Prater
Susan Ross, 55
Edward Ross, 45
Samuel ___, 7
Susan Letton,
Samuel Jones, 22
William Jones, 21
Elick Adams, 40
Kitty Nichols, 60
___ Boswell, 30
Susan Watts, 28
Kitty Watts, 14
Betty Watts, 12
___ Watts, 8
Louis Watts, 10
V ___ Ann Watts, 5
Modecai Bellows, 61
___ Bellows, 45
Cassy Adams, 22
Kitty Bellows, 6
___ Bellows, 11
Isaac Bellows, 33
Priscilla Bellows, 25
Mordecai Bellows Jr. 33
Nancy Ann Bellows, 6
Mary Bellows, 11 months
Cephas Hall, 52
Jane Hall, 38
Cassandra Hall, 13
Kitty Hall, 10
Joseph Hall, 8
Louisa Hall, 5
Sarah Bacon, 40

Eliza Bacon, 16
Barbara Bacon, 12
Otho Bacon, 9 months
James Barrett, 57
Edward Adams, 52
Harriett Boswell, 38
Sarah Bacon Jr. 26
William Brown, 18
Nelly ___, 13
Andrew Boswell, 10
Nancy Boswell, 9
Jane Adams, 18
Thomas Boston, 21
William Shipley, 22
Lewes Jackson, 53
Lutetia Davis, 28
James Henry Davis, 10
Mahala Davis, 7
Mary Ann Davis, 7
Charlotte Davis
Martha Ellen Davis
Martha Ann Diggs, 18
William Diggs, 3
Rebecca Canter, 50
Ara Canter
Mira Canter
Rachel Canter, 1
George Canter, 14
Ann Canter, 13
John Canter, 10
Richard Lancaster, 60
Jemina Lancaster, 60
Elliot Adams
Thomas Lancaster, 35
Margaret Lancaster, 27
Louisa Lancaster, 5
Benjamin Lancaster, 7
Isiah Lancaster, 5
Theophilis Lancaster, 4
Edward Lancaster, 2
Francis Lancaster, 5 months
Benjamin Adams, 18
John C. Adams, 15
Silvia Wallace, 42
Charity Wallace, 17
Isaac Wallace, 15

Free African Americans of Maryland - 1832

Wesley Williams, 13
David Wallace, 11
Libby Ann Wallace, 9
Uriah Wallace, 7
Sarah Ann Dutton, 1
Robert Adams, 25
Rachel Adams, 25
Rosetta Adams, 2
Caleb Adams, 4
    months
Basil Stephens, 45
___ Ray, 65
Eliza Ann Taylor, 19
Julia Ann Taylor, 1
Ellen Taylor, 60
Abraham Kellom, 65
Sarah Kellom, 46
Martha Anne Kellom,
    9 months
C___ Burgess, 44
Mary ___, 40
John Baker, 56
Henry Baker, 54
Milly Baker, 8
Mary Baker, 6
Rachel Williams, 47
Jacob Holland, 30
Christina Holland,
    28
John Holland, 20
Nancy Holland, 15
Elisha Holland, 15
Elizabeth Holland,
    11
William Holland, 8
Sarah Holland, 5
William Becket, 27
Verlina Becket, 27
Joseph Becket, 6
William Henry
    Becket, 4
Enoch George
    Becket, 2
Theophilis Becket, 8
    months
Edward ___, 12
Charlotte Pla___, 9
Rachel Berry, 55
Elijah Webster, 9
Henry Webster, 6
Ho___ Webster, 38
Nancy Webster, 18
Franklin Webster, 14
Deborah Webster, 12
Levi Webster, 9
Mary Ann Webster, 7

Elizabeth Webster, 2
James Webster, 1
Samuel Powell, 56
Flora Powell, 16
Basil Powell, 17
Ann Denny, 9
William Henry
    Powell, 4
Grorge Franklin
Rachel Franklin
Nancy Franklin
Nelly Franklin
Nicholas Thomas
Ellen Thomas
Otho Garrett,, 16
Henrietta Garrett, 13
Thomas F___
Flora Brown, 35
Priscilla Brown, 7
Isaac Brown, 6
Susan Matthews, 45
Betsy Brown, 5
Rebecca Matthews,
    16
Richard Matthews 14
Clement Matthews, 8
Susanna Matthews,
    6
Sarah Elizabeth
    Matthews, 3
Caleb Briggs, 29
William Lancaster,
    37
Eliza Lancaster, 16
_____ Lancaster, 14
Edward Lancaster, 8
Horatio Sedgewick,
    28
Ellen Dorsey, 27
William Pumphrey,
    42
Hester Dorsey, 26
Samuel Dorsey, 7
John Dorsey, 4
Lavinia Dorsey, 1
Henry Todd, 35
Mariah Todd, 40
Mary Todd, 9
Joseph Todd, 7
Ann Todd, 5
William Webster, 57
Henny Webster, 57
Louisa Gassaway, 11
Mary Dorsey, 7
Jesse Hodges, 14

Samuel Pumphrey,
    30
Darius Pumphrey,
    24
John Edward
    Pumphrey, 4
Samuel Pumphrey
    Jr. 2
Sarah Pumphrey, 12
Mary Pumphrey, 48
Rachel Pumphrey,
    18
Henry Pumphrey, 1
Alfred Pumphrey, 1
Sarah Brown, 40
John Chew, 19
Samuel Booth, 40
Priscilla Booth, 40
Nicholas Berry, 10
Hanson Nugent, 10
Caroline Thomas, 15
Charles Powell, 65
Katy Powell, 70
Henny Bond, 60
Rachel Bond, 39
Maranda Bond, 13
Kitty Bond, 8
Thomas John Bond,
    6
Moses Lynn, 14
Alfred Barlow, 17
Jack Thomas, 45
Lavinia Thomas, 40
Rachel Ann Thomas,
    17
Thomas John
    Thomas, 9
Elizabeth Thomas, 5
Margaret Thomas, 3
Charles Washington
    Thomas, 1
Susan Beall, 11
Fanny Ducker, 55
Rozier Ducker, 30
Margart Dorsey, 70
Washington Lynn, 23
Letty Carter, 24
Mary Ellen Carter,
    10
William Carter, 4
John Wesley Carter,
    1
Philip Hamilton, 40
James Hamilton
George Moody, 55
George Askins, 4

111

Montgomery County

Harriet Bradley, 13
Rezin Webster, 35
Nicholas Waters, 60
Kate Waters, 45
Kitty Waters, 13
Urania Waters, 10
Sarah Ann Waters, 8
Amelia Waters, 5
Thomas Pumphrey, 17
Henry Taylor , 27
Sarah Taylor, 11
Edward Taylor, 12
Lydia Taylor, 8
Phillip Taylor, 5
Eliza Taylor, 3
Chester Taylor, 6 months
John Hamilton, 31
Philis Hamilton, 40
Barney Hamilton, 13
John Hamilton Jr. 9
Nicholas Hamilton, 4
Sarah Hamilton, 11 months
Lena Mitchell, 33

William Mitchell, 13
Rachel Mitchell, 8
Tilghman Mitchell, 6
Elizabeth Mitchell, 4
Hezekiah Mitchell, 2
Jacob Jones, 31
Freda Jones, 29
___ Ann Jones, 13
John Henry Jones, 11
Lucinda Jones, 9
Elizabeth Jones, 7
Mary Ellen Jones, 5
Perryander Jones, 3
William Henderson Jones, 1
Alfred Hopkins, 18
Thomas Price, 49
Tabitha Price, 31
Martha Price, 3
Caroline Calvert, 39
George Calvert, 49
Charlotte Calvert, 36
Henry Calvert, 17
Henrietta Calvert, 15
Thomas Calvert, 12

Maryetta Calvert, 10
Richard Calvert, 8
Hannah Calvert, 6
Robert Calvert, 4
Alexander Calvert, 2
Ann Maria Calvert, 10
Louisa Calvert, 5
Luc___ Calvert, 2
John Calvert, 34
Elizabeth Smith, 17
William Chase, 30
Eliza Taylor, 25
John Chew, 26
Lucy, 17
Hannah Lyles, 19
Priscilla Lyles, 17
Vachel Lyles, 15
Barnabas Lyles, 13
John Key, 8
Nicholas Hamilton, 3
Sarah Ellen Hamilton, 1
Thomas Willson, 24

Rockville, Montgomery County, Md.
Sept. 14th. 1832

To The Board of State Colonization Managers,

Gentlemen

Owing to the indisposition of my clerk & the press of other Business has prevented my making this return earlier.
There is none of the foregoing list that is willing to go to Liberia.

Very Respectfully
Your Obedient
Servant

William O'neale Jr. Sheriff.

Free African Americans of Maryland - 1832

A List of the Names and Ages of the Free People of Color Residing in Queen Anne's County, Maryland in 1832.

John Thomas, 45
Joseph Thomas, 40
Jenkins Browne, 5
Charles Wally, 16
John Charles
    Thomas, 2
    months
Issac Hill, 57
William Hill, 13
Charles Hill, 5
James Thomas, 12
Clinton Thomas, 6
Charles Thomas, 44
Henry Tillman, 65
Edward Wilson, 34
Peter Wilson, 13
William James
    Stansbury, 6
James Busley, 37
Samuel Deward, 12
William Johnson, 35
William Johnson Jr,
    9
Edward Johnson, 6
Jacob Johnson, 3
    months
Thomas Johnson, 2
Henry Hines, 16
Charles Wilson, 35
James Peaker, 54
Charles Miller, 33
Henry Johnson, 25
Nathaniel Hinson, 45
Clinton Hinson, 12
Samuel Baynard, 13
Alexander Baynard,
    6
Jeremiah Baynard, 6
Anthony Ayres, 47
Pere Hambleton, 26
Thomas Pritchett, 13
Pompey Damson, 52
Abram Hardcastle,
    36
James Hawkins, 49
James Hawkins Jr.
    14
Frisby Hawkins, 11
Charles Hutchins, 40
Charles A, Hutchins,
    12

James Dickinson, 8
Lambert Green, 24
Lymus Thomas, 47
William James
    Holland, 1
John Cole, 34
John C. Askins, 6
    months
Robert Gibbs, 19
Thomas Miller, 40
Thomas Miller, 3
Edward Downes, 60
George A. Hynson, 4
William Braccer, 50
James Wilmer, 9
Chester Hawkins, 26
Jefferson Grant, 21
John Emory, 15
Solomon Dickson, 50
Jerry Dobson, 14
Edward Elbert, 72
Gerald Elbert, 14
George Peck, 43
John Harris, 60
William Johnson, 12
Harry Ayres, 40
Jacob Midwinter, 70
Jerry Wallis, 60
James Wallis, 15
John Wallis, 9
Robert T. Wallis, 18
    months
David Colter, 2
Peter Hynson, 33
Charles Plater, 66
Dick Plater, 6
William Plater, 3
Solomon Johnson,
    50
William Pauls, 61
Solomon Plater, 1
Matthew Glasgow, 30
Lena Sullivan, 50
Richard L. Sullivan,
    2
William Jobes, 30
Bradford Harrison,
    20
Hercules Green, 70
Jacob Robinson, 7
Isaac Robinson, 3

Daniel Dunn, 60
Jack Jackson, 50
William Heath, 46
Darden N. Heath, 14
John L. Heath, 12
Pere Ringgold, 18
Daniel Dunn, 46
James Dunn, 5
Benjamin Browne,
    15
Charles Weeks, 38
Charles Weeks Jr. 4
Burton Weeks, 2
Levi White, 50
Arthur White, 15
Pere Smith, 3
Philemon Jobes, 60
Thomas Green, 10
Robert Green, 8
Samuel Green, 17
Jesse Lee, 46
Pere Johnson, 23
John Wilson, 50
Charles Dunn, 13
Nathan Wilson, 12
Richard Dunn, 19
John Dunn, 12
Lloyd Smith, 24
Pere Smith, 51
James Smith, 18
Pere Smith, 22
Jacob Wilson, 10
Henry Bowser, 3
James Barton, 45
James Barton Jr. 4
Jacob Barton, 3
James Griffin. 60
James Griffin, 18
Stephen Griffin, 10
Pere Griffin, 12
James Robinson, 6
Charles Dunn, 80
Samuel Johnson, 46
Philemon Baynor, 46
Richard Lee, 55
Jacob Harris, 12
Jeffrey Elliot, 80
John Wright, 14
Daniel Tolson, 48
Daniel Tolson, 15

Queen Ann's County, Maryland

John T. Tolson, 6 months
George Goldsbourgh, 26
Dick Robinson, 7
James Robinson, 10
Pere Robinson, 22
Samuel Roll, 10
Cesar Johnson, 46
William Anderson, 6
Pere Anderson, 4
Charles Anderson, 3
David Moore, 44
John T. Bayley, 11
Andrew Jobe, 35
Robert Wright, 19
George Lewis, 35
Walter Grinage, 14
Asbury Grinage, 12
Jessey Grinage, 17
David Nicholson, 14
Jobe Browne, 8
Andrew Browne, 6
Isaac Browne, 4
Harry Wilson, 58
Charles Turner, 4
William Wilson , 50
Pere Wilson, 18
Thomas Landman, 80
Thomas Landman Jr. 23
James Landman, 8
John Grinage, 10
Pere Browne, 21
Arthur Robinson, 13
David Nicholson, 12
James Green, 60
Jacob Harris, 14
Charles Clayton, 55
William Ringgold, 30
Charles Robinson, 10
Harry Crowner, 64
Henry Thomas, 6
Richard Jefferson, 55
Pere Stansbury, 30
James Harvey, 48
Joshua Harvey, 17
James Harvey, 11
Joseph Browne, 65
Thomas Wilson, 45
James Wilson, 20
Matthew Hazzard, 52
Richard Hazzard, 25
Daniel Watkins, 45

Samuel T. Watkins, 3
Alexander Watkins, 1
Pere Robinson, 50
Pere Robinson, 17
Richard Robinson, 2
Henry Robinson, 7
William C. Robinson, 4 months
Benjamin Nicholson, 22
Charles Nicholson, 19
David Nicholson, 14
Caleb L. Nicholson, 2
Nason Bouyer, 60
James Arthur Wilson, 2
Thomas Roberts, 10
Adam Roberts, 35
Jacob Meredith, 49
Richard Meredith, 14
John W. Meredith, 5
Frederick Lee, 24
James Heath, 2
Jacob Lee, 2 months
William Scott, 12
John Henry Meredith, 3
Jacob Hudson Mitchell, 4 months
James Mitchell, 41
Richard Mitchell, 9
James H. Mitchell, 9
Daniel Mitchell, 6
Thomas Mitchell, 4
Richard Wilson, 34
Arthur Browne, 3
Horace Browne, 33
Jacob Browne, 14
Frederick Browne, 34
John Ringgold, 18
Emory Muncy, 35
Richard Moore, 60
Charles Nicholson, 23
James Cook, 25
William Cook, 14
Henry Cook, 17
John Dyer, 55
Clinton Cook, 9
Samuel Griffin, 35
Charles Robinson, 50

Frederick Robinson, 26
William Moody, 45
Isaac Griffin, 80
Charles Hazzleton, 35
Philip Hazelton, 2 months
James Foreman, 40
Pere Bolden, 16
William Bolden, 14
Richard Bolden, 6
Solomon Bolden, 5
Samuel Bolden, 4
Sidney Bolden, 2
James Hazleton, 50
Robert Hazleton, 3
Henry Dobson, 4
James Dobson, 2
Philip Hutcheons, 58
Thomas Hutcheons, 14
Edward Jobe, 48
Aaron Little, 44
William Henry Little, 20
Robert Little, 15
John West Little, 4 months
Benjamin Wilmer, 4
Daniel Wilmer, 2
William Wilmer, 1
Jacob Simson, 30
Philemon Johnson, 45
Nat Hinson, 10
John Johns, 6
Robert Allen, 35
Solomon Wilson, 40
Contel Wilson, 33
John Wilson, 32
John Leeks, 35
William Browne, 34
Philip Gibson, 30
David Wilson, 45
Asbury Wilson, 18
Arthur Wilson, 17
David Thomas, 28
Polyps Collins, 70
William Jenkins, 45
Henry Thompson, 26
Nat Johnson, 1
James Browne, 33
John Gould, 35
Daniel Ashley, 6
John Godd, 5

Free African Americans of Maryland - 1832

James Godd, 6
Nathaniel Harris, 44
James Warwick, 9
Philip Thompson, 8
Philip Gibson, 30
Samuel Warwick, 16
Simon Morris, 12
Frank Anderson, 35
Robert Ashley, 35
Robert McHenny, 23
Samuel Anderson, 68
David Ashley, 11
Frank Anderson, 30
George Jones, 30
George Devoris, 25
Pere Nailer, 38
Levi Elliot, 27
Peter Dawson, 35
Thomas Chambers, 18
Caesar Faulkner, 69
George Bishop, 33
Henry Jackson, 11
James Lively, 40
Thomas Miller, 46
Benjamin Grimes, 20
Henry Clark, 50
William Wilmer, 33
Aaron Johnson, 30
Aaron Hans, 10
Philip Johnson, 45
Asbury Johnson, 9
Christopher Belicin, 50
Alfred Johnson, 5
James Emory, 65
James Demby, 35
Richard Massey, 39
Robert Warrick, 40
David Hawkins, 36
Stephen Granger, 12
Dowale Thompson, 40
William H. Ringgold, 15
Peter Dawson, 50
Pere Browne, 30
James Green, 35
Benjamin Blake, 40
George Heckster, 48
John Rochester, 1
Charles Browne, 70
Richard Brinkley, 68
Frisby Rice, 39
Aaron Price, 11

James Elliot, 17
Isaac Freeman, 38
Pere Landman, 11
James Johnson, 23
Jacob Price, 75
Charles H. Price, 1
William Starling, 25
William Aldridge, 25
Richard Rochester, 59
Isaac Mote, 67
William Williams, 73
Thomas Williams, 7
Alfred Johnson, 5
Authur Moray, 35
Henry Moody, 17
Samuel Moody, 14
Charles Moody, 11
William Moody, 18
Thomas Hacket, 40
Wesley Trusty, 8
William Roberts, 33
Henry Roberts, 7
Authur Roberts, 4
Arthur Griffin, 26
William Griffin, 22
Benjamin Griffin, 18
William H. Griffin, 4
James A. Griffin, 1
John Greenage, 25
Thomas C. Browne, 3
David Ashley, 30
David Ashley, 11
William Ashley, 8
Benjamin Smith, 6
William Anthony, 35
John W. Anthony, 7
William Anthony, 11
James Wilson, 45
Charles Wilson , 10
Joseph Line, 20
Henry Clark, 20
Thomas Steward, 15
George W. Massey, 11
Joseph Sena, 25
Sewell Nacky, 13
George Masey, 60
Asbury Tilghman, 10
Joshua Masey, 11
Joseph Masey, 1
Pere Nailer, 19
Frisby Price, 11
John B. Offley, 25
Authur Offley, 7

James Masten, 20
Jacob Freeman, 30
Jacob Potts, 45
Charles E. Offley, 20
Jacob Manson, 60
William Landman, 8
Charles Landman, 4
Wilson Brinkley, 32
Adam Brinkley, 30
Wilson Brinkley, 4
Wesley Brown, 4
Thomas Prior, 14
John Offley, 27
Charles E. Offley, 20
Alexander Offley, 17
Greenbury Offley, 23
Stephen Downes, 31
Charles Green, 84
Henry Con, 49
Ellenoyer, Parker, 46
Stepney Gould, 45
John W. Gould, 6
Jacob Freeman, 28
Pere I. Freeman, 1
Emery Harrison, 19
____ Harrison, 20
James Harrison, 10
William Harrison, 6
Thomas Harrison, 6
William Simpson, 18
Nat Johnson, 49
Greenbury Bright, 48
Pere Simpson, 35
William Browne, 55
Thomas Browne, 15
Greenbury Brown, 3
Charles Browne, 31
Jacob Wright, 17
Harrison Wright, 13
James Miller, 70
John Young, 6
Charles Potts, 46
Charles Potts, 10
Pompey Carpenter, 97
Edward Hawkins, 47
Jacob Farewell, 55
Jacobs Hopkins, 13
Samuel Gibson, 17
Phil Hines Jr. 45
Henry Hines, 18
Pere Hines, 13
William Hines, 3
Thomas Griffin, 55
Samuel Hackett, 47
John Green, 25

Queen Ann's County, Maryland

Dick Warrick, 13
Ben Warrick, 13
William H. Hackett, 5
Samuel Baleman, 60
Charles Wilson, 20
Elijah Wilson, 18
Charles Wilson, 15
Charles Wilson, 6
Peter Griffin, 25
Pere Griffin, 4
Samuel Wells, 56
William Knotts, 14
Samuel Knotts, 9
Samuel Warner, 22
Henry Hollyday, 27
Alexander _____, 7
Robert Wright, 60
Samuel Hemsley, 46
Richard Hemsley, 15
James Hemsley, 14
Samuel Hemsley, 12
Alexander Hemsley, 6
Ester Rino, 49
William Henry Rino, 18
John Rino, 15
James Rino, 13
Asbury Rino, 4
Basil Browne, 34
Esau Browne, 55
Benjamin Elliot, 65
William Henry Wright, 1
Nathaniel Trueman, 55
Acco Cook, 100
James Browne, 8
Eliphalett Browne, 16
Thomas McDaniel, 40
James Henry McDaniel, 3
Aaron Griffin, 12
James Kent, 6
Thomas Johns, 2
James H. Johns, 1
James Thomas, 55
George Wicks, 14
Benjamin Downes, 3
William Downes, 9
Phill Johns, 62
Michael Young, 40
Michael Young, 11 months

Joseph Hollis, 35
Mark Dood, 25
Thomas Dood, 16
Benjamin Dood, 18
Solomon Stephens, 35
Daniel Browne, 16
Samuel Freak, 17
James Freak, 9
David Wally, 60
John Brandiford, 3
James Griffin, 27
Mathias Sampson, 70
Henry Sampson, 24
William Cuff, 40
Perre Earle, 43
Noah Earle, 7
Perre Earle, 6
Michael Thomas, 48
George Anderson, 13
Jesse Reese, 4
William Levi Rice, 1
Thomas Askins, 15
Epiphany Pembrook, 41
William Pembrook, 2
Charles Pembrook, 18 months
William Mitchell, 22
William Pearce, 45
Jeremiah Fisher, 55
William Fisher, 2
James Jackson, 18
William Hercules, 32
Elisha Warner, 65
James Wilkins, 45
Charles Griffin, 51
Thomas Griffin, 17
Charles Griffin, 6
John Holland, 55
Pere Carter, 35
William Johnson, 26
John Carter, 15
Pere Carter, 10
Charles Carter, 4
Isaac Holiday, 48
Jacob Johnson, 55
Henry Johnson, 2
John Holliday, 2
Richard Bias, 20
John Murphey, 40
Thomas Moore, 30
John Moore, 7
Samuel Murry, 4
Henry Chair, 7

John Cain, 14
Moses Thomas, 18
Aron Thomas, 8
John Thomas, 7
Jacob Taylor, 53
Isaac Taylor, 27
Major Dyoto, 27
John Johnson, 18
Alexander Johnson, 16
James Mackey, 11
Richard French, 80
George Peck, 30
George Peck, 3
London Gould, 35
Thomas Nichols, 39
Mark Corner, 14
Thomas H. Nichols, 4
Joshua Smallwood, 65
Joshua Smallwood, 26
Asbury Bias, 5
James Corner, 6
Anthony Thomas, 40
Harriston Thomas, 14
Garretson Thomas, 13
Jossia Thomas, 12
Anthony Thomas, 4
James Thomas, 2
Pere Coge, 60
Joshua Martin, 16
Madison Giles, 7
Clinton Giles, 4 months
Richard Dutron, 60
George Sampson, 60
Henry Comegys, 3
Jacob Moody, 20
Joshua Hines, 35
Shadrach Sands, 60
John Darnold, 35
Alexander Jones, 27
Samuel Hall, 55
David Laddy, 37
James Moody, 37
Thomas Griffin, 45
Esau Eccleston, 30
Phileman Eccleston. 14
Ervin Curtis, 8
Daniel Curtis, 3
John Burkett, 40

116

Free African Americans of Maryland - 1832

James Burkett, 6 months
George Waters, 30
Alexander Knotts, 11
William Heath, 50
William Heath, 11
John W. Heath, 8
Charles Dickerson, 22
James Dickerson, 17
Thomas Heath, 2
George Ayres, 32
James Jackson, 15
Arthur Ayres, 32
Joseph Dobson, 55
Charles Ayres, 6
Joseph Ayres, 13
Luther Ayres, 8
Robert Roseberry, 60
Perre Roseberry, 4
Francis Roseberry, 3
Henry Wilson, 28
Jacob Wright, 19
George Baccer, 40
Mark Hutchins, 50
Toby Hicks, 60
Daniel McDaniel, 50
William Noke, 60
William Noke, 23
Ezekial Noke, 12
William Pritchett, 24
Thomas Pritchett, 16
Samuel Pritchett, 10
William H. Pritchett, 1
Solomon Griffin, 16
Anderson Parsons, 60
Joseph Adke, 60
Robert Farewell, 64
William Boson, 64
Ben Wright, 58
Cloudbury Jones, 38
Benjamin Clemonts, 80
Isaac Benson, 55
Jacob Kent, 27
Pere Johnson, 45
William James Johnson, 3
John Green, 15
Charles Wright, 15
Charles Costen, 10
Benjamin Costen, 1
William Costen, 4

Thomas Chickeman, 8
John Tranor, 65
Aaron Wisher, 40
Frank Bordley, 43
George Norman, 2
Henry Eccleston, 30
Pere Anderson, 38
Joseph Anderson, 10
John Johnson, 57
William Johnson, 6
Henry Farenton, 22
Levin Jackson, 54
James Jackson, 16
Asbury Jackson, 13
Alexander Jackson, 12
Samuel Jackson, 9
Andrew Jobe, 35
Solomon Wright, 35
James Howard, 50
Pere Gleaves, 35
John Tack, 30
Arnor Stinson, 30
Solomon Miers, 8
Pompey Miers, 7
Jefferson Daws, 21
Henry Wilson, 58
Solomon Wilson, 32
Philip Pritchett, 4
Oster Pritchett, 1
James Gould, 35
John Pritchett, 4
Lynford Prichett, 6 months
William Wilson, 22
Benjamin Wilson, 88
Solomon WilsonSamuel Wilson, 13
Benjamin Wilson, 1
Joseph Lockerman, 55
William Lockerman, 7
Solomon Thompson, 40
Hugh Fox, 17
Charles Fox, 20
Philemon Hines, 60
Cornelious Comegys, 50
William Johnson, 50
Daniel Johnson, 9
Solomon Johns, 6
Robert Johns, 4

Wesley Groice, 35
James H. Wilmer, 10
Richard Wilmer, 5
Charles Black, 40
Edward Fullerman, 5
John Black, 3
David Gould, 3
Samuel Gould, 6
Benjamin Hackett, 60
Thomas Lingo, 1
Pere Copper, 40
John Buck, 60
William H. Stinson, 6
Arnold Stinson, 36
Robert Wilson, 25
Garretson Wilson, 10
Clemus Hughston, 60
Samuel Stinson, 65
Samuel Comegys, 6
Samuel Griffin, 30
Samuel Griffin, 7
William H. Griffin, 6
Alexander Griffin, 5
Arthur Griffin, 2
Harrison Dolens, 9
Charles Smith, 40
Charles Smith, 6
John Smith, 5
Emory Smith, 2
Richard Smith, 21
John White, 18
Alexander White, 16
Jervis Gasaway, 69
John German, 5
Abraham Young, 30
Robert Wright, 50
James Johnson, 25
Frank Johnson, 60
John H. Johnson, 6
Robert Scott, 35
James Scott, 8
Richard Scott, 4
Pere Leatherberry, 55
Thomas Johnson, 18
Charles Wicks, 46
Robert Rollins, 33
Robert S. Rollins, 4
Samuel W. Rollins, 2
Hemsley Brooks, 50
Charles Keene, 60
Samuel Keene, 33
Henry Keene, 1
Jacob Keene, 22

Queen Ann's County, Maryland

James Furell, 13
Pere Frisby, 40
James P. Frisby, 1
John Wilson, 14
Isaac Woodling, 18
Joseph Bowyer, 27
Adam Hackett, 56
Isaac Goldsberry, 66
Robert Smith, 56
Robert Wilson, 60
James Duckey, 21
Jacob Duhamel, 62
William H. Duhamel.
  15
Benjamin Duhamel,
  7
John Duhamel, 2
Frisby Hood, 2
James Green, 2
William Green, 3
Samuel Green, 1
Moses Bradley, 40
James Bradley, 7
Luser Gafford, 55
Mike Cooper, 52
John Cooper, 12
James Cooper, 10
John Burgess, 10
Jacob Gafford, 36
Willam H. Tilghman,
  10
Thomas Gafford, 5
James Fogwell, 68
Henry Potts, 16
Samuel Johnson, 50
Thomas Cook, 20
James Simmons, 53
Alfred Simmons, 26
Richard Simmons,
  15
William Simmons, 10
Arthur Simmons, 8
Benjamin Price, 40
Luther Price, 3
Jonathan Price, 1
Joseph Lewis, 40
James Grinage, 52
Joseph Hollis, 35
Mark Dodd, 25
Thomas Dodd, 16
Mark Dood, 60
Benjamin Dodd, 18
Solomon Stephens,
  35
Daniel Browne, 16
Samuel Freak, 17

James Freak, 9
David Wally, 60
John Brandyford, 20
William H.
  Brandyford, 3
James Griffin, 27
Mathias Sampson,
  70
Henry Sampson, 24
William Cuff, 40
Perre Earle, 43
Noah Earle, 7
Griffin, 51
Thomas Griffin, 17
Charles Griffin, 6
John Holland, 55
Pere Carter, 35
William Johnson, 26
John Carter, 15
Perre Carter, 10
Charles Carter, 4
Isaac Holliday, 48
Jacob Johnson, 55
Henry Johnson, 2
John Holliday, 2
Richard Bias, 20
John Murphey, 40
Thomas Murray, 30
John Murray, 7
Samuel Murray, 4
Henry Chairs, 7
John Cain, 14
Moses Thomas, 18
Aron Thomas, 8
John Thomas, 7
Jacob Taylor, 53
Isaac Taylor, 27
Major Dyoto, 27
John Johnson, 18
Alexander Johnson,
  16
James Mackey, 11
Richard French, 80
George Peck, 30
George Peck, 2
London Gould, 35
Thomas Nichols, 39
Mark Corner, 14
Thomas H. Nichols, 4
Joshua Smallwood,
  65
Joshua Smallwood,
  26
Asbury Byas, 5
James Corner, 6
Anthony Thomas, 40

Harrison Thomas, 14
Garrettson Thomas,
  13
Gassia Thomas, 12
Anthony Thomas, 4
James Thomas, 2
Pere Coge, 60
Joshua Martin, 16
Madison Giles, 7
Clinton Giles, 4
  months
Richard Dutron, 60
George Sampson, 60
Henry Comedies, 3
Jacob Moody, 20
Joshua Hines, 35
Shadrach Sands, 60
John Darnels, 55
Alexander Jones, 27
Samuel Hall, 65
David Laddy, 37
James Moody, 37
Thomas Griffin, 65
Esau Eccleston, 30
Philemon Eccleston,
  14
Ervin Curtis, 8
Daniel Curtis, 3
John Burkett, 40
James Burkett, 6
  months
George Waters, 30
Alexander Knotts, 11
William Heath, 50
William Heath, 10
John W. Heath, 8
Charles Dickerson,
  22
James Dickerson, 17
Thomas Heath, 2
George Ayres 32
James Jackson, 15
Arthur Ayres, 14
Joseph Dobson, 55
Charles Ayres, 60
Luther Ayres, 6
Robert Roseberry, 61
Perre Roseberry, 4
Francis Roseberry, 3
Henry Wilson, 28
Jacob Wright, 19
George Bauer, 40
Mark Hutchins, 50
Toby Hicks, 60
Daniel McDaniel, 50
William Noke, 60

Free African Americans of Maryland - 1832

William Noke, 23
Ezekial Noke, 12
William Pritchett, 24
Thomas Pritchett, 16
Samuel Pritchett, 10
William H. Pritchett,
1
Solomon Griffin, 16
Anderson Parsons,
60
Joseph Adke, 60
Robert Farewell, 64
William Boson, 64
Ben Wright, 58
Cloudberry Jones,
38
Benjamin Clements,
80
Isaac Benson, 55
Jacob Kent, 27
Perre Johnson, 45
William James
Johnson, 3
John Green, 15
Charles Wright, 15
Charles Costen, 10
Benjamin Costen, 1
William Costen, 4
Thomas Chickeman,
8
John Teanor, 65
Aaron Wisher, 40
Frank Bordley, 45
George Norman, 2
Henry Eccleston, 30
William H. Eccleston,
4
Perre Anderson, 38
Joseph Anderson
John Johnson, 57
William Johnson, 6
Henry Farenton, 22
Levin Jackson, 54
James Jackson, 16
Asbury Jackson, 13
Alexander Jackson,
12
Samuel Jackson, 9
Andrew Jobe, 35
Solomon Wright, 35
James Howard, 50
Pere Cleaves, 35
John Tack, 30
Ann Hinson, 30
Solomon Miers, 8
Pompey Miers, 7

Jefferson Davis, 21
Perry Wilson, 58
Solomon Wilson, 32
Philip Pritchett
Oster Pritchett, 1
James Gould, 35
Lynford Pritchett, 64
William Wilson, 22
Benjamin Wilson, 88
Solomon Wilson, 18
Samuel Wilson, 13
Joseph Lockerman,
55
William Lockerman,
7
Solomon Thompson,
40
Hugh Fox, 17
Charles Fox, 20
Philemon Hines, 60
Cornelious Comegys,
50
William Johnson, 50
Daniel Johnson, 9
Solomon Johns, 6
Robert Johns, 4
Wesley Groie, 35
James H. Wilmer, 10
Richard Wilmer, 5
Charles Black, 40
Edward Fullerman, 5
John Black, 3
David Gould, 3
Samuel Gould, 6
Benjamin Hackett,
60
Thomas Lingo, 1
Pere Copper, 40
John Buck, 60
William H. Stinson, 6
Arnold Stinson, 36
Robert Wilson, 25
Garrettson Wilson,
10
Clenus Hughston, 60
Samuel Hinson, 65
Samuel Comegys, 6
Samuel Griffin, 30
Samuel Griffin, 7
William H. Griffin, 6
Alexander Griffin, 5
Arthur Griffin, 2
Harrison Dalons, 9
Charles Smith, 6
John Smith, 5
Emory Smith, 2

Richard Smith, 21
John White, 18
Alexander White, 16
Jervis Gasaway, 69
John German, 5
Abraham Young, 30
Robert Wright, 50
James Johnson, 25
Tank Johnson, 60
John H. Johnson, 6
Robert Scott, 35
William Scott, 10
James Scott, 8
Richard Scott, 4
Pere Leatherberry,
55
Thomas Johnson, 18
Charles Weeks, 46
Robert Rollins, 2
Samuel W. Rollins, 2
Hemsley Brooks, 50
Charles Kune, 60
Samuel Kune, 53
Henry Kune, 1
Jacob Kune, 22
James Sorrell, 13
Pere Frisby, 40
James P. Frisby, 1
John Wilson, 14
Isaac Woodling, 18
Joseph Bouyer, 27
Adam Hackett, 56
Anthony Hackett, 10
George Hackett, 6
Isaac Goldsberry, 66
Robert Smith, 56
Robert Witson, 60
James Duckey, 21
Jacob Duhamel, 62
William H. Duhamel,
15
Benjamin Duhamel,
15
John Duhamel, 2
Frisby Hood, 2
James Green, 2
William Green, 3
Samuel Green, 1
Moses Bradley, 40
James Bradley, 7
Luser Gafford, 55
Mike Cooper, 52
John Cooper, 10
James Cooper, 10
John Burgess, 10
Jacob Gafford, 36

119

Queen Ann's County, Maryland

William H. Tilghman, 10
Thomas Gafford, 5
James Fogwell, 68
Henry Potts, 16
Samuel Johnson, 50
Thomas Crook, 20
James Simmons, 53
Alfred Simmons, 16
Richard Simmons, 15
William Simmons, 10
Arthur Simmons, 8
Benjamin Price, 40
Luther Price, 3
Jonathan Price, 1
Joseph Lewis, 40
James Grinage, 52
Thomas Grinage, 22
James Grinage, 19
William Grinage, 18
Wesley Grinage, 16
Emmanuel F. Anderson, 13
John T. Anderson, 9
James Baynard, 50
Pere Tiller, 40
Henry Gould, 35
John Holland, 28
James Gould, 4
Joshua Lung, 25
Moses Lung, 11
Robert Ferrell, 45
Levi Downes, 5
John Benton, 40
Charles H. Downes, 1
Jacob Gibson, 35
George Gibson, 5
William Gibson, 3
John Price, 30
Samuel Rochester, 4
Abraham Rochester, 65
Clemus Lowman, 65
Mingo Holliday, 45
Robert Bauske, 12
Theodore Cooper, 4
Jacob Cooper, 1
Abraham Gibb, 71
Daniel Gilbert, 18
James Gibb, 12
David Massey, 60
Benjamin Massey, 21
Emory Jackson, 23
George Benson, 30

Charles Blackiston, 40
Samuel Blackiston, 3
Benjamin Sands, 70
Thomas Coursey, 16
John Coursey, 13
William Coursey, 6
Benjamin Warwick, 55
James Warwick, 10
Robert Warwick, 6
Joseph Warwick, 5
William Warwick, 1
James F. Casey, 3
William Hollis, 7
James Hollis, 3
Henry Monday, 60
William Browne, 55
Lloyd Browne, 25
Joseph Wright, 23
Jacob Rochester, 35
William Rochester, 10
Samuel Rochester, 4
Joseph Ferrell, 45
John Ferrell, 9
Shadrach Tiller, 7
Pere Tiller, 7
William J. Wright, 1
Benjamin Hanson, 5
John Hanson, 29
John Carsons, 30
John Carsons Jr. 6
Jacob Barton, 15
John L. Benton, 12
Levi Benton, 10
James Wilson, 3
James Kelly, 19
Daniel Kelly, 21
Benjamin Harison, 35
James Green, 35
William Green, 7
James Green, 7
John Green, 5
Benjamin Green, 3
Chester Jackson, 70
Elias Johnson, 36
John Johnson, 20
Joseph Lewis, 40
Joseph Seegar, 30
Benjamin Dixon, 60
Samuel Gulen, 90
Nathaniel Walttum, 45
John Bordler, 29

Frank Coppage, 18
Noah Coppage, 9
Joseph Seegar, 80
Joseph Gibb, 3
James Fogwill, 3
Benjamin Massey, 27
Solomon Leary, 21
James Fare, 40
James A. Fare, 4
Henry Browne, 40
James Browne, 19
John Browne, 14
Pere Bradshaw, 44
Pere Bradshaw, 7
James Medford, 90
Abraham Gibbs, 30
Joseph Hutchins, 8
Philemon Hutchins, 5
Oneal Comegys, 35
Henry New, 18
Joseph New, 10
Jacob Bordly, 44
Lunan Bordly, 38
John W. Bordly, 2
George Coys, 50
Joseph Ferrell, 38
Levi Ferrell, 15
Henry Kelson, 28
James Wilson, 30
John Wilson, 13
James Wilson, 11
Thomas Wilson, 9
Robert Wilson, 6
Therey Wilson, 1
James Hawkins, 6
James Darnal, 45
James Price, 45
Frisby Price, 17
Moses Price, 14
Joseph Price, 6
Charles Price, 5
Joshua Price, 4
James Hoges, 24
Clinton Hoges, 10
Andrew Raisin, 29
Thomas Bau, 90
Charles Bordly, 7
Jacob Bordley, 3
William Raisin, 4
John Raisin, 3
Andrew Raisin, 2
Samuel Little, 50
John Browne, 26
Lemuel Wilmer, 58
Charles Bell, 70

Free African Americans of Maryland - 1832

Joseph Oliver, 62
Daniel Smith, 60
Warner Gibbs, 16
Joshua Oliver, 17
Abraham Cook, 8
David Hatcheson, 7
William Cook, 4
Jacob Jeffers, 70
William Jeffers, 31
John Jeffers, 18
George Jeffers, 17
Isiah Jeffers, 5
William Anthony, 40
Thomas Anthony, 2
Thomas Henderson, 32
Thomas Browne, 3
William Smith, 7
Solomon SmithThomas Hackett, 45
Thomas Sharp, 17
Samuel Kelson, 55
Samuel Kelson Jr. 25
Pere Kelson, 20
George Perrel, 25
James Ferrell, 20
Abraham Ferrell, 25
William Rochester, 2
George Monday, 45
Alfred Simmons, 4
Joshua Kelson, 25
Henry Kelson, 15
James French, 45
George Coge, 40
Jacob Daniel, 13
William Daniel, 19
Jacob Daniel, 13
Robert Daniel, 11
Samuel Daniel, 4
Simon Daniel, 5
Pere Daniel, 3
John Daniel, 2
George Daniel, 22
Cuffy Rowe, 58
Daniel Rowe, 20
James Rowe, 15
Samuel Perkins, 48
John Green, 27
Robert Warrick, 21
John Green, 5
Richard Masey, 57
Adam Wilson, 27
Samuel Kelly, 65

Joshua Kelly, 8 months
Samuel W. Kelly, 6
William H, Kelly, 7
Lewis Comegys, 75
James Wadkins, 18
Falin Thompson, 80
Walter Thompson, 25
William H. Woodling, 5
Edward S. Mason, 2
Isaac Nailor, 35
Pere Nailor, 1
Philip Dixon, 37
Levi Dixon, 3
George Dixon, 1
Emory Temples, 43
Emory Temples, 12
Samuel Temples, 6
Pere Wilson, 26
Philip Davis, 3
Solomon Scott, 45
Isaac Masey, 34
Isaiah Masey, 5
George Masey, 50
Henry Stevens, 45
Samuel Wilmer, 80
Robert Kasy, 40
Henry Mason, 9
Robert Mason, 6
Henry Nichols, 26
Richard Emory, 60
Pere Miers, 70
Harrison Miers, 38
Isaiah Miers, 32
William Anderson, 45
Phil Wye, 21
Benjamin Thomas, 70
Cain Thomas, 20
Daniel Thomas, 18
John Thomas, 11
Hannibal Thompson, 55
James Thompson, 20
Benjamin Thompson, 16
Frisby Gannon, 25
Phil Sewel, 35
William Sewel, 6
Benjamin Grinage, 35

Benjamin Grinage, 11
George Grinage, 9
Jacob Grinage, 6
Mingo Mason, 45
Emory Mason, 13
Henry Mason, 8
Stephen Thomas, 30
Richard Thomas, 3
James Brown, 2
Samuel Wright, 35
George Brown, 70
Williams Ferguson, 35
Samuel Ferguson, 4
Charees Gooby, 4
Charles Gooby, 35
Joseph Reed, 50
Joe Garain, 70
Jacob Downes, 45
Jace Freeman, 40
William Freeman, 35
James Clayton, 40
Jonas Asbury, 15
George Rine, 6
Phill Johns, 65
George Waters, 35
John A. J. Griffin, 9 months
Abram Sutton, 50
Joseph Anderson, 13
William Thompson, 13
Henry Thompson, 6
David Deford, 13
William Kirby, 5
Samuel Kirby, 1
Samuel Kiry, 100
Joseph Hawkins, 30
Charles Hawkins, 3
Joseph Hawkins, 4 months
Jervis Hutchenson, 8
Wake Miers, 70
Charles Chairs, 45
Jefferson Chairs, 14
Bill Pindar, 12
Henry Kelson, 30
Samuel Kelson, 60
Pere Kelson, 21
Joshua Kelson, 23
Henry Kelson, 20
George Monday, 65
George Dyer, 40
Henry Dyer, 10
Sherry Flamer, 30

121

Queen Ann's County, Maryland

Nicholas Flamer, 15
Lazarus Little, 35
Harry Hinson, 50
Ben Barrick, 60
John Foreman, 35
Jacob Hutchinson, 40
Henry Sampson, 30
Alexander Hutchins, 28
Pere Lee, 26
William Hutchins, 27
Barnett Hollyday, 25
John, 32
Arthur Rochester, 25
William Pindar, 12
Theodore Pindar, 12
Jesse Hughes, 50
Nathan Pearce, 33
James Pearce, 28
Pere Pindar, 24
Samuel Pindar, 20
Isaac Freeman, 60
Edward Goldsbourough, 35
Joseph Harrod, 35
Richard Scott, 30
Infant No Name, 3 months
Henry Muncy, 45
William H. Muncy, 11
Samuel T. Dawson, 27
James Hinson, 14

Names of Females

Dinah Thomas, 40
Mary Smith, 39
Mary E. Smith, 12
Angelina Smith, 4
Littilla Thomas, 39
Susan Browne, 30
Harriet Browne, 7
Margaret Thomas, 26
Mary Dally, 13
Henrietta Thomas, 3
Hannah Hill, 40
Anamaria Hill, 12
Hester Thomas, 38
Eliza Thomas, 7
Harriet Thomas, 4
Augusta Thomas, 57
Lucy Cox, 40
Rachel Bell, 8

Mary Bell, 8
Ann Stansbury, 25
Mary Wilson, 18
Maria R. Stansbury, 8
Rachel Bruss, 55
Elizabeth Burley, 40
Rachel Hambleton, 59
Caroline Kant, 10
Anamaria Lary, 17
Milly Johnson, 35
Susan A, Johnson, 10
Kitty Wye, 39
Margaret Wye, 60
Eliza Browne, 8
Lucy Dawson, 19
Nelly Griffin, 40
July Ann Hutchins, 40
Tena Ann Hutchens, 6
Nelly Hutchens, 4
Mary Ann Hutchens, 2
Hannah Raker, 54
Hannah Hinson, 51
Sophia Spencer, 7
Mary Baynard, 50
Susan Harrod, 14
Henny Lingo, 45
Charlotte Hambleton, 23
Maria Dawson,. 28
Fanny Grant, 64
Anna Hardcastle, 23
Nancy Hardcastle, 3
Anamaria Hutchens, 7
Mary E. Hutchens, 4
Sarah J. Hutchens, 2 weeks
Elizabeth Smith, 20
Susan Lingo. 60
Ann Caldwell, 9
Hannah Thomas, 48
Elizabeth Thomas, 13
Charlotte Ann Thomas, 7
Harriet Thomas, 9
Mary Cole, 45
July Ann Cole, 4
Susan Harrod, 17
Laura Harod, 6

Maria Miller, 33
Adeline Miller, 2
Sarah Miers, 30
Elizabeth Downes, 35
Henrietta Brace, 59
Margaret Bracer, 22
Mary Elizabeth Richards, 42
Fanny Wilmer, 56
Jane Harden, 17
Daphnay Ann Jackson, 1
Ann Hawkins, 22
Anamaria Bryan, 10
Tena Wallys, 35
Dinah Peckham, 58
Rachel Emory, 47
Henrietta Emory, 24
Mary Emory, 20
Emoly Ann Emory, 2
Rebecca Maxwell, 50
Dolly Browne, 70
Mary Ors, 80
Sarah Elbert, 70
Louisa Elbert, 3
Frances Ann Elbert, 11
Dolly Peeke, 43
Ruth Johnson, 53
Rosetta Wallis, 45
Sally Ann Wallis, 11
Louisa Wallis, 5
Phillis Colter, 32
Mary Colter, 4
Rebecca Plater, 65
Charity Browne, 40
Rachel Plater, 36
Sarah Johnson, 27
Louisa Plater, 8
Sally Ann Plater, 3
Margaret Paul, 50
Margaret Hinson, 18
Mary Chairs, 40
Mary Chamberlain, 8
Statia Chamberlain, 17
Margaret Patterson, 70
Sophia Silivan, 65
Fanny Few, 25
Pindar Harvey, 50
Ann Harvey, 19
Mary Ann Robinson, 45
Chloe Dunn, 62

Free African Americans of Maryland - 1832

Darky Jacobs, 90
Ruth Jackson, 54
Harriet Jackson, 10
Nancy Heath, 48
Milly Heath, 7
Rachel Heath, 18
Henny Hazleton, 39
Sarah Green, 50
Dinah Hutchins, 13
July Ann Heath, 25
Phoeby Dunn, 46
Abarelly Dunn, 8
Eliza Weeks, 5
Mary Green, 17
Harriet Anderson, 4
Mary Thomas, 22
Sarah Skinner, 60
Henny Tolson, 41
Elizabeth Tolson, 13
Henny Tolson, 4
Polly Robinson, 45
Henny Green, 65
Ann Green, 23
Rachel Green, 3
Rachel Johnson, 36
Henrietta Johnson, 8
Anamaria Johnson, 4
Sophia Anderson, 32
Harriet Anderson, 16
Rachel Anderson, 7
Mary Anderson, 1
Nancy Moore, 60
Margaret Granger, 65
Esther Wright, 25
Ann Gains, 13
Jane Griffin, 29
Phillis Browne, 39
Kitty U. Browne, 10
Margaret Ann Browne, 2
Patty Griffin, 30
Priscilla Griffin, 3
Cassy Sutton, 70
Ally Wilson, 58
Susan Wilson, 20
Harriet Wilson, 2
Sylvia Turner, 28
Tena Turner, 8
Eliza Turner, 6
Susan Wilson, 15
Rebecca Ann Wilson, 15
Sarah Ann Wilson, 12

Henrietta Wilson, 6
Mary Ann Wilson, 2
Rose Landman, 70
Kitty Landman, 32
Rose Landman, 5
Susan Landman, 3
Emeline Landman, 1
Fanny Landman, 8
Jenny Browne, 50
Ann Willams, 26
Priscilla Anderson, 10
Sarahall I. Tilghman, 16
Delia Tilghman, 16
Hannah Clayton, 40
Rebecca Clayton, 2
Mary Robinson, 10
Phoeby Snead, 50
Sarah Ringgold, 30
Elizabeth Lucas, 6
Mary Ringgold, 6
Ann Ringgold, 4
Rose Baily, 60
Hannah Baily, 40
Fanny Wright, 3
Henny Crowner, 49
Catherine Jefferson, 60
Melia Gains, 15
Hannah Harvey, 45
Lydia Harvey, 7
Rachel Cox, 68
Mary Williams, 18
Margaret Wilson, 40
Esther Barton, 50
Esther Barton, 14
Sara Barton, 19
Mary Barton, 20
Hariett Whitaker, 26
Eliza Whitaker, 3
Ruth Gibson, 50
Sally Gibson, 50
Sally Anderson, 7
Esther Hazzard, 70
Jane Cower, 12
Anamaria Worthington, 35
Queen Grinage, 40
Mary Ann Grinage, 21
Adeline Grinage, 10
Dinah Carroll, 70
July E. Green, 24
Harriet I. E. Green, 3
Sarah Robinson, 30

Hester Robinson, 15
Rachel Robinson, 13
Eliza Robinson, 20
Charlotte Nicholson, 50
Cusby Frasier, 23
Elizabeth Bouyer, 49
Daphny Wilson, 30
Lucretia Roberts, 70
Ann Meridith, 47
Mary Lee, 21
Priscilla Meridith, 12
Juliet Meridith, 9
Rachel Meridith, 4
Catherine Meridith, 2
Judy Berry, 49
Jane Garretson, 75
Darky Mitchell, 23
Ann Johnson, 20
Henny Waters, 16
Phillis Davis, 50
Ann Mitchell, 29
Ann Mitchell, 2
Margaret A. Mitchell, 2 days
Minty Landers, 50
May Ann Landers, 13
Elizabeth Browne, 7
Harriet Ann Browne, 65
Martha Ann Wright, 33
Mary Ringgold, 50
Henny Dyer, 40
Sally Ann Dyer, 3
Letty Griffin, 22
Margaret Griffin, 7 months
Henny Cook, 22
Henny Hazleton, 40
Jenny Robinson, 50
Mary Woody, 40
Henny Hutchins, 60
Henny Hazleton, 27
Anamaria Hazleton, 2
Lucy Bolden, 40
Mary Bolden, 12
Nancy Allen, 35
Matilda Bolden, 12
Nancy Allen, 35
Matilda Bolden, 10
Lucy Hazleton, 13

Queen Ann's County, Maryland

Margaret Hazleton, 50
Sally Hazleton, 11
Eleanor Dobson, 30
Rosetta Hutchins, 40
Mary Ann I. Hutchins, 17
Candis Hutchins, 7
Margaret Hutchins, 8
July Ann Hutchins, 50
Caroline Hinson, 16
Elizabeth Hinson, 6 months
Maria Little, 38
Eliza Little, 14
Ellen Little, 6
Henny Little, 4
Rosetta Little. 3
Etheline Little, 1
Eliza Robinson, 22
Eliza M. Wilmer, 24
July Ann Cook, 16
Mina Browne, 60
Nancy Johns, 40
Priscilla Wright, 9
Sophia Wright, 8
Selina Wright, 5
Rosetta Miller, 30
Rachel Potts, 35
Louisa Hawkins, 47
Lydia Farewell, 55
Maria Hines, 45
Charlotte Hines, 23
Mary Hines, 15
Sarah Hines, 9
Minty Bateman, 60
Caroline Bateman, 4
Kitty Bateman, 19
Sarah Griffin, 57
Nancy Hackett, 30
Nancy Tack, 50
Henny Johnson, 40
Nancy Johnson, 7
Elizabeth Johnson, 7
Elizabeth Johnson, 2
Susan Wilson, 50
Betsy Griffin, 23
Henny Browne, 39
Margaret Gross, 12
Elizabeth Willis, 49
Nancy Willis, 60
Betsy Hopkins, 30
Tena Port, 40
Violet Port, 16
Mary Port, 11

Sally Ann Port, 9
Henny Port, 4
Eliza Port, 4
Henry Hemsley, 40
July Hemsley, 20
Priscilla Hemsley, 17
Jenny Hemsley, 8
Elizabeth Hemsley, 3
Frances Ann Hemsley, 7 months
Charlotte Hemsley, 1
Mary Rine, 38
Henny Rine, 11
Henrietta Jane Rine, 2
Lydia Browne, 5
Judy Adams, 17
Margaret Browne, 41
Henrietta Browne, 5
Dolly Ann Browne, 10
Litilla Elbert, 60
Littilah Wright, 25
Milly Wright, 4
Rachel Freeman, 45
Rachel Cook, 60
Emily Browne, 16
Litilla Browne, 12
Sarah McDaniel, 40
Mary Ann McDaniel, 4
Ibby Kent, 50
Lucy Osten, 50
Susan Thomas, 95
Mary L. Johns, 4
Dianna Thomas, 57
Ellen Downes, 5
Maria Downes, 32
Sarah Downes, 8
Eliza Wilson, 33
Harriet Chandler, 36
Henrietta Wilson, 4
Nancy Johns, 62
Mary Stootley, 35
Hetty Stootly Hawkins, 19
Dianna Emory, 80
Margaret Rigby, 15
Harriet R____, 15
Kitty Dodd, 17
Ann Dodd, 1
Ibby Dodd, 60
Charlotte Stevens, 22
Sarah Dodd, 4

Elizabeth Lavage, 18
Ibby Dodd, 17
Henny True, 45
Fanny True, 10
Elizabeth Gray, 3
Susan Wally, 55
Betsy Brandiford, 25
Anna M. Brandiford, 11
Henrietta Brandiford, 3 months.
Hannah Griffin, 35
Mary Matthews, 12
Nelly Beck, 19
Rachel Thomas, 22
Priscilla Sampson, 55
Susan Lylwan, 70
Henny Earle, 10
Lucy Earle, 3
Maria Earle, 43
Rachel Ruth, 50
Margaret Thompson, 6
Sally Ann Thompson, 5
Jane Thomas, 52
Anna Ruse, 26
Susan Lylwan, 70
Henny Earle, 10
Lucy Earle, 3
Maria Earle, 43
Rachel Smith, 50
Margaret Thompson, 30
Sally Thompson, 5
Jane Thomas, 52
Anna Reese, 26
Mary Emory, 4
Henny Bryann, 25
Harriet Pembrook, 28
Sarah Pearce, 38
Eliza Pearce, 20
Nancy Pearce, 2 weeks
Nancy Green, 40
Henny Sulivan, 45
Rachel Fisher, 45
Ann fisher, 16
Mary Fisher, 10
Elizabeth Warner, 16
Susan Warner, 11
Minty Warner, 50
Mary Wilkins, 55
Rachel Griffin, 50

124

Free African Americans of Maryland - 1832

Henny Griffin, 21
Clarissa Griffin, 19
Darky Griffin, 15
Maria Griffin, 13
Rachel Griffin, 11
Elizabeth Griffin, 9
Elizabeth Griffin, 5
Kitty Griffin, 3
Isabelly Dickerson, 50
Eliza Ann Dickerson, 15
Charlotte Carter, 25
Mary Carter, 12
Fanny Carter, 5
Maria Carter, 9 months
Eliza Holliday, 43
Henny Holliday, 85
Darky Johnson, 4 months
Margaret Johnson, 8
Ann Johnson, 6
Fanny Bias, 24
Ibby Browne, 40
Sarah Murphy, 9
Harriet Roth, 33
Attice Bias, 50
Eliza Roll, 3
Ellen Roll, 2
Sarah Murry, 30
Mary Chairs, 40
Mary Gaither, 17
Rachel Thomas, 6
Sarah Taylor, 49
Mary Byott, 34
Sally Taylor, 27
Rosetta Stewart, 69
Hannah Wilkes, 68
Chloe Peck, 30
Sarah Peck, 5
Unnamed infant, 2 months
July Gould, 30
Jane Canada, 16
Ferny Dickerson, 30
Minty Sampson, 50
Emeline Ayres, 10
Henny Ayres, 7
Rachel Ayres, 6
Ann Brown, 16
Sarah Dobson, 40
July Clayton, 20
Lela Demby, 80
Ann Clayton, 6 months

Henny Ayres, 55
Phillis Ayres, 8
Arrey Ayres, 55
Kitty Ayres, 17
Charlotte Johnson, 4 months
Sally Johnson, 3
Lela Nichols, 45
Ann Nichols, 12
Sarah Ellen Nichols, 5
Kitty Smallwood, 55
Mary Smallwood, 18
Priscilla Nichols, 65
Henny Corner, 7
Milly Thomas, 37
Nancy Thomas, 6
Vickey Cole, 80
Daphny Downes, 70
Litilla Gibbs, 20
July Lingo, 20
Rachel Martin, 60
Mary Comegys, 2
Henny Pullman, 14
Prisey Wilkes, 65
Nancy Griffin, 47
Henny Eccleston, 30
Ellen Curtis, 12
Mary Eccleston, 8
Rebecca Eccleston, 35
Louisa Eccleston, 2
Rebecca Curtis, 35
Sarah Curtis, 2
Ann Curtis, 2 months
Susan Hutchins, 40
Kitty Masters, 25
Maria Knotts, 35
Henny Knotts, 3
Charlotte Thompson, 45
Rachael Murrey, 15
Rachael Handy, 80
Rachael Heath, 35
Ann Ayres, 30
Mary Bell, 26
Priscilla Noke, 50
Kitty Noke, 17
Elizabeth Noke, 3
Adeline Noke, 5
Hannah Pritchett, 46
Sally Pritchett, 21
Hannah A. Pritchett, 1

Fanny Farewell, 80
Nancy Farewell, 65
Nancy Price, 30
Susan Jones, 30
Grace Clemans, 60
Fanny Dunn, 82
Rachael Griffin, 60
Rachael Griffin, 17
Frances Benson, 15
Darky Benson, 56
Elizabeth Kent, 27
Jane Kent, 5
Henny Johnson, 35
Maria Johnson, 12
Mercy Johnson, 9
Sarah Johnson, 6
Elizabeth Johnson, 4 months
Ann E. Johnson, 3 months
Massey Easter, 35
Sarah Costen, 7
Hester Ann Costen, 7
Mary Eccleston, 12
Rebecca Chickaroom, 35
Fanny Chickaroom, 13
Serena Teanor, 20
Ann Teanor, 14
Lydia Benson, 40
Sela Benson, 50
Memory Bordley, 35
Sophia Jackson, 40
Henrietta Bordly, 7
Henny Bordly, 22
Uriah Jackson, 7
Adeline Jackson, 5
Unnamed infant, 1 day
Henny Murray, 3
Henny Newnam, 50
Prissy Newnam, 45
Milly Newnam, 25
Prissy Newnam, 1
Kitty Newnam, 3
Rachael Eccleston, 25
Frances Ann Eccleston, 5
Elizabeth Eccleston, 2
Mary Eccleston, 1
Mary Anderson, 52
Ellen Anderson, 16

Queen Ann's County, Maryland

Ann Anderson, 12
Jenny Johnson, 52
Susan Cook, 55
Caroline Cook, 17
Ann Jackson, 45
Rebecca Jackson, 18
Ann Jackson, 6
Fanny Wilson, 35
Masy Wilson, 4
Maria Wilson, 25
Minty Carmichael, 60
Jane Wright, 60
July Roberts, 2
Rettia Miers, 30
Judy, 12
Nancy Cooper, 60
Mary Ann Cooper, 22
Richard Wright, 30
Martha Browne, 58
Mary Pritchett, 15
Ann Pritchett, 15
Mary Wilson, 16
Ann Wilson, 1
Jenny Lockerman, 50
Rachael Cook, 45
Ann Faulkner, 17
Rebecca Blake, 45
Wittey A. Browne, 22
Catherine Browne, 1
Eliza Rochester, 35
Jane Rochester, 35
Susan Rochester, 2
Martha Gould, 67
Rachel Roberts, 62
Rosetta Browne, 60
Julia Price, 36
Elizabeth Price, 12
Mary Ann Price, 1
Rachael Freeman, 11
Deborah Elliot, 42
Augusta Elliot, 17
Elizabeth Elliot, 13
Milky Elliot, 16
Mary E. J. Elliot, 2
Julia A. Elliott, 1
Rachael Greenwood, 12
Leah Bowyer, 40
Charlotte Anthony, 21
Hester Coursey, 27
Harriet Tilden, 20
Fanny Gould, 40
Sarah Moody, 45

Maria Moody, 9
Julia Moody, 5
Henny Ashley, 20
Elizabeth A. Ashley, 17
Elizabeth Hackett, 36
Fanny Gould, , 40
Hester Mann, 87
Hester Browne, 6
Harriet Browne, 6
Esther Wilmer, 80
Esther Hackett, 78
Mary Martin, 16
Mary Martin, 1
Milky Elliott, 18
Grace Landman, 16
Rebecca Landman, 16
Nancy Landman, 3
July Green, 14
Hester Johnson, 20
Mary Blake, 10
Sarah Johnson, 2
Hester Massey, 35
Susan Graves, 10
Henrietta Offley, 50
Henrietta Offley, 10
Martha Miller, 7
Sarah Cox, 46
Julia A. Hollis, 17
Charlotte Parker, 32
Ann Parker, 7
Catherine Parker, 3
Barbary Parker, 1
Martha Gould, 43
Charlotte Gould, 14
Julia Freeman, 27
Ann Gould, 18
Charlotte A. Ringgold, 2
Ann M. Harrison, 16
Judy Gibbs, 60
Henny Harrison, 40
Hannah Baily, 30
Daphny Green, 35
Mary Baily, 13
Emeline Thompson, 15
Susan Browne, 19
Maria Browne, 39
Sarah Gibson, 23
Esther Gould, 60
Henny Wilson, 40
Hester A. Wilson, 14
Rachael Wilson, 7

Harriet Gould, 32
Charlotte Johnson, 26
Netta Williamson, 90
Adeline Johnson, 3
Ana Maria Johnson, 2
Elizabeth Gould, 16
Esther A. Gould, Ibby Harris, 35
Henny Warwick, 45
Mary Warwick, 6
Sarah Gibson, 29
Sophia Green, 33
Charlotte Green, 17
Mary E. Wilson, 9
Ally Warwick, 90
Ann Green, 32
Ann R. Potts, 12
Christiana Bordley, 8
Henny A. Bordley, 14
Mary Miller, 25
Mary A. Miller, 1
Ruth Cooper, 39
Jane Cooper, 13
Martha Cooper, 9
Henrietta Cooper, 6
Lucy A. Cooper, 4
Emily Cooper, 1
Lucy A. Dias, 80
Darky Burgess, 30
Henrietta Burgess, 12
Alsy Gafford, 32
Martha H. Tilghman, 12
Sarah A. Tilghman, 6
Nicey Fogwell, 52
Rachael Johnson, 63
Dolly Crook, 80
Henny Simmons, 15
Maria Price, 35
Elizabeth Lewis, 35
Nancy Grinage, 50
Mary Julious, 50
Mary Miller, 32
Maria Anderson, 35
Charlotte A. Anderson, 11
Delia Baynard, 50
Nancy Benton, 14
Rebecca Tiller, 50
Harriet Johnson, 15
Henny Clayton, 35
Rachael Gould, 35
Henny Gould, 10

Free African Americans of Maryland - 1832

Margaret Gould, 7
Ann Gould, 5
Rachael Gould, 2
Isabella Gould, 3
Jane Hawkins, 55
Mary Looney, 55
Milly Looney, 27
Mary Looney, 14
Eliza Simmons, 20
Sarah E. Simmons, 2
Frances A. Simmons, 1
Darky Ferrell, 35
Charity Ferrell, 11
Emeline Ferrell, 8
Grace Ferrell, 5
Harriet Ferrell, 3
Ann M. Ferrell, 3
Caroline Primrus, 24
Sarah A. Nickerson, 3
Rose Benton, 35
Sarah A. Gibson, 21
Martha A. Gibson, 21
Charity Rochester, 17
Milly Price, 25
Sarah E. Price, 1
Mary Travis, 7
Fanny Rochester, 50
Jane Rochester, 20
Sarah Rochester, 13
Ann Rochester, 6
Alsy Lowman, 50
Hester Hollyday, 30
Rachael Dobson, 80
Charlotte Cooper, 25
Elizabeth Cooper, 2
Dolly Gibbs, 75
Darky Massey, 42
Elizabeth Massey, 16
Fanny Benson, 21
Harriett Benson, 7
Ann L. Benson, 5
Nancy Benson, 2
Nancy Blackiston, 30
Susan Blackiston, 10
Lydia Blackiston, 1
Nancy Lingo. 50
Ann Jackson, 12
Rose Sands, 60
Bina Casy, 49
Sarah Casy, 8
Nancy Warwick, 30
Henny Warwick, 14

Rosetta Warwick, 12
Mary Warwick, 3
Kitty Warwick, 1
Creasy Hollis, 70
Rachael Hollis, 3
Jennie Browne, 40
Kitty Monday, 20
Charlotte Browne, 30
Delila Rochester, 27
Elizabeth Rochester, 17
Louisa Rochester, 7
Lucy A. Rochester, 1
Jane Ferrell, 35
Rachael Ferrell, 16
Ary A. Ferrell, 13
Rachael Ferrell, 11
Charlotte A.Ferrell, 7
Henny Ferrell, 5
Minty Tiller, 25
Ann Tiller, 6
Elizabeth Tiller, 5
Henny Tiller, 1
Maria Smith, 55
Ritty U. Smith, 9
Mary Jane Smith, 6
Delia Miller, 30
Ruth Miller, 1
Maria Segar, 23
Elizabeth Segar, 6
Ann U. Price, 60
July A. Hanson, 24
Margaret Carsons, 26
Ann Carsons, 2
Mary Benton, 30
Darky Benton, 9
Elizabeth Benton, 7
Mahala Benton, 5
Priscilla Graves, 40
Susan Kune, 80
Charlotte Thomas, 25
Elily Green, 30
Elizabeth Green, 1
Hester Fogwell, 40
Nancy Fogwell, 13
Rachael Johnson, 65
Sarah Johnson, 14
Henrietta Lewis, 35
Hager Goldsberry, 75
Eleanor Seegar, 85
Ann Dixon, 43
Emeline Dixon, 14
Rachael Jackson, 50
Rebecca Boardly, 60

Hester Bordley, 30
Ruth Coppage, 45
Ann Coppage, 9
Elizabeth Seegar, 25
Ruth Segar, 2
Rachael Fogwell, 60
Jane Fogwell, 60
Fanny Fogwell, 2
Caroline Fase, 40
Delia Fase, 1
Sarah Browne, 30
Rachael Browne, 17
Sarah A. Browne, 4
Louisa Bradshaw, 44
Eliza S. Bradshaw, 9
Rachael Bradshaw, 2
Mary Cooper, 21
Hessy Gibbs, 25
Mary Gibbs, 2
Ann Gibbs, 1
Emily Demby, 6
Rachael Hutchins, 45
Minty Bateman, 55
Kitty Bateman, 12
Rebecca Bateman, 80
Hannah Niew, 63
Elizabeth, 12
Henny Bradly, 46
Linta Bradly, 9
Mary Bradly, 5
Sarah E. Bradly, 2
Sarah Bradly, 20
Hannah Coge, 35
Elizabeth Ferrell, 25
Ann Kelson, 25
Mary Kelson, 9
Rachael Duhamel, 60
Henny Wilson, 25
Nancy Hawkins, 35
Jane Hawkins, 16
Mary Hawkins, 9
Alsy Baynard, 45
Sarah A. Baynard, 1
Elizabeth Darmel, 30
Phillis Price, 44
Julia Price, 12
Sarah Price, 9
Louisa Price, 3
Mahala Price, 2
Susan Price, 1
Ann Bouyer, 12
Alsy Hoges, 45
Rose Garnett, 86

Queen Ann's County, Maryland

Ann Hoges, 14
Kitty Reason, 27
Julia Demby, 1
Sarah Browne, 45
Hannah Little, 45
Rebecca Demby, 18
Elizabeth Demby, 14
Emeline Demby, 4
Elizabeth Demby, 3
Esther Wilmer, 55
Mary Bill, 30
Margaret Oliver, 50
Hannah Smith, 48
Henny Jeffers, 26
Rachael Jeffers, 26
Mary Jeffers, 23
Rebecca Jeffers, 20
Runy Jeffers, 15
July Jeffers, 10
Mary H. Jeffers, 6
Susanna Jeffers, 4
Milly E. Jeffers, 1
Henny Anthony, 31
Hester Anthony, 12
Elizabeth Anthony, 8
Eliza Anthony, 5
Hester Browne, 30
Hester Browne, 12
Elizabeth Browne, 8
Elizabeth I. Browne,
    5
Hannah Smith, 35
Rachael Smith, 14
Kitty Smith, 9
Elizabeth Hackett,
    33
Hannah Sharp, 35
Henny Sharp, 9
Rebecca Calder, 64
Jane Kelson, 8
Elizabeth Ferrell, 20
Hester Rochester, 16
Fanny Monday, 40
Sarah Hackett, 16
Mary Gibbs, 5
July French, 40
Sophia Ferrell, 55
Lydia Massey, 55
Hanna Coge, 30
Harriet Daniel, 30
Rachael Daniel, 17
Elizabeth Daniel, 15
Charity Daniel, 9
Martha Daniel, 7
Chloe Daniel, 1
Ann Miller, 45

Margaret H. Miller, 4
Lydia Roe, 50
Mary Roe, 18
Matilda Roe, 13
Elizabeth Roe, 12
Martha Roe, 4
Sarah E. Green, 30
Emily Green, 21
Sarah I. Green, 1
Alsy Massey, 75
Elizabeth Granger,
    16
Margaret Wilson, 22
Thamar Carmichael
Sarah I. Wilson, 4
Mary Wilson, 1
Minty Kelly, 45
Sarah H. Kelly, 17
Mary I. Kelly, 15
Hannah Kelly, 12
Milly U. Kelly, 7
Desey Cooper, 25
Nancy Thompson, 45
Elizabeth Thompson,
    16
Mary Woodling, 25
Henny Munson, 25
Sarah E. Munson, 1
Rebecca Nailer, 25
Eliza Nailer, 5
Ann Jane Wood, 9
Louisa Nailer, 4
Mary Dixon, 25
Emily Dixon, 9
Priscilla Dixon, 7
Masy R. Dixon, 4
Phillis Temples, 48
Rebecca Temples, 3
Hannah Davis, 40
Tilla Davis, 3
Caroline Davis, 3
Caroline Davis, 2
Matilda Massey, 25
Hannah Shary, 70
Mary Massey, 1
Henny Stevens, 40
Esther Wilmer, 55
Grace Black, 55
Elizabeth Sutton, 22
Mary Sutton, 12
Rachael Thompson,
    20
Mary Thompson, 10
July Ann Thompson,
    9 months
Rachael Potts, 23

Ann R. Potts, 3
Henrietta Potts, 1
Charlotte Matthews,
    16
Kitty Kirby, 25
Ann Kirby, 50
Henry Hawkins, 25
Mary Hawkins, 8
Elizabeth Hawkins, 5
Minty Bateman, 12
Tilly Bateman, 6
Nancy Chairs, 35
Casy Richardson, 60
Mary Richardson, 15
Richard Potts, 60
Ann Potts, 36
Ann Freeman, 30
Rachael Kelson, 70
Priscilla Kelson, 20
July French, 25
Milly Thomas, 40
Nancy Chairs, 23
Elizabeth Dyer, 8
Angelina Dyer, 5
Margaret Dyer, 45
Hannah Martin, 26
Ellen Martin, 26
Rosetta Anderson,
    60
Elizabeth Anderson,
    14
Rebecca W. Kenny,
    60
Charlotte Browne, 18
Margaret Brown, 1
Maria Roberts, 9
Amy Faulkner, 62
Nancy Rollins, 28
Violet Dudley, 16
Rachael Brooks, 44
Jane Carsons,
    10Grace Keene,
    70
Louisa Greens, 31
Emily Keen, 2
Mary Danes, 8
Dinah Frisby, 35
Ann Frisby, 5
Henny Hackett, 45
Henny Hackett. 13
Elizabeth Hackett,
    13
Fanny
    Goldsbourough,
    56
Minty Smith, 60

Free African Americans of Maryland - 1832

Ruth Wilson, 55
Elizabeth Jacobs, 30
Kitty Duhamel. 37
Nancy Duhamel, 12
Sarah Duhamel, 9
Kitty Duhamel, 5
Lucy Green, 56
Charlotte Flamer, 49
Rebecca Flamer, 18
Mary Flamer, 13
Nancy Lee, 25
Candis Lee, 21

Priscilla Hutchenson,
    25'Ellen Pindar,
    40
Charlotte Pindar, 14
Debby Ann Pindar, 8
Fanny Hughes, 45
Jane Hughes, 70
Ann Gibson, 24
Martha Ann Gibson,
    5
Minty Gibson, 2
Mary Hawkins, 35
Jane Roseberry, 55
Ruth Rasberry, 17

Rachael Ann
    Hawkins, 24
Louisa Thomas, 58
Mary Massey, 20
Mary Fogwell, 6
Nancy Hutchens, 8
Charlotte Hutchens,
    5
Margaret Hutchens,
    4
Mary E Hutchens, 2
Charity Hutchens, 1
Kitty Hinson, 50
Ann Martha Lee, 2

Thomas Ashcomb, Sheriff of Queen Anns County
August 28th 1832
****

ST. Mary's County

To the Board of Managers of the Maryland State Colonization Society.
    By virtue of an act of the General Assembly of Maryland entitled "An Act
Relating to the People of Color in This State": passed the twelfth day of March
eighteen hundred and thirty two requiring the Sheriffs of the several counties of
this State to ascertain the number of the ___ people of color inhabiting their
respective counties to be taken and caused to be made a list of the names of the
said people of color residing in their respective counties, the Sheriff of Saint
Mary's County makes this following report to wit,.

Adams, Henry, 27
Adams, Samuel, 4
Adams, Charles, 12
Adams, Henry, 60
Adams, Henry Jr, 14
Alexander, Joseph, 32
Abott, Barney, 45
Allen Cornelius, 16
Barnes, Jacob, 17
Barnes, Gabriel, 14
Barnes, Stephen, 35
Barnes, John, 10
Barnes, Richard, 4
Barnes, Phillip, 20
Barnes, Abraham, 15
Barnes Philip, 65
Barnes, Robert, 10
Bryan, Richard, 3
Bryan, William F, 1
Bryan, William, 35
Bryan, William, 14
Bryan, Henry, 16
Barnes, William, 25

Barnes, Charles, 35
Barnes, Joseph, 9
Barnes, Jesse, 50
Barnes, Jesse Jr, 25
Barnes, Richard, 10
Barnes, Charles, 8
Barnes, John, 7
Bryan, Wellington, 5
Bryan, John, 11
Barnes, Thomas, 16
Barnes, Charles, 11
Barnes, George, 3
Bean Zachariah, 19
Barnes, John, 16
Barnes, Richard, 16
Barnes, Jacob, 30
Barnes, Moses L, 1 month
Barnes, John, 21
Barnes, William, 20
Barnes, Edward, 45
Barnes, Joseph, 58
Barnes, Joseph Jr, 5
Adams, Elizabeth, 30

St. Mary's County

Barnes, Eleanor, 12
Barnes, Jane, 7
Barnes, Sarah, 23
Barnes, Martha A, 5
Barnes, Sarah, 40
Barnes, Mary Ann, 17
Barnes, Eliza, 50
Butler, Polly, 42
Butler, Mary, 8
Butler, Eliza, 4
Beal, Charity, 5
Beal Maria, 33
Beal, Elizabeth, 5
Beal Joanna, 1
Beal, Jane, 70
Beal, Ann, 40
Beal. Charity, 8
Beal, Henny, 4
Beal, Celia, 4
Butler, Mary, 30
Butler, Shady A, 8
Butler, Henrietta, 6
Barnes, Catherine, 22
Barnes, Jane, 1
Bryan, Catherine, 35
Bean, Elizabeth, 45
Bean, Eliza Ann, 18
Bean, Mary C, 11
Barnes, Catherine, 50
Barnes, Elizabeth, 18
Barnes, Sarah, 14
Barnes, Ann, 10
Barnes, Rose, 8
Barnes, Rebecca, 6
Barnes, Priscilla, 3
Barnes, Ann, 45
Barnes, Henrietta, 18
Barnes, Eliza, 15
Barnes, Lucinda, 7
Barnes, Ann, 45
Barnes, Minny, 45
Barnes, Margaret, 23
Barnes, Rose, 20
Barnes, Abraham, 21
Barnes, John, 17
Barnes, William, 13
Barnes, Hanson, 12
Barnes, Charles, 60
Barnes, Jeremiah, 9
Barnes, Abraham, 4
Barnes, Bennett, 56
Barnes, Reveredy, 36
Barnes, Peter, 45
Butler, Robert, 24
Butler, Henry, 18
Butler, Thomas, 15

Brown, Henry, 45
Butler, Cyrus, 40
Butler, James, 8
Bailey, John, 56
Bryan, John G.. 18
Bryan, James, 15
Bryan, Samuel, 5
Bryan, Ignatious, 3
Barnes, John, 37
Butler, Lewis, 46
Bryan, Richard, 22
Barnes, Jesse, 38
Barnes, Michael, 11
Barnes, Abraham, 9
Barnes, James, 2
Barnes, Robert, 40
Barnes, Benedict, 11
Barnes, Walter, 9
Barnes, Frances, 7
Barnes, Alexander, 5
Barnes, George Washington, 1
Butler, Alexander, 30
Butler, Francis, 5
Butler, Benedict, 1
Barnes, Lewis, 10
Barnes, Benedict, 8
Barnes, Alexander, 2
Butler, Richard, 21
Butler, Joe, 16
Butler, Philip, 8
Butler, Boy unnamed, 1 month
Butler, John, 26
Boarman, Charles, 45
Butler, Eli, 23
Butler, Raphael, 40
Butler, Thomas, 21
Butler, Henry, 17
Butler, William J, 12
Butler, John, 16
Butler, James, 12
Butler, Charles Henry, 10
Butler, William, 10
Butler, Charles, 4
Barnes, Nancy, 19
Barnes, Ann, 18
Barnes, Jane, 16
Barnes, Treacy, 16
Barnes, Ann M, 2
Barnes, Elizabeth, 4
Butler, Sarah, 42
Barnes, Dorcas, 68
Barnes, Henrietta, 35
Barnes, Elizabeth, 7
Barnes, Catherine, 6
Barnes, Eliza, 25
Barnes, Priscilla, 70

Free African Americans of Maryland - 1832

Adams, Matilda, 21
Adams, Ann, 7
Adams Eliza, 5
Adams Sophia, 5
Adams, Charity, 6
Adams, Jane, 10
Adams, Sarah, 36
Adams, Ann, 17
Adams, Ellen, 13
Adams, Mary E, 8
Adams, Jane U, 4
Adams Celia, 37
Adams, Frances, 3
Allen, Milly, 50
Barnes, Elizabeth, 44
Barnes, Eliza, 9
Allen, Milly, 50
Barnes, Elizabeth, 11
Barnes, Eliza, 9
Barnes, Charity, 30
Barnes, Sarah Ann, 15
Barnes, Elizabeth, 13
Barnes, Margaret, 8
Barnes, Margaret, 35
Barnes, Sarah Ann, 16
Barnes, Mary Jane, 5
Barnes, Charlotte B. 2
Barnes, Elizabeth, 40
Barnes, Fanny, 17
Barnes, Mary, 35
Barnes, Ann, 14
Barnes, Sarah, 28
Barnes, Eliza, 23
Barnes, Ann E, 8
Barnes, Ester, 5
Barnes, Plymer, 4
Barnes, Eliza Ann, 1
Barnes, Catherine, 22
Barnes, Priscilla, 18
Barnes, Eleanor, 2
Barnes, Henrietta, 14
Barnes, Mary, 4
Bryan, Mary, 24
Bryan, Juliet, 33
Bryan, Maria, 7
Barnes, John, 2
Barnes, Lewis, 29
Butler, Thomas, 52
Butler, Reverdy, 48
Beal, George, 41
Beal, John, 7
Beal, George A, 3
Beal, William, 55
Beal, Henry, 1
Butler, Lewis, 34
Butler, William H, 4
Butler, John L, 2
Barnes, Henry, 25

Bryan, John, 35
Bryan, Nelson, 3
Bean, Jeremiah, 69
Bean, Jeremiah, 16
Bean, James L, 13
Bean Joseph, 9
Barnes, Abraham, 65
Barnes, James, 22
Barnes, Charles, 16
Barnes, Michael, 12
Barnes, Charles, 23
Barnes, Gabriel, 17
Barnes, Lewis, 27
Barnes, William H, 1 month
Barnes, Charles, 5
Barnes, Reverdy, 3
Barnes, Jackson, 2
Barnes, John H, 2
Butler, Joseph, 48
Butler, Lewis, 3
Butler, Basill, 2
Barnes, Titus, 78
Barnes, William H, 11
Barnes, Robert, 9
Barnes, Joseph, 35
Barnes Josiah, 6
Barnes, John, 3
Barnes, Arnold, 75
Barnes, William, 22
Barnes, Abraham, 7
Barnes, Richard, 6
Butler, Henry, 25
Butler, James, 21
Barnes, Abraham, 19
Barnes, John F, 7
Barnes, Peter, 2
Barnes, Elijah, 1
Barnes, Charles, 9
Barnes, William, 3
Barnes, Jeremiah, 44
Barnes, John, 60
Barnes, Joe, 26
Barnes, Ambrose, 24
Barnes, Primus, 24
Bryan, Sarah, 3
Bean, Tawny, 50
Bryan, Elizabeth, 63
Barnes, Ann, 15
Barnes, Elizabeth, 14
Bryan, Elizabeth, 26
Bryan, Ann, 10
Bryan, Elizabeth, 2
Barnes, Rose, 24
Barnes, Mary E, 1
Brown, Lydia, 83
Barnes, Jane, 41
Barnes, Sophia, 17
Barnes, Mary, 16

St. Mary's County

Barnes, Eleanor, 12
Barnes, Jane, 7
Barnes, Sarah, 23
Barnes, Martha A, 5
Barnes, Sarah, 40
Barnes, Mary Ann, 17
Barnes, Eliza, 50
Butler, Polly, 42
Butler, Mary, 8
Butler, Eliza, 4
Beal, Charity, 5
Beal Maria, 33
Beal, Elizabeth, 5
Beal Joanna, 1
Beal, Jane, 70
Beal, Ann, 40
Beal. Charity, 8
Beal, Henny, 4
Beal, Celia, 4
Butler, Mary, 30
Butler, Shady A, 8
Butler, Henrietta, 6
Barnes, Catherine, 22
Barnes, Jane, 1
Bryan, Catherine, 35
Bean, Elizabeth, 45
Bean, Eliza Ann, 18
Bean, Mary C, 11
Barnes, Catherine, 50
Barnes, Elizabeth, 18
Barnes, Sarah, 14
Barnes, Ann, 10
Barnes, Rose, 8
Barnes, Rebecca, 6
Barnes, Priscilla, 3
Barnes, Ann, 45
Barnes, Henrietta, 18
Barnes, Eliza, 15
Barnes, Lucinda, 7
Barnes, Ann, 45
Barnes, Minny, 45
Barnes, Margaret, 23
Barnes, Rose, 20
Barnes, Abraham, 21
Barnes, John, 17
Barnes, William, 13
Barnes, Hanson, 12
Barnes, Charles, 60
Barnes, Jeremiah, 9
Barnes, Abraham, 4
Barnes, Bennett, 56
Barnes, Reveredy, 36
Barnes, Peter, 45
Butler, Robert, 24
Butler, Henry, 18
Butler, Thomas, 15
Brown, Henry, 45
Butler, Cyrus, 40

Butler, James, 8
Bailey, John, 56
Bryan, John G., 18
Bryan, James, 15
Bryan, Samuel, 5
Bryan, Ignatious, 3
Barnes, John, 37
Butler, Lewis, 46
Bryan, Richard, 22
Barnes, Jesse, 38
Barnes, Michael, 11
Barnes, Abraham, 9
Barnes, James, 2
Barnes, Robert, 40
Barnes, Benedict, 11
Barnes, Walter, 9
Barnes, Frances, 7
Barnes, Alexander, 5
Barnes, George Washington, 1
Butler, Alexander, 30
Butler, Francis, 5
Butler, Benedict, 1
Barnes, Lewis, 10
Barnes, Benedict, 8
Barnes, Alexander, 2
Butler, Richard, 21
Butler, Joe, 16
Butler, Philip, 8
Butler, Boy unnamed, 1 month
Butler, John, 26
Boarman, Charles, 45
Butler, Eli, 23
Butler, Raphael, 40
Butler, Thomas, 21
Butler, Henry, 17
Butler, William J, 12
Butler, John, 16
Butler, James, 12
Butler, Charles Henry, 10
Butler, William, 10
Butler, Charles, 4
Barnes, Nancy, 19
Barnes, Ann, 18
Barnes, Jane, 16
Barnes, Treacy, 16
Barnes, Ann M, 2
Barnes, Elizabeth, 4
Butler, Sarah, 42
Barnes, Dorcas, 68
Barnes, Henrietta, 35
Barnes, Elizabeth, 7
Barnes, Catherine, 6
Barnes, Eliza, 25
Barnes, Priscilla, 70
Barnes Eleanor, 33
Butler, Elizabeth, 27
Barnes, Rose, 44
Barnes, Elizabeth, 23

132

Free African Americans of Maryland - 1832

Barnes, Jane, 16
Barnes, Caroline, 15
Barnes, Eliza, 1
Barnes, Jane, 35
Barnes, Henny, 50
Barnes, Monacy, 30
Barnes, Polly, 28
Barnes, Sarah, 56
Barnes, Matilda, 7
Barnes, Ann, 20
Barnes, Jane, 12
Barnes, Maria, 7
Barnes, Milly, 55
Butler, Charity, 20
Butler, Henny, 60
Butler, Sarah, 30
Butler, Susan, 25
Brown, Polly, 1 month
Butler, Casia, 35
Butler, Mary, 10
Butler, Matilda, 6
Butler, Jane, 4
Butler, Milly, 3
Butler, Hope, 1
Butler, Monica, 60
Butler, Henny 35
Butler, Milly, 55
Baily, Mary, 45
Baily, Celia, 56
Bryan, Eleanor, 38
Bryan Abigail, 12
Bryan, Mary, 11
Bryan, Elizabeth, 8
Bryan, Sarah A, 8
Barnes, Drady, 42
Barnes, Mary, 16
Barnes Aunt, 7
Butler, Margaret, 36
Barnes, Cecelia, 35
William Butler, 55
Butler, John, 53
Butler, John, 17
Butler, Leonard, 70
Brady, Charles, 67
Brown, Robert, 35
Briscoe, Barton, 45
Briscoe, George, 76
Butler, Rezin, 39
Blackiston, Baptist, 45
Brooks, Hendly, 38
Butler, Henry, 30
Butler, Henry, 2
Butler, Shadrack, 28
Butler, Henry, 1
Butler, James, 4
Bete, Robert, 28
Bete, Thomas, 1
Butler, James, 18

Bush, John, 26
Butler, Richard, 24
Butler, Mores, 17
Butler, Anthony, 28
Cole, Alexander, 32
Cole, James, 9
Cole, George, 4
Cole, Charles H, 1 month
Curtis, William,
Custy, John, 5
Curtis, James M, 1
Crawley, William, 25
Crawley, Bennett, 72
Curtis, Michael, 50
Curtis, Philip, 27
Curtis, William, 22
Curtis, Leonard, 16
Curtis, Gusty, 15
Crawley, John, 17
Crawley, Merritt, 13
Cooper, Lewis, 40
Cooper, John, 12
Cooper, Joseph, 12
Cole, John, 6
Curtis, Charles, 35
Curtis, Hillery, 24
Curtis, Cornelius, 18
Curtis, George, 14
Curtis, Gilbert, 19
Curtis, John, 18
Curtis, Augustus, 57
Cooper, John, 4
Cooper, Charles, 26
Carpenter, George, 9
Carpenter, John, 11
Carpenter, William, 4
Curtis, William, 4
Carter, Ignatius, 30
Butler, Sarah, 22
Barnes, Susan, 35
Barnes, Ann, 6
Barnes, Susan, 4
Butler, Permelia, 40
Butler, Rachael, 65
Butler, Harriet, 30
Butler, Eveline, 25
Butler, Mary, 1 month
Butler, Juliana F, 18
Butler, Margaret, 70
Bennett, Jane, 10
Beaton, Matilda, 20
Butler, Charity, 40
Butler, Ellen, 30
Butler, Rebecca, 19
Butler, Ann, 12
Butler, Celia, 45
Butler, Alcey, 14
Butler, Celia, 35

133

St. Mary's County

Butler, Jane, 14
Butler, Mary, 2
Butler, Susan, 50
Butler, Monica, 65
Brady, Ann, 65
Barnes, Letty, 68
Blackiston, Pricilla, 6
Blackiston, Jane U. #
Butler, Rebecca, 13
Butler, Susan, 4
Butler, Margaret Ann, 1
Butler, Mary, 58
Butler, Ann, 48
Butler Nancy, 44
Butler, Rebecca, 26
Brooks, Rebecca, 70
Butler, Henry, 24
Butler, Charity, 3
Butler, Eleanor, 28
Butler, Marth, 8
Butler, Milly, 5
Butler, Rachael, 24
Butler, Mary Eleanor, 3
Butler, Mary, 14
illegible
Butler, Bynee, 16
Bell, Letty, 22
Bell, Eliza, 6
Butler, Catherine, 30
Butler, Ann, 30
Butler, Rebecca, 9
Corum, Rachael, 70
Cole, Mary, 28
Collings, Henry, 28
Cadden, Francis, 55
Cadden, William, 13
Cadden, John, 15
Cadden, Francis H, 2
Collins, William, 52
Cole, Thomas, 40
Curtis, Washington, 25
Curtis, James, 8
Curtis, William, 5
Cooper, Jere, 67
Cooper, Cyrus, 47
Cooper, Washington, 29
Cole, Joseph, 45
Carter, James, 25
Carter, Thomas, 28
Carter, Jesse, 48
Carter, Enoch, 45
Chilton, Samuel, 45
Curtis, Ignatius, 10
Curtis, James. 8
Curtis, George, 45
Cole, William, 9
Curtis, Alexander, 36
Curtis, Dellary, 30

Cole, Benedict, 20
Cole, Elias, 17
Cole, Joseph, 12
Cole, Thomas, 3
Carter, Isaiah, 1 month
Curtis, James, 12
Curtis, William, 7
Cooper, Gerard, 25
Crawley, Bernard, 18
Crawley, James, 14
Crawley, John B. 4
Collins, Jonah, 8
Collins, Philip, 14
Collins, William, 11
Collins, Pere, 11
Custis, Somerville, 7
Cole, William, 9
Carter, Henry, 19
Carter, John, 14
Carter, Thomas, 12
Carter, Lewis, 40
Curtis, Anthony, 7
Curtis, John, 3
Curtis, John Henry, 2
Curtis, George, 40
Curtis, Henry, 9
Curtis, Charles, 8
Curtis, Benjamin, 6
Cole, Walter, 51
Cole, William W. 7
Curtis, John Francis, 8
Cole, Sussanna, 7
Cole, Jane, 3
Cole, Araminta, 55
Curtis, Margaret, 45
Curtis, Henny, 25
Curtis, Emeline, 7
Curtis, Lethia A, 3
Crawley, Elizabeth, 70
Crawley, Ann, 33
Cole, Milly, 57
Curtis, Sophia, 12
Curtis, Martha, 10
Culchamber, Charlotte, 8
Cooper, Ann, 38
Cole, Maria, 25
Cole, Sally, 45
Cooper, Maria, 25
Curtis, Sally, 45
Curtis, Mary, 48
Curtis, Margaret, 14
Curtis, Jane, 1
Carpenter, Ann, 16
Cooper, Charlotte, 30
Curtis, Ally, 50
Curtis, Mary, 40
Curtis, Matilda, 14
Carpenter, Eleanor, 6

134

Free African Americans of Maryland - 1832

Castes, Eleanor, 29
Caster, Mary, 7
Castes, Ann, 5
Castes, Elizabeth, 3
Castes, unnamed, 1 month
Cadden, Harriet, 16
Cadden, Ann, 26
Cadden, Mary, 20
Cadden, Jeanna, 6
Cadden, Leanna, 4
Crawley, Elizabeth, 13
Crawley, Ann, 10
Curtis, Sarah, 26
Curtis, Jane, 3
Curtis, Sarah, 30
Curtis, Ann, 3
Curtis, Mary, 1 month
Curtis, Caroline, 6
Curtis, Mary Jane, 4
Cooper, Polly, 65
Caster, Sarah, 65
Cooper, Ann, 20
Curtis, Mary, 35
Curtis, Matilda, 17
Curtis, Juliett, 13
Cole, Mary, 30
Cole, Ann, 8
Cole, Ellen, 10
Caster, Sarah, 25
Curtis, Alexander, 46
Cooper, William, 3
Cooper, Alexander, 14
Curtis, Thomas, 3
Crutis, Henry, 6
Curtis, John 36
Curtis, Mesheck, 35
Cole, Henry Thomas, 11
Cole, John G. 3
Curtis, Joseph, 26
Curtis, James, 24
Curtis, Isaac, 22
Curtis, Charles, 20
Curtis, George, 18
Curtis, Ambrosia, 16
Curtis, James, 15
Curtis, John, 4
Curtis, Thomas, 1
Curtis, Henry A, 23
Curtis, Charles, 2
Curtis, George, 12
Curtis, Moses, 38
Curtis, Henry, 35
Curtis, Ignatious, 5
Curtis, Robert, 1
Curtis, John, 14
Curtis, George, 38
Curtis, Edward, 39
Curtis, William, 11

Curtis, Aloysius, 2
Curtis, Spencer, 20
Curtis, Gustavius, 70
Curtis, Leonard, 36
Crawley, William, 67
Davis, Charles, 60
Dorson, James, 7
Davis, Allen, 40
Dickinson, Meloy, 52
Fowler, William A, 23
Fowler, Fergerson, 19
Fowler, William H, 23
Fowler, Hanson, 19
Fowler, Josiah, 16
Fowler, John Maxwell, 14
Fowler, Henry H, 4
Fowler, George, 1
Fenwick, George, 24
Fletcher, Maxwell, 30
Fletcher, Isaac, 20
Fenwick, John, 45
Fenwick, Abraham, 1
Fenwick, George, 26
Fenwick, Ignatius, 3
Fenwick, William, 23
Ford, John Francis, 16
Garner, John, 18
Caster, Caroline, 7
Carter, Jane, 3
Carter, Mary J, 4
Cooper, Lydia, 45
Cole, Ellen, 10
Caster, Sarah, 25
Caster, Caroline, 7
Carter, Jane, 3
Caster, Mary J, 4
Cooper, Lydia, 45
Cooper, Minta, 16
Cooper, Henrietta, 16
Cooper, Maria, 10
Crawley, Sarah, 40
Crawley, Elizabeth, 10
Crawley, Ann L, 7
Collins, Matilda, 27
Collins, Mary, 42
Collins, Ann, 18
Collins, Eleanor, 9
Collins, Juliet, 16
Collins, Sarah, 12
Collins, Elizabeth, 7
Collins, Margaret, 45
Curtis, Helen, 23
Curtis, Adeline, 27
Curtis, Rebecca, 4
Curtis, Rebecca, 4
Cole, Eliza, 19
Cole, Ann, 16
Cole, Elizabeth, 12

St. Mary's County

Carter, Jane, 6
Carter, Mary, 25
Curtis, Lydia, 35
Curtis, Sabria, 20
Curtis, Mary Jane, 6
Carter, Martha, 64
Crawley, Elizabeth, 18
Crawley, Jane Ellen, 2
Cooper, Ann, 22
Curtis, Susan, 27
Curtis, Jane Eliza, 1 month
Curtis, Mary E, 12
Cole, Sarah Ann, 5
Curtis, Rosetta, 28
Cooper, Elizabeth, 9
Cooper, Avis, 28
Cooper, Jane, 6
Curtis, Elizabeth, 9
Curtis, Caroline, 26
Curtis, Sarah, 4
Curtis, Celia, 5
Curtis, Martha, 15
Cole, Jane, 44
Cole, Emely, 24
Cole, Mary Jane, 8
Galloway, Samuel, 12
Galloway, Lewis, 26
Hill, Henry, 89
Hutchins, Samuel, 30
Holly, Joseph, 36
Holly, John, 10
Holly, Thomas, 8
Holly, Thomas, 50
Hick, Thomas, 32
Hawkins, James, 60
Holly, Thomas, 38
Holly, Lewis, 43
Holly, George, 47
Holly, John, 5
Holly, George, 3
Holly, William, 16
Holly, Stephen, 10
Hall, John, 30
Hall, John G, 4
Harris, James, 12
Harris, Arthur, 12
Holly, Jacob, 36
Holly, John B. 7
Hicks, Martin H, 12
Hicks, William, 7
Hicks, John, 3
Hicks, George W, 7
Holly, Ignatius, 58
Holly, Emanuel, 2 1
Holly, Charles, 50
Holly, Charles H, 2
Holly, Frederick, 30
Holly, Charles, 66

Holly, William, 5
Holly, Joseph, 37
Holly, Henry, 16
Hutchins, William, 16
Hutchins, Ignatius, 14
Hutchins, James B, 5
Hutchins, Robert, 11
Hutchins, John H, 6
Harris, George, 30
Harris, Thomas, 10
Holly, Joseph, 30
Holly, Thomas, 28
Holly, Causin, 3
Hero, Old Lew, 75
Holly, Michael, 36
Jenkins, Thomas, 7
Jenkins, Joseph, 17
Jenkins, Joseph, 19
Jenkins, Charly, 3
Jenkins, William, 3
Jenkins, unnamed, 1 month
Jenkins, Peter, 15
Jones, Thomas, 47
Cole, Dorothy J, 6
Curtis, Elizabeth, 50
Curtis, Rebecca, 30
Curtis, Nancy, 28
Curtis, Jane, 14
Curtis, Elizabeth, 14
Curtis, Mary, 7
Curtis, Celia, 2
Curtis, Ann, 50
Curtis, Charlotte, 25
Curtis, Jane Eliza, 7
Curtis, Mary, 5
Curtis, Sarah, 18
Curtis, Henrietta, 15
Curtis, Elizabeth, 5
Cole, Ann, 12
Curtis, Sarah, 26
Curtis, Sarah Ann, 8
Curtis, Eleanor A, 5
Curtis, Amilaly, 30
Curtis, Julia, 3
Curtis, Maria, 1
Curtis, Eliza, 48
Curtis, Mary, 10
Curtis, Maria, 1
Curtis, Eliza, 48
Curtis, Mary, 10
Curtis, Maria, 38
Curtis, Sarah Maria, 6
Curtis, Elizabeth, 40
Curtis, Milly, 1
Davis, Elizabeth, 45
Davis, Fanny, 17
Fowler, Sarah, 79
Fowler, Elizabeth, 44

Free African Americans of Maryland - 1832

Fowler, Margaret, 20
Fowler, Luiza, 25
Fowler, Celia, 23
Fowler, Sarah Ann, 9
Fowler, Margaret, 55
Fletcher, Charlotte, 40
Fenwick, Margaret, 25
Fenwick, Jane, 22
Garner, Mary, 80
Garner, Monica, 60
Garner, Mary Ann, 5
Garner, Susanna, 65
Garner, Jane, 68
Hill, Margaret, 76
Holly, Ann G, 6
Holly, Priscilla, 35
Holly, S___, 12
Holly, Susanna, 10
Holly, Lucinda, 21
Hopewell, Maria, 2
Hopewell, unnamed, 1 month
Jenkins, Michael, 60
Jones, Shadrick, 40
Jones, Henry, 10
Kirby, George, 40
Laurence, John, 44
Lawrence, James, 3
Lawrence, Cornelius, 2
Lawrence, John, 8
Lawrence, William F, 4
Lawrence, Ignatius, 33
Lawrence, Alexander, 19
Lawder, Thomas, 25
Lawder, James, 58
Lawrence, John, 65
Lawrence, Joseph, 8
Lawrence, Alexander, 3
Lawrence, unnamed, 1 month
Lee, Daniel, 65
Mason, Joseph, 43
Mason, Henry, 14
Mason, James, 10
McClain, Abraham, 60
McClain, Abraham, 7
McClain, John, 5
McClain, Hanson, 3
McClain, Richard, 2
McClain, Jesse, 1
Mason, Henry, 28
Mason, William, 26
Mason, Perry, 30
Mason , John, 50
Mason, Henry, 15
Mason, Alexander, 14
Mason, Washington, 8
Milburn, George, 8
Milburn, John, 6
Morgan, John, 55

Mason, James E, 12
McGinty, Uriah, 37
Mason, Lewis, 22
Mason, Benjamin, 60
Mason, Joseph B, 10
Mason, Barton, 8
Mason, William G, 5
Mason, Abraham, 50
Mason, George, 13
Mason, William, 11
Mason, John P, 5
Murry, John, 22
Murray, Edward, 20
Murray, James, 18
Murray, Ignatius, 16
Murray, Michael. 8
Murray, Joseph, 6
Morgan, Jesse, 48
Morgan, James, 66
Holly, Hannah, 60
Holly, Elizabeth, 30
Holly, Ann, 60
Hicks, Elizabeth, 30
Hicks, Mary, 70
Hicks, Margaret, 35
Hicks, Fanny, 22
Hicks, Susanna, 18
Hicks, Lucinda, 14
Hicks, Eliza, 9
Hicks, Pamelia, 4
Hicks, Ann, 2
Hicks, Priscilla, 55
Holly, Drady A, 6
Holly, Susanna, 4
Holly, Sarah, 40
Holly, Elizabeth, 6
Holly, Harriett, 28
Holt, Alcis, 45
Holt, Elizabeth, 27
Holt, Mary E, 7
Holly, Lydia, 30
Holly, Mary, 3
Holly, Henny, 2
Holly, Elizabeth, 1 month
Harris, Eliza, 15
Hutchins, Sarah, 35
Hutchins, Harriett, 10
Harris, Jane, 13
Harris, Sarah Ann, 6
Harris, Elizabeth, 4
Holly, Jane, 15
Holly, Mary, 35
Higden, Elizabeth, 22
Holly, Eleanor, 35
Holly, Louisa, 14
Holly, Mary, 16
Hayden, Lucy, 60
Hayden, Letty, 60

St. Mary's County

Holly, Eunice, 20
Holly, Phoebe, 38
Holly, Sarah, 60
Holly, Ann, 40
Holly, Harriett, 12
Jenkins, Mary, 40
Jenkins, Ann, 17
Jenkins, Eliza, 15
Jenkins, Mary U, 9
Jenkins, Catherine, 22
Jones, Edy, 35
Jones, Juliet, 20
Lawrence, Rebecca, 64
Lawrence, Ann, 7
Lawrence, unnamed, 1 month
Lawrence, Helen, 30
Lawrence, Sarah, 35
Moses, John, 48
Miller, George, 35
Medary, Thomas, 88
Morgan, Jerre, 50
Morgan, John, 15
Morgan, Bennett, 8
Morgan, Columbus, 5
Murry, Henry, 65
Mattingly, John G, 13
Mattingly, William L, 10
Mattingly, Samuel, 2
Neale, John, 1
Neale, William, 22
Neale, John, 1
Neale, James, 48
Powell, James, 38
Powell, Henry, 11
Pinkerton, Joseph, 13
Parker, Jackson, 4
Parker, Joseph, 2
Parker, John Henry, 1 month
Payne, Joseph, 35
Queen, George, 4
Roberson, Frank, 60
Read, John A, 3
Read, Charles M, 1
Read, William H, 10
Read, Joseph A, 6
Read, Lafayette, 1
Read, Benjamin, 1 month
Read, Charles Hanson, 1 month
Reston, James, 60
Read, Anthony, 4
Read, William, 12
Read, Thomas, 8
Read, Josias, 6
Somervill, William, 25
Somervill, William, 46
Shadrick, Alexander, 30
Somervill, Philip, 65
Somervill, Thomas, 15

Spriggs, Charles, 60
Shilton, Charles, 60
Somervill, Lewis, 16
Somervill, Henry, 11
Somervill, Nelson, 8
Somervill, George, 18
Somervill, Joseph, 35
Somervill, Joseph, 3
Somerville, Peter, 2
Somervill, Samuel, 25
Somervill, Henry, 8
Somervill, Robert, 6
Somervill, Clement, 10
Somervill, Charles, 8
Somervill, William H, 14
Lawrence, Polly, 65
Lawder, Catherine, 27
Lawder, Ann, 65
Lawrence, Ann, 51
Lawrence, Priscilla, 20
Lawrence, Attaway, 18
Lawrence, Mary, 51
Mason, Milly, 84
Mason, Salah, 42
Mason, Mary, 12
Mason, Sarah Ann, 11
McClain, Elizabeth, 56
McClain, Henries, 44
McClain, Lydia, 40
McClain, Maria, 35
McClain, Margaret, 20
McClain, Roseann, 12
McClain, Elizabeth, 3
Mason, Charity, 40
Mason, Eliza Ann, 17
Mason, Mary, 12
Mason Elizabeth, 10
Mason, Olivia, 6
Milburn, Jane, 55
Milburn, Eliza, 18
Morgan, India, 30
McQuirty, Mary, 24
Mason, Sarah, 47
Mason, Maria, 25
Mason, Elizabeth, 17
Mason, Sarah B. 7
Mahoney, Ally, 70
Mason, Elizabeth, 65
Mason, Ann C, 12
Mason, Susanna D, 6
Mason, Ann40
Mason, Catherine, 15
Mason, Mary, 7
Murray, Eleanor, 3
Morgan, Priscilla, 45
Mince, Clara, 46
Moore, Rachael, 48
Mack, Juliet, 45

138

Free African Americans of Maryland - 1832

Mack, Sarah Ann, 12
Mack, Celista, 3
Mendy, Sylvia, 75
Morgan, Emeline, 1
Murry, Elizabeth, 53
Mattingly, Elizabeth, 33
Mattingly, Sarah, 16
Mattingly, Rebecca, 11
Mattingly, Ann, 6
Mattingly, Elizabeth, 9
Mattingly, Eliza, 22
Mattingly, Catherine, 7
Neale, Drady, 24
Somervill, Nehemiah, 6
Saxton, Joseph, 56
Saxton, James, 13
Somervill, Peter, 14
Somervill, John, 25
Somervill, Andrew, 66
Somervill, George, 18
Somervill, Thomas, 14
Somervill, William, 23
Somervill, Francis, 7
Somervill, Robert, 6
Somervill, Thomas, 5
Somervill, Moses, 46
Stewart, James, 13
Stewart, John L, 11
Shorter, George, 22
Sotherose, Charles, 65
Simmonds, John, 42
Steward, Edward, 35
Stone, Jere, 35
Shorter, Edward, 75
Somervill, Henry, 5
Shorter, George, 22
Shorter, Hillary, 14
Turner, David, 50
Thomas, Washington, 21
Thomas, Benedict, 19
Thomas, George, 17
Thomas, John, 24
Teer, James, 40
Teer, Joseph, 55
Teer, Isaac, 45
Teer, Alexander, 7
Teer, Joseph, 6
Teer, Samuel, 4
Teer, Peter, 1 month
Taney, Alexander, 15
Taney, Dominick, 13
Taney, John F, 11
Taney, Ilank, 2
Thomas, Henry, 30
Thompson, Samuel, 54
Thompson, Henry, 54
Thompson, Charles, 8
Thomas, William, 6

Thomas, James. 3
Tippett, John, 5
Trent, Neal, 6
Trent, P___, 4
Trent, G___, 12
Trent, Nace, 20
Thompson, Abraham, 32
Taney, Anthony, 20
Taney, Ignatius, 20
Taney, Octavius, 13
Taney, Robert, 11
Neale, Eliza, 22
Neale, Ann. 20
Nelson, Minty, 45
Powell, Ann, 15
Powell, Louisa, 14
Parker, Ann, 35
Parnham, Henny, 55
Queen, Ester, 26
Queen, Rebecca, 2
Riner, Sabra, 60
Read, Elizabeth, 14
Read, Attaway, 24
Read, Elizabeth, 1
Read, Catherine Ann, 7
Read, Sarah Maria, 5
Read, Mary, 25
Read, Susan, 30
Read, Mary Ann, 8
Read, Sarah Ann, 23
Read, Mary E, 4
Somervill, Henrietta, 65
Somervill, Henrietta, 40
Shadrick, Lucretia, 25
Spriggs, Susanna, 50
Somervill, Ann E, 4
Somervill, Hannah, 40
Somervill, Ann, 15
Somervill, Jane, 17
Somervill, Eliza, 13
Somervill, Priscilla, 6
Somervill, Emeline, 3
Somervill, unnamed, 1 month
Somervill, Lydia, 60
Somervill, Letty, 25
Somervill, Elizabeth, 3
Somervill, Mary, 25
Somervill, Henny, 60
Somervill, Catherine, 40
Somervill, Appalonia, 23
Somervill, Susanna, 3
Somervill, Susanna, 19
Smith, Elizabeth, 1 month
Somervill, Jane, 45
Somervill, Sophia, 50
Somervill, Attaway, 21
Somervill, ellen I, 16
Somervill, Mary L, 1 month

St. Mary's County

Somervill, Mary Eliza, 2
Somervill, Kesiah, 31
Saxton, Mary, 50
Saxton, Henny, 15
Saxton Mary A, 14
Saxton, Sophia, 7
Somervill, Elizabeth, 69
Somervill, Nancy, 30
Somervill, Elizabeth, 4
Taney, Calestis, 3
Tippett, Robert, 9
Tippett, Shadrick, 50
Tippett, Alexander, 28
Tippett, Raphael, 70
Watts, Rupert, 14
Watts, Isaac, 20
Williams, Robert, 36
Williams, William H, 7
Woodland, John, 6
Woodland Stephen, 22
Woodland, Ignatius, 45
Woodland, Thomas, 8
Woodland, Marcellus, 4
Woodland, John, 2
Woodland, Thomas, 24
Woodland, Nase, 19
Woodland, Charles, 14
Woodland, Joseph, 30
Williams, Barney, 58
Williams, Henry, 16
Woodland, Joseph A, 1
Woodland, William, 25
Woodland, Joseph, 25
Warran, Peter, 56
Warran, Abraham, 20
Woodland, Ignatius, 17
Woodland, Charles, 16
Woodland, ___, 30
Woodland, John, 35
Woodland, Robert, 4
Woodland, Primus, 65
Woodland, Henry, 26
Woodland, Washington, 35
Young, Robert, 53
Young, James, 9
Young, Raphael, 25
___, Josiah, 60
Leigh, Ratliff, 58
Barnes, Thomas, 20
Barnes, Benedict, 19
Somervill, Eliza, 20
Somervill, Ann, 24
Somervill, Catherine, , 50
Somerville, Henny, 20
Somervill, Susan, 11
Somervill, Eliza Ann, 1 month
Stewart, Harriet, 30
Stewart, Caroline A, 12

Stewart, Susan, A, 8
Stewart, Mary A, 5
Stewart, Teresia A, 1 month
Somervill, Ann, 30
Somervill, Caroline, 50
Simmonds, Jane, 33
Somervill, Elizabeth, 90
Somervill, Jane, 24
Somervill, Maria, 3
Shorter, Henny, 74
Shorter, Lucinda, 19
Shorter, Ann, 17
Shorter, Jane, 10
Thomas, Susan, 15
Teer, Susan, 30
Teer, Mary, 5
Tabels, Emeline, 30
Taney, Barbary, 35
Thomas, Caroline, 25
Thompson, Tersia, 50
Thomas, Mary, 2
Trent, Sarah, 30
Trent, Henny, 38
Trent, Susan, 25
Trent, Judy, 37
Trent, Ann, 25
Taney, Ann, 25
Taney, Monica, 38
Taney, Matilda, 18
Taney, Sophia, 16
Taney, Ann Josephine, 15
Tippett, Sabria, 38
Tippett, Mary, 6
Thomas, Monica, 66
Thomas, Charity, 75
Tippett, Mary, 52
Woodland, Ann, 65
Whaling, Monica, 50
Willis, Geasy, 55
Williams, Mary, 22
Williams, Henrietta, 2
Woodland, Henny, 57
Woodland, Lucy, 40
Woodland, Ann, 10
Woodland, Polly, 65
Woodland, Jane, 16
Williams, Cicely, 60
Woodland, Elizabeth, 43
Woodland, Charlotte, 7
Woodland, Mary, 40
Woodland, Jane, 18
Woodland, Mary, 28
Woodland, Polly, 22
Woodland, Caroline, 1 month
Weach, Mary, 14
Weach, Sarah, 37
Young, Henny, 53
Young, Mary Ann, 1 month

140

Free African Americans of Maryland - 1832

Young, Elizabeth, 25
Young, Eleanor, 18

Zachary, Sarah, 50
Hoyle, Catherine, 70

Males over 1 year old	582		
Males under 1 years old	13	Total Number	595
Females over 1 years old	602		
Females under 1 year old	16	Total Number	618

Gross Amount   1213

25th August 1832

All of which is respectfully submitted,
Benjamin G. Coles, Sheriff
Of Saint Marys County

■■

SCHEDULE OF THE FREE PERSONS OF COLOR IN WASHINGTON COUNTY (1832)

Phillip Smith
Lewis Minner
John Brawdon
Jeremiah Hammilton
Abraham Hess
James Gibson
Henry Miles
William Porter
Douglass Carter,
Emily Beed,
Nelly Gray,
William Barnes
Samuel Burnes
Philemon Barnes.
    Henry Miller
    Levy Davis
    Barney
    Montgomery
    Rachel Bromley
    William E. Butler
    Maria Dasha
    John Blackford
    James Hands
    Samuel Harrison
    Lewis Howard
    Joseph Jacobs
    Harriet
    Burke
    Charles Adams
    West Callaman
    John Ingram,
    *Archibald
    Patterson,
John Callaman,
William Callaman
___ Patterson,
Jonathon Patterson,
Solomon Patterson
Thomas Callaman

Widow Lott,
Betsy Callaman,
William Hays,
Frederick Jackson,
Fowler
Basil Taylor
 John Lee
Charles Walker
Charles Herbert
John Gelwicks
D. Chaneys,
Esther Chase,
A. Kennedys,
Thomas Edwards,
    Lewis Fletcher
William Douglass
Joseph Weast
Nancy Carter
Oliver Chesley
Berry Simson
Jeremiah
    Livearingen
Walter Scott
Levy Lee
 Jacobs Higgs
Bachus Motts
Thomas Motts
Thomas Jurricks
Nace Luckett
James Adler
George Washington
    Miller
Frank Matthews
Henry Rollins
James Row
Zachariah Patterson
Thomas Ducket
Jeremiah Hall
A Wares

Levi Hall
Jacob Egelston
Conter
Tucker
Minty
Peter Hopewell
Mary Turner
Aquila Yarrow
George Pinkney
Isaac Warfield
Henry
Prince Williams
Susan Kelly
Samuel Hayden
Robert Hayden
John Adams
Perry Green
John Bowens
Harry Sands
Sarah Cooper[3]
Hanah Gray
Nancy Borrell
Ned
    Snowden(Slowde
    n ?)
Henry Barnes
Jones Darker
Joseph
Jacob Diggs
Perry Noel
Eliza Sands
Thomas Harry
Briston Anderson
Jamaes Twang
Mahala Edwards
Thomas Butler

[3]lined out

141

Washington County

Jesse Gwin
Jane Lane[4]
Priscila Gruber
Delia Dorsey
Ludia Waggoner
Kitty Francis
Charles Brison
Mary Ann Burrell
James Brooks
Philis Job & Chloe
  Brooks
George Coney
Thomas Russell
Jesse Ryder
Lloyd Mackey
Harry
Shaakie Shears
Tobias Miller
Charles Grace
John Burke
Ruth Cook
Rachel Booth
Leonard McGinty
George
Esther Briscoe
Charles Briscoe
Ferry Briscoe
Nelly Thomas
Henry Clarke
John Gats
Samuel Williams
Henry Williams
Richard Miles
Samuel Miller
Thomas Sanders
Jacob Berris
Henry V.Nancy
Solomon Stocks
Wiliam Duncan
Rebecca Watts
Thomas Watts
George Coal
Samuel Lake
*Charity Lake
John Green
Harry Beltzoover
William Brown
James Grace
Harry Grace
Levin Grace
Caty Michael
Abraham Barnes
Matthew
  Truman/Triman
John Truman
Ambrose Bender

James Young
Seaborn/Sebrun
  Brooks
A. ____
Samuel Ryley
Perry Riley
Rebecca Compton
Franis Dirham
Patty Peters
Nancy Miner
Lydia Jordan
Lucy Blake
Nathan Brooks
James Scott
Kitty Thomas
Frank Chessley
Nancy Cooper
Sarah Butler
Mary Butler
*Sophia Butler
Fanny Baker
Harrison Jones
Nace & wife
Ceaser Monday
Sarah Diggs
James Handy
Samuel Harris
Eveline Cobert
Benjamin Smot
Richard Harrison
Charles Gats
Frisby Miller
Lewis Nailor
Berry Gats
Dick Briscoe
Isaac Draper
Samuel Green
Adam Tims
Washington Lucas
Cato Smith
Berry Jackson
Daniel Hanson
John Grace
John Boss
Nancy Hines
Charles ____
John Marshall
Jeremiah Hall
George Dorsey
Hagard Livan
Cesar Duffy
Henry McKay
*Jacob Beiner
Otho Snyder
Matilda Chase
Mary Brown
Mary Tilghman
  Alexander

Stephen Dorsey
Rachel____
Peter Richardson
Reuben Johnston
John McDaniel
Richard Boyer
Fanny Johnston
James Crawford[5]
Kitty Brown
Patience Summers
Patrick Turman
Jack Helmesley
John Cook
Samuel Galloway
Samuel Richardson
Rachel Booth
Geofery Booth
David Booth
Nancy Barnes
Thomas Harvey
Maria Bond
Maria Pheonix
* Hannah Steward
George Handy
Betsy Snyder
Kitty Shorter
Letty Williamson
Judy Taylor
Ceasor Russell
Celia Jones
Margaret Francis
Polly Dorsey
William Brown
Susan Bevans
Polly Hatton
Jane Statton
Sarah
Harry Bell
Jane Mc____
James Brown
Richard Smith
Elvia Williams
Joseph Green
Stephen N. Herris

William H. Fitzhugh,
  Sheriff
Washington County.

---
[4]lined out

---
[5]lined out

142

SURNAME INDEX

Index

Index

Ferguson, 121
Ferrell, 120, 127
Festus, 101
Few, 122
Fidd, 18
Fieds, 79
Fields, 45, 51, 79, 81, 98
Fish, 45, 69
Fisher, 12, 14, 17, 19, 21, 23, 35, 36, 40, 45, 51, 61, 62, 74, 85, 86, 89, 105, 106, 116, 124
Fitzhugh, 104, 142
Flamer, 121
Fletcher, 60, 63, 65, 70, 72, 76, 83, 84, 137
Flood, 22, 25, 26
Fogwell, 118, 120, 126, 127
Fogwill, 120
Folks, 17
Foot, 11, 25, 29
Ford, 17, 18, 45, 51, 56, 57, 59, 79, 80, 81, 94, 95, 135
Foreman, 28, 77, 106, 114, 122
Forgewell, 45, 51
Forman, 51, 95, 99, 109
Forty, 18
Fosset, 17
Foster, 40, 61, 66, 73, 75
Fountain, 36, 37, 38, 40, 45, 51, 91
Fowler, 7, 135, 136
Fox, 51, 97, 117, 119
Foxwell, 35
Fraling, 83
France, 23
Frances, 86
Francis, 84, 142
Frank, 23
Franklin, 16, 22, 25, 109, 111
Frasier, 104, 123
Frasser, 23
Fray, 97

Frazier, 29, 65, 72, 102
Freak, 116
Frederick, 106
Freeland, 30, 32
Freeman, 32, 34, 35, 45, 84, 89, 90, 91, 95, 99, 100, 101, 104, 115, 121, 122, 124, 126
French, 19, 116, 118, 121, 128
Friend, 40, 42
Frisby, 35, 91, 93, 94, 95, 96, 97, 101, 102, 118, 119
Frost, 18
Fry, 27, 31
Fullerman, 117, 119
Fuly, 82
Furell, 118
Furl, 45, 51
Furman, 51

G

Gaddis, 96, 99, 100
Gadis, 95
Gafford, 118, 119, 126
Gainby, 62, 72
Gaines, 69, 77
Gains, 26, 30, 123
Gaither, 11, 15, 20, 80, 81, 86, 104, 106, 125
Galaway, 79, 81
Gale, 45, 51, 85, 92, 94, 95, 98
Gales, 30
Galloway, 7, 136, 142
Gambrill, 2, 15, 19
Gamby, 69, 77
Gannon, 76, 121
Gannons, 68
Gant, 79, 86
Gante, 6
Gantt, 109
Garain, 121
Gardner, 13, 23, 25

Garner, 35, 38, 58, 79, 135, 137
Garnett, 45, 127
Garret, 82
Garretson, 123
Garrett, 2, 6, 7, 8, 17, 45, 46, 93, 95, 96, 111
Garrettson, 93, 95
Garrison, 18
Garrott, 45, 51
Garry, 26
Gasaway, 29, 33, 39, 80, 87, 119
Gasby, 45, 51
Gassaway, 27, 110, 111
Gassoway, 22
Gates, 103
Gats, 142
Gault, 26, 28, 32, 33
Geddis, 99, 101
Gelwicks, 141
Genson, 22
George, 45, 51, 83
German, 117, 119
Gibb, 51, 120
Gibbings, 45, 51
Gibbons, 22, 106
Gibbs, 16, 34, 82, 94, 97, 100, 102, 103, 113, 120, 121, 125, 126, 127, 128
Gibson, 19, 27, 28, 33, 37, 43, 45, 61, 67, 68, 69, 73, 76, 92, 114, 115, 120, 123, 126, 127, 129, 141
Gidley, 92, 93, 98
Gilbert, 58, 90, 92, 102, 120
Giles, 22, 66, 93, 116, 118
Gill, 16
Gittings, 108
Givens, 51
Givings, 46
Givins, 29
Gladden, 64, 71
Glasgan, 61
Glasgow, 113

Index

Free African Americans of Maryland - 1832

17, 18, 19, 20, 24,
45, 56, 93, 95, 106,
120, 127, 137, 142
Hardaker, 28
Hardcastle, 74, 113,
122
Harden, 11, 24, 27,
30, 102, 122
Hardester, 107
Hardesty, 27, 33,
109
Harding, 19, 35, 46,
52
Hardman, 27, 28,
30, 31, 32, 87
Hardy, 22, 24, 25, 33
Harkens, 13
Harkey, 55
Harley, 57
Harper, 10, 36, 79,
80, 81, 84, 94
Harres, 29
Harress, 69, 70, 77
Harris, 1, 5, 14, 17,
18, 22, 35, 38, 40,
41, 46, 52, 60, 64,
66, 67, 71, 80, 85,
96, 98, 99, 102,
109, 113, 114, 115,
126, 136, 137, 142
Harris, Joseph, 5
Harrison, 10, 12, 14,
17, 18, 25, 33, 35,
43, 67, 83, 84, 113,
115, 118, 126, 141,
142
Harrod, 32, 122
Harrot, 32
Harry, 63, 141
Hart, 52, 59
Hartshorn, 46, 52,
98
Harttwood, 28
Hartwood, 31
Harvey, 96, 114, 122,
123, 142
Harwood, 7, 11, 17,
26, 27, 29
Hary, 71
Hasket, 41
Haskins, 68, 76
Hasmon, 46

Hatcheson, 100, 121
Hatton, 142
Hawk, 14
Hawkins, 2, 3, 4, 9,
11, 13, 14, 16, 17,
18, 19, 20, 21, 23,
28, 29, 32, 34, 35,
36, 41, 46, 52, 59,
80, 98, 104, 113,
115, 120, 121, 122,
124, 127, 128, 129,
136
Hayden, 137, 141
Haylent, 99
Haynes, 64
Hays, 38, 141
Hayward, 62
Haywood, 60, 72, 74
Hazleton, 123
Hazzard, 97, 114,
123
Hazzleton, 114
Heath, 113, 114, 117,
118, 123, 125
Heckman, 10
Heckster, 115
Heinz, 88
Helmesley, 142
Helms, 102
Hemming, 18
Hemsley, 37, 116,
124
Henderson, 46, 52,
108, 121
Henry, 1, 23, 26, 34,
35, 36, 39, 46, 66,
67, 68, 71, 72, 73,
77, 84, 96, 100, 101
Henson, 7, 31, 46
Hepburn, 108
Herbert, 11, 141
Hercules, 116
Herd, 81
Hero, 136
Herris, 142
Hess, 141
Hewes, 46, 52
Hicks, 37, 38, 117,
137
Higden, 137
Higgins, 80, 81, 108
Higgs, 141

Higins, 80
Hill, 1, 2, 3, 4, 13, 14,
15, 30, 31, 41, 52,
55, 60, 61, 63, 64,
71, 73, 79, 82, 83,
84, 85, 86, 88, 89,
105, 109, 113, 122,
136, 137
Hillery, 80
Hindman, 19, 96
Hindsman, 12
Hines, 37, 79, 113,
115, 116, 117, 119,
124, 142
Hinson, 31, 52, 67,
76, 113, 114, 119,
122, 124
Hiteh, 39
Hitt, 66, 67
Hnson, 31
Hodge, 109
Hodges, 58, 90, 91,
93, 108, 111
Hodson, 60, 64, 72
Hogan, 1, 46
Hogans, 31, 52
Hoges, 120, 127
Holiday, 61, 64, 72,
73, 80, 116
Hollan, 73, 74
Hollan/Holland, 76
Holland, 24, 28, 37,
46, 52, 67, 68, 77,
91, 104, 111, 113,
116, 118, 120
Hollander, 32
Hollen, 61
Holley, 1
Holliday, 118, 120,
125
Hollin, 64
Hollingsworth, 46
Hollins, 61
Hollis, 52, 65, 70, 71,
91, 96, 116, 118,
120, 126, 127
Holly, 23, 95, 96, 136,
137
Hollyday, 116, 122
Holmes, 34, 41, 43,
81, 82, 86
Holt, 59, 137

151

Index

Holton, 23
Homely, 98
Homes, 75
Hood, 10, 28, 105, 118, 119
Hooper, 10, 14, 40, 66, 67, 68, 69, 73, 76, 77, 78
Hopewell, 83, 85, 137, 141
Hopkins, 12, 22, 26, 37, 46, 52, 64, 65, 66, 77, 87, 88, 90, 98, 101, 104, 105, 106, 112, 115, 124
Hopp, 80
Horner, 65, 72
Horsey, 21, 62, 74
Hosper, 76
Houston, 93, 95, 103
Howard, 3, 12, 14, 16, 18, 19, 21, 23, 24, 26, 36, 52, 56, 82, 83, 84, 85, 86, 88, 104, 117, 119, 141
Howe, 52
Hoyle, 141
Hubbard, 41, 63, 65, 70, 87
Huchinson, 46, 52
Hudson, 90
Hughes, 60, 61, 62, 63, 66, 67, 72, 73, 74, 75, 122
Hughs, 46
Hughston, 117, 119
Huison, 46
Human, 72, 75
Humbird, 87
Humby, 60, 73
Humphries, 57
Hunt, 7, 19, 62
Hurlock, 63
Hurtt, 101, 102, 103
Hussan, 52
Hustron, 29
Hutchens, 122
Hutchenson, 121
Hutcheons, 114
Hutchins, 36, 113, 117, 118, 120, 122,

123, 124, 125, 136, 137
Hutchinson, 52, 122
Hute, 38
Hutson, 36, 61, 73
Hutton, 12
Hynson, 90, 91, 93, 94, 95, 96, 98, 99, 100, 102, 113
Hythe, 68, 77

I

Ijams, 16
Inglish, 65, 72
Ingram, 141
Ireland, 17, 26, 29
Isaac, 15

J

Jacks, 26, 29, 81
Jackson, 6, 11, 13, 14, 15, 16, 17, 18, 19, 22, 24, 25, 26, 27, 28, 29, 30, 32, 33, 37, 39, 41, 42, 43, 46, 47, 52, 56, 58, 59, 60, 62, 63, 65, 66, 67, 69, 70, 71, 72, 73, 74, 75, 76, 77, 80, 81, 84, 86, 87, 89, 95, 96, 99, 100, 104, 108, 110, 113, 115, 116, 117, 118, 119, 120, 122, 123, 125, 126, 127, 141
Jacob, 16
Jacobs, 17, 18, 41, 47, 52, 92, 123, 129, 141
James, 41, 42, 47, 52, 61, 65, 74, 80, 81, 82, 83, 86, 87
James, Benjamin, 5
Jamison, 92
Jasby, 30
Jason, 106
Jay, 47, 52
Jeff, 46, 52

Jeffers, 121, 128
Jefferson, 25, 26, 89, 114, 123
Jenifer, 88
Jenkins, 2, 19, 40, 52, 58, 59, 68, 82, 85, 91, 92, 93, 98, 103, 107, 113, 114, 136, 137, 138
Jennings, 7, 8, 10
Jenny, 1, 30
Jew, 60, 73
Jiles, 52
Jinkins, 64, 68, 71, 76
Job, 16, 62, 80
Jobe, 114, 117, 119
Jobes, 88, 113
Jocks, 81
Johns, 40, 41, 42, 46, 52, 63, 67, 70, 76, 116, 117, 119, 124
Johnson, 1, 7, 8, 9, 10, 12, 13, 14, 15, 16, 17, 18, 19, 20, 21, 22, 23, 24, 25, 26, 27, 28, 29, 30, 31, 32, 33, 34, 36, 38, 39, 40, 41, 43, 46, 47, 52, 60, 61, 62, 63, 64, 65, 66, 67, 68, 69, 70, 71, 72, 73, 74, 75, 76, 77, 78, 82, 83, 84, 85, 86, 87, 90, 92, 93, 94, 95, 96, 99, 101, 104, 105, 106, 107, 110, 113, 114, 115, 116, 117, 118, 119, 120, 122, 123, 124, 125, 126, 127
Johnston, 89, 142
Joice, 18, 21, 84
Joiner, 98
Jolley, 62
Jolly, 61, 63, 73, 74, 75
Jones, 1, 8, 9, 11, 13, 14, 16, 18, 19, 20, 23, 24, 25, 26, 27, 28, 29, 30, 31, 32, 33, 46, 47, 52, 59,

152

Index

Index

P

Paca, 93
Pace, 108
Pack, 16
Page, 91, 92, 97, 98
Palmer, 96, 97
Palmore, 48
Parker, 1, 4, 7, 8, 9,
    10, 17, 26, 28, 29,
    35, 47, 48, 53, 54,
    62, 63, 67, 69, 75,
    76, 89, 99, 101,
    115, 126, 138, 139
Parker, Fanny
    Elizabeth
        Ann
            Althea
                James, 4
Parks, 20, 21
Parnham, 139
Parran, 28, 30, 32
Parris, 47
Parrott, 48
Parsons, 117, 119
Patchatt, 34
Paterson, 10
Patrick, 108
Patterson, 122, 141
Pattison, 66, 69, 77
Paul, 122
Pauls, 113
Payne, 68, 138
Pea, 12
Peach, 23, 85
Peacock, 94
Peaker, 98, 99, 113
Pearce, 53, 90, 93,
    94, 95, 97, 116, 122
Pearman, 6, 86, 87
Peck, 48, 113, 116,
    125
Peckham, 122
Peeke, 122
Pellton, 20
Pelton, 20
Pembrook, 116
Penae, 47, 53
Pendleton, 36
Penn, 82
Pennington, 14, 37,
    42, 47, 53, 68, 76

Penny, 56, 57, 58, 59
Perdy, 80
Perkins, 92, 97, 98,
    100, 103, 121
Perrel, 121
Perry, 1, 5, 7, 12, 20,
    23, 28, 34, 44, 46,
    48, 56, 60, 61, 73,
    74, 75, 83, 137
Pervine, 90
Peterkin, 78
Peters, 28, 47, 53, 80,
    142
Peterson, 13, 18
Petrkin, 69
Phelps, 17, 18
Pheonix, 142
Philips, 8, 39, 40, 42,
    47, 53, 92
Phillingham, 91
Phillips, 10, 63, 70,
    76, 77, 93
Pierson, 81
Pillens, 31
Pindar, 121, 122
Pinder, 60, 61, 62,
    63, 73, 74, 75
Piner, 53
Pines, 93, 99
Pinkerton, 138
Pinket, 63, 65
Pinkett, 64, 71
Pinkney, 21, 24, 28,
    29, 32, 81, 141
Pinor, 53
Pinow, 48
Piper, 102
Plater, 68, 77, 84,
    113, 122
Plemeth, 48, 53
Ploughman, 43
Plumer, 84
Plummer, 7, 22, 104,
    106, 110
Pointer, 108
Pokety, 66, 68
Polly, 101
Poolman, 102
Pope, 40
Porgety, 72
Port, 124
Porter, 1, 21, 53, 85,

    141
Posey, 96
Possum, 72, 73
Potter, 36, 38
Potts, 25, 100, 118,
    120, 124
Powell, 9, 12, 20, 48,
    53, 105, 106, 109,
    111, 138, 139
Powers, 21
Prater, 110
Pratt, 2, 3, 29, 31, 38,
    41, 42, 93
Prattes, 40, 41, 42
Price, 9, 16, 17, 21,
    34, 35, 38, 40, 48,
    53, 67, 73, 75, 82,
    94, 112, 115, 118,
    120, 125, 126, 127
Prices, 61
Prig, 48
Primrose, 12
Primrus, 127
Prior, 115
Prises, 22
Pritcett, 126
Pritchett, 113, 117,
    119, 125
Proby, 79
Procter, 86
Proctor, 56, 57, 59
Promus, 53
Prout, 8, 9, 15, 17,
    79, 80, 81, 87
Pruitt, 30, 101
Pullman, 125
Pully, 18
Pully,, 19
Pumphrey, 21, 24,
    111, 112
Purnell, 102
Pye, 88

Q

Quash, 67, 76
Queen, 7, 8, 9, 11,
    12, 13, 14, 15, 55,
    89, 113, 129, 138,
    139
Quicks, 86
Quill, 29, 31, 32, 33

Index

Free African Americans of Maryland - 1832

Wicks, 31, 116, 117
Wiggins, 97
Wilcox, 98
Wilkes, 19, 125
Wilkins, 91, 94
Wilkinson, 15
Willams, 123
Willet, 29, 31, 32
Willett, 26, 29
Willey, 76
Williams, 8, 11, 12, 13, 14, 15, 16, 17, 19, 20, 21, 22, 23, 24, 25, 26, 35, 39, 49, 55, 62, 68, 70, 72, 79, 80, 81, 82, 84, 86, 88, 89, 90, 92, 99, 105, 106, 109, 111, 115, 123, 140, 141, 142
Williamson, 18, 126, 142
Willing, 66
Willis, 49, 64, 66, 71, 102, 124, 140
Willison, 35, 41
Willitt, 33
Wills, 49, 55
Willson, 43, 107, 109, 112
Wilmer, 55, 94, 95, 99, 100, 101, 102, 113, 114, 117, 119, 120, 121, 124, 126, 128
Wilson, 1, 7, 8, 10, 12, 19, 23, 30, 49, 55, 61, 66, 67, 69, 74, 77, 78, 81, 91, 92, 93, 94, 95, 96, 97, 99, 100, 101, 102, 103, 113, 114, 115, 116, 117, 118, 119, 120, 121, 122, 123, 124, 126, 127, 128, 129
Winder, 62
Wing, 63, 68, 75, 76
Wiseman, 56, 57
Wisher, 37, 42, 117, 119
Witman, 101
Witson, 119
Wolford, 41
Wolley, 90
Wolly, 95
Wood, 28, 29, 32, 89, 109
Woodard, 31, 88
Woodland, 35, 59, 97, 101, 102, 140
Woodling, 118, 119, 121
Woodward, 105
Woody, 123
Woodyear, 88
Woolford, 61, 62, 65, 66, 72, 73, 74, 77
Wooton, 3
Wormsley, 96
Wornar, 107
Worrell, 93, 95
Worthington, 49, 123
Wotton, 104
Wrider, 74

Wright, 12, 16, 19, 21, 37, 39, 40, 41, 49, 55, 63, 65, 79, 90, 91, 92, 93, 94, 95, 96, 97, 99, 100, 101, 102, 113, 114, 115, 116, 117, 118, 119, 120, 121, 123, 124, 126
Wrotten, 66
Wyatt, 34
Wye, 122
Wyncoop, 91

Y

Yakin, 55
Yarrow, 141
Yawkin, 49
Yeates, 93
York, 10, 49, 55
Yorke, 10
Yorkes, 92
Young, 10, 19, 28, 49, 55, 62, 63, 64, 65, 71, 72, 74, 75, 92, 95, 97, 99, 100, 115, 116, 117, 119, 140, 142
Younger, 81

Z

Zachary, 141

Made in United States
Orlando, FL
09 December 2023